# ENCYCLOPEDIA

## OF

# HITS

## The 1960s

# ENCYCLOPEDIA
## OF
# HITS
## The 1960s

Dave McAleer

BLANDFORD

## Dedication

To Little Inkie & The Penpals, The Gutbucket Simmons Group and thousands of other bands who, for one reason or another, never made the grade.

**A Blandford Book**

First published in the UK 1996 by Blandford

A Cassell Imprint

Cassell Plc, Wellington House,
125 Strand, London  WC2R 0BB

Copyright © 1996 Dave McAleer

The right of Dave McAleer to be identified as author of this work has been asserted by him in accordance with the provisions of the UK Copyright, Designs and Patents Act 1988.

All rights reserved. No part of this book may be reproduced or transmitted in any form or by any means, electronic or mechanical, including photocopying, recording or any information storage or retrieval system without permission in writing from the publisher.

Distributed in the United States by Sterling Publishing Co., Inc.,
387 Park Avenue South, New York, NY 10016–8810

Distributed in Australia by Capricorn Link (Australia) Pty Ltd
2/13 Carrington Road, Castle Hill, NSW 2154

**British Library Cataloguing-in-Publication Data**
A catalogue entry for this title is available from the British Library

ISBN 0-7137-2609-1

Compiled and entries fully created by Dave McAleer on disk using Word for Windows 6
Design, typesetting and page make up from the above by Ben Cracknell on an Apple Macintosh

Printed and bound in Great Britain by Hartnolls Limited, Bodmin, Cornwall

# Contents

# Acknowledgements

My thanks to Stuart Booth, Billie Gordon and Jon Philibert for their help on this project.

Also, thanks over the years to Derek Brecknock, Malcolm Carrick, Alan Hood, the massed McAleers and my numerous record business associates and friends.

Finally, a tip of the hat to the many record papers, music books and magazines that have kept me entertained and informed over the decades.

# Introduction

The 1960s was an exciting and innovative decade for music, and the aim of this book is to cover the whole gamut of musical milestones from the Twist to Woodstock, calling at all the stops along the way.

In the quarter century since the 'swinging sixties' passed into history many books have been written about its music, but until now none has included information on *every* US and UK Top 10 single of that era. In this first volume of *The Encyclopedia of Hits*, all the 2,000-plus hits from the years that saw the arrival of acts like The Beatles, The Rolling Stones, Bob Dylan and Michael Jackson are put under the microscope – from the most successful and influential to the often overlooked and imitative.

Even before the dawn of the decade, the rebellious and untamed brand of rock'n'roll that had exploded on to the peaceful music scene in the mid 1950s had been defused. The sound that had so excited teenagers and so shocked adults, both outside and inside the record business had been turned into Teen Beat – a hybrid of rock'n'roll and pop – which had adult as well as teen appeal. The majority of record buyers were not unhappy about that situation. In fact, quite the opposite: sales were healthy and there was no shortage of transatlantic teen idols and fresh new faces for most people's tastes.

However, there was a small minority of diehard rock'n'roll fanatics who still yearned for a wilder, more exuberant brand of music and many turned to American R&B for their kicks. Numbered among these were members of such groups as The Beatles, The Rolling Stones, The Animals and the Yardbirds, whose later attempts at reproducing R&B gave birth to the British Beat Boom and helped shape the sound of the decade.

There is no doubt that the 1960s was the most important decade of the century for British recording artists. After The Beatles broke down the barriers that had held back British acts for so long, UK records were finally given a fair listening by the vast American audience. It would be fair to say that in the US during the mid 1960s it was a positive advantage to be British: after decades of being 'also-rans', Britannia ruled the airwaves. Nevertheless, by the end of the decade American acts had regained much of their lost ground.

The 1960s was the last decade in which cover versions were still prevalent. Unlike today (the 1990s), when the vast majority of performers write their own songs, only a handful of 1960s acts could claim to have been 100 per cent original in their choice of material. The British may have rewritten the book of rock, but most of the era's biggest hits still emanated from the US.

As the 1970s approached, an increasing number of recording artists on both sides of the Atlantic were writing their own material and starting to experiment with sounds and ideas; unlike their predecessors, many stars of the late 1960s refused to be manipulated by producers and A&R men.

The whole spectrum of 1960s music can be viewed by delving into this book. Song by song, record by record, it comprehensively charts the many changes that took place over this ten-year period in the Top 10s of the US and UK, and helps to explain why the 1960s has now been acknowledged as the most important and influential decade in popular music.

# How to Use This Book

This volume in *The Encyclopedia of Hits* contains information about every single that reached the US or UK Top 10 during the 1960s. The records are listed chronologically and when two or more entered the chart simultaneously the highest entry is listed first and the lowest last. If a record appeared in both the US and UK Top 10, the information appears under the entry in the artist's home country.

Included are details about original versions, cover recordings, follow-ups, record-breaking feats, answer records and success on the other side of the Atlantic. When a chart placing is mentioned within the text, it refers to the country under which the entry appears unless stated otherwise. When the R&B or country chart is mentioned, this refers to the US charts.

The heading for each entry shows the artist's name, record title, label, peak position and the act's total number of Top 10 entries up to that point (these running totals being calculated from the first published chart in the 1950s, plus the record's placing in the Top 500 singles of the decade, if applicable. The book also includes separate listings of these Top 500 singles and of the Top 100 acts on both sides of the Atlantic.

Please note that where a word is spelt differently in the US and the UK, the British spelling is used, eg favourite (not favorite) or colour (not color).

## Top 100 Artists

The positions in these lists (see pages 307–308) are calculated by a complex points system which takes into account each record's weekly chart position, peak position, weeks in the Top 10 and time spent at No 1. Only points earned by an artist within the decade are included; thus, if an act's record entered the chart in the last week of 1969 and reached the top in 1970, only the points amassed in its first chart week will be included in that act's total.

## Top 500 singles

It is impossible to obtain completely accurate sales figures for the era, and these lists (see pages 309–320) are therefore based on each record's chart performance. It is thus 'longevity biased', so that a record which spent a long time in the Top 10 will score more points than a bigger-selling single which made a quick exit.

The positions are calculated by a complex points system which takes into account each record's weekly chart position, peak position, weeks in the Top 10 and time spent at No 1. Only points earned within the decade are included; thus, if a record entered the chart in the last week of 1969 and reached the top in 1970 only the points amassed in its first chart week will be included.

## British Record Paper Abbreviations

*MM    Melody Maker       RM    Record Mirror       NME  NewMusical Express*
US chart information © BPI Communications Inc used courtesy of *Billboard* magazine. Billboard ® is a registered trademark of BPI Communications. All rights reserved and are used under licence from VNU Business Press Syndication International BV.

UK chart information © *Music Week*

## Record Heading Information

The heading for each record contains the following information

### Example

**JOHNNY PRESTON**
RUNNING BEAR
*Mercury*

| | |
|---|---|
| **JOHNNY PRESTON** | Act name |
| RUNNING BEAR | Song title |
| *Mercury* | Record label in country concerned |

▲ 1 = Peak position in country concerned

⑩ 8 = Number of Top 10 entries act has had in country concerned to this point, in this case 8 – when followed by ● indicates it was also the last top ten hit

45/500 = Position in country's Top 500 for the decade, where applicable

# UNITED STATES
# JANUARY 1960

## JOHNNY PRESTON
RUNNING BEAR
*Mercury*

▲ 1
⑩ 1
45/500

Texas-born John Preston Courville had a transatlantic No 1 with his first chart entry. His early mentor, the Big Bopper (J.P. Richardson), was inspired by a commercial for Dove soap to write this tragic tale of love between Red Indians from warring tribes. Both the Big Bopper and country legend George Jones sang backing vocals on the track recorded shortly before the composer's death (in the February 1959 plane crash that also killed Buddy Holly). Preston's 1965 re-recording went nowhere, but a 1969 version by Sonny James topped the country list.

## JIMMY CLANTON
GO JIMMY GO
*Ace*

▲ 5
⑩ 2
—/500

The teen idol from Louisiana had his biggest hit since the million-selling 'Just A Dream' (1958). Doc Pomus and Mort Shuman had originally written the catchy up-tempo tune for Bobby Rydell as 'Go Bobby Go', but when his A&R team rejected it they altered the title and submitted it to Clanton. Ironically, Clanton subsequently rejected Pomus & Shuman's chart-topping 'Save The Last Dance For Me'.

## MARK DINNING
TEEN ANGEL
*MGM*

▲ 1
⑩ 1•
83/500

After several unsuccessful singles, the singer from Oklahoma scored with a teen disaster lament penned for him by his sister Jean, who had been in the best-selling 1940s group, The Dinning Sisters. 'Teen Angel' was a tale about a 16-year-old killed by a train as she searched for her boyfriend's high school ring in his car stalled on the railroad track. The record was banned in the UK on the grounds of 'bad taste'. Dinning, who was unable to add to his Top 40 score, died in 1986.

## ANDY WILLIAMS
THE VILLAGE OF
ST BERNADETTE
*Cadence*

▲ 7
⑩ 5
—/500

This semi-religious ballad about the wonders of Lourdes added to the hit tally of the popular singer. It was written by British-based Australian singer Eula Parker, who had replaced Marie Benson in the UK's leading vocal group, The Stargazers, in 1955. The song, which veteran vocalist Anne Shelton had failed to take into the UK charts in 1959, won the prestigious (British) Ivor Novello Award for Top Song of 1959.

## DION & THE BELMONTS
WHERE OR WHEN
*Laurie*

▲ 3
⑩ 2•
372/500

One of the most popular teen vocal groups of the late 1950s said goodbye to the Top 10 with a smooth harmony version of a well-known standard penned by Rodgers & Hart for the 1937 musical *Babes In Arms*. It was the doo-wop-based quartet's second million seller, following in the footsteps of 'A Teenager In Love' (1958). Later that year Dion left for a successful solo career. The group have reunited on several occasions since.

# UNITED KINGDOM
# JANUARY 1960

## MAX BYGRAVES
JINGLE BELL ROCK
*Decca*

The British hit version of this well-known Christmas novelty was by popular all-round entertainer Bygraves, who had been a UK chart regular in the 1950s. Joe Beal and Jim Boothe's only hit composition had reached the US Top 40 in 1957, 1958, 1959 and 1960 by the often covered country artist Bobby Helms. In 1961, the rock-oriented opus registered again in the US for the duo of Chubby Checker and Bobby Rydell.

## MARTY WILDE
BAD BOY
*Philips*

After four UK Top 10 entries with cover versions of American hits, this British teen idol had a hit with with one of his own compositions. He was one of the Larry Parnes stable of rock acts, which also included Tommy Steele and Billy Fury. In the US, Wilde's recording beat several covers (including one by teenage hitmaker Robin Luke) and only narrowly missed the Top 40.

## ANTHONY NEWLEY
WHY
*Decca*

The actor turned singer/composer and entertainer added to his string of UK hits with an effective interpretation of Frankie Avalon's recent US No 1. It was the Londoner's third Top 10 entry and his first chart topper. 'Why' (which musically bore a passing resemblance to 'In A Little Spanish Town') was composed by Peter De Angelis and Bob Marcucci, who not only produced Avalon's version but also owned his record label. Newley's 1992 re-recording with his daughter Tara was a non-starter.

## MICHAEL HOLLIDAY
STARRY EYED
*Columbia*

The first Liverpool act to top the UK chart in the Swingin' Sixties was a Bing Crosby sound-alike with his version of a minor US hit by Gary Stites. 'Starry Eyed' was the only Top 10 hit this decade for the vocalist whose cover of Burt Bacharach's 'The Story Of My Life' had been a No 1 in 1958. Regular hit writers Earl Shuman and Mort Garson composed the engaging pop ditty.

## FREDDY CANNON
WAY DOWN YONDER IN
NEW ORLEANS
*Top Rank*

After clicking with original material like 'Tallahassee Lassie', the Philadelphia-based rocker (born Freddy Picariello) gave a batch of standards his unique 'boom boom' treatment. Cannon's revival of the 1922 composition 'Way Down Yonder In New Orleans' earned him his biggest transatlantic hit. The track was included on *The Explosive Freddy Cannon* – the first rock album to top the UK chart.

## GUY MITCHELL
HEARTACHES BY THE
NUMBER
*Philips*

One of the biggest-selling singers of the early 1950s returned after a couple of relatively quiet sales years. The popular performer, who had topped the transatlantic charts in 1956 with 'Singing The Blues', had his last major hit with another cover of a country smash. Noted Nashville tunesmith Harlan Howard wrote the number, which was originally cut by Ray Price. Mitchell (born Al Cernick) re-recorded it for the country market with minimal success in 1969.

## CLIFF RICHARD
VOICE IN THE
WILDERNESS
*Columbia*

▲ 2
🔟 5
232/500

Producer Norrie Paramor and noted British songsmith Bunny Lewis wrote this semi-religious ballad for Cliff's second film, *Expresso Bongo*. In the movie, the song became a big hit for Bongo Herbert, played by Cliff.

# UNITED STATES
# FEBRUARY 1960

## JIMMY JONES
HANDY MAN
*Cub*

▲ 2
🔟 1
213/500

The falsetto-voiced R&B performer from Alabama penned his first major hit with Otis Blackwell, and originally recorded it with the Sparks Of Rhythm in 1956. Jones, who had previously sung in gospel and doo-wop outfits, was backed on this 1959 version by celebrated session group The Cues. 'Handy Man' returned to the US chart courtesy of Del Shannon in 1964 and of James Taylor in 1977. Culture Club's top 1983 hit 'Karma Chameleon' also allegedly owed a little to Jones' debut hit.

## CONWAY TWITTY
LONELY BLUE BOY
*MGM*

▲ 6
🔟 3•
—/500

Presley-esque rocker Conway's last Top 10 pop hit was originally titled 'Danny', and Fred Wise and Ben Weisman wrote it for Elvis Presley's much acclaimed *King Creole* (in which he played Danny Fisher). Elvis recorded it, but it did not appear in the movie. Dion & The Belmonts, Cliff Richard and Marty Wilde also cut 'Danny', before Twitty (born Harold Jenkins) changed its title and took it into the charts. He turned to country music in 1968 and had stockpiled 40 No 1 hits prior to his death in 1993.

## JACK SCOTT
WHAT IN THE WORLD'S
COME OVER YOU
*Top Rank*

▲ 5
🔟 3
463/500

The deep-voiced Canadian rockabilly performer joined Top Rank Records from Carlton for a staggering $50,000 in late 1959. His first release for the label was a transatlantic Top 10 entry and, like his previous US Top 10 hits, 'My True Love' and 'Goodbye Baby', it was self-composed. The memorable beat ballad was also a Top 10 country hit for Sonny James in 1975.

## JIM REEVES
HE'LL HAVE TO GO
*RCA*

▲ 2
🔟 1•
205/500

Shortly after signing a new five-year deal with RCA, the velvet-voiced country singer from Texas had his biggest US hit with a Joe and Audrey Allison composition, which also became his first UK Top 20 entry. The song had been recorded earlier by Billy Brown and subsequently charted for R&B star Solomon Burke in 1964. It inspired many answer versions, including the Top 5 hit 'He'll Have To Stay' by Jeannie Black.

## MARV JOHNSON
YOU GOT WHAT IT TAKES
*UA*

This R&B singer from Detroit, who in 1958 had been the first artist on the Tamla label, cracked the Top 10 with his third chart single. Berry Gordy Jr, the record's producer, penned it with his sister Gwen and Tyran Carlo (aka Billy Davis); they were the team that had written many early Jackie Wilson hits. In Britain, the Dave Clark Five charted with the song in 1967 and Showaddywaddy steered it to No 2 in 1977.

## PERCY FAITH
THEME FROM *A SUMMER PLACE*
*Columbia*

The title song from a movie starring Richard Egan, Dorothy McGuire and teen pin-ups Sandra Dee and Troy Donahue gave the orchestra leader and musical director from Canada his third No 1 single. Mack Discant and Max Steiner composed the instrumental, which headed the US list for nine weeks and won the Grammy for Record of the Year. A vocal version by The Lettermen reached the Top 20 in 1965. Faith died in 1976 – shortly after his disco re-recording of this chart topper failed to ignite any interest.

## EVERLY BROTHERS
LET IT BE ME
*Cadence*

Early rock music's biggest-selling duo clocked up another transatlantic Top 20 entry with a song composed by Frenchmen Gilbert Becaud and Pierre Delanoe as 'Je t'Appartiens'. The English version (with lyrics by Mann Curtis) was first released by Jill Corey in 1957 and was the theme to a CBS TV drama about payola. Unlike the brothers' previous hits, this string-laden track was not cut in Nashville but at Bell Studios in New York, where their good friend Buddy Holly had recorded.

## BOBBY DARIN
BEYOND THE SEA
*Atco*

This multi-talented entertainer from New York followed his transatlantic No 1 'Mack The Knife' with another cabaret-styled reworking of a European-penned pop standard. This time it was 'La Mer', composed by noted French tunesmith Charles Trenet, that was afforded the distinctive Darin treatment.

## DINAH WASHINGTON & BROOK BENTON
BABY (YOU GOT WHAT IT TAKES)
*Mercury*

Teaming the top 1950s female R&B vocalist with one of the early 1960s biggest-selling R&B song stylists proved to be a highly successful move. The well-matched pair's first hit came with an upbeat offering, penned for them by Benton's long-time writing partner, Clyde Otis.

## BOBBY RYDELL
WILD ONE
*Cameo*

Cameo Records' in-house writers Dave Appell, Bernie Lowe and Kal Mann penned the stomping hit which shipped the photogenic singer with the standout quiff into the transatlantic Top 20 for the first time. This confirmed Rydell's position as the top-selling Philadelphia-born teen idol, replacing late 1950s pin-ups Frankie Avalon and Fabian (Forte).

# UNITED KINGDOM
# FEBRUARY 1960

## ADAM FAITH
POOR ME
*Parlophone*

▲ 1
🔟 2
86/500

Like its predecessor 'What Do You Want', Faith's second chart topper was conceived by singer/songwriter Johnny Worth (under the name Les Vandyke). Only Cliff Richard sold more singles in the UK in 1960 than this diminutive pop star, whose records, thanks in part to arrangements by John Barry, had a definite Buddy Holly feel to them. Soon afterwards, Faith published his autobiography, *Poor Me*.

## BOBBY DARIN
BEYOND THE SEA (LA MER)
*London American*

▲ 8
🔟 3
—/500

See US entry.

## EMILE FORD & THE CHECKMATES
ON A SLOW BOAT TO CHINA
*Pye*

▲ 3
🔟 2
385/500

West Indian vocalist Ford fronted the multi-racial British beat group who followed their No 1 debut 'What Do You Want To Make Those Eyes At Me For' with another update of an old favourite. This time it was a much-recorded Frank Loesser composition from the late 1940s. As it sailed up the chart, the act's first single was battling it out Stateside with covers by hitmakers Ray Peterson and Sunny Gale.

## CRAIG DOUGLAS
PRETTY BLUE EYES
*Top Rank*

▲ 5
🔟 2
462/500

This amiable ex-milkman from the Isle of Wight had topped the UK chart with his previous release, a version of Sam Cooke's 'Only Sixteen'. He quickly returned to the Top 10 with this faithful cover of Steve Lawrence's US hit, which was penned by early rock 'n' roll star Teddy Randazzo (who had fronted The Chuckles in the mid-1950s).

## JOHNNY PRESTON
RUNNING BEAR
*Mercury*

▲ 1
🔟 1
95/500

See US entry (January).

## MR. ACKER BILK & HIS PARAMOUNT JAZZ BAND
SUMMER SET
*Columbia*

▲ 10
🔟 1
—/500

Bearded British trad jazz band leader Bilk named his first hit after his home county, Somerset. He co-wrote this instrumental with ex-band member Dave Collett and it started life as a piano solo. Bilk's instantly recognizable Edwardian stage outfit, complete with colourful waistcoat and bowler hat, made him the most conspicuous of the UK trad jazz performers. In the US, a cover version by trumpeter Monty Kelly cracked the Top 40.

# UNITED STATES
# MARCH 1960

## PAUL ANKA
PUPPY LOVE
*ABC Paramount*

▲ 2
⑩ 6
273/500

The first teenager to top the transatlantic charts (with 'Diana' in 1957) collected his ninth US Top 20 entry before his nineteenth birthday. The self-composed song was reportedly written about actress Annette Funicello, who had a hit with 'Tall Paul' a year earlier. Interestingly, Annette later married Anka's manager. This teen love song was also a transatlantic hit in 1972 for another young performer, the incredibly popular Donny Osmond.

## PLATTERS
HARBOR LIGHTS
*Mercury*

▲ 8
⑩ 7•
—/500

British song writer Jimmy Kennedy penned the last major hit for the biggest-selling vocal group of the early rock years. 'Harbor Lights' previously charted for such notables as Frances Langford (1937), Bing Crosby (1950), Sammy Kaye (1950) and Guy Lombardo (1950), and was one of the first tunes Elvis Presley recorded. The top doo-wop quintet, originally fronted by Tony Williams, were one of the first groups inducted into the Rock and Roll Hall of Fame in 1990.

## BRENDA LEE
SWEET NOTHIN'S
*Decca*

▲ 4
⑩ 1
381/500

The most successful female teenage performer of the 1960s was born Brenda Tarpley in Georgia. She signed to Decca at age 11 in 1956, and after several so-so sellers had her first big hit with a cute Ronnie Self-composed rocker. The record, which cracked the transatlantic Top 5, also featured top Nashville session musicians Floyd Cramer, Bob Moore and Boots Randolph.

## LITTLE DIPPERS
FOREVER
*University*

▲ 9
⑩ 1•
—/500

Top country music publisher Buddy Killen penned this ballad, which charted for a quartet of session singers assembled by Anita Kerr (and including later country hitmaker Darell McCall). Kerr's main act, the Anita Kerr Singers, were the most in-demand Nashville session group in the 1950s and 1960s, backing such headliners as Connie Francis, Brenda Lee, Perry Como, Eddy Arnold and Jim Reeves. Amazingly, in 1965, at the height of the British invasion, the Anita Kerr Singers grabbed the Grammy for Best Vocal Group Performance.

## ANNETTE
O DIO MIO
*Vista*

▲ 10
⑩ 2•
—/500

Hot tunesmiths Al Hoffman and Dick Manning wrote the last Top 10 entry for this popular singer and actress. The pair's other recent hits had included 'The Three Bells', 'Secretly' and 'Hawaiian Wedding Song'. Annette (Funicello) first came to national prominence as a cute little Mousketeer on Mickey Mouse's mid-1950s TV series, and her debut hit 'Tall Paul' also introduced writers Richard and Robert Sherman (*Mary Poppins* etc) to the charts.

# UNITED KINGDOM
# MARCH 1960

## PERRY COMO
DELAWARE
*RCA*

▲ 3
⑩ 11
384/500

The balladeer from Pennsylvania was one of the most popular post-war vocalists and TV personalities. His only British Top 10 entry of the 1960s was a novelty which artificially linked the names of numerous US states. 'Delaware' was written by Irving Gordon, who is better known for such 1950s hits as 'Unforgettable' and 'Be Anything (But Be Mine)'. As the single was charting, Como visited the UK to record a show for his TV series.

## LANCE FORTUNE
BE MINE
*Pye*

▲ 4
⑩ 1•
—/500

Eminent impresario Larry Parnes discovered singer Chris Morris at the famous 2 I's coffee bar. Parnes rechristened him with a name he had previously given to singing keyboard player Clive Powell, whose name was then changed to Georgie Fame. Fortune's sole hit was a Joe Meek-produced version of a German composition, 'Alles Madchen Wollen Kussen', with English lyrics by Marcel Stellman. The record had an Adam Faith/Buddy Holly sound, thanks to the string arrangements by Faith's musical director John Barry.

## PERCY FAITH
THEME FROM *A SUMMER PLACE*
*Philips*

▲ 2
⑩ 1•
229/500

See US entry (February).

## LONNIE DONEGAN
MY OLD MAN'S A DUSTMAN
*Pye*

▲ 1
⑩ 12
55/500

The UK's biggest-selling star of the late 1950s collected his third No 1 with his own arrangement of an old music hall favourite, which was recorded live at the Gaumont Cinema, Doncaster. Donegan launched the skiffle craze of the late 1950s, and by 1960 was the genre's sole successful survivor. The single entered the *NME* chart at No 1 – the first UK record to achieve this feat.

## CLIFF RICHARD
FALL IN LOVE WITH YOU
*Columbia*

▲ 2
⑩ 7
200/500

Cliff narrowly failed to notch up his third No 1 with this track. The song was penned by his one-time backing musician Ian Samwell, who wrote several earlier hits for Cliff including another No 2, 'Move It'.

## BOBBY RYDELL
WILD ONE
*Columbia*

▲ 7
⑩ 1•
—/500

See US entry (February).

## MAX BYGRAVES
FINGS AIN'T WHAT THEY USED T'BE
*Decca*

▲ 5
⑩ 7•
—/500

The popular radio and TV entertainer achieved his last Top 10 single with a version of the title tune from Lionel Bart's cockney theatrical musical. A decade later, Bygraves had a string of hit 'sing-along' albums.

## BILLY FURY
COLETTE
*Decca*

This teenage rock'n'roll singer's third self-penned single gave him his first Top 10 entry. Fury was the latest Larry Parnes protégé to make the big time, following in the footsteps of Tommy Steele and Marty Wilde. He went on to stockpile more UK chart records than any Liverpool act of the 1960s, including The Beatles.

## MARV JOHNSON
YOU GOT WHAT IT TAKES
*London American*

See US entry (February).

---

# UNITED STATES
# APRIL 1960

---

## JOHNNY HORTON
SINK THE BISMARCK
*Columbia*

The Texas-based country singer recorded 1959's biggest-selling single, 'The Battle Of New Orleans'. The Singing Fisherman struck again with the title song from a Kenneth More movie, which he co-wrote with well-regarded country composer Tillman Franks.

## STEVE LAWRENCE
FOOTSTEPS
*ABC Paramount*

This well-respected easy listening vocalist followed-up his Top 10 hit 'Pretty Blue Eyes' with a catchy Barry Mann and Hank Hunter song. New Yorker Lawrence (born Sidney Leibowitz), together with his wife and singing partner Eydie Gorme, has remained a top-line cabaret entertainer for almost 40 years.

## CONNIE FRANCIS
MAMA
*MGM*

The biggest-selling female singer of the early rock decades had her first smash of the 1960s with a powerful Italian ballad taken from her first hit album, *Italian Favorites*. The Paul Anka-composed

B side 'Teddy', also made the Top 20. For the record books, the singer, who was born Concetta Franconero in New Jersey, had released ten unsuccessful singles before starting a staggering string of 22 American Top 20 singles in 1958.

## BROTHERS FOUR
GREENFIELDS
*Columbia*

Four fraternity brothers from the University of Washington earned a gold record for their plaintive version of a Terry Gilkyson folk song that Roberta Lee had recorded without success in 1958. They subsequently had several minor hits, including 'The Green Leaves Of Summer' from the film *The Alamo*.

## MARV JOHNSON
I LOVE THE WAY YOU LOVE
*UA*

Berry Gordy Jr, later head of Motown Records, penned Johnson's last major US hit. It was one of two simultaneous Top 40 entries for Gordy, the other being the meritorious 'Money' by Barrett Strong. Johnson, who subsequently recorded for Motown, died in 1993 when appearing at The Drifters fortieth anniversary show.

### ELVIS PRESLEY
STUCK ON YOU
*RCA*

▲ 1
⑩ 18
28/500

Elvis hated his first release after leaving the army, but his fans loved it enough to take him to the top for the twelfth time in four years. The B side 'Fame And Fortune' also attained a US Top 20 position.

### BROWNS
THE OLD LAMPLIGHTER
*RCA*

▲ 5
⑩ 2•
—/500

This family vocal trio notched up their third Top 20 pop entry in a row with a revival of a plaintive Charles Tobias and Nat Simon song that had headed the charts in 1946 by label-mate Sammy Kaye. Lead singer Jim Ed Brown went solo in 1965 and had a string of top country hits.

### CONNIE STEVENS
SIXTEEN REASONS
*Warner*

▲ 3
⑩ 2•
308/500

The actress/singer from New York (born Concetta Ingolia) first hit with Edward Byrnes on the *77 Sunset Strip*-inspired novelty 'Kookie Kookie (Lend Me Your Comb)' in 1959. Her version of this teen love lament, written by Bill and Doree Post, was the only transatlantic Top 20 entry for the woman who was once married to 1950s heart-throb Eddie Fisher. At the time of the hit she was starring as Cricket Blake in the top TV series *Hawaiian Eye*.

### BILL BLACK'S COMBO
WHITE SILVER SANDS
*HI*

▲ 9
⑩ 1•
—/500

Elvis Presley's ex-bass player's instantly recognizable instrumental team had six successive Top 20 entries, but only their remake of Don Rondo's 1957 vocal smash climbed into the Top 10. The influential Memphis-based combo were voted Top Instrumental Group of 1960. They re-charted with a Twist version of this hit in 1962. Black's band appeared on The Beatles' 1964 US tour and continued recording after he died in 1965 from a brain tumour.

# UNITED KINGDOM
# APRIL 1960

### ANTHONY NEWLEY
DO YOU MIND
*Decca*

▲ 1
⑩ 4
103/500

The instantly recognizable performer's second successive chart topper was also the second No 1 for composer Lionel Bart (following Cliff Richard's 'Living Doll'). Both this version of the finger-snapping song and a cover by Andy Williams reached the bottom of the US Top 100.

### ELVIS PRESLEY
STUCK ON YOU
*RCA*

▲ 3
⑩ 19
391/500

See US entry.

### JIMMY JONES
HANDY MAN
*MGM*

▲ 3
⑩ 1
192/500

See US entry (February).

## JOHNNY & THE HURRICANES
BEATNIK FLY
*London American*

This popular Ohio-based instrumental outfit's last transatlantic Top 20 entry was their interpretation of the old folk favourite 'Blue Tail Fly' (aka 'Jimmie Crack Corn'). Like most of the band's other hits, the composer credits listed the group's agents Irv Micahnik and Harry Balk (known as Tom King and Ira Mack).

## BOBBY DARIN
CLEMENTINE
*London American*

The Las Vegas-styled pop star continued his run of transatlantic smashes with a swinging cabaret treatment of the traditional folk song about a gold miner's daughter. 'Clementine' was arranged by Woody Harris, the co-writer of Darin's 'Queen Of The Hop'.

## JOHN BARRY SEVEN
HIT AND MISS
*Columbia*

The trumpeter/band leader and composer from Yorkshire penned his only Top 10 entry. It was used as the theme music to the popular TV series *Juke*

*Box Jury* and featured Barry's instantly recognizable pizzicato string sound which he had made famous on records by Adam Faith. His band had been regulars on earlier UK rock TV shows *6-5 Special*, *Oh, Boy!* and *Wham!*. The multi-talented artist (born John Prendergast) became one of the best-known movie score writers in Hollywood.

## ADAM FAITH
SOMEONE ELSE'S BABY
*Parlophone*

Faith almost achieved three No 1s with his first three hits. Perry Ford (later of the Ivy League) co-wrote the song with Les Vandyke (who had penned the No 1s). Both this and his previous single, 'Poor Me', were covered in the US by Marty Evans.

## EVERLY BROTHERS
CATHY'S CLOWN
*Warner*

See US entry (May).

## BRENDA LEE
SWEET NOTHIN'S
*Brunswick*

See US entry (March).

# UNITED STATES
# MAY 1960

## JACKIE WILSON
NIGHT
*Brunswick*

The ex-lead vocalist of Billy Ward & The Dominoes was arguably the No 1 R&B star of the early 1960s. After a string of up-tempo hits, mostly penned by Berry Gordy Jr, he turned his hand successfully to the classics. 'Night', which was based on Saint-Saens' aria 'My Heart At Thy Sweet Voice', was the biggest US hit of his long career.

## JOHNNY PRESTON
CRADLE OF LOVE
*Mercury*

Preston followed his chart-topping 'Running Bear' with a nursery rhyme rocker that gave composers Jack Fautheree and Wayne Gray their only hit. His follow-up, a re-tread of Shirley & Lee's 'Feel So Fine', was his last big seller. In later years Preston recorded demos for acts such as Charlie Pride and occasionally sang in The Jordanaires.

## BILLY BLAND
LET THE LITTLE
GIRL DANCE
*Old Town*

▲ 7
🔟 1•
—/500

The R&B performer from North Carolina, who helped popularize the Chicken dance craze in the mid-1950s, had a transatlantic Top 20 entry with a pop-oriented opus penned by Carl Spencer of The Halos. Titus Turner was meant to record the song but could not get the right feel, and so Bland (who happened to be working in the same studio) added his vocal to the track. Among his subsequent unsuccessful singles was a similar-sounding sequel, 'Can't Stop Her From Dancing'.

## EVERLY BROTHERS
CATHY'S CLOWN
*Warner*

▲ 1
🔟 8
18/500

Don and Phil Everly's first Warner Brothers release was recorded in the same Nashville studio as their Cadence hits and utilized the same session men. They wrote the song about a high school sweetheart of Don's, and the duo's single headed the charts on both sides of the Atlantic. In 1990 Reba McEntire's version was the top country record of the year.

## NEIL SEDAKA
STAIRWAY TO HEAVEN
*RCA*

▲ 9
🔟 2
—/500

The composer of the Connie Francis hits 'Stupid Cupid' and 'Frankie' followed his own Top 20 singles, 'The Diary', 'I Go Ape' (in the UK) and 'Oh! Carol' with another infectious self-penned pop hit. The New York-based performer became a frequent transatlantic chart entrant in the early 1960s, which more than justified the huge promotional push that RCA had put behind the launch of his recording career.

## JIMMY JONES
GOOD TIMIN'
*CUB*

▲ 3
🔟 2•
326/500

Celebrated songsmiths Clint Ballard Jr and Fred Tobias wrote Jimmy Jones' second successive million seller. The record, which topped the UK chart, was produced by Otis Blackwell, who penned many great rock'n'roll hits. It was the last major hit for the singer who had fronted the noteworthy doo-wop group The Pretenders.

## JEANNE BLACK
HE'LL HAVE TO STAY
*Capitol*

▲ 4
🔟 1•
485/500

This country-oriented singer's answer record to Jim Reeves' gold single 'He'll Have To Go' sold a million copies. Surprisingly, Black's recording also inspired other answer songs such as 'He'd Better Go' and 'I Can't Stay'. Later in 1960 the Californian singer, who was discovered by country hitmaker Cliffie Stone, had a minor hit with 'Oh, How I Miss You Tonight', released as an answer to 'Are You Lonesome Tonight' by Elvis.

## ANITA BRYANT
PAPER ROSES
*Carlton*

▲ 5
🔟 1
—/500

Successful 1950s tunesmith Fred Spielman composed this sad sing-along ballad with Janice Torre. It was recorded with little success in 1955 by Lola Dee, but in 1960 it gave ex-beauty queen Bryant her biggest hit, and in the UK it was a Top 10 entry for the Kaye Sisters. Thirteen years later, 14-year-old Marie Osmond turned the song into a transatlantic Top 10 hit.

## JACK SCOTT
BURNING BRIDGES
*Top Rank*

▲ 3
🔟 4•
335/500

The distinctive Canadian rockabilly performer (born Jack Scafone Jr) was accompanied on his last major hit by The Chantones, who sang backing vocals on all his nine Top 40 hits. The B side, 'Oh, Little One', also charted. Glen Campbell's revival of 'Burning Bridges' reached the country Top 20 in 1967.

# UNITED KINGDOM
# MAY 1960

## KING BROTHERS
STANDING ON THE
CORNER
*Parlophone*

▲ 4
🔟 2•
—/500

Essex vocal and instrumental trio Michael, Tony and Dennis King were the top group in the UK before The Beatles. The youthful, though old-fashioned, act had been TV stars since the mid-1950s and had several chart singles, including an Anglicized cover of 'A White Sports Coat' in 1957. Their last major hit was a version of the best-known song from Frank Loesser's musical *The Most Happy Fella*, which had been a US hit for The Four Lads in 1956.

## STEVE LAWRENCE
FOOTSTEPS
*HMV*

▲ 4
🔟 1•
445/500

See US entry (April).

## DUANE EDDY
SHAZAM
*London American*

▲ 4
🔟 2
437/500

The bass guitar star from Phoenix Arizona, who made the 'Twang' the 'in thang' in the late 1950s, was more successful in the UK in the 1960s than in the US. Like most of his hits, he composed this rocking instrumental with producer Lee Hazlewood. Eddy introduced it on his sell-out debut UK tour, where he received the lion's share of audience response over fellow American headliner Bobby Darin.

## JOHNNY PRESTON
CRADLE OF LOVE
*Mercury*

▲ 2
🔟 2•
233/500

See US entry.

## CRAIG DOUGLAS
HEART OF A TEENAGE
GIRL
*Top Rank*

▲ 10
🔟 3
—/500

Bill Compton and Morgan 'Thunderclap' Jones (a wild piano pounder from the pre-rock days) penned this tender teen ballad for the regular British hit maker, who was born Terry Perkins.

# UNITED STATES
# JUNE 1960

## CONNIE FRANCIS
EVERYBODY'S
SOMEBODY'S FOOL
*MGM*

▲ 1
⑩ 7
98/500

The first of Francis' three US No 1 hits was a country-styled composition with a very catchy chorus. It was co-written by Howard Greenfield, who had part-penned her British No 1, 'Stupid Cupid'.

## RON HOLDEN
LOVE YOU SO
*Donna*

▲ 7
⑩ 1•
—/500

This West Coast-based singer/songwriter's only chart entry was recorded with his band The Thunderbirds at the small home studio of ex-police officer Larry Nelson. He based his self-composed opus on The Diamonds' 1957 hit 'Little Darlin'. Although the band were not always in tune, the track had a magic that Holden was unable to reproduce later in more expensive studios. The B side, 'My Babe', was popular with rock'n'roll fans.

## BOBBY RYDELL
SWINGIN' SCHOOL
*Cameo*

▲ 5
⑩ 3
—/500

One of the many early rock hits from the pens of Kal Mann, Dave Appell and Bernie Lowe was sung by Rydell in the Dick Clark movie *Because They're Young*.

## PAUL EVANS
HAPPY-GO-LUCKY-ME
*Guaranteed*

▲ 10
⑩ 2•
—/500

The New Yorker who wrote the Kalin Twins' 1958 smash 'When' had the last of three consecutive American Top 20 entries with this bouncy self-composed song. Frank Ifield (in his pre-hit period)

and Britain's World War II star George Formby covered Evans' hit in the UK. In 1977, Evans had his first UK Top 20 hit with 'Hello This Is Joannie'.

## HOLLYWOOD ARGYLES
ALLEY-OOP
*Lute*

▲ 1
⑩ 1•
154/500

Gary Paxton, who had been Skip of the hit duo Skip & Flip, co-produced and sang lead on this novelty about the cartoon caveman from the funny papers. 'Alley-Oop' was penned by his friend Dallas Frazier, who went on to become one of the most accomplished country writers of the 1960s and 1970s. Covers by Dante & The Evergreens and R&B super-session group The Dyna-Sores also charted. The Hollywood Argyles was one of many names the entrepreneurial Paxton sang under. Among his later releases was 'Alley-Oop Was A Two-Dab Man'.

## DUANE EDDY
BECAUSE THEY'RE YOUNG
*Jamie*

▲ 4
⑩ 3•
461/500

The most popular solo instrumentalist of the early rock years had his biggest transatlantic hit with the string-laden title theme from a movie starring Dick Clark and Tuesday Weld. The song was penned by Aaron Schroeder, Wally Gold and Don Costa.

## BRENDA LEE
I'M SORRY
*Decca*

▲ 1
⑩ 2
31/500

Fifteen-year-old Brenda Lee's first No 1 hit was an impassioned love ballad written by Ronnie Self, who had penned her breakthrough hit 'Sweet Nothin's'. It was one of the first Nashville recordings to utilize a string section, and was rushed off in five minutes at the end of a session.

## DINAH WASHINGTON & BROOK BENTON
A ROCKIN' GOOD WAY
*Mercury*

▲ 7
⑩4/3
—/500

The R&B dream team clicked again with a happy rocker penned by Benton, Clyde Otis and Luchi Dejesus. The song, which was first recorded by Priscilla Bowman, was a Top 5 hit in the UK in 1984 by Shakin' Stevens and Bonnie Tyler.

---

# UNITED KINGDOM
# JUNE 1960

---

## EDDIE COCHRAN
THREE STEPS TO HEAVEN
*London American*

▲ 1
⑩ 2•
93/500

The influential American rocker, who had died in a car crash at the end of a UK tour, headed the UK chart with an ironically titled song that never even dented the US Top 100. The noted singer and guitarist composed it and he was backed on the single by The Crickets, the late Buddy Holly's group. 'Three Steps To Heaven' narrowly missed the top of the UK chart in 1975 when recorded by Showaddywaddy.

## LONNIE DONEGAN
I WANNA GO HOME
*Pye*

▲ 5
⑩13
—/500

Skiffle's sole survivor scored with his interpretation of a traditional folk song. The Beach Boys had a transatlantic hit with it six years later under the title 'Sloop John B'.

## CONNIE FRANCIS
MAMA/ROBOT MAN
*MGM*

▲ 2
⑩ 5
315/500

See US entry (April). The double A side 'Robot Man', composed by Sylvia Dee (who had written Nat 'King' Cole's 1951 chart topper 'Too Young') was not released in the USA.

## NEIL SEDAKA
STAIRWAY TO HEAVEN
*RCA*

▲ 8
⑩ 3
—/500

See US entry (May).

## TOMMY BRUCE & THE BRUISERS
AIN'T MISBEHAVIN'
*Columbia*

▲ 3
⑩ 1•
352/500

Bruce, whose style was reminiscent of the Big Bopper, hit with a unique rock update of the old Fats Waller hit. Similar-sounding follow-ups failed to return him to the heights. Hank Williams Jr's version topped the country chart in 1986.

## NAT 'KING' COLE
THAT'S YOU
*Capitol*

▲ 10
⑩ 12
—/500

The legendary song stylist and pianist had a UK-only hit with his unmistakable treatment of a ballad composed by Sammy Gallop, Sidney Mitchell and arranger Nelson Riddle.

## JIMMY JONES
GOOD TIMIN'
*MGM*

▲ 1
⑩ 2•
64/500

See US entry (May).

## ADAM FAITH
WHEN JOHNNY COMES
MARCHING HOME/MADE
YOU
*Parlophone*

Faith's A side, an update of the US civil war tune, was heard in his film *Never Let Go*. It was coupled with a suggestive John Barry song from another Faith film, *Beat Girl*. The BBC banned the latter, as did many radio stations in the US, where fellow teen idol Fabian covered it with no noticeable success.

## MICHAEL COX
ANGELA JONES
*Triumph*

The singer from Liverpool briefly found fame with a Joe Meek-produced version of a hum-along John D. Loudermilk song which Johnny Ferguson had taken into the US Top 40. Cox, who was frequently seen on UK pop shows in the late 1950s, released several other singles, including the similar 'Along Came Caroline', but failed to chart again.

# UNITED STATES
# JULY 1960

## BRENDA LEE
THAT'S ALL YOU GOTTA
DO
*Decca*

Singer/songwriter/guitarist Jerry Reed composed the catchy uptempo cut which was initially intended to be the A side of Lee's chart-topping 'I'm Sorry'.

## FENDERMEN
MULE SKINNER BLUES
*Soma*

Named after the Fender guitars they played, this act hit with an unusual upbeat revival of a country/folk favourite originally made famous in the early 1930s by 'The Singing Brakeman', Jimmie Rodgers. The Wisconsin duo's raucous rendition was picked up from the Cuca label by Soma. Subsequent singles, including an equally exciting version of Huey 'Piano' Smith's 'Don't You Just Know It', achieved only minimal success.

## PAUL ANKA
MY HOME TOWN
*ABC Paramount*

The Canadian singer, who made his first record at age 15 in 1956, had his fifth self-composed Top 10 hit in a row.

## ROY ORBISON
ONLY THE LONELY
*Monument*

One of the most successful solo artists of the 1960s had his first major hit with a song he had hoped that either Elvis or the Everly Brothers would record. The unmistakable Texas vocalist took his version to the runner-up position in the US and right to the top in the UK. 'Only The Lonely' headed the country chart in 1969 by Sonny James.

## EVERLY BROTHERS
## WHEN WILL I BE LOVED
*Cadence*

Phil Everly's composition was recorded at the duo's last session for Cadence in February 1960. Linda Ronstadt's 1975 remake reached No 2 in the chart.

## RAY PETERSON
## TELL LAURA I LOVE HER
*RCA*

The Texas singer crashed into the Top 10 with a tragic tale about the stock car race Tommy entered in order to pay for Laura's ring. At first, his UK label refused to release the record, which they considered in 'bad taste' – leaving the way clear for a cover version to motor to the top. The singer, who possessed a four-and-a-half octave vocal range, re-recorded the Jeff Barry and Ben Raleigh song in 1971, but it was a non-starter.

## BRIAN HYLAND
## ITSY BITSY TEENIE WEENIE YELLOW POLKA DOT BIKINI
*Leader*

The 16-year-old New York high school student's second single went all the way to No 1. Lee Pockriss and Paul Vance wrote the jaunty pop novelty, which was inspired by Vance's two-year-old daughter Paula's beach escapades. Jeri Lynn

Foster recorded an answer version, 'Poor Begonia Caught Pneumonia', which was not even a teenie weenie hit. In 1990 an update by Bombalurina topped the UK chart.

## SAFARIS
## IMAGE OF A GIRL
*Eldo*

This LA quartet's only hit was the first release on Eldo – a label owned by R&B star Johnny Otis. It was a haunting doo-wop-styled song penned by members Marv Rosenberg and Richard Clasky. The act were backed by a team of session musicians under the name The Phantom's Band, and among them was Bobby Rey, whose wood-block playing created the tick-tock sound that helped make the record so popular. In the UK, versions by Mark Wynter and Nelson Keene outsold the original.

## HANK LOCKLIN
## PLEASE HELP ME, I'M FALLING
*RCA*

The veteran country performer notched up his only big pop hit with a Don Robertson-penned slipping-around song that Jim Reeves had rejected. The transatlantic Top 10 entry also headed the country chart for 14 weeks. Added to that, an answer version, '(I Can't Help You) I'm Falling Too' by Skeeter Davis, attained a pop Top 40 position.

# UNITED KINGDOM
# JULY 1960

## TOMMY STEELE
WHAT A MOUTH
*Decca*

▲ 5
⑩ 7•
—/500

Days after the one-time target of teen adoration was married, he collected the last of his 13 Top 20 hits with a chirpy update of an old cockney music hall favourite. In a few short years, the UK's first home-grown rock'n'roll star (born Tommy Hicks) had achieved his goal of becoming an all-round entertainer. R.P. Weston penned the music hall novelty in 1906, and five years later he composed 'I'm Henry VIII, I Am' – a US No 1 in 1965 by Herman's Hermits.

## CLIFF RICHARD
PLEASE DON'T TEASE
*Columbia*

▲ 1
⑩ 8
34/500

The Shadows' rhythm guitarist Bruce Welch wrote Cliff's first No 1 of the decade with Peter Chester, who had led Welch's previous group The Five Chesternuts.

## JOHNNY & THE HURRICANES
DOWN YONDER
*London American*

▲ 8
⑩ 3
—/500

The early 1920s song, which had been a major hit for Nashville pianist Del Wood in 1951, charted again for this Ohio instrumental group, which featured keyboard player Paul Tesluk and saxophonist Johnny Paris.

## JOHNNY KIDD & THE PIRATES
SHAKIN' ALL OVER
*HMV*

▲ 1
⑩ 1
105/500

In need of a B side to record, eyepatch-wearing Kidd (born Frederick Heath) hurriedly wrote this song in a coffee bar while waiting for the session

to begin. It went on to become his highest placed hit and is generally regarded as one of the few outstanding UK rock songs of the pre-Beatles era. In 1965, 'Shakin' All Over' introduced Canadian rockers Guess Who to the US Top 40.

## CONNIE STEVENS
SIXTEEN REASONS
*Warner*

▲ 9
⑩ 1•
—/500

See US entry (April).

## ANTHONY NEWLEY
IF SHE SHOULD COME TO YOU
*Decca*

▲ 6
⑩ 5
—/500

The one-time husband of actress Joan Collins charted on both sides of the Atlantic with his unique interpretation of a Spanish love ballad originally entitled 'La Montana'.

## EVERLY BROTHERS
WHEN WILL I BE LOVED
*London American*

▲ 4
⑩ 8
327/500

See US entry.

## GARRY MILLS
LOOK FOR A STAR
*Top Rank*

▲ 7
⑩ 1•
—/500

A&R man Dick Rowe spotted the teenager from Surrey singing at London's famous 2 I's coffee bar. After several overlooked cover versions, Mills had his only hit with a song that also introduced celebrated composer Tony Hatch to the chart. The romantic ballad, which was rejected for inclusion in the Norman Wisdom film *Follow A Star*, was heard in the Hammer movie *Circus Of Horrors*. In the US, four versions reached the Top 100, the biggest seller being a cover by the similarly named Gary Miles.

# UNITED STATES
# AUGUST 1960

## ELVIS PRESLEY
IT'S NOW OR NEVER
*RCA*

The King of Rock's decision to record the turn-of-the-century Italian classical aria 'O Sole Mio' proved to be an inspired choice. Previously associated with such non-rock artists as Enrico Caruso, Mario Lanza and Tony Martin, the track marked a turning point for Presley. It introduced him to a vast new audience and sold an estimated 20 million copies worldwide.

## VENTURES
WALK–DON'T RUN
*Dolton*

The US's biggest-selling instrumental act of the rock era kick-started their career with a version of an instantly memorable tune they knew from Chet Atkins' version on his LP *Hi-Fi In Focus*. 'Walk–Don't Run', penned by jazz musician Johnny Smith, became an instrumental that every budding guitarist learned. The group released it as the second single on their own Blue Horizon label, and after Dolton took over distribution it ran up the charts on both sides of the Atlantic.

## FATS DOMINO
WALKIN' TO
NEW ORLEANS
*Imperial*

One of the true greats of rock'n'roll last strolled into the Top 10 with a tune he co-wrote with Robert Guidry (aka Bobby Charles) and his long-term collaborator Dave Bartholomew. In total, the unique R&B singer/songwriter from New Orleans, who could make 'hand' rhyme with 'shame', is credited with composing and performing 20 million sellers. He was one of the first acts inducted into the Rock and Roll Hall of Fame.

## HANK BALLARD &
## THE MIDNIGHTERS
FINGER POPPIN' TIME
*King*

This top-selling mid-1950s R&B act had their first Top 40 pop hit with an infectious dance track penned by the band's leader. The Detroit group had initially made a name for themselves with such controversial R&B hits as 'Work With Me Annie', 'Annie Had A Baby' and 'Sexy Ways'. They re-recorded 'Finger Poppin' Time' in 1972 with little notable success.

## CHUBBY CHECKER
THE TWIST
*Parkway*

The biggest dance craze of the 1960s was launched by this cover version of Hank Ballard's 1959 R&B hit. When composer Ballard's record and dance took off with teenagers in Philadelphia, DJ Dick Clark had pop/R&B performer Checker cut a similar-sounding version. After Checker's interpretation was featured on Clark's top-rated TV show, *Bandstand*, it quickly overtook Ballard's version on the chart.

## BOBBY RYDELL
VOLARE
*Cameo*

The Italian-American teen pin-up (born Robert Ridarelli) was successful with an early revival of the Italian song that had topped the chart in 1958 by Domenico Modugno.

## DONNIE BROOKS
MISSION BELL
*Era*

▲ 7
🔟 1•
—/500

The Texas singer (born John Faircloth) recorded with minimal success under a variety of names and styles before scoring with his sixth Era release. The happy-go-lucky pop opus which gave him his only Top 20 entry was composed by William Michael. Brooks' only other visit to the Top 40 came with the follow-up, 'Doll House', which charted for the King Brothers in the UK.

## ANITA BRYANT
IN MY LITTLE CORNER OF
THE WORLD
*Carlton*

▲ 10
🔟 2•
—/500

The pop songstress, who came third in the 1958 Miss America pageant, had her second successive Top 10 entry with a song from the pens of regular hit writers Bob Hilliard and Lee Pockriss. Like her erstwhile hit 'Paper Roses', this ballad was also subsequently revived successfully by Marie Osmond. Bryant is now best known as a top inspirational singer and spokesperson for middle America.

# UNITED KINGDOM
# AUGUST 1960

## DUANE EDDY
BECAUSE THEY'RE
YOUNG
*London America*

▲ 2
🔟 3
195/500

See US entry (June).

## ELVIS PRESLEY
A MESS OF BLUES
*RCA*

▲ 2
🔟 20
181/500

RCA in the UK were unable to issue Presley's US hit 'It's Now Or Never' due to copyright problems. Therefore, they released its Pomus and Shuman-penned B side which narrowly missed the top. The UK B side, 'Girl Of My Best Friend', also fared well.

## BRIAN HYLAND
ITSY BITSY TEENIE
WEENIE YELLOW POLKA
DOT BIKINI
*London American*

▲ 8
🔟 1
—/500

See US entry (July).

## SHADOWS
APACHE
*Columbia*

▲ 1
🔟 1
22/500

The first hit for Cliff Richard's backing band came with the quartet's fourth single. Their recording of the Jerry Lordan-composed instrumental (which renowned guitarist Bert Weedon had cut earlier in 1960) featured Cliff on bongos. It was No 1 for five weeks, sold a million in Europe and was voted Record of the Year in *NME*. A later version by Denmark's Jorgen Ingmann narrowly missed the top of the US chart.

## ROLF HARRIS
TIE ME KANGAROO
DOWN SPORT
*Columbia*

▲ 9
🔟 1
—/500

This Australian entertainer, who is a popular TV personality in the UK, sold a million copies of his self-composed novelty. It climbed into the US Top 10 three years later, beating an unexpected cover version by Pat Boone. Among the answer records were 'Tie Me Hunting Dog Down Jed' and 'Tie Me Surfing Board Down Sport'.

## KEN DODD
LOVE IS LIKE A VIOLIN
*Decca*

▲ 8
🔟 1
—/500

The popular comedian started his run of UK hits with an English lyric version (by Jimmy Kennedy) of a French song, 'Mon Coeur Est Un Violin', which Bing Crosby had sung in his 1953 movie *Little Boy Lost*.

---

## UNITED STATES
# SEPTEMBER 1960

---

## CONNIE FRANCIS
MY HEART HAS A MIND
OF ITS OWN
*MGM*

▲ 1
🔟 8
70/500

Francis' second successive chart topper came with another contagious Howard Greenfield and Jack Keller country-slanted opus. Susan Raye and Debby Boone brought the song into the country Top 20 in 1972 and 1979 respectively.

## FERRANTE & TEICHER
THEME FROM THE
APPARTMENT
*UA*

▲ 10
🔟 1
—/500

Classically trained pianists Arthur Ferrante and Louis Teicher's first hit was the theme from the Oscar-winning Billy Wilder film *The Apartment*. Charles Williams originally composed the instrumental under the name 'Jealous Lover'.

## LARRY VERNE
MR CUSTER
*Era*

▲ 1
🔟 1•
186/500

Writer Fred Darian, Al DeLory and Joseph Van Winkle needed someone with a southern accent to perform their novelty 'Mr Custer'. They recruited Verne, a photographer's assistant, who worked in the office opposite. The record, which numerous labels had rejected, hit the top. For Verne it was to be a brief flirtation with fame; his seven follow-ups, including 'I'm A Brave Little Soldier', 'The Coward That Won The West' and the inevitable 'Return Of Mr Custer', refused to fight their way up the charts. In the UK, comedian Charlie Drake had the hit version.

## SAM COOKE
CHAIN GANG
*RCA*

▲ 2
🔟 2
227/500

RCA Records guaranteed this soulful singer/songwriter a reported $100,000 to sign with them. His self-penned debut single for the label gave the influential vocalist his first transatlantic Top 10 entry. Theola Kilgore released an answer single entitled 'Chain Gang (The Sound Of My Man)'.

## BROOK BENTON
KIDDIO
*Mercury*

▲ 7
🔟 5
—/500

The top R&B record of the year was another song from the team of Benton and his A&R man Clyde Otis. It had been originally released by Teddy Randazzo in 1957.

## IVY THREE
YOGI
*Shell*

▲ 8
⑩ 1•
—/500

A trio of New York students tickled the nation's funny bone with a 'Alley-Oop'-styled novelty which combined the subject of Yoga with the popular Yogi Bear cartoon. Other follow-ups, including the similar 'Bagoo', fell flat. Label owners Sid Jacobson and Lou Stallman (who penned Perry Como's No 1 'Round And Round') wrote the song with group member Charles Koppelman. Before long the Ivy Three were history, but Koppelman went on to become one of the music industry's most successful recording executives.

## JIMMY CHARLES
A MILLION TO ONE
*Promo*

▲ 5
⑩ 1•
—/500

This teenage R&B vocalist from New Jersey had his only foray into the Top 40 with a track he recorded as a song demo for composer Phil Medley (best known for 'Twist And Shout'). The youthful-sounding singer was backed by The Revelletts. His subsequent releases, including the children's Christmas classic 'I Saw Mommy Kissing Santa Claus' were chart casualties. 'A Million To One' was a perfect teen love lament and subsequently charted for Donny Osmond, Bryan Hyland and the Five Stairsteps.

## EVERLY BROTHERS
SO SAD (TO WATCH GOOD LOVE GO BAD)
*Warner*

▲ 7
⑩ 10
—/500

Even though the duo's recording of Don Everly's lost-love lament did not make the country chart at the time, it later reached it on four separate occasions. In the UK, their single was a double-sided hit – the B side being an update of Little Richard's 'Lucille'.

## DRIFTERS
SAVE THE LAST DANCE FOR ME
*Atlantic*

▲ 1
⑩ 2
52/500

This top R&B group's first transatlantic Top 10 entry was with a Doc Pomus and Mort Shuman composition that they had intended to record with Jimmy Clanton. An answer, 'I'll Save The Last Dance For You' by veteran Damita Jo, also waltzed into the Top 40. A revival by The Defranco Family entered the Top 20 in 1974, and it made the country Top 20 by Buck Owens (1962), Emmylou Harris (1979) and Dolly Parton (1984). Ben E. King, who sang lead on The Drifters' recording, re-cut it without success in 1987.

---

# UNITED KINGDOM
# SEPTEMBER 1960

---

## SHIRLEY BASSEY
AS LONG AS HE NEEDS ME
*Columbia*

▲ 2
⑩ 4
157/500

The most successful song from Lionel Bart's musical *Oliver* added to the chart regular's hit total. It spent 30 weeks on the hit parade and was one of the year's top-selling singles. In the US, Sammy Davis Jr had the only successful version of this show-stopper in 1963.

## KAYE SISTERS
PAPER ROSES
*Philips*

▲ 7
⑩ 3•
—/500

This unrelated female pop trio, who had originally recorded as the Three Kayes, had the UK hit version of the lost-love ballad which Anita Bryant had just taken into the US Top 10. It was the last major hit for the act, whose previous successes had been in the company of Frankie Vaughan.

## CONNIE FRANCIS
EVERYBODY'S
SOMEBODY'S FOOL
*MGM*

| ▲ 5 |
| ⑩ 6 |
| —/500 |

See US Entry (June).

## LONNIE DONEGAN
LORELEI
*Pye*

| ▲ 10 |
| ⑩ 14 |
| —/500 |

Jerry Leiber and Mike Stoller, who had written many great rock songs including 'Jailhouse Rock' and 'Hound Dog', penned and produced this single for Donegan in New York.

## RICKY VALANCE
TELL LAURA I LOVE HER
*Columbia*

| ▲ 1 |
| ⑩ 1• |
| 73/500 |

When Decca Records deemed that Ray Peterson's original version was in 'bad taste' and decided not to release it, EMI producer Norrie Paramor quickly recorded a version with Welsh singer Valance (born David Spencer). The publicity this 'death disc' attracted helped it race to the top. Subsequent singles by Valance, including a cover of the equally controversial 'Bobby', were left at the starting line.

## ROY ORBISON
ONLY THE LONELY
*London American*

| ▲ 1 |
| ⑩ 1 |
| 51/500 |

See US entry (July).

## CLIFF RICHARD
NINE TIMES OUT OF TEN
*Columbia*

| ▲ 3 |
| ⑩ 9 |
| 365/500 |

Cliff's ninth time in the Top 10 was courtesy of a wild rocker from the pen of Otis Blackwell, composer of many of the era's top songs including 'Don't Be Cruel', 'All Shook Up', 'Handy Man' and 'Great Balls of Fire'.

## ADAM FAITH
HOW ABOUT THAT
*Parlophone*

| ▲ 4 |
| ⑩ 5 |
| 447/500 |

The ex-member of the Worried Men skiffle group charted again with a song penned by Les Vandyke (born Yani Skordalides), who recorded cover versions of hits for Woolworth's Embassy label as Johnny Worth.

# UNITED STATES
# OCTOBER 1960

## BOBBY VEE
DEVIL OR ANGEL
*Liberty*

| ▲ 6 |
| ⑩ 1 |
| —/500 |

Vee, whose cover of 'What Do You Want' failed to interest record buyers, found fame with his fourth single release. It was a Buddy Holly-influenced remake of a 1956 R&B hit by The Clovers, recorded in Norman Petty's New Mexico studio – where most of Holly's hits had been cut.

## BRENDA LEE
I WANT TO BE WANTED
*Decca*

| ▲ 1 |
| ⑩ 4 |
| 185/500 |

The singer, who appeared on the Perry Como, Ed Sullivan and Steve Allen TV shows before she was 13, chalked up her second successive chart topper with a heartfelt Italian ballad (originally heard in *Never On Sunday*), for which Kim Gannon had supplied the English lyrics.

## BOB LUMAN
LET'S THINK ABOUT LIVING
*Warner*

▲ 7
⑩ 1•
—/500

As an anecdote to the many 'death-discs' in the charts, Texas singer Luman asked fellow songwriters to 'forget about the dying' in this up-tempo country novelty. The single was the well-regarded rockabilly performer's only pop hit on either side of the Atlantic. It also became the first of over three dozen country hits for the singer, who died at the age of 41 in 1978.

## JOE JONES
YOU TALK TOO MUCH
*Roulette*

▲ 3
⑩ 1•
451/500

This veteran R&B singer/songwriter and pianist had five minutes of pop fame with a self-composed ode that, for a change, did not wax lyrical about a partner's charms. He recorded it for two labels, Ric and Roulette, and after a legal tussle Roulette secured the hit. A spirited cover by fellow New Orleans performer Frankie Ford was a minor hit. Jones' subsequent singles, including 'One Big Mouth' and 'California Sun', made little headway. However, a recording of the latter by The Rivieras in 1964 reached the Top 10.

## JOHNNY TILLOTSON
POETRY IN MOTION
*Cadence*

▲ 2
⑩ 1
255/500

The country-rooted pop performer from Florida had his only transatlantic Top 10 entry with this percolating pop ditty. Producer Archie Bleyer (who was responsible for the early Everly Brothers hits) first cut the track in New York, but it needed a Nashville re-recording before he deemed it right for release. Country star Ferlin Husky released a parody version, 'Enormity in Motion', under the name Simon Crum.

## RAY CHARLES
GEORGIA ON MY MIND
*ABC Paramount*

▲ 1
⑩ 2
205/500

ABC Paramount's $50,000 a year guarantee to Charles began to seem a wise investment when his soul-soaked revival of the Hoagy Carmichael classic hit the top. The song, which was produced in New York by Sid Feller, was a personal favourite of the R&B legend from Georgia. In 1978, Willie Nelson guided it to No 1 on the country chart. Overall, 'Georgia On My Mind' has amassed over four million plays on American radio.

# UNITED KINGDOM
# OCTOBER 1960

## EVERLY BROTHERS
LUCILLE/SO SAD
(TO WATCH GOOD
LOVE GO BAD)
*Warner*

▲ 4
⑩ 9
467/500

See US entry (September).

## VENTURES
WALK–DON'T RUN
*Top Rank*

▲ 8
⑩ 1
—/500

See US entry (August).

## SAM COOKE
CHAIN GANG
*RCA*

▲ 9
⑩ 1
—/500

See US entry (September).

## HANK LOCKLIN
PLEASE HELP ME,
I'M FALLING
*RCA*

▲ 9
⑩ 1•
—/500

See US entry (July).

**BOB LUMAN**
LET'S THINK ABOUT LIVING
*Warner*

▲ 6
⑩ 1•
—/500

See US entry.

---

# UNITED STATES
# NOVEMBER 1960

**MAURICE WILLIAMS
& THE ZODIACS**
STAY
*Herald*

▲ 1
⑩ 1•
202/500

At 97 seconds, 'Stay' is the shortest million-selling single of the rock era. The group's leader penned the catchy composition which gave them their only noticeable hit. Williams had earlier written and originally recorded (as The Gladiolas) 'Little Darlin', which earned The Diamonds a gold disc in 1957. 'Stay' also reached the US Top 20 by The Four Seasons (1964) and Jackson Browne (1978). A later live re-recording by this act went almost unnoticed.

**HANK BALLARD &
THE MIDNIGHTERS**
LET'S GO, LET'S GO,
LET'S GO
*King*

▲ 6
⑩ 2•
—/500

Soon after Chubby Checker's cloned cover of Ballard's 'The Twist' topped the chart, this groundbreaking R&B combo cracked the Top 10 themselves with another self-composed floor-filler. Six months later Ballard clicked with 'Let's Go Again'. In the late 1980s, Ballard was inducted into the Rock and Roll Hall of Fame.

**ROY ORBISON**
BLUE ANGEL
*Monument*

▲ 9
⑩ 2
—/500

The unmistakable Nashville-based vocalist made it two transatlantic Top 20s in a row with a self-composed song that 1980s star Cyndi Lauper

named a group after. Co-incidentally, one of the last tracks Orbison recorded was his version of Lauper's hit 'I Drove All Night'.

**FLOYD CRAMER**
LAST DATE
*RCA*

▲ 2
⑩ 1
209/500

The pianist most responsible for the 'Nashville Sound' in the early rock years narrowly missed the top spot with a self-penned instrumental, which also charted for popular band leader Lawrence Welk. Simultaneously, a vocal interpretation, 'My Last Date (With You)', entered the Top 40 by both Skeeter Davis and Joni James. In 1972, a new lyric version, '(Lost Her Love) On Our First Date', headed the country list by Conway Twitty and ten years later returned to No 1 by Emmylou Harris.

**KATHY YOUNG WITH
THE INNOCENTS**
A THOUSAND STARS
*Indigo*

▲ 3
⑩ 1•
269/500

This California singer, with a child-like vocal quality, scored two Top 40 entries before her sixteenth birthday. Young's highest-ranked hit was a revival of The Rivileers' 1954 doo-wop hit, which their lead singer Gene Pearson composed. She was backed on her single by a West Coast trio who had earlier recorded as The Echoes. Young later married John Maus of the Walker Brothers. In the UK, pop idol Billy Fury had the chart entry with the song.

## ELVIS PRESLEY
ARE YOU LONESOME
TONIGHT?
*RCA*

Elvis had his fourth consecutive No 1 with an update of a 25-year-old standard that Al Jolson had included in his repertoire. The song inspired several answer records, and in 1974 Donny Osmond took it back into the Top 20.

## U.S. BONDS
NEW ORLEANS
*Legrand*

The records of this R&B singer/songwriter from Virginia had a unique muzzy live-sound, which added excitement to a somewhat staid scene. Among his subsequent releases was the similar 'Take Me Back To New Orleans'.

## JOHNNY HORTON
NORTH TO ALASKA
*Columbia*

As his recording of the title song from a John Wayne movie climbed the chart, Horton died in an automobile accident. He was returning from a show at the Skyline Club in Austin – the same venue where his wife's first husband, the legendary Hank Williams, had played his last gig. The Mike Phillips song was originally titled 'Go North'.

## JACKIE WILSON
ALONE AT LAST
*Brunswick*

The energetic live performer repeated the formula that had made 'Night' a million seller by recording another classical piece arranged by Johnny Lehmann. This time it was Tchaikovsky's 'Piano Concerto In B Flat' that was given an unmistakable Wilson work-out.

# UNITED KINGDOM
# NOVEMBER 1960

## ELVIS PRESLEY
IT'S NOW OR NEVER
*RCA*

After copyright problems were finally sorted out, Presley's first adult-oriented single crashed into the chart at No 1. It sold a million in the UK in a record six-and-a-half weeks. See also US entry (August).

## JOHNNY & THE HURRICANES
ROCKING GOOSE
*London American*

One-time rockabilly musician Johnny Paris' combo from America had their last major hit with a novelty rock instrumental composed as usual by Tom King and Ira Mack. Like most of the band's hits from the 1960s, it was more successful in the UK than in the US. Interestingly, they were supported by The Beatles at Hamburg's Star Club in 1962.

## JOHNNY BURNETTE
DREAMIN'
*London American*

The leader of the legendary, although little-heralded rockabilly band, the Johnny Burnette Rock n' Roll Trio, had his first transatlantic Top 20 single with a bouncy pop song composed by Barry DeVorzon. The singer from Memphis had earlier written hits such as 'Believe What You Say', 'Waitin' In School' and 'Just A Little Too Much' for Ricky Nelson.

## JOHNNY MATHIS
MY LOVE FOR YOU
*Fontana*

Despite the fact that this record failed to crack the US Top 40, it delivered the instantly recognizable song stylist from San Francisco into the UK Top 20 for the fifth time in two years.

## CONNIE FRANCIS
MY HEART HAS A
MIND OF ITS OWN
*MGM*

See US entry (September).

## SHADOWS
MAN OF MYSTERY/THE
STRANGER
*Columbia*

The A side of the group's second hit came from the pen of veteran Michael Carr ('Washing On The Seigfried Line', 'South Of The Border' etc). 'Man Of Mystery' was the theme from the popular Edgar Wallace film series and Chet Atkins covered it in

the US. 'The Stranger' gave writers Bill Compton and Morgan Jones their second Top 10 of the year (following 'Heart Of A Teenage Girl').

## DRIFTERS
SAVE THE LAST DANCE
FOR ME
*London American*

See US entry (September).

## PETER SELLERS &
## SOPHIA LOREN
GOODNESS GRACIOUS ME
*Parlophone*

The UK comedian/actor and the top Italian film star had a hit together with a novelty based on the characters they played in the film *The Millionairess*. The song was written by David Lee, who also wrote another left-field duet hit, 'Kinky Boots' by Patrick MacNee and Honor Blackman. George Martin produced 'Goodness Gracious Me' and the follow-up hit 'Bangers And Mash' – which was originally intended to be the B side of their debut hit.

# UNITED STATES
# DECEMBER 1960

## JERRY BUTLER
HE WILL BREAK
YOUR HEART
*Vee Jay*

The Impressions' current lead singer Curtis Mayfield composed the first solo hit by the group's ex-lead singer. Astoundingly, the 'Ice Man', who went on to log over three dozen American pop chart entries, never cracked the UK list. In 1975, Tony Orlando & Dawn transported the song to the top under the new name 'He Don't Love You (Like I Love You)'.

## LOLITA
SAILOR (YOUR
HOME IS THE SEA)
*Kapp*

Austrian songstress Lolita (Ditta) had her only US hit with her European success 'Seemann'. Aside from a short English monologue, it was performed completely in German – the first Top 10 hit in that language by a female artist.

## BERT KAEMPFERT
WONDERLAND BY NIGHT
*Decca*

▲ 1
⑩ 1•
42/500

The German orchestra leader/composer and producer hit the summit with the haunting trumpet-led title tune from the German film *Wunderland Bei Nacht*. It was the last song to have three versions reach the Top 20 – the others being Louis Prima's instrumental interpretation and Anita Bryant's vocal version. Soon afterwards Kaempfert became the first producer to work with The Beatles, and later in the 1960s he wrote a transatlantic No 1 for Frank Sinatra ('Strangers In The Night') and the Elvis Presley (UK)/Joe Dowell (US) chart topper 'Wooden Heart'.

## CONNIE FRANCIS
MANY TEARS AGO
*MGM*

▲ 7
⑩ 9
—/500

Respected writer Winfield Scott, who composed the oft-recorded 'Tweedle Dee' and several Elvis Presley hits, penned Francis' fourth transatlantic Top 20 entry in a row.

## FERRANTE & TEICHER
EXODUS
*UA*

▲ 2
⑩ 2
208/500

Celebrated composer Ernest Gold penned the theme to Otto Preminger's Oscar-winning film *Exodus*, which provided the classically trained pianists with their only transatlantic Top 10 entry. Recordings by Mantovani and jazz saxophonist Eddie Harris also reached the Top 40, while Pat Boone had the most successful vocal version.

## JOHNNY BURNETTE
YOU'RE SIXTEEN
*Liberty*

▲ 8
⑩ 1•
—/500

Bob and Dick Sherman, writers of many later Walt Disney soundtracks, penned the one-time Memphis truck driver's biggest hit. The respected performer, who had two more Top 20 entries, 'Little Boy Sad' and 'God, Country And My Baby', died in a boating accident in 1964. The song returned to the transatlantic Top 10 in 1974 by Ringo Starr.

## RAY PETERSON
CORINNA, CORINNA
*Dunes*

▲ 9
⑩ 2•
—/500

The composition that had given Joe Turner (the 'Grandfather of Rock') his biggest pop hit in 1956 took this emotional vocalist into the Top 10 for the second and last time. It was on Peterson's own label, Dunes, which is also remembered for hits by Curtis Lee.

# UNITED KINGDOM
# DECEMBER 1960

## NINA & FREDERICK
LITTLE DONKEY
*Columbia*

▲ 3
⑩ 1•
406/500

The first Scandinavian act to have a major UK hit were Danish duo Baron Frederick Van Pallandt and his wife Nina. Their folk-styled interpretation of Eric Boswell's Christmas song outsold versions by Gracie Fields and the Beverley Sisters.

## CLIFF RICHARD
I LOVE YOU
*Columbia*

▲ 1
⑩ 10
92/500

After two months at the top, Elvis' 'It's Now Or Never' was dethroned by Cliff's tenth Top 10 entry in just over two years. Like his previous No 1, 'Please Don't Tease', it was composed by Shadow Bruce Welch.

## ANTHONY NEWLEY
STRAWBERRY FAIR
*Decca*

▲ 3
🔟 6
355/500

The singer, whose theatrically mannered cockney phrasing influenced David Bowie, registered with a unique treatment of the traditional folk song. It charted as his quirky TV series *The Strange World Of Gurney Slade* was launched.

## JOHNNY TILLOTSON
POETRY IN MOTION
*London American*

▲ 1
🔟 1•
88/500

See US entry (October).

## ADAM FAITH
LONELY PUP (IN A CHRISTMAS SHOP)
*Parlophone*

▲ 4
🔟 6
—/500

This Christmas novelty gave the singer his sixth successive Top 5 hit – the first time a UK artist had achieved such a feat. Simultaneously, Faith's interview on TV's *Face To Face* showed that he was more intelligent than most people expected pop stars to be.

# UNITED STATES
# JANUARY 1961

## ROSIE & THE ORIGINALS
ANGEL BABY
*Highland*

▲ 5
⑩ 1•
498/500

A ballad that 15-year-old Rosalie Hamlin wrote about her first boyfriend gave the Californian act its only chart entry. The doo-wop dirge was crudely recorded and featured a noticeably inexperienced saxophonist (the young act's regular player was grounded by his mother!). Perhaps not surprisingly then, the track was rejected by many West Coast labels. The group were musically inadequate and some listeners considered the high-pitched vocalist off-putting, but the primitive platter had a certain magic. Rosie's later well-produced tracks fared poorly – her 15 minutes of fame were over.

## SHIRELLES
WILL YOU LOVE ME TOMORROW
*Scepter*

▲ 1
⑩ 1
111/500

This R&B quartet's only transatlantic Top 10 entry was a Carole King and Gerry Goffin composition that at first they considered 'too country' for them. The song served as a sequel to the group's previous release, the controversial Top 40 entry 'Tonight's The Night'. 'Will You Love Me Tomorrow', which was originally intended for Johnny Mathis, returned to the US Top 40 by the Four Seasons (1968) and Dave Mason (1978). There were answer records, including 'Not Just Tomorrow But Always' by Tony Orlando (as Bertell Dache).

## BOBBY VEE
RUBBER BALL
*Liberty*

▲ 6
⑩ 2
—/500

Gene Pitney penned this bouncy pop tune with top publisher Aaron Schroeder. At the outset, they had hoped Jimmy Jones would cut the song, but obviously were not disappointed when Vee's version reached the transatlantic Top 10.

## LAWRENCE WELK
CALCUTTA
*Dot*

▲ 1
⑩ 1•
88/500

A German instrumental that had started life in 1958 as 'Tivoli Melody' became the King Of Champagne Music's only No 1. The performer that *Life* magazine called 'The most popular musician in US history' recorded the harpsichord-led track as a B side. However, it was quickly flipped over when it started picking up heavy airplay. TV personality Welk's mix of polka and 'sweet music' resulted in more than 40 chart albums including the No 1 *Calcutta*.

## MIRACLES
SHOP AROUND
*Tamla*

▲ 2
⑩ 1
294/500

Motown's first million seller was a song Smokey Robinson penned in just ten minutes for singer Barrett Strong. On hearing Robinson sing it, co-writer and label head Berry Gordy Jr insisted Smokey record it with his group The Miracles. They cut it twice and it was the second, more up-tempo treatment that almost hit the summit. An answer, 'Don't Let Him Shop Around' by Debbie Dean, also charted. In 1976, Captain & Tennille steered 'Shop Around' back into the Top 5.

## NEIL SEDAKA
CALENDAR GIRL
*RCA*

▲ 4
🔟 3
481/500

The unmistakable singer attained his third transatlantic Top 10 entry with another of his own contagious compositions. Stacy Adams released an answer version, 'Calendar Boy'.

## BRENDA LEE
EMOTIONS
*Decca*

▲ 7
🔟 5
—/500

Country composer Mel Tillis penned the latest ballad hit for the talented young entertainer, who went on to have a string of country hits in the 1970s.

# UNITED KINGDOM
# JANUARY 1961

## VENTURES
PERFIDIA
*London American*

▲ 4
🔟 2•
—/500

The American instrumental combo, who also sold millions of records in Japan, had a transatlantic Top 20 entry with their update of a Latin American smash from the early 1940s.

## MATT MONRO
PORTRAIT OF MY LOVE
*Parlophone*

▲ 3
🔟 1
358/500

Producer Norman Newell and noted UK tunesmith Cyril Ornadel composed the enduring ballad which gave this Londoner his first chart entry. The one-time London bus driver's debut hit was voted Record of the Year by readers of *MM*. In America, a cover version by Steve Lawrence entered the Top 20.

## EMILE FORD & THE CHECKMATES
COUNTING TEARDROPS
*Pye*

▲ 4
🔟 3•
494/500

The group, voted Best New Act of 1960, had their last Top 10 entry with an infectious pop piece written and originally recorded by successful young American Barry Mann. Ford (born Emile Sweatman), the first British-based black rock artist to top the UK chart, relocated to Sweden when his British hits dried up.

## DUANE EDDY
PEPE
*London American*

▲ 2
🔟 4
313/500

This bouncy German-written instrumental theme from the star-studded film, *Pepe*, charted in the UK by pianist Russ Conway and was a transatlantic Top 20 entry for frequent hit maker Eddy.

## ELVIS PRESLEY
ARE YOU LONESOME TONIGHT?
*RCA*

▲ 1
🔟22
54/500

See US entry (November).

## MR. ACKER BILK & HIS PARAMOUNT JAZZ BAND
BUONA SERA
*Columbia*

▲ 7
🔟 2
—/500

In the early 1960s, trad jazz was almost as popular as rock in the UK, and clarinettist Bilk's band led the genre. His first major vocal hit was a revival of a Carl Sigman composition which Louis Prima had previously recorded.

## JOHNNY BURNETTE
YOU'RE SIXTEEN
*London American*

▲ 3
🔟 ••
392/500

See US entry (December).

---

# UNITED STATES
# FEBUARY 1961

---

## JACKIE WILSON
MY EMPTY ARMS
*Brunswick*

▲ 9
⑩ 4
—/500

The influential performer's last semi-classical hit came with Al Kasha and Hank Hunter's arrangement of 'Vesti La Giubba (On With The Motley)'. Incidentally, the legendary Enrico Caruso's 1903 interpretation of the original operatic opus is acknowledged as the first million seller.

## CHUBBY CHECKER
PONY TIME
*Parkway*

▲ 1
⑩ 2
56/500

Checker's faithful cover of a dance track written and originally recorded by Don Covay (with his group The Goodtimers) was the teenager's second No 1 in six months. Incidentally, the song bore a resemblance to Hank Ballard's 'Sexy Ways'.

## CAPRIS
THERE'S A MOON
OUT TONIGHT
*Old Town*

▲ 3
⑩ 1•
445/500

A single that completely stiffed in 1958 on the tiny Planet label became a surprise hit (beating a cash-in cover by Pat Boone) when there was an upsurge of interest in doo-wop music. The belated success of the single, which had one of the most memorable endings in rock music, convinced the quintet from Queens to re-form briefly. They re-united again in 1982 and recorded a handful of tracks, including the very similar 'There's A Moon Out Again'.

## SHIRELLES
DEDICATED TO THE
ONE I LOVE
*Scepter*

▲ 3
⑩ 2
268/500

A re-issue of their 1959 revival of the outstanding Five Royales ballad quickly returned the hot girl group to the heights. The song was a transatlantic No 2 in 1967 by The Mamas & The Papas and a major UK hit in 1994 by Bitty McLean. The Shirelles' 1971 re-recording was overlooked.

## STRING-A-LONGS
WHEELS
*Warwick*

▲ 3
⑩ 1•
375/500

This quintet from New Mexico recorded two tracks at the Norman Petty studio (where Buddy Holly cut most of his hits). By mistake, the titles were switched on the tape boxes and a chirpy pop instrumental, penned by members Jimmy Torres and Richard Stephens as 'Tell The World', was released under the B side title, 'Wheels'. It was a bestseller on both sides of the Atlantic (despite stiff UK opposition from Joe Loss). Nonetheless, they failed to string together a run of hits, and subsequent singles, including 'Spinnin' My Wheels', stalled outside the charts.

## ELVIS PRESLEY
SURRENDER
*RCA*

▲ 1
⑩ 21
129/500

Elvis followed his multi-million seller 'It's Now Or Never' with another old Italian aria. 'Surrender' started out in 1911 as 'Torna A Sorrento', and had new English lyrics by Doc Pomus and Mort Shuman. Incidentally, this transatlantic topper coincided with Presley's last live appearance for eight years.

## MARTY ROBBINS
DON'T WORRY
*Columbia*

▲ 3
⑩ 3•
320/500

The country superstar from Arizona, who headed the pop charts with 'El Paso' as the decade began, had a top seller with a self-penned song that led the C&W list for 10 weeks. It is often said to be the first hit that featured fuzz guitar. Gloria Lambert released an answer version 'Each Time I Hear Don't Worry'. For the record books, Robbins, who died in 1982, had a 30-year span of country hits, which included 14 No 1s.

## CONNIE FRANCIS
WHERE THE BOYS ARE
*MGM*

▲ 4
⑩ 10
460/500

Connie's regular writers, Howard Greenfield and Neil Sedaka, were given just four days to pen a title song for her first movie *Where The Boys Are* – they composed two of that title, and the ballad one was chosen. The record became her fourth transatlantic Top 10 entry of the decade.

## EVERLY BROTHERS
EBONY EYES
*Warner*

▲ 8
⑩ 11
—/500

Noted songwriter John D. Loudermilk wrote this tearjerker about a plane crash for the act voted Top Vocal Group in the US and the UK. Both sides of the single separately reached the Top 10, while in the UK it was a double-sided hit.

---

## UNITED KINGDOM
# FEBRUARY 1961

---

## PETULA CLARK
SAILOR
*Pye*

▲ 1
⑩ 5
150/500

The singer, who had first come to the UK public's attention at the age of nine in 1942, had her first chart topper with a version of Austrian singer Lolita's international hit, 'Seemann'. The song, with English lyrics by producer Norman Newell, also attained a UK Top 10 position by another World War II star, Anne Shelton.

## ANNE SHELTON
SAILOR
*Philips*

▲ 10
⑩ 2•
—/500

Shelton's version of Lolita's hit was her last UK chart entry. She had been one of the top UK record sellers in the pre-rock era, working with such notables as Ambrose, Bing Crosby and Glenn Miller during World War II. The veteran vocalist, who achieved a UK No 1 in 1956 with 'Lay Down Your Arms', also notched up a couple of minor US hits.

## BOBBY VEE
RUBBER BALL
*London American*

▲ 4
⑩ 1
—/500

See US entry (January).

## SHADOWS
FBI
*Columbia*

▲ 6
⑩ 3
499/500

The group, whose first three self-composed singles (the first two released as The Drifters) failed to chart, finally hit with a number of their own.

## EVERLY BROTHERS
WALK RIGHT BACK
*Warner*

▲ 1
⑩ 10
47/500

See US entry (March).

## MARTY WILDE
RUBBER BALL
*Philips*

▲ 9
⑩ 6•
—/500

One of the UK's bestselling recording stars of the late 1950s visited the Top 10 for the last time with his performance of a Gene Pitney composition that introduced Bobby Vee to the UK chart. When the hits stopped, Wilde (born Reg Smith) continued to be an in-demand performer and wrote hits for several other acts including his daughter, Kim Wilde.

## ADAM FAITH
WHO AM I/THIS IS IT
*Parlophone*

▲ 5
⑩ 7
—/500

Parlophone's hottest act before The Beatles added to his enviable hit list with a double-sided smash. Both songs were composed by Les Vandyke.

## SHIRELLES
WILL YOU LOVE ME TOMORROW
*Top Rank*

▲ 4
⑩ 1•
396/500

See US entry (January).

## NEIL SEDAKA
CALENDAR GIRL
*RCA*

▲ 8
⑩ 4
—/500

See US entry (January).

# UNITED STATES
# MARCH 1961

## BUZZ CLIFFORD
BABY SITTIN' BOOGIE
*Columbia*

▲ 6
⑩ 1•
—/500

The 18-year-old vocalist had a one-off transatlantic Top 20 entry with his second Columbia release, which was a cute rock novelty penned by his producer Johnny Parker. The record, first known as 'Baby Sitter Boogie', featured baby noises from Parker's two children Mike (aged 4) and Lulu (aged 2). The follow-up, an update of the novelty 'Three Little Fishes' (on which he was backed by The Teenagers), returned Clifford to obscurity.

## BEN E. KING
SPANISH HARLEM
*Atco*

▲ 10
⑩ 1
—/500

The ex-lead vocalist of The Drifters (born Ben E. Nelson) had a major hit with his first solo single. Jerry Leiber and Mike Stoller produced the haunting Latin-oriented record which Leiber and his apprentice Phil Spector composed. In the UK, a cover version by Jimmy Justice grabbed the honours. A revival ten years later by Aretha Franklin reached the transatlantic Top 20.

## JORGEN INGMANN
APACHE
*Atco*

▲ 2
⑩ 1•
288/500

Denmark's best known guitarist had the American hit with a Jerry Lordan-composed instrumental that The Shadows had previously taken to the top in the UK. At the outset, it was intended to be the B side of his composition 'Echo Boogie', but radio play forced Atco to change their plans. A vocal version by country singer Sonny James also graced the Top 100. Rap pioneers The Sugarhill Gang's version of 'Apache' entered the R&B Top 20 in 1982.

## EVERLY BROTHERS
WALK RIGHT BACK
*Warner*

The other side of 'Ebony Eyes' was written for the instantly recognizable harmony duo by Sonny Curtis, a sometimes member of The Crickets (who on occasion backed the brothers). This irresistible foot stomper was their third UK No 1.

## MARCELS
BLUE MOON
*Colpix*

Producer Stu Phillips liked this Pittsburgh group's over-the-top doo-wop version of The Cadillacs' song 'Zoom', and asked them to give a similar treatment to the standard 'Blue Moon' (which had the same chord changes as 'Zoom'). They finished

the track in less than ten minutes and the resulting record topped the chart on both sides of the Atlantic. Interestingly, the music was originally written in 1933, and 'Blue Moon' was the third lyric that composers Rodgers and Hart set to the tune.

## CARLA THOMAS
GEE WHIZ (LOOK AT HIS EYES)
*Atlantic*

The 18-year-old daughter of noted Memphis R&B performer/DJ Rufus Thomas had her biggest hit with a self-composed love ballad. Among Carla's subsequent singles was the similarly titled 'Gee Whiz (It's Christmas)'. In 1980 actress/singer Bernadette Peters' version reached the Top 40.

# UNITED KINGDOM
# MARCH 1961

## ALLISONS
ARE YOU SURE
*Fontana*

John Alford and Bob Day, who were then known as John & Bob Allison, were the first UK rock duo to crack the Top 10. An unprecedented amount of publicity accompanied the release of their debut single, which represented the UK in the sixth Eurovision Song Contest. They were runners up in the competition, and the single, which reached the runner-up spot, went on to sell over a million in Europe. Despite this great start, the Everly Brothers-styled duo had little further chart success.

## RAMRODS
RIDERS IN THE SKY
*London American*

A Duane Eddy-influenced update of the Vaughn Monroe/Bing Crosby hit of 1949 was the

Connecticut-based combo's only hit. Group members Vincent Bell and female drummer Claire Lane arranged the Stan Jones-composed western opus, adding such sound effects as whip cracks and cattle noises. The similar follow-up, 'Take Me Back To My Boots & Saddles', failed to stop them riding off into the sunset.

## CLIFF RICHARD
THEME FOR A DREAM
*Columbia*

Americans Mort Garson and Earl Shuman, who had recently written the UK chart topper 'Starry Eyed' (sung by Michael Holliday), composed the first of four Top 5 hits in 1961 for Cliff.

### ELVIS PRESLEY
WOODEN HEART
*RCA*

In his film *GI Blues*, Presley sang this old German folk tune to a puppet, and it helped confirm his intention to change from rebellious rocker to all-round family entertainer. RCA declined to release the single in the US, and a cover by Joe Dowell hit the top. Composer credits included noted German orchestra leader Bert Kaempfert, who soon afterwards produced the first recordings by The Beatles.

### STRING-A-LONGS
WHEELS
*London American*

See US entry (February).

### MATT MONRO
MY KIND OF GIRL
*Parlophone*

The Sinatra-styled singer had his only US Top 20 entry with a Leslie Bricusse composition which came runner-up in the ITV Song Contest. The ballad went on to win an Ivor Novello award and helped Monro pick up the *Billboard* DJ award as Best International Act and Best New Male Artist

for 1961. Incidentally, Monro's idol, Frank Sinatra, later recorded the track.

### FERRANTE & TEICHER
EXODUS
*London American*

See US entry (December 1960).

### ANTHONY NEWLEY
AND THE HEAVENS CRIED
*Decca*

A UK-aimed cover of Ronnie Savoy's US hit gave the talented, quavery-voiced performer his last Top 10 entry. Newley, who had appeared in over 20 films before making his recording debut, was one of the most successful UK composers of the 1960s, penning such standards as 'What Kind Of Fool Am I', 'Who Can I Turn To' and 'Candy Man'.

### BOBBY DARIN
LAZY RIVER
*London American*

Soon after Hoagy Carmichael's 1930 composition 'Georgia On My Mind' earned Ray Charles a gold disc, the multi-talented Darin added to his hit tally with an update of this Carmichael classic from 1932.

# UNITED STATES
# APRIL 1961

### FLOYD CRAMER
ON THE REBOUND
*RCA*

The noted pianist from Louisiana, who had played on countless hits (including ones by Elvis and Jim Reeves), took this lively self-composed instrumental to the top of the UK chart.

### DEL SHANNON
RUNAWAY
*Big Top*

This Michigan rocker made the top of the transatlantic charts with his first hit. The instantly recognizable vocalist co-wrote the song with his band's keyboard player Max Crook. Shannon said the song was autobiographical, as he felt he was always running away from relationships. Crook's musitron (a forerunner of the synthesizer, which clipped under the piano) solo helped make the single one of the definitive records of the rock era.

## CLARENCE 'FROGMAN' HENRY
BUT I DO
*Argo*

The noteworthy New Orleans R&B singer, whose nickname was inspired by the frog-like vocals on his 1956 hit 'Ain't Got No Home', had a transatlantic Top 10 entry with a Fats Domino-influenced beat ballad. Veteran New Orleans musician Paul Gayten wrote the song with Robert Guidry (aka Bobby Charles), the composer of such rock classics as 'See You Later Alligator' and 'Walkin' To New Orleans'.

## ERNIE K-DOE
MOTHER-IN-LAW
*Minit*

This R&B performer from New Orleans had his only major hit with a novelty number penned by celebrated pianist/composer/producer Allen Toussaint. The singer, who was born Ernest Kador Jr, was vocally assisted by Benny Spellman (the deep voice on the title line). Toussaint said that musically it was based on a Harmonizing Four track, and K-Doe commented that lyrically it suited his family situation at the time. Louise Brown and The Blossoms charted with answers, both entitled 'Son-In-Law'. Among K-Doe's subsequent small sellers was 'My Mother-In-Law (Is In My Hair Again)'.

## KOKOMO
ASIA MINOR
*Felsted*

Classically trained jazz pianist Jimmy 'Wiz' Wisner recorded a beat version of Greig's Piano Concerto in the key of A minor (hence the title). When it was rejected by most majors, he released the single on his own Future label under the pseudonym Kokomo. Futher releases under that name, included the cleverly titled 'Theme From A Silent Movie', did not make the grade. Wisner went on to become one of the decade's busiest producers, working with such acts as The Cowsills, The Buckinghams, Dion, Paul Evans and Len Barry.

## GENE MCDANIELS
A HUNDRED POUNDS OF CLAY
*Liberty*

This talented performer from Kansas City had his first national hit with his third single on Liberty. McDaniel's million-selling recording of the lively Luther Dixon, Bob Elgin and Kay Roger's song, about God's creation of woman, was banned in the UK on religious grounds (an amended version by Craig Douglas took the honours there).

## LINDA SCOTT
I'VE TOLD EVERY LITTLE STAR
*Canadian American*

Her updated version of a song from Oscar Hammerstein's 1932 musical *Music In The Air* lifted this 16-year-old New York schoolgirl (born Linda Sampson) into the Top 10 on both sides of the Atlantic. Scott, one of the most successful new singers in 1961, revived several standards during her brief career, including the 1931 hit 'I Don't Know Why' which reached the Top 20 seven months later.

## BRENDA LEE
YOU CAN DEPEND ON ME
*Decca*

'Little Miss Dynamite' exploded on to the US Top 10 for the sixth time in 15 months with a song that, coincidentally, had given Louis Armstrong his sixth Top 10 entry back in 1932.

## ADAM WADE
TAKE GOOD CARE OF HER
*Coed*

1961 was a good year for the smooth balladeer from Pittsburgh. The first of his three Top 10s in six months came with a stand-out ballad which Ed Warren and Arthur Kent had written. The song also entered the Hot 100 by Mel Carter (1966) and Elvis Presley (1974), and in 1966 topped the country chart by Sonny James.

## RAY CHARLES
ONE MINT JULEP
*Impulse*

▲ 8
⑩ 3
—/500

The multi-talented blind R&B performer registered with a jazzy organ-led instrumental update of a Rudy Toombs tune, which The Clovers had taken up the R&B charts in 1952.

# UNITED KINGDOM
# APRIL 1961

## CONNIE FRANCIS
WHERE THE BOYS ARE
*MGM*

▲ 5
⑩ 8
—/500

See US entry (February).

## MARCELS
BLUE MOON
*Pye International*

▲ 1
⑩ 1•
130/500

See US entry (March).

## TEMPERANCE SEVEN
YOU'RE DRIVING ME CRAZY
*Parlophone*

▲ 1
⑩ 1
154/500

Britain's biggest novelty act of 1961 were a zany nine-piece band that recreated the sound and look of 1920s/1930s society jazz bands. The group, who were George Martin's last major artists before The Beatles, had four Top 20 singles and two Top 20 albums in the year. Their highest-ranking hit came with a carefully cloned version (complete with megaphone vocals) of a 1930 smash for Guy Lombardo & His Royal Canadians. Style-wise, later transatlantic hit makers the New Vaudeville Band borrowed freely from them.

## BROOK BROTHERS
WARPAINT
*Pye*

▲ 5
⑩ 1•
—/500

This UK duo, who conjured up images of the Everly Brothers, had their biggest successes with covers of little-known US records. The act's top seller was a Tony Hatch-produced version of a potent pop ditty penned and originally released by Barry Mann. The follow-up, 'Ain't Gonna Wash For A Week' (previously an Eddie Hodges B side), also reached the Top 20. In total, the duo amassed five Top 40s before vanishing beneath the sea of Merseybeat groups.

## CLIFF RICHARD
GEE WHIZ IT'S YOU
*Columbia*

▲ 4
⑩ 12
—/500

Cliff's only hit from his 1960 album, *Me And My Shadows*, became his thirteenth consecutive Top 20 entry. It came from the pens of Shadow Hank Marvin and ex-Shadow Ian Samwell.

# UNITED STATES
# MAY 1961

## STEVE LAWRENCE
PORTRAIT OF MY LOVE
*UA*

Matt Monro had the original UK hit with this tasteful Norman Newell and Cyril Ornadel ballad. However, in the US, Lawrence's rendition gave him his third Top 10 entry in a row. The song reappeared in the Top 40 in 1967 by The Tokens.

## SHEP & THE LIMELITES
DADDY'S HOME
*Hull*

In 1956, stylish vocalist/songwriter James Sheppard and The Heartbeats had a R&B hit with 'A Thousand Miles Away'. A year later they recorded a sequel, '500 Miles To Go', and in 1961 'Daddy' finally arrived home, thanks to another sequel from Sheppard (and new group The Limelites). The song inspired several answer versions, including 'Mommie's Gone', 'Daddy's Gone' and 'Daddy's Going Away Again'. Sheppard also returned to the theme with 'What Did Daddy Do'. 'Daddy's Home' subsequently hit for Jermaine Jackson (1973) and Cliff Richard (1982).

## RICKY NELSON
TRAVELIN' MAN
*Imperial*

Minor rock star Jerry Fuller composed this song with Sam Cooke in mind. However, he was far from unhappy when teen icon Nelson recorded it and took it to the top.

## SHIRELLES
MAMA SAID
*Scepter*

The most successful girl group of the early 1960s made it three hits in a row with a song written for them by producer Luther Dixon. 'Mama Said' was their third consecutive Top 5 record.

## ROY ORBISON
RUNNING SCARED
*Monument*

Six years after making his recording debut, 'The Big O' had his first US chart topper with an atmospheric beat ballad penned in just five minutes with regular co-writer Joe Melson.

## CONNIE FRANCIS
BREAKIN' IN A BRAND
NEW BROKEN HEART
*MGM*

Howard Greenfield and Jack Keller, who composed Francis' chart-topping 'My Heart Has A Mind Of Its Own', also penned this contagious country-flavoured transatlantic hit for the Italian-American Queen of Rock and Roll.

## RICKY NELSON
HELLO MARY LOU
*Imperial*

The top-selling singer/actor had his biggest transatlantic hit with a infectious song written and originally recorded by up-and-coming singer Gene Pitney. It was the B side of his US No 1 'Travelin' Man'.

## ELVIS PRESLEY
I FEEL SO BAD
*RCA*

A reworking of R&B star Chuck Willis' self-composed 1954 success added to Presley's staggering hit tally. In the UK, the B side 'Wild In The Country' was a bigger seller.

## FLEETWOODS
TRAGEDY
*Dolton*

▲ 10
⑩ 3•
—/500

This instantly recognizable soft rock vocal trio's last venture into the Top 10 was with their rendition of Thomas Wayne's heartfelt 1959 million seller. The Washington-based trio (who started life as Two Girls & A Guy) are best remembered for the 1959 chart toppers, 'Come Softly To Me' and 'Mr Blue'.

# UNITED KINGDOM
# MAY 1961

## HELEN SHAPIRO
DON'T TREAT ME LIKE A CHILD
*Columbia*

▲ 3
⑩ 1
366/500

The first major British female singer of the 1960s had her debut hit when she was still a 14-year-old London schoolgirl. Regular hit maker Norrie Paramor produced the single, which his assistant John Schroeder and Mike Hawker had written especially for the youthful singer with the mature voice, who was tagged 'the UK's Brenda Lee'.

## DUANE EDDY
THEME FROM DIXIE
*London American*

▲ 7
⑩ 5
—/500

This old rebel song was afforded a wild workout by the twangy guitarist and his backing band, The Rebels. In total, Eddy chalked up nine UK Top 20 LPs and 17 Top 20 singles (the last being in 1986).

## JOHNNY DANKWORTH
AFRICAN WALTZ
*Columbia*

▲ 9
⑩ 2•
—/500

The internationally respected UK modern jazz band, who often featured Dankworth's vocalist wife Cleo Laine, had a left-field instrumental hit with this George Martin production. The catchy tune was composed by Galt MacDermot (who later co-wrote the rock musical *Hair*). 'African Waltz' picked up an Ivor Novello award and an American cover version by fellow saxophonist Cannonball Adderley narrowly missed the US Top 40.

## BOBBY VEE
MORE THAN I CAN SAY
*London American*

▲ 4
⑩ 2
418/500

Although only a minor hit in his homeland, the Buddy Holly-influenced singer scored with his version of a Crickets B side, penned by ex-Holly sidemen Jerry Allison and Sonny Curtis. In 1980, Leo Sayer turned the song into a transatlantic Top 3 hit.

## FLOYD CRAMER
ON THE REBOUND
*RCA*

▲ 1
⑩ 1•
185/500

See US entry (April).

## CRAIG DOUGLAS
A HUNDRED POUNDS OF CLAY
*Top Rank*

▲ 9
⑩ 4
—/500

When Gene McDaniel's original US hit was banned by the BBC on religious grounds, the clean-cut UK teen idol's lyrically amended rendition added to his hit score. Among the song's composers was Luther Dixon, known for his work with The Shirelles.

## DEL SHANNON
RUNAWAY
*London American*

See US entry (April).

## SHADOWS
FRIGHTENED CITY
*Columbia*

The combo's second film theme hit was penned by producer Norrie Paramor. It gave the act, named as Top Instrumental Group in the *NME* poll, their fourth Top 10 entry in less than a year.

# UNITED STATES
# JUNE 1961

## BEN E. KING
STAND BY ME
*Atco*

King originally wrote this classic song (with producers Jerry Leiber and Mike Stoller) for his group The Drifters – they did not see its potential, so he recorded it as a solo. The ever popular tune revisited the Top 20 by Spyder Turner (1967) and John Lennon (1975). In 1980, Mickey Gilley took it to the top of the country list. Amazingly, King's version re-entered the Top 10 in 1986 and the following year headed the UK chart.

## PAT BOONE
MOODY RIVER
*Dot*

Elvis' major rival in the late 1950s returned to the Top 10 after a three-year absence with a praiseworthy cover of a controversial suicide song first cut by Chase Webster. It was to be the award-winning rock balladeer's third and last chart topper.

## DEE CLARK
RAINDROPS
*Vee Jay*

The soulful vocalist from Arkansas, who sang on Red Saunders' 1952 ground-breaking success 'Hambone', had the biggest of his five R&B Top 10 hits with one of his own compositions. The heartfelt ballad, which came complete with storm sounds, was covered in the UK by noted vocal team The Raindrops! Clark revived the song (with far less success) a dozen years later as 'Raindrops '73'. The distinctive vocalist, whose sole UK hit was 'Ride A Wild Horse' in 1975, died in 1990.

## ADAM WADE
THE WRITING ON
THE WALL
*Coed*

Mark Barkan, Sandy Baron and George Eddy composed the second successive Top 10 entry for the classy song stylist who had been cast in the Johnny Mathis-mould. The UK's first rock star, Tommy Steele, had his last UK chart record with a cover version.

## THE PIPS
EVERY BEAT OF MY HEART
*Vee Jay*

In 1952, eight-year-old Gladys Knight (singing the aptly titled 'Too Young') won first prize on the prestigious 'Original Amateur Hour' hosted by Ted Mack. Nine years later, family group The Pips, fronted by Knight, had their first hit with a song written shortly before her talent show win. Johnny Otis penned it and Henry Booth & The Midnighters recorded it first. The Pips' single, which appeared on three labels – Huntom, Fury and Vee Jay – was produced by Felton Jarvis, who subsequently produced many hits for Elvis Presley.

## U.S. BONDS
QUARTER TO THREE
*Legrand*

▲ 1
🔟 2
116/500

R&B instrumental combo The Church Street Five had a minor success with 'A Night With Daddy G' (named after sax-playing front man Gene Barge). Their label-mate Bonds added lyrics to the track at a rather drunken session, and the atmospheric party-like record gave him his biggest US hit and his only UK Top 10 entry.

## BROOK BENTON
THE BOLL WEEVIL SONG
*Mercury*

▲ 2
🔟 6
235/500

The instantly recognizable R&B baritone from South Carolina had his highest-ranked hit with his own adaptation of an old folk song. This hit inspired the answer record 'DDT And The Boll Weevil' by Lyn Earlington.

## BOBBY LEWIS
TOSSIN' AND TURNIN'
*Beltone*

▲ 1
🔟 1
4/500

1961's biggest hit was by an R&B singer from Indiana who had been recording with negligible sales since the mid-1950s. The single, which spent a staggering seven weeks in first position, was written by Ritchie Adams, the ex-lead singer of white doo-wop act, The Fireflies. Among Lewis' other recordings was the similar-sounding, though far lower-selling, 'I'm Tossin' And Turnin' Again'.

## LITTLE CAESAR & THE ROMANS
THOSE OLDIES BUT GOODIES (REMIND ME OF YOU)
*Del-Fi*

▲ 9
🔟 1•
—/500

David 'Little Caesar' Johnson fronted the toga-wearing vocal quintet, who notched up their sole Top 40 hit with a tribute to the great doo-wop ditties of the past. The song, which the act were not too keen on, was composed by teenager Paul Politi, who later wrote with Barry White. Coincidentally, Johnson previously sang with The Upfronts, who at times included White. Among this group's subsequent attempts to return to the heights was the similarly styled 'Memories Of Those Oldies But Goodies'.

# UNITED KINGDOM
# JUNE 1961

## ELVIS PRESLEY
SURRENDER
*RCA*

▲ 1
🔟 24
58/500

See US entry (February).

## SHIRLEY BASSEY
YOU'LL NEVER KNOW
*Columbia*

▲ 6
🔟 5
—/500

Britain's foremost female cabaret entertainer added to her hit portfolio with a revival of a song from the 1943 Alice Faye and John Payne film *Hello Frisco Hello*. It was written by award-winning composers Mack Gordon and Harry Warren, and originally hit by Frank Sinatra and Dick Haymes.

## JERRY LEE LEWIS
WHAT'D I SAY
*London American*

▲ 10
🔟 4•
—/500

One of the original rock'n'roll greats achieved his last transatlantic Top 40 hit with a rockin' re-work of the classic Ray Charles call-and-response song. It was the first hit for 'The Killer' since his marriage to a 13-year-old second cousin had put the brakes on his career in 1958. Lewis, one of the top country artists of the late 1960s and 1970s, is still rockin' his life away.

### CLARENCE 'FROGMAN' HENRY
BUT I DO
*Pye International*

▲ 3
⑩ 1
306/500

See US entry (April).

### LONNIE DONEGAN
HAVE A DRINK ON ME
*Pye*

▲ 8
⑩15
—/500

Both this song and Donegan's first major success, 'Rock Island Line', were originally recorded by folk/blues legend Leadbelly. The single was one of 28 Top 30 hits in succession for the performer.

### BILLY FURY
HALFWAY TO PARADISE
*Decca*

▲ 4
⑩ 2
199/500

The 20-year-old Liverpudlian's highest-placed hit to date was a suggestive Carole King and Gerry Goffin song that had given Tony Orlando his first US Top 40 entry. Fury's album of the same name was also a Top 5 entry.

### LINDA SCOTT
I'VE TOLD EVERY LITTLE STAR
*Columbia*

▲ 7
⑩ 1•
—/500

See US entry (April).

### RICKY NELSON
HELLO MARY LOU/TRAVELLIN' MAN
*London American*

▲ 2
⑩ 4•
193/500

See US entry (May).

### NEIL SEDAKA
LITTLE DEVIL
*RCA*

▲ 9
⑩ 5
—/500

This ex-member of The Tokens, who during his long career penned Top 10 hits for Connie Francis,

Captain & Tennille, The Partridge Family and Andy Williams, clocked up another transatlantic Top 20 entry with this commercially compelling Sedaka composition.

### TEMPERANCE SEVEN
PASADENA
*Parlophone*

▲ 4
⑩ 2•
334/500

The trad era's biggest novelty act followed their chart-topping debut with an equally tongue-in-cheek recreation of a song written in 1924 by Harry Warren, Grant Clarke and Edgar Leslie. The popular left-field live band, who wore formal 1920s evening wear on stage, had two more Top 40 entries, 'Hard Hearted Hannah' and 'Charleston', before they finally faded into musical history.

### EVERLY BROTHERS
TEMPTATION
*Warner*

▲ 1
⑩ 11
129/500

Even though it failed to crack the Top 20 in the US, the dynamic duo achieved their second successive UK chart topper with an imaginative reworking of a song written by Arthur Freed and Nacio Herb Brown for Bing Crosby's movie *Going Hollywood*.

### ROY ORBISON
RUNNING SCARED
*London American*

▲ 9
⑩ 2
—/500

See US entry (May).

# UNITED STATES
# JULY 1961

## ARTHUR LYMAN
YELLOW BIRD
*Hi Fi*

▲ 4
🔟 1•
497/500

An old West Indian folk song that celebrated choir leader Norman Luboff had arranged became the biggest-selling single for Lyman (ex-member of the hit-making Martin Denny Trio). Advertisements proclaimed that the Hawaiian multi-instrumentalist's vibraphone-led recording sold over 250,000 in just two weeks. A version by Lawrence Welk also reached the Top 100.

## DEL SHANNON
HATS OFF TO LARRY
*Big Top*

▲ 5
🔟 2
—/500

Harry Balk and Irving Micahnik, the team behind Johnny & The Hurricanes' organ-fronted hits, also produced Shannon's successes, which again relied heavily on a keyboard sound – this time Max Crook's musitron. 'Hats Off To Larry', which the singer wrote with the Everly Brothers in mind, gave him his second successive transatlantic Top 10 entry.

## PAUL ANKA
DANCE ON LITTLE GIRL
*ABC Paramount*

▲ 10
🔟 8
—/500

The talented teenager not only penned this hit but also later composed top sellers for Frank Sinatra and Tom Jones, wrote with Michael Jackson and was inducted into the Songwriters Hall of Fame. He returned to the charts in the mid-1970s with a string of hit singles with Odia Coates.

## FLOYD CRAMER
SAN ANTONIO ROSE
*RCA*

▲ 8
🔟 3•
—/500

One of country music's best-known compositions ushered the unmistakable Nashville-based pianist into the US Top 10 for the third time in eight

months. The song had been a top seller in 1939 for Bing Crosby and also for its composer, the King of Western Swing, Bob Wills.

## CHRIS KENNER
I LIKE IT LIKE THAT (PT 1)
*Instant*

▲ 2
🔟 1•
279/500

Top R&B producer/musician Alan Toussaint co-wrote this contagious R&B pounder with the record's New Orleans-based vocalist. It was the only major hit for the singer, who also penned such gems as 'Land Of 1,000 Dances, 'Sick & Tired' and 'Something You Got'. An answer version, 'I Don't Like It Like That' by The Bobbettes also charted. In 1965, The Dave Clark Five reinstated 'I Like It Like That' in the Top 10.

## BRENDA LEE
DUM DUM
*Decca*

▲ 4
🔟 7
443/500

The teenage vocalist added to her transatlantic hit tally with an infectious foot-tapper composed by singer/songwriter Jackie DeShannon and the late Eddie Cochran's girl friend, Sharon Sheeley.

## CONNIE FRANCIS
TOGETHER
*MGM*

▲ 6
🔟 12
—/500

The artist, who was frequently voted World's Top Female Singer on both sides of the Atlantic, continued her run of hits with a moving rendition of Paul Whitman's 1928 chart topper.

## CHUBBY CHECKER
LET'S TWIST AGAIN
*Parkway*

▲ 8
🔟 3
156/500

After turning Hank Ballard's 'The Twist' into a chart topper, Checker clicked with a twister penned by Cameo/Parkway Records' in-house tunesmiths, Kal Mann and Dave Appell. The song, which hit again six months later, was not unlike Ballard's recent single, 'Let's Go Again (Where We Went Last Night)'.

**MAR-KEYS**
LAST NIGHT
*Satellite*

▲ 3
⑩ 1•
392/500

One of the year's hottest and most original R&B instrumentals was a riveting blues-based track performed by an all-white septet which included Steve Cropper and Donald 'Duck' Dunn. Soon after 'Last Night' turned gold, Satellite Records changed its name to Stax, The Mar-keys were installed as the Stax house-band, and this hit served as a blueprint for the world-famous 'Stax Sound'. Follow-ups, including a sequel 'The Morning After', sold less well, and Cropper and Dunn left to form Booker T. & The MGs.

# UNITED KINGDOM
# JULY 1961

**CLIFF RICHARD**
A GIRL LIKE YOU
*Columbia*

▲ 3
⑩ 13
333/500

Jerry Lordan, who had earlier written the No 1 'Apache' for Cliff Richard's backing band The Shadows, composed the singer's third Top 5 single of the year.

**EDEN KANE**
WELL I ASK YOU
*Decca*

▲ 1
⑩ 1
69/500

The UK's last major home-grown teen idol before The Beatles hit the top with his second single. Johnny Worth, who had written Adam Faith's biggest hits (under the name Les Vandyke), composed it especially for Kane. The song was unsuccessful in the US despite being covered by a handful of acts, including 1950s chart regular Kay Starr and the up-and-coming Bobby Vinton.

**HELEN SHAPIRO**
YOU DON'T KNOW
*Columbia*

▲ 1
⑩ 2
33/500

The 14-year-old schoolgirl, who was voted Top UK Female Singer in 1961 and 1962, became the youngest UK act to reach No 1. This teenage love lament, written for her by John Schroeder and Mike Hawker, sold over a million copies worldwide.

**CRAIG DOUGLAS**
TIME
*Top Rank*

▲ 9
⑩ 5
—/500

Eight of Douglas' nine UK Top 20 entries were covers of US singles. The least successful of the songs Stateside was Buddy Kaye and Phil Springer's composition 'Time', which had failed to chart there by its original vocalist Jerry Jackson.

**PETULA CLARK**
ROMEO
*Pye*

▲ 3
⑩ 6
345/500

The popular entertainer, who had appeared in more than 20 films before the start of the decade, had her second German-composed hit of the year. This time it was with Jimmy Kennedy's English lyric version of 'Salome', a song written 40 years earlier by Robert Stolz.

# UNITED STATES
# AUGUST 1961

## CURTIS LEE
PRETTY LITTLE ANGEL
EYES
*Dunes*

Singer Ray Peterson, the co-owner of the Dunes label, brought in Phil Spector (who had produced his last hit 'Corinna, Corinna') to record Curtis Lee. Tommy Boyce and Lee co-wrote the song and doo-wop act The Halos backed him on what was to be Lee's biggest hit. UK group Showaddywaddy shipped both this and his follow-up 'Under The Moon Of Love' into the UK Top 5 in the 1970s.

## JOE DOWELL
WOODEN HEART
*Smash*

When it was decided that Elvis' version of this German folk song from his film *GI Blues* would not be released in the US, a handful of acts quickly recorded it and Dowell's version shot to the top. Producer Shelby Singleton Jr gave the clean-cut singer just three hours to learn the multi-lingual song and called in hit maker Ray Stevens to play organ. Dowell had one further Top 40 hit, the novelty 'Little Red Rented Rowboat', before he was drafted and learned about GI blues first hand.

## HIGHWAYMEN
MICHAEL
*UA*

According to a poll of American DJs, this university-based folk quintet's adaptation of a Georgia slave song, 'Michael Row The Boat Ashore', was 1961's Best Record. The group's Dave Fisher was given composer's credits on the single, which topped the chart on both sides of the Atlantic. Before returning to their studies, the act put another folk opus, 'Cotton Fields', into the Top 20. The Highwaymen's re-recording of 'Michael' in 1965 failed to create any waves.

## GARY U.S. BONDS
SCHOOL IS OUT
*Legrand*

The exciting performer (born Gary Anderson) made it three Top 10 entries in nine months with an anthemic stomper that he penned with saxophonist Gene Barge. The similar-sounding follow-up 'School Is In' also cracked the Top 40.

## RAL DONNER
YOU DON'T KNOW WHAT
YOU GOT (UNTIL YOU
LOSE IT)
*Gone*

One of the earliest and certainly the foremost Elvis sound-alikes followed his version of Presley's 'Girl Of My Best Friend' into the Top 20 with a stand-out beat ballad. It was penned by Paul Hampton, whose song 'Sea Of Heartbreak' was simultaneously charting by Don Gibson. Donner, who followed this hit with two more Top 40 entries, was the narrator on the 1981 film *This Is Elvis*. Coincidentally, like his idol, Donner died in his early 40s.

## LINDA SCOTT
DON'T BET MONEY HONEY
*Canadian American*

Sixteen-year-old Scott penned her second successive Top 10 entry, which was joined in the chart by its B side, 'Starlight, Starbright'. Despite this enviable career start her hit days were numbered, and after 1961 she never returned to the Top 40. Later in the decade, she co-hosted the popular TV series *Where The Action Is*.

## TIMI YURO
HURT
*Liberty*

▲ 4
⑩ 1•
—/500

The ground-breaking, soulful white female song stylist had her biggest hit with an emotional rendition of a Roy Hamilton R&B hit from 1954.

The record sold few in Europe at the time but was a top hit in Holland in 1981. Among the Chicago-born singer's other successful singles was her heartfelt 1962 Top 20 entry 'What's A Matter Baby (Is It Hurting You)'. In 1976, US soul group The Manhattans took 'Hurt' into the UK Top 5.

# UNITED KINGDOM
# AUGUST 1961

## CLARENCE 'FROGMAN' HENRY
YOU ALWAYS HURT THE ONE YOU LOVE
*Pye International*

▲ 6
⑩ 2•
—/500

This Fats Domino-influenced performer collected his second successive transatlantic Top 20 entry with a revival of a song that the Mills Brothers had taken to the top in 1944. Interestingly, fellow New Orleans R&B artist Bobby Mitchell had cut a similar version in 1957 and, also interestingly, Domino himself recorded it after Henry.

## JOHN LEYTON
JOHNNY REMEMBER ME
*Top Rank*

▲ 1
⑩ 1
48/500

The photogenic actor-turned-singer followed his neglected treatment of 'Tell Laura I Love Her' with another death disc produced by the legendary Joe Meek. This record amassed 40,000 advance orders after Leyton sang it on the popular TV series *Harpers West One*. To make the lyric less ghoulish, composer Geoff Goddard amended it from 'The girl I loved who died a year ago' to 'The girl I loved and lost a year ago'. An updated treatment by Bronski Beat in 1985 also reached the Top 3.

## SHIRLEY BASSEY
REACH FOR THE STARS/CLIMB EV'RY MOUNTAIN
*Columbia*

▲ 1
⑩ 6
138/500

A second chart topper from this celebrated vocalist coupled a German composition (originally titled 'Woner Ich Auch Komm, Wohin Ich Auch Geh') with the well-known song from *The Sound Of Music*. Norman Newell, the record's producer, penned the English lyric for the A side.

## GARY U.S. BONDS
QUARTER TO THREE
*Top Rank*

▲ 7
⑩ 1•
—/500

See US entry (June).

## KARL DENVER
MARCHETA
*Decca*

▲ 8
⑩ 1
—/500

Flexible-voiced Scottish singer Denver (born Angus McKenzie) was one of the most recognizable new UK acts of the early 1960s. The pop/folk/country singer/yodeller and his trio first charted with a reworking of a song which the legendary Irish tenor John McCormack had helped popularize in the early 1920s.

# UNITED STATES
# SEPTEMBER 1961

## BOBBY VEE
TAKE GOOD CARE OF MY BABY
*Liberty*

This early 1960s transatlantic teen idol's biggest seller was written by Carole King and Gerry Goffin and first recorded by Dion. The song also entered the Top 40 in 1968 by Bobby Vinton and the UK Top 40 in 1980 by Smokie. Vee released a ballad version in 1973 under his real name of Robert Thomas Velline.

## JIVE FIVE
MY TRUE STORY
*Beltone*

One of the last hit-making doo-wop groups was fronted by Eugene Pitt, who also penned their highest-ranked hit. Pitt, who had been an early member of late 1950s hit act The Genies, said he based the ballad on a true story concerning himself, an ex-girlfriend and a good friend of his that she married. The New York-based quintet have maintained a performing profile and still work 'oldies' venues around the world.

## ADAM WADE
AS IF I DIDN'T KNOW
*Coed*

Kusik and David composed the last notable hit by one of the year's top ballad singers. For the record books, none of Wade's 11 US chart entries cracked the UK list. In the 1970s, the singer/actor hosted the TV game show *Musical Chairs*, and in the 1980s helmed his own TV talk show.

## LONNIE DONEGAN
DOES YOUR CHEWING GUM LOSE ITS FLAVOR (ON THE BEDPOST OVERNIGHT)
*Dot*

The skiffle superstar, whose 'Rock Island Line' was a transatlantic Top 10 hit in 1956, became the first UK act in the rock era to score two US Top 10 singles. He hit with a novelty song that had been a top seller for Hare & Jones in 1924. Donegan's record was a 'sleeper', having originally been released with little fanfare in the US in 1959 (when it made the UK Top 3).

## BARRY MANN
WHO PUT THE BOMP (IN THE BOMP, BOMP, BOMP)
*ABC*

One of the most successful composers of the rock era had his only vocal hit with a tongue-in-cheek doo-wop novelty. He wrote it with Gerry Goffin and was ably backed on the record by The Halos. His earth-shattering question was answered by such acts as Frankie Lymon with 'I Put The Bomp' and Bob & Jerry with 'We're The Guys (Who Put The Bomp In The Bomp, Bomp, Bomp). In the UK, The Viscounts' version entered the Top 20, and in 1982 Showaddywaddy re-introduced it to the Top 40.

## ELVIS PRESLEY
LITTLE SISTER
*RCA*

The hit team of Doc Pomus and Mort Shuman penned this blues-based Elvis hit, which R&B star Lavern Baker answered in 'Hey Memphis'. In 1987, Dwight Yoakam steered the song into the country Top 10.

## ELVIS PRESLEY
(MARIE'S THE NAME) HIS
LATEST FLAME
*RCA*

The other side of 'Little Sister', which was written by Doc Pomus and Mort Shuman, also reached the Top 10. In the UK, where both sides were listed together, it was another chart topper for the King.

## ROY ORBISON
CRYIN'
*Monument*

The unmistakable Texan wrote this moving ballad after seeing an old flame that he still carried a torch for. Astonishingly, it was only a minor UK hit. However Don McLean's 1980 US Top 5 revival reached No 1 in the UK.

## JOHNNY TILLOTSON
WITHOUT YOU
*Cadence*

The success of this single not only proved that Tillotson was no one-hit-wonder, it also added his name to the list of singers who had penned their own Top 10 entries.

## BOBBY LEWIS
ONE TRACK MIND
*Beltone*

Jackie Wilson's protégé Lewis had his second successive Top 10 entry with a song he co-wrote with Malou Rene (who also penned his previous

chart topper 'Tossin' And Turnin'). It was the last big hit for the singer, who started recording in 1952 and was still singing these hits to appreciative audiences in the 1990s.

## DREAMLOVERS
WHEN WE GET MARRIED
*Heritage*

The vocal quintet, who had backed Chubby Checker on 'The Twist', had a major hit of their own with a top-notch doo-wop ballad composed by ex-member Don Hogan. Fellow Philadelphia group The Intruders re-introduced the song to the R&B Top 10 in 1970 and Larry Graham repeated that feat ten years later.

## DICK & DEEDEE
THE MOUNTAIN'S HIGH
*Liberty*

After several poor-selling solo singles, Dick St John Gosting teamed with fellow LA native Dee Dee Sperling. One of Gosting's songs, which they had recorded as a B side for the tiny Lama label, was picked up by Liberty and only narrowly missed the top. It was the first of their five Top 40s, which included 'Young And In Love' (1963) and 'Thou Shalt Not Steal' (1964). Dick subsequently turned his hand to the culinary arts and his *Country Music Cookbook* in 1994 sold well.

# UNITED KINGDOM
# SEPTEMBER 1961

## ACKER BILK
THAT'S MY HOME
*Columbia*

▲ 7
⑩ 3
—/500

The best-known personality of the trad jazz boom charted with his treatment of a song previously cut by Louis Armstrong. As a sign of his popularity, Bilk appeared in the 1961 Royal Variety Show.

## ELVIS PRESLEY
WILD IN THE COUNTRY
*RCA*

▲ 4
⑩25
484/500

The title song from Presley's latest movie was a bigger hit on the other side of the Atlantic. Soon afterwards, its composers Hugo (Peretti) and Luigi (Creatore) and George David Weiss penned the celebrated ballad 'Can't Help Falling In Love' for the singer's next film.

## SHADOWS
KON-TIKI
*Columbia*

▲ 1
⑩ 5
172/500

As their self-titled debut LP became the first album by a group or indeed by any UK recording artist to top the UK chart, the innovative instrumental combo clicked with another Michael Carr composition.

## BOBBY VEE
HOW MANY TEARS
*London American*

▲ 1
⑩ 3
—/500

This teenager, who had once had Bob Dylan in his backing band, continued his run of hits with a Carole King and Gerry Goffin song that failed to reach the Top 40 in the US.

## LONNIE DONEGAN
MICHAEL ROW THE
BOAT/LUMBERED
*Pye*

▲ 6
⑩16
—/500

The frequent chart visitor scored with an upbeat treatment of The Highwayman's US No 1. His version was coupled with a novelty number from Anthony Newley's musical *Stop The World – I Want To Get Off*. Coincidentally, The Highwaymen later recorded 'Putting On The Style', a song Donegan had earlier taken to the top in the UK.

## SAM COOKE
CUPID
*RCA*

▲ 7
⑩ 2
—/500

Arguably the most influential R&B singer/songwriter of the decade had a transatlantic Top 20 entry with another of his irresistibly commercial self-composed pop classics. The timeless tune returned to the transatlantic charts in 1969 by Johnny Nash and in 1980 by The Spinners.

## BILLY FURY
JEALOUSY
*Decca*

▲ 2
⑩ 3
328/500

A melodramatic ballad, which had given Frankie Laine a Top 10 hit ten years earlier, now gave the UK pop idol his biggest hit. The song started life in Denmark in the late 1920s as 'Jalousie'.

## HIGHWAYMEN
MICHAEL
*HMV*

▲ 1
⑩ 1•
173/500

See US entry (August).

## CLEO LAINE
YOU'LL ANSWER TO ME
*Fontana*

▲ 5
⑩ 1•
—/500

This celebrated song stylist, who was born Clementina Campbell, had her only major hit single with a ballad originally recorded in the US by Patti Page. It was written by regular chart visitors Hal David and Sherman Edwards. The singer, who had been the featured vocalist with husband Johnny Dankworth's band since 1951, went on to make a big name for herself on the US entertainment scene.

## CONNIE FRANCIS
TOGETHER
*MGM*

▲ 6
⑩ 9
—/500

See US entry (July).

## DEL SHANNON
HATS OFF TO LARRY
*London American*

▲ 6
⑩ 2
—/500

See US entry (July).

# UNITED STATES
# OCTOBER 1961

## RAY CHARLES
HIT THE ROAD JACK

*ABC Paramount*

▲ 1
⑩ 4
124/500

Veteran R&B singer/songwriter Percy Mayfield penned this call and response classic for the first popular music act to be tagged a genius. Answer records included 'Well, I Told You' by The Chantels and 'I Changed My Mind Jack' by Jo Ann Campbell.

## BOB MOORE & HIS ORCHESTRA
MEXICO
*Monument*

▲ 7
⑩ 1•
—/500

One of Nashville's most respected session musicians had a one-off hit with a compelling instrumental composed by Felice and Boudleaux Bryant, the team responsible for many hits by the Everly Brothers. Bass player Moore, who had worked with such greats as Elvis Presley, Connie Francis, Brenda Lee and Pat Boone, was also Roy Orbison's musical director. The success of 'Mexico' may well have influenced Herb Alpert's decision to form the gold-plated Tijuana Brass.

## BOBBY DARIN
YOU MUST HAVE BEEN A BEAUTIFUL BABY

*Atco*

▲ 5
⑩ 6
—/500

A song Dick Powell performed in the 1938 movie *Hard To Get* upped the number of standards Darin returned to the Top 40 to five. Some rock historians believe that noted producer Phil Spector had a hand in the recording.

## DOVELLS
BRISTOL STOMP
*Parkway*

▲ 2
⑩ 1
217/500

Blue-eyed soul vocalist Len Barry (born Leonard Borisoff) led this quintet from Philadelphia, whose second single told the nation about the dance craze that had started in nearby Bristol. Like many of the other hits from the Cameo/Parkway group of labels, it was composed by Kal Mann and Dave Appell. Among the act's subsequent chart singles was a sequel, 'Bristol Twistin' Annie'.

## DION
RUNAROUND SUE
*Laurie*

The ex-leader of Dion & The Belmonts' fourth solo single was the highest-placed hit of his long career. He penned the 'Quarter To Three'-influenced rocker with fellow Laurie recording artist Ernie Maresca, and recalls that it was inspired by a girl named Roberta, not Sue. An answer, 'Stay-At-Home Sue' by Linda Laurie, narrowly missed the chart. Actor-turned-singer Leif Garrett brought the song back to the US Top 20 in 1978 and pop group Racey had a UK Top 20 entry with it in 1980.

## HAYLEY MILLS
LET'S GET TOGETHER
*Vista*

Richard and Robert Sherman wrote this bouncy item for the Walt Disney film *The Parent Trap*, and it transported the 14-year-old English actress into the transatlantic Top 20 for the only time. Could this mop-topped vocalist's hit, with its 'yeah yeah yeah' refrain have been a harbinger of the UK Beat Boom?

## SUE THOMPSON
SAD MOVIES (MAKE ME CRY)
*Hickory*

Ten years after she launched her recording career, the singer (born Eva McKee) with the distinctive child-like vocal style had an impressive stockpile of pop successes. Noted Nashville tunesmith John D. Loudermilk penned her first major hit, which easily out-pointed a rendition by the popular Lennon Sisters.

## JIMMY DEAN
BIG BAD JOHN
*Columbia*

The tall Texan (born Seth Ward) had his biggest hit with a song he wrote while flying to Nashville to record. The story, which told of a miner killed while rescuing others, was fiction but the character was based on a 6ft 5in actor friend, Johnny Mento. The single was Dean's only major transatlantic hit and it inspired many answer records, including the Top 40 hit 'Small Sad Sam' by Phil McLean. Dean later resurrected John in his hit 'The Cajun Queen' and in 'Little Bitty Big John'.

## LEE DORSEY
YA YA
*Fury*

It took about 15 minutes for New Orleans R&B singer Dorsey and New York record company head Bobby Robinson jointly to compose this song, which they based on a children's playground rhyme. In Europe, Petula Clark had the hit version, which was retitled 'Ya Ya Twist'.

## TROY SHONDELL
THIS TIME
*Liberty*

Before 'Tragedy' struck gold in 1959, Memphis singer Thomas Wayne had released this Chips Moman composition without success. A couple of years later, Shondell revived the heartfelt rockaballad. It was released on the Writers & Artists, Gaye and Golden Crest (his own company) labels, before Liberty picked up the master and made it the singer/songwriter's biggest hit. Multi-instrumentalist Shondell recorded for many more labels during his career but never returned to the heights.

## PARIS SISTERS
I LOVE HOW YOU LOVE ME
*Gregmark*

The US radio watchdog, the Radio Trade Practices Committee, deemed this Barry Mann and Larry Kolber composed love song was 'too suggestive'. Their comments, however, did not stop the Phil Spector-produced single from taking the California trio into the Top 20 for the only time. In the UK, it was a cover by Jimmy Crawford that reached the Top 20. Bobby Vinton returned the ballad to the Top 10 in 1968, and both Lynn Anderson (1979) and Glen Campbell (1983) had country Top 20 entries with it.

## CHUBBY CHECKER
THE FLY
*Parkway*

▲ 7
⑩ 4
—/500

As the Twist started to take off for the second time, the dance master, who was born Ernest Evans, launched a new dance craze. John Madera and Danny White (from Danny & The Juniors) penned the hit.

# UNITED KINGDOM
# OCTOBER 1961

## EDEN KANE
GET LOST
*Decca*

▲ 10
⑩ 2
—/500

The British pop idol, with the easily recognizable growl in his voice, proved he was no one-hit-wonder when he launched another Johnny Worth song into the Top 10.

## HELEN SHAPIRO
WALKIN' BACK TO HAPPINESS
*Columbia*

▲ 1
⑩ 3
40/500

This jaunty, up-tempo John Schroeder and Mike Hawker composition amassed a record 300,000 advance orders and was the 15-year-old's second successive No 1. It went on to sell over a million copies around the globe and even managed to dent the bottom of the US chart.

## JOHN LEYTON
WILD WIND
*Top Rank*

▲ 2
⑩ 2•
321/500

The team of producer Joe Meek, composer Geoff Goddard and vocalist John Leyton amassed four Top 20 singles in nine months, and Leyton was voted Best New Singer of 1961. Nonetheless, as for many early 1960s UK headliners, the arrival of the beat groups brought a premature end to his recording career. He subsequently appeared in several top movies, including *The Great Escape* and *Von Ryan's Express*.

## CLIFF RICHARD
WHEN THE GIRL IN YOUR ARMS IS THE GIRL IN YOUR HEART
*Columbia*

▲ 3
⑩14
376/500

Veteran US songsmiths Sid Tepper and Roy Bennett, who were responsible for Cliff's earlier chart topper 'Travellin' Light', penned this romantic ballad for inclusion in his film *The Young Ones*. In the US, a cover version by Connie Francis cracked the Top 10.

## TONY ORLANDO
BLESS YOU
*Fontana*

▲ 5
⑩ 1•
—/500

The 17-year-old New York session singer, who had cut the original version of Billy Fury's hit 'Halfway To Paradise', placed this powerful Barry Mann and Cynthia Weil song into the transatlantic Top 20. The singer, born Michael Cassavitis, recorded under various names throughout the 1960s, and forged a chain of hits fronting the group Dawn in the 1970s.

# UNITED STATES
# NOVEMBER 1961

## BRENDA LEE
FOOL #1
*Decca*

The one-time regular on the top-rated country TV show *The Ozark Jubilee* had a hit with a country ballad first recorded by coal miner's daughter Lorettta Lynn. Interestingly, it was Lynn's version of the song that got her a deal with Decca and started her on the road to success.

## GENE MCDANIELS
TOWER OF STRENGTH
*Liberty*

Burt Bacharach and Bob Hillliard wrote the third of the pop/R&B baritone's six US Top 40 entries. For the second time in succession his hit was successfully covered in the UK – where Frankie Vaughan took it to the top. Gloria Lynne answered the hit with 'You Don't Have To Be A Tower of Strength'.

## MARVELETTES
PLEASE MR. POSTMAN
*Tamla*

Motown's first No 1 hit was achieved by a female quartet from Detroit, who had 23 US chart entries in the decade. The song was co-written by founder member Georgia Dobbins, who left the group before they recorded it. The Beatles cut it on their second album and in 1975 The Carpenters' version also reached the top. The Marvellettes' follow-up was the similarly themed 'Twistin' Postman'.

## JAMES DARREN
GOODBYE CRUEL WORLD
*Colpix*

Actor James Darren (born James Ercolani) had his first major hit with a Gloria Shayne song in which he threatened to go off and join the circus. It was the first of four consecutive Top 40 hits by the star of such top teen movies as *Gidget* and *Because They're Young*.

## MARCELS
HEARTACHES
*Colpix*

An over-the-top doo-wop rendition of a 1931 composition, which Ted Weems had turned to gold in 1947, reinstalled the unmistakable vocal team into the Top 10. The quintet, who helped renew interest in the 1950s R&B vocal group sounds, recorded several similar singles but with little commercial success.

## PATSY CLINE
CRAZY
*Decca*

In 1992, America's jukebox owners voted 'Crazy' their all-time top hit. The song introduced country singer/composer Willie Nelson to the pop charts and gave Cline her highest-placed hit. The legendary singer, who was born Virginia Hensley in Virginia, died in a plane crash in 1963. Amazingly, 'Crazy' finally entered the UK Top 20 in 1991. It was also a Top 10 country hit for Linda Ronstadt in 1977.

# UNITED KINGDOM
# NOVEMBER 1961

**ELVIS PRESLEY**
HIS LATEST FLAME/
LITTLE SISTER
*RCA*

See US entry (September).

**RAY CHARLES**
HIT THE ROAD JACK
*HMV*

See US entry (October).

**KARL DENVER**
MEXICALI ROSE
*Decca*

A song which Bing Crosby had made famous before World War II quickly returned the versatile vocalist, with the multi-octave range, to the Top 10 for the second successive time.

**BOBBY DARIN**
YOU MUST HAVE BEEN A
BEAUTIFUL BABY
*London American*

See US entry.

**JIMMY DEAN**
BIG BAD JOHN
*Philips*

See US entry (October).

**ADAM FAITH**
THE TIME HAS COME
*Parlophone*

The singer/actor (born Terry Nelhams) charted with a Les Vandyke song that was featured in his film *What A Whopper*. When his record sales ceased, Faith's acting career blossomed and he starred in two successful TV series, *Budgie* and *Love Hurts*.

**DAVE BRUBECK QUARTET**
TAKE FIVE
*Fontana*

The biggest-selling modern jazz group of the era had their top single with a re-release of a track that had been overlooked in late 1959. The California-based quartet was led by award-winning pianist Brubeck (born Dave Warren), and included saxophonist Paul Desmond who composed this hypnotic tune. Even though 'Take Five' was featured on the combo's fifth US Top 10 album, *Time Out*, it was not a Top 20 hit in America. Follow-ups 'It's A Raggy Waltz' and 'Unsquare Dance' were mid-table UK hits.

**BOBBY VEE**
TAKE GOOD CARE OF MY
BABY
*London American*

See US entry (September).

**LAURIE JOHNSON**
SUCU-SUCU
*Pye*

UK bandleader/composer Johnson had the biggest hit version of one of the year's most recorded songs in the UK. The Argentinean composition, which also charted by Nina & Frederick, Ted Heath, Joe Loss and the nattily named duo Ping Ping and Al Verlaine, was the theme tune for TV production *Top Secret*. Johnson later composed the themes to the top TV series *The Avengers* and *The Professionals*.

## FRANKIE VAUGHAN
TOWER OF STRENGTH
*Philips*

▲ 1
⑩ 9
89/500

Burt Bacharach and Bob Hilliard's powerful pop song gave the frequent chart visitor his first No 1 since 'Garden Of Eden' in early 1957. His lively version easily outpaced both the original American hit by Gene McDaniels and teenager Paul Raven's (aka Gary Glitter) rendition. Vaughan (born Frankie Abelson) was arguably the UK's best-known male entertainer in the US, and had recently starred in the film *Let's Make Love* with Marilyn Monroe.

## DANNY WILLIAMS
MOON RIVER
*HMV*

▲ 1
⑩ 1
94/500

Henry Mancini's perennially popular theme from the acclaimed film *Breakfast At Tiffany's* was taken to the top by a South African-born singer whose voice inspired comparisons to Johnny Mathis. In the US, Mancini's instrumental version of 'Moon River' reached the Top 20 alongside Jerry Butler's vocal interpretation.

## SHADOWS
THE SAVAGE
*Columbia*

▲ 10
⑩ 6
—/500

Britain's most imitated group played this Norrie Paramor composition in the film *The Young Ones,* in which they starred alongside Cliff Richard. In the US it was cut by The Ventures.

# UNITED STATES
# DECEMBER 1961

## CHUBBY CHECKER
THE TWIST
*Parkway*

▲ 1
⑩ 5
1/500

The only single to reach No 1 in the US on two separate occasions spent a record-breaking 39 weeks in the Top 100. This time the Twist craze caught on with American adults and it soon spread right around the globe. Thanks to Checker, and Twist music, the album charts were finally opened wide to rock-oriented music too.

## LEROY VAN DYKE
WALK ON BY
*Mercury*

▲ 5
⑩ 1•
457/500

The polished performer from Missouri spent a staggering 19 weeks at the top of the country chart with this Kendall Hayes-composed 'slipping around' song. It was one of the few country hits to reach the Top 5 on both sides of the Atlantic. Nonetheless, the one-time auctioneer failed in his bid to become a regular pop hit maker, although he managed to notch up a healthy number of country bestsellers in the 1960s and 1970s.

## G-CLEFS
I UNDERSTAND
(JUST HOW YOU FEEL)
*Terrace*

A ballad that the Four Tunes had written and charted with in 1953 became the quintet from Massachusetts' biggest hit. They made it sound seasonal by adding the chorus of the well-known Scottish song 'Auld Lang Syne', and the resulting record was a transatlantic Top 20 hit. In the mid-1960s, a revival by Freddie & The Dreamers was also a transatlantic success.

## TOKENS
THE LION SLEEPS
TONIGHT
*RCA*

An adaptation of a 1930s Zulu folk song, 'Mbube' (aka 'Wimoweh'), was the New York vocal group's highest-ranked hit. It inspired answer records such as 'The Lion Is Awake' and 'The Tiger's Wide Awake'. In 1972, the act produced a faithful cover by Robert John which hit the Top 3. In the UK, a remake by Tight Fit hit the top in 1982. In 1994, The Tokens' original version returned to the Top 100 after being heard in the successful movie *The Lion King*.

## BOBBY VEE
RUN TO HIM
*Liberty*

Eighteen-year-old Vee's third transatlantic Top 10 entry in 15 months was a Gerry Goffin and Jack Keller composition, which had originally been written with the Everly Brothers in mind.

## FERRANTE & TEICHER
TONIGHT
*UA*

The pianists, who first played together at New York's prestigious Juilliard School of Music in the 1930s, hit with a lush treatment of the oft-recorded Leonard Bernstein song. 'Tonight' was taken from their Top 10 LP *West Side Story & Other Motion Picture & Broadway Hits*.

## SANDY NELSON
LET THERE BE DRUMS
*Imperial*

Nelson, who had played drums on countless hits recorded on the West Coast, scored his second transatlantic Top 10 hit with this self-penned instrumental. Among the legendary session drummer's later-forgotten 45s were 'Let There Be Drums '66' and 'Let There Be Drums And Bass'. A bad road accident in 1963 helped put the brakes on his successful career.

## NEIL SEDAKA
HAPPY BIRTHDAY,
SWEET SIXTEEN
*RCA*

Sedaka and long-time co-writer Howard Greenfield composed this sing-along pop pearl which gave him his biggest UK hit of the decade. It inspired an answer record, 'Happy Birthday Mr 21'.

## JOEY DEE &
## THE STARLITERS
PEPPERMINT TWIST (PT 1)
*Roulette*

Alongside Chubby Checker's 'The Twist', this record was largely responsible for the renewed interest in the dance craze. The band also helped break easy-listening music's stranglehold on the Top 5 album chart with their set *Doin' The Twist At The Peppermint Lounge* (cut at the New York club where they were the house band). It was the first of four Top 20 hits in nine months for the New Jersey group, which at times included Jimi Hendrix and a couple of Young Rascals.

## ELVIS PRESLEY
CAN'T HELP FALLING
IN LOVE
*RCA*

The team who adapted 'The Lion Sleeps Tonight', producers Hugo (Peretti) and Luigi (Creatore) and top tunesmith George David Weiss, also composed this beautiful ballad which was based on a French song, 'Plaisir d'Amour'. It reappeared in the UK Top 10 courtesy of American acts Andy Williams (1970) and The Stylistics (1976) and became a transatlantic No 1 in 1993 by UB40.

# UNITED KINGDOM
# DECEMBER 1961

## KENNY BALL
MIDNIGHT IN MOSCOW
*Pye Jazz*

▲ 2
⑩ 1
222/500

Before The Beatles broke down the barriers for good, only a handful of UK singles had reached the US Top 10. One of the few was this top UK trad jazz band's Dixieland adaptation of a Russian tune originally known as 'Padmeskoveeye Vietchera'. Interestingly, the band returned behind the Iron Curtain musically for later tracks 'Red Square' and 'From Russia With Love'.

## SHIRLEY BASSEY
I'LL GET BY
*Columbia*

▲ 10
⑩ 7
—/500

The ever-popular Welsh songstress charted with an oft-recorded standard written before she was born by top tunesmiths Roy Turk (the composer of the recent No 1 'Are You Lonesome Tonight') and Fred Ahlert.

## PETULA CLARK
MY FRIEND THE SEA
*Pye*

▲ 7
⑩ 7
—/500

Soon after riding high with 'Sailor', the one-time child star reappeared with another nautical number. Like many of her earlier singles, it was released in the US but sank without trace.

## PAT BOONE
JOHNNY WILL
*London American*

▲ 4
⑩ 11
471/500

A jaunty Paul Evans-composed single, which failed to reach the US Top 20, conveyed the one-time teen icon into the UK Top 10 for the first time in over three years. Boone, who had been voted World's Top Male Singer in the 1957 *NME* poll, failed to chart again after the arrival of the UK beat groups.

## MR. ACKER BILK
STRANGER ON THE SHORE
*Columbia*

▲ 2
⑩ 4
38/500

Bilk's biggest hit also topped the US chart. It sold over a million in the UK and was in the Top 50 for over a year. It was the No 1 transatlantic instrumental of 1962. Bilk originally called the song after his daughter 'Jenny'; its title changed when it became the theme to a children's TV series *Stranger On The Shore*.

## SANDY NELSON
LET THERE BE DRUMS
*London American*

▲ 3
⑩ 2•
369/500

See US entry.

## RUSS CONWAY
TOY BALLOONS
*Columbia*

▲ 7
⑩ 7•
—/500

1959's most successful singles artist in the UK, pianist/composer Conway (born Trevor Stanford), had the last of his 11 Top 20 entries with an instrumental composed by American musician/band leader Billy Mure. Among his very impressive hit tally were two consecutive self-composed chart toppers, 'Side Saddle' and 'Roulette'.

## NEIL SEDAKA
HAPPY BIRTHDAY, SWEET SIXTEEN
*RCA*

▲ 3
⑩ 6
275/500

See US entry.

# UNITED STATES
# JANUARY 1962

## LETTERMEN
WHEN I FALL IN LOVE
*Capitol*

This oft-recorded love song, written for Robert Mitchum's 1952 movie *One Minute To Zero*, followed the group's previous single, 'The Way You Look Tonight', into the Top 20. The smooth West Coast vocal trio were one of the most popular easy-listening acts of the 1960s, clocking up six Top 20 singles and albums. Donny Osmond re-introduced the love ballad to the transatlantic charts in 1973, and in 1987 both Nat 'King' Cole's 1957 recording and a version by Rick Astley returned to the UK Top 10.

## RAY CHARLES
UNCHAIN MY HEART
*ABC Paramount*

Ray Charles, who was now regarded as the singer's singer on both sides of the Atlantic, achieved his fourth US Top 10 entry in just over a year with his thirty-fifth R&B chart entry.

## BARBARA GEORGE
I KNOW (YOU DON'T LOVE ME NO MORE)
*AFO*

This R&B singer/songwriter from New Orleans based her biggest hit on the gospel gem 'Just A Closer Walk With Thee'. The single was released on the newly launched AFO (All For One) label owned by accomplished producer/arranger Harold Battiste. Soon after it topped the R&B chart, she signed to the renowned Sue label, but no other hits were forthcoming. The million seller inspired the answer record 'Oh Yes (I Don't Love You No More)' by Peter Buck.

## CONNIE FRANCIS
WHEN THE BOY IN YOUR ARMS (IS THE BOY IN YOUR HEART)
*MGM*

The award-winning singer, who in her early days had supplied the screen singing voice for both Tuesday Weld and Jayne Mansfield, hit with a cover of a song first heard in Cliff Richard's film *The Young Ones*.

## SUE THOMPSON
NORMAN
*Hickory*

A cute novelty written by John D. Loudermilk made it two consecutive Top 5 entries for the youthful-sounding songstress. In the UK, a cover by Carol Deene (who had also recorded Thompson's previous hit, 'Sad Movies') grabbed the honours. Thompson, who had started as a C&W singer in 1952, had a run of mid-table country charters in the 1970s.

## DION
THE WANDERER
*Laurie*

This renowned rock anthem was hitting as its composer Ernie Maresca's own record 'Shout! Shout! (Knock Yourself Out)' climbed the chart. Dion was backed on both 'The Wanderer' and 'Runaround Sue' by The Del-Satins. In the UK, it re-entered the Top 10 in 1976 and a revival by Status Quo reached the Top 10 in 1984.

## SHIRELLES
BABY IT'S YOU
*Scepter*

▲ 8
⑩ 4
—/500

Burt Bacharach and Hal David's rewrite of their song 'I'll Cherish You' added to the New Jersey quartet's hit tally. The single was simply the writer's demo plus Shirley Owens' lead vocal. A version by Smith went into the Top 5 in 1969 and a live recording by The Beatles was a UK Top 10 entry in 1995.

---

# UNITED KINGDOM
# JANUARY 1962

---

## BOBBY DARIN
MULTIPLICATION
*London American*

▲ 5
⑩ 7
—/500

A semi-suggestive song that its composer Darin sang in the film *Come September* gave him his twelfth UK chart entry in three years. In the US, the other side, a cover of Bobby Peterson's 'Irresistible You', reached the Top 20.

## BILLY FURY
I'D NEVER FIND ANOTHER YOU
*Decca*

▲ 5
⑩ 4
495/500

Fury, who had earlier hit with his treatment of Tony Orlando's 'Halfway To Paradise', registered with his rendition of a Carole King and Gerry Goffin song that both Orlando and Paul Anka had earlier recorded.

## CLIFF RICHARD
THE YOUNG ONES
*Columbia*

▲ 1
⑩ 15
15/500

The title song from Cliff Richard's latest movie amassed over 500,000 advance orders and was the first UK record to enter the chart at No 1 in the decade. It was another Sid Tepper and Roy Bennett composition, and went on to sell over a million copies. A noted reviewer called the film 'The best musical the UK has ever made'.

## DEL SHANNON
SO LONG BABY
*London American*

▲ 10
⑩ 3
—/500

Shannon's fourth of his 14 UK Top 40 hits was another self-composed, up-tempo stomper which as usual featured Shannon's instantly recognizable semi-falsetto vocals.

## BOBBY VEE
RUN TO HIM
*Liberty*

▲ 6
⑩ 5
—/500

See US entry (December 1961).

## EDEN KANE
FORGET ME NOT
*Decca*

▲ 3
⑩ 3
302/500

The combination of a Johnny Worth song and Kane's vocal took 1961's hottest new UK act back up the chart. Incidentally, Kane's real name was Richard Sarstedt and he was born in India. His brothers Peter and Clive (aka Robin) both had major hits of their own in later years.

## LEROY VAN DYKE
WALK ON BY
*Mercury*

▲ 5
⑩ 1•
482/500

See US entry (December 1961).

# UNITED STATES
# FEBRUARY 1962

## GENE CHANDLER
DUKE OF EARL
*Vee Jay*

▲ 1
⑩ 1•
68/500

For contractual reasons, semi-successful Chicago group The Dukays released their composition 'Duke Of Earl' under lead singer Gene Chandler's (born Eugene Dixon) name. Inspired by the name of member Earl Edwards, it was one of the year's biggest hits, and an answer version, 'Duchess Of Earl' by The Pearlettes, also charted. Chandler became one of the most consistent R&B record sellers of the decade, although his sound-alike follow-up 'Walk On With The Duke' fell by the wayside. 'Duke Of Earl' finally entered the UK Top 10 in 1979 by The Darts.

## BRENDA LEE
BREAK IT TO ME GENTLY
*Decca*

▲ 4
⑩ 9
429/500

The first teenage artist to put two albums in the Top 5 added to her hit tally with a big ballad that would also carry Juice Newton into the Top 20 twenty years later.

## BURL IVES
A LITTLE BITTY TEAR
*Decca*

▲ 9
⑩ 1
—/500

This popular folk singer/actor reappeared in the Top 10 after an 11-year absence with a sing-along country composition from the pen of regular Nashville hit writer Hank Cochran. The record reached the Top 10 on both sides of the Atlantic, and was the first of three US Top 20 hits in a row for the likeable troubadour.

## GARY U.S. BONDS
DEAR LADY TWIST
*Legrand*

▲ 9
⑩ 4
—/500

'Do the Twist and you'll never grow old' was the advice Bonds imparted on the first of his two top Twist hits. The commercially solid composition came from the pen of his long-time producer Frank Guida.

## EVERLY BROTHERS
CRYIN' IN THE RAIN
*Warner*

▲ 6
⑩ 13
—/500

Despite the fact that they were now in the Marines, the Everlys chalked up another hit with this lilting Carole King and Howard Greenfield ballad. The song returned to the US Top 20 in 1990 by A-Ha.

## BRUCE CHANNEL
HEY! BABY
*Smash*

▲ 1
⑩ 1•
73/500

A song that took the singer from Texas ten minutes to write and a quarter of an hour to record only narrowly failed to top the chart on both sides of the Atlantic. The single's distinctive harmonica introduction (by Delbert McClinton) influenced The Beatles' debut disc, 'Love Me Do'. Among Channel's subsequent non-starters were the similarly titled 'Come On Baby', 'Oh Baby' and 'No Other Baby'. He achieved his only other Top 20 hit in the UK in 1968 with 'Keep On'.

# UNITED KINGDOM
# FEBRUARY 1962

### CHUBBY CHECKER
LET'S TWIST AGAIN
*Columbia*

▲ 2
⑩ 1•
196/500

The King of the Twist's biggest UK hit was the sequel single to his US No 1 'The Twist'. It reached the UK Top 10 in both 1962 and 1975. See also US entry (December 1961).

### ELVIS PRESLEY
ROCK-A-HULA-
BABY/CAN'T HELP
FALLING IN LOVE
*RCA*

▲ 1
⑩27
21/500

See US entry (December 1961).

### EVERLY BROTHERS
CRYIN' IN THE RAIN
*Warner*

▲ 6
⑩12
—/500

See US entry.

### KARL DENVER
WIMOWEH
*Decca*

▲ 4
⑩ 3
372/500

As the US smash 'The Lion Sleeps Tonight' by The Tokens climbed the UK chart, Denver overtook it with his eardrum-piercing interpretation of the traditional South African song on which it was based. Denver's 1989 re-recording with the Happy Mondays was a minor success.

### BURL IVES
A LITTLE BITTY TEAR
*Brunswick*

▲ 9
⑩ 1•
—/500

See US entry.

# UNITED STATES
# MARCH 1962

### KENNY BALL
MIDNIGHT IN MOSCOW
*Kapp*

▲ 2
⑩ 1•
276/500

See UK entry (December 1961).

### GENE MCDANIELS
CHIP CHIP
*Liberty*

▲ 10
⑩ 3•
—/500

The pop/R&B singer's second successive Top 10 entry was also his last major hit as a vocalist. It was a potent Jeff Barry, Arthur Resnick and Cliff

Crawford composition, which featured a 'chipping' sound created by hitting a hammer on a steel bar. Later in the decade McDaniels turned his hand to writing and penned several successful soul songs, including Roberta Flack's international hit 'Feel Like Making Love'.

### CONNIE FRANCIS
DON'T BREAK THE HEART
THAT LOVES YOU
*MGM*

▲ 5
⑩14
192/500

Benny Davis, who wrote such standards as 'Baby

Face' and Connie's earlier UK No 1 'Carolina Moon', wrote the last of her three US No 1 singles. The song also topped the country charts in 1978 by Margo Smith.

## SENSATIONS
LET ME IN
*Argo*

Yvonne Baker, who composed this infectious R&B song, also fronted the Philadelphia vocal quartet who sold a million copies of it. It was the biggest hit for the act that had earlier charted with distinctive revivals of 'Yes Sir That's My Baby' (1956) and 'Music, Music, Music' (1961).

## JAMES DARREN
HER ROYAL MAJESTY
*Colpix*

The photogenic actor from Philadelphia scored his second consecutive Top 10 entry with a Gerry Goffin and Carole King composition. Before returning full time to acting, Darren notched up another Top 20 hit with the follow-up, 'Conscience'. All his US hits were only minor successes in the UK, where he is primarily remembered as Tony Newman in the cult TV series *The Time Tunnel*.

## DON & JUAN
WHAT'S YOUR NAME
*Big Top*

Two members of the late 1950s chart act The Genies, Claude Johnson and Roland Trone, briefly found fame with a self-composed, jazz-influenced R&B ballad. The doo-wop-styled New York duo released several more singles but failed to make a real name for themselves.

## BILLY JOE &
## THE CHECKMATES
PERCOLATOR (TWIST)
*Dore*

One-time comedian Louis Bideu fronted this session group who had a one-off hit with a xylophone-led instrumental he had written with noted arranger Ernie Freeman. They named the track 'Percolator' as it reminded them of the sound made by percolating coffee. The word Twist was added in brackets simply to increase its potential sales market. Record buyers did not thirst for more hits and follow-ups such as 'One More Cup' were ignored.

## ROY ORBISON
DREAM BABY
*Monument*

Country composer Cindy Walker penned the unique vocalist's third Top 5 entry in under a year. An update in 1971 by Glen Campbell also reached the transatlantic Top 40.

## CHUBBY CHECKER
SLOW TWISTIN'
*Parkway*

The internationally renowned dance master hit again with an atmospheric Jon Sheldon Twister that also featured newcomer Dee Dee Sharp. This hit came soon after Checker had put an amazing four albums simultaneously in the US Top 12.

## SAM COOKE
TWISTIN' THE NIGHT AWAY
*RCA*

The legendary singer had one of the biggest Twist hits with one of his own compositions. Rod Stewart, one of the many singers influenced by Cooke's vocal style, guided the floor-filling song into the US chart in 1973 and 1987.

## SHELLEY FABARES
JOHNNY ANGEL
*Colpix*

The actress from California, who played Mary Stone in the popular TV series *The Donna Reed Show*, had her biggest hit with another cute pop song from the pen of Lee Pockriss. The follow-up 'Johnny Loves Me' was Fabares' only other notable success. After she left the series she starred in several movies and her leading men included Elvis Presley, Fabian and Peter Noone (Herman's Hermits).

## ELVIS PRESLEY
GOOD LUCK CHARM
*RCA*

▲ 1
⑩ 26
127/500

Elvis' sixth transatlantic No 1 hit was a bouncy pop rocker composed by Aaron Schroeder and Wally Gold, who had written the English lyric to his earlier chart topper 'It's Now Or Never'.

# UNITED KINGDOM
# MARCH 1962

## KENNY BALL
MARCH OF THE
SIAMESE CHILDREN
*Pye Jazz*

▲ 4
⑩ 2
—/500

Trumpet-toting trad jazz star Ball and his band topped the *NME* chart with his Dixieland interpretation of the well-known Richard Rodgers number from the hit musical *The King And I*.

## HELEN SHAPIRO
TELL ME WHAT HE SAID
*Columbia*

▲ 2
⑩ 4
210/500

The first four releases by this award-winning young singer/actress all entered the Top 5 – a record-breaking feat. It was her first American-written single and was penned by Brill Building tunesmith Jeff Barry.

## SHADOWS
WONDERFUL LAND
*Columbia*

▲ 1
⑩ 7
4/500

Jerry Lordan, who had written their breakthrough single 'Apache', composed the biggest hit for the UK's most popular group of the early 1960s. The track had been recorded 12 months earlier but the act did not feel the sound was quite right. 'Wonderful Land' was finally deemed suitable for release after a string section was added. In 1993, Shadow Hank Marvin released a version with Mark Knopfler of Dire Straits.

## ROY ORBISON
DREAM BABY
*London American*

▲ 2
⑩ 3
231/500

See US entry.

## DION
THE WANDERER
*HMV*

▲ 10
⑩ 1•
—/500

See US entry (January).

## BERNARD CRIBBINS
HOLE IN THE GROUND
*Parlophone*

▲ 3
⑩ 1
—/500

Celebrated character actor Cribbins, who appeared in many UK films during the decade, had three Top 40 entries in the early 1960s with novelty items. His biggest chart single was written for him by Ted Dicks and Myles Rudge and produced by George Martin.

## MATT MONRO
SOFTLY AS I LEAVE YOU
*Parlophone*

▲ 10
⑩ 3
—/500

The UK song stylist recorded the original version of this ballad, which Frank Sinatra and Elvis Presley subsequently added to their repertoires.

# UNITED STATES
# APRIL 1962

### RICK NELSON
YOUNG WORLD
*Imperial*

Jerry Fuller, composer of Nelson's recent No 1 'Travelin' Man', wrote this easy-on-the-ear pop nugget, which rocketed Rick (he had now dropped the 'Y' in Ricky) into the Top 20 for the twenty-second time.

### KETTY LESTER
LOVE LETTERS
*Era*

The singer/actress, born Revoyda Frierson in Arkansas, had her only major hit with the title song from a 1945 Jennifer Jones film. Ed Cobb produced the recording, which featured an innovative piano arrangement by top session man Lincoln Mayorga. His arrangement was also used on subsequent hit singles by Elvis Presley (1966) and Alison Moyet (1987). Talented vocalist Lester is probably best known for her many TV roles, including that of Hestor Sue in *Little House On The Prairie*.

### DEE DEE SHARP
MASHED POTATO TIME
*Cameo*

Soon after Sharp and Chubby Checker's duet 'Slow Twistin' charted, the R&B singer from Philadelphia topped some lists with her first solo hit. The song, which turned the Mashed Potato into a national dance craze, was part written by ex-Marvelette Georgia Dobbins. It was the first of four consecutive Top 10 hits for the singer born Dione LaRue.

### CLYDE MCPHATTER
LOVER PLEASE
*Mercury*

One of the 1950s most recognizable and innovative vocalists had his highest-placed hit of the 1960s with a song written by later hit-maker Billy Swann. 'Lover Please' had previously been recorded by Swann's group Mirt Mirley & The Rhythm Steppers and by Dennis Turner. In the UK, the Vernon Girls escorted it into the Top 20. Falsetto-voiced McPhatter, who in 1953 had formed The Drifters, died of a heart attack in 1972, at the age of only 39.

### SHIRELLES
SOLDIER BOY
*Scepter*

The top-selling female group's biggest hit was written in five minutes at a recording session by producer Luther Dixon and label owner Florence Greenberg. It inspired several answer versions, including 'I'm Your Soldier Boy' by the Soldier Boys.

### JOEY DEE & THE STARLITERS
SHOUT (PT. 1)
*Roulette*

Dee (born Joseph DiNicola) and his talented combo returned to the Top 20 with their imaginative interpretation of the Isley Brothers' celebrated 1959 composition, which they featured in the movie *Hey Let's Twist*. Dee helped put the Twist on the international map and his tenure at the top ended as interest in the dance faded.

## MR ACKER BILK
STRANGER ON THE
SHORE
*Atco*

See UK entry (December 1961).

## GARY U.S. BONDS
TWIST, TWIST SENORA
*Legrand*

The last of the exciting performer's top sellers of the 1960s came with a Twister based on the calypso single 'Shake Shake Senora' by Lord Flea. During the 1970s Bonds wrote and produced many critically acclaimed soul sides, and in the early 1980s he made a chart comeback as an artist with records produced by Bruce Springsteen and Southside Johnny.

# UNITED KINGDOM
# APRIL 1962

## SAM COOKE
TWISTIN' THE NIGHT AWAY
*RCA*

See US entry (March).

## DEL SHANNON
HEY LITTLE GIRL
*London American*

Even though it was only a mid-table US hit, this stomper made it four UK Top 10s in a row for the prolific Michigan singer/songwriter (born Charles Westover).

## BRUCE CHANNEL
HEY! BABY
*Mercury*

See US entry (February).

## JOHNNY KEATING
THEME FROM *Z CARS*
*Piccadilly*

In the mid-1950s Keating was one of the most in-demand UK big band arrangers, working with such notables as Count Basie and Ted Heath. He had his only hit with the theme from a very popular UK TV police series. The instrumental, which was adapted from the old folk number 'Johnny Todd', also charted for top producer/bandleader Norrie Paramor.

## KARL DENVER
NEVER GOODBYE
*Decca*

A song which failed in its bid to become the UK's Eurovision entry in 1962, nevertheless presented the Jack Good-produced vocalist from Glasgow with his fourth Top 10 entry in succession. Denver was another casualty of the beat boom, but before fading from the scene he put two more singles into the Top 20, 'A Little Love, A Little Kiss' and 'Still'.

## CRAIG DOUGLAS
WHEN MY LITTLE GIRL IS
SMILING
*Top Rank*

Both Douglas and Jimmy Justice reached No 9 with covers of a bouncy Carole King and Gerry Goffin composition that had first been recorded by The Drifters.

## BRENDA LEE
SPEAK TO ME PRETTY
*Brunswick*

The singer who spent over 200 weeks on the UK chart without ever reaching No 1 had her biggest UK hit with a mid-tempo track taken from her film *Two Little Bears*. Astonishingly, the single was not released in the US.

# UNITED STATES
# MAY 1962

## JIMMY DEAN
PT 109
*Columbia*

Dean, who first recorded in 1952, returned to the Top 10 with a Marijohn Wilkin ode, which told of the sinking of President Kennedy's torpedo boat during World War II. The easy-going country entertainer, who hosted his own very popular TV series between 1963 and 1966, had several more country chart entries during the decade.

## JAY & THE AMERICANS
SHE CRIED
*UA*

John 'Jay' Traynor only sang on one of the New York vocal group's hits before being replaced by Jay Black (born David Blatt). The group opened their chart account with a dramatic ballad, which composer Ted Daryl had previously released with few sales.

## WALTER BRENNAN
OLD RIVERS
*Liberty*

The three-time Oscar-winning actor's recitation of a story about an old farmer and his mule transported the 68-year-old star of TV's *The Real McCoys* to the upper reaches of the chart. 'Old Rivers', which every country singer from Johnny

Cash down had rejected, was intended to be the B side of Brennan's single. However, producer Snuff Garrett was convinced he had a hit on his hands, even when arranger Ernie Freeman told him it was the worst song he had ever done!

## ERNIE MARESCA
SHOUT! SHOUT! (KNOCK
YOURSELF OUT)
*Seville*

By the time this New York singer/songwriter had a hit of his own he had already co-written several for his friend Dion, including 'The Wanderer' and the No 1 single 'Runaround Sue'. Maresca's only chart entry came with a similar-sounding good time rock opus. In 1982, Rocky Sharpe & The Replays shipped 'Shout! Shout!' into the UK Top 20 for the only time. Maresca's forgotten follow-ups included 'Something To Shout About'.

## BRENDA LEE
EVERYBODY LOVES ME
BUT YOU
*Decca*

Rockabilly performer Ronnie Self, who composed the teenage hit machine's first two major hits, also wrote her tenth US Top 10 entry of the decade.

## BURL IVES
FUNNY WAY OF LAUGHIN'
*Decca*

The 53-year-old folk singer and Oscar-winning actor's second successive Top 10 entry grabbed the Grammy for Best C&W Performance of 1962. Like his previous hit, it was composed by top country writer Hank Cochran. The popular performer died in 1995 aged 85.

## RAY CHARLES
I CAN'T STOP LOVING YOU
*ABC Paramount*

Three years earlier Charles and Don Gibson battled it out with revivals of the country No 1 'I'm Moving On'. Now, the former's soulful remake of Gibson's

self-composed 1958 million seller gave him his only transatlantic No 1. Conway Twitty took the song to the top of the country list in 1972 – ten years before Charles finally debuted on that chart.

## DION
LOVERS WHO WANDER
*Laurie*

The similar-sounding follow-up to 'The Wanderer' was written by Dion and Ernie Maresca. The B side, '(I Was) Born To Cry', also charted.

# UNITED KINGDOM
# MAY 1962

## B. BUMBLE & THE STINGERS
NUT ROCKER
*Top Rank*

A West Coast session group, which included saxophonist Plas Johnson, drummer Earl Palmer and pianist Lincoln Mayorga, clicked with a rock rendition of Tchaikovsky's 'Nutcracker'. It was arranged by Kim Fowley, who produced the original recording by the equally oddly named Jack B. Nimble & The Quicks. Among Bumble's other releases were the similar 'Apple Knocker' and 'Dawn Cracker'. Surprisingly, this record returned to the UK Top 20 in 1972.

## KETTY LESTER
LOVE LETTERS
*London American*

See US entry (April).

## DANNY WILLIAMS
WONDERFUL WORLD OF THE YOUNG
*HMV*

Veteran US tunesmiths Sid Tepper and Roy Bennett, who had penned hits for Cliff Richard, composed the ultra-smooth vocalist's last major UK hit. Norman Newell produced this version, which had previously been recorded by Andy Williams. In 1964, after the UK hits dried up, Danny Williams had a big US hit with 'White On White'.

## LONNIE DONEGAN
THE PARTY'S OVER
*Pye*

The most successful and influential UK recording star before The Beatles registered his last Top 10 hit ironically with 'The Party's Over'. It was a string-filled treatment of the torch song from the 1956 Jule Styne, Betty Comden and Adolph Green musical *Bells Are Ringing*.

## ELVIS PRESLEY
GOOD LUCK CHARM
*RCA*

See US entry (March).

## CLIFF RICHARD
I'M LOOKING OUT THE
WINDOW/DO YOU WANNA
DANCE
*Columbia*

Cliff coupled a revival of a beautiful ballad, which Peggy Lee had previously recorded, with his rendition of Bobby Freeman's top-notch rock'n'roll song from 1958.

## ADAM FAITH
AS YOU LIKE IT
*Parlophone*

Regular hit maker Faith, who was often named the UK's Best-Dressed Artist, delivered another Les Vandyke song into the Top 10. He may not have been the strongest vocalist of his era, but this diminutive teen idol became one of the UK's most instantly recognizable and popular singers.

## JIMMY JUSTICE
WHEN MY LITTLE GIRL IS
SMILING
*Pye*

A song written by Carole King and Gerry Goffin was the first of three UK Top 20 singles in a row for this blue-eyed soul singer (born James Little) from Surrey. In the UK, the Tony Hatch-produced single outsold the original recording by The Drifters, and joined another cover version by Craig Douglas in the Top 10.

## BRIAN HYLAND
GINNY COME LATELY
*HMV*

This pretty ballad composed by Peter Udell and Gary Geld gave the 18-year-old American his second major UK hit and only narrowly missed the US Top 20.

## BILLY FURY
LAST NIGHT WAS MADE
FOR LOVE
*Decca*

The singer, who was born Ronald Wycherley, added to his hit tally with a tune that UK singer/songwriter Alan Fielding had written especially for him.

## MIKE SARNE AND
## WENDY RICHARD
COME OUTSIDE
*Parlophone*

Actor Sarne (born Michael Scheuer) hit the top with the first of four consecutive Top 40s. This cockney pop novelty (which owed a little to Alma Cogan and Frankie Vaughan's 'Do Do Do Do Do Do It Again') was written by his musical arranger Charles Blackwell, and the Londoner duetted with teenage actress Wendy Richard. Sarne became a Hollywood film producer and Richard later starred in the TV shows *Are You Being Served?* and *EastEnders*. A 1986 retread by Richard and singer/actor Mike Berry tempted few buyers.

## EDEN KANE
I DON'T KNOW WHY
*Decca*

A few months after Linda Scott's update of this 1931 hit reached the US Top 20, Kane clocked up his fourth successive UK Top 10 entry with a completely different arrangement of it. The song's co-writer Roy Turk also composed Elvis' earlier No 1 'Are You Lonesome Tonight'.

# UNITED STATES
# JUNE 1962

## MARY WELLS
THE ONE WHO REALLY
LOVES YOU
*Motown*

In 1961, this 17-year-old singer/songwriter from Detroit became the first artist to chart on the Motown label. A year later, the Smokey Robinson-composed and produced 'The One Who Really Loves You' made her the first solo act from the Tamla/Motown group of labels to crack the Top 10.

## GENE PITNEY
(THE MAN WHO SHOT)
LIBERTY VALENCE
*Musicor*

This Burt Bacharach and Hal David opus was inspired by (but did not appear in) the James Stewart and John Wayne film of the same name. The single followed Pitney's version of the title theme from *Town Without Pity* into the Top 20. It was the first of a very impressive run of hits for the unmistakable singer from Connecticut. Reportedly, the song was originally intended for Vito Picone (ex-leader of The Elegants).

## JOHNNY TILLOTSON
IT KEEPS RIGHT ON
A-HURTIN'
*Cadence*

The hit-making vocalist also attained a country Top 10 position with this song that he penned with Nashville tunesmith Lorene Mann. In 1968, Tillotson re-recorded it specially for the country market but, like his other country-targeted singles, it generated few sales.

## CONNIE FRANCIS
SECOND HAND LOVE
*MGM*

The biggest-selling female singer of the rock era (until Madonna came on the scene) chalked up her thirteenth Top 20 of the decade with a song written and produced by Phil Spector.

## FREDDY CANNON
PALISADES PARK
*Swan*

After a two-year absence, the rocker from Massachusetts reappeared with a lively stomper composed by Chuck Barris – who went on to host TV's *Gong Show*. The singer, whose career many had already written off, also reached the US Top 20 twice in the mid-1960s with 'Abigail Beecher' and 'Action'.

## MARVELETTES
PLAYBOY
*Tamla*

The group, who started life as The Casinyets, revisited the Top 10 with a song partly composed by member Gladys Horton.

## DAVID ROSE &
## HIS ORCHESTRA
THE STRIPPER
*MGM*

A left-field novelty instrumental, which the orchestra leader had written as throw-away background music for a 1958 TV show called *Burlesque,* surprisingly topped the chart. The track, recorded in less than 15 minutes at the end of a session, was originally intended to be the B side of 'Ebb Tide'. The veteran London-born Grammy winner also composed the music for many TV shows including *Bonanza, Little House On The*

*Prairie, High Chaparral* and *Highway To Heaven*. Rose, the one-time husband of Judy Garland, died in 1990.

## JOHNNY CRAWFORD
CINDY'S BIRTHDAY
*Del-Fi*

The 15-year-old star of TV's *The Rifleman* had three consecutive Top 20 hits in 1962. The biggest was this teen love song penned by Jeff Hooven and Hal Winn (later owners of Double Shot Records). In the UK, 'Cindy's Birthday' became the first Top 20 hit for Shane Fenton (aka Alvin Stardust).

## EVERLY BROTHERS
THAT'S OLD FASHIONED
(THAT'S THE WAY LOVE
SHOULD BE)
*Warner*

The Everlys last US Top 10 entry was written by Bill Giant, Bernie Baum and Florence Kaye. The duo, who influenced many subsequent hit groups, broke up for ten years in 1973. In 1986 they were the first non-solo act inducted into the Rock and Roll Hall of Fame.

## BOBBY VINTON
ROSES ARE RED
(MY LOVE)
*Epic*

Epic Records signed Vinton as a big band leader and released several singles with minimal success. Before dropping his contract they let him record two more vocal tracks – both of which topped the chart. The song that started his staggering run of US hits was a retro-sounding pop ballad composed by hit writer Paul Evans. Vinton later returned to the rose theme with 'Red Roses For Mom', 'Bed of Roses' and 'The Last Rose'.

## EMILIO PERICOLI
AL DI LA
*Warner*

Thanks in part to a show-stopping performance by top Italian star Betty Curtis, this big ballad won the 1961 San Remo Festival. Italian singer/actor Pericoli was asked to sing it in the Troy Donahue movie *Rome Adventure*, and his recording went on to sell over a million copies. In 1964, the song that was also featured in the film *Lovers Must Learn* was taken back into the Top 40 by The Ray Charles Singers. Pericoli's follow-up, 'Romantico Amore', sold few copies outside his homeland.

# UNITED KINGDOM
# JUNE 1962

## JOE BROWN & THE BRUVVERS
A PICTURE OF YOU
*Piccadilly*

Before his first major hit, Brown was already a leading UK rock star thanks to his many TV and live appearances. The country-oriented song that took the accomplished singer/guitarist to the top of the *NME* chart was composed by two members of The Bruvvers, Johnny Beveridge (who had recently left) and Pete Oakman. In the US, neither Brown's original recording nor covers by such notables as Paul Evans and the Kalin Twins developed into hits.

## KENNY BALL
THE GREEN LEAVES OF SUMMER
*Pye Jazz*

A song from the 1960 John Wayne film *The Alamo*, which The Brothers Four had taken into the US chart, became the top-selling trad jazz band's third Top 10 hit in a row.

## JIMMIE RODGERS
ENGLISH COUNTRY
GARDEN
*Columbia*

One of America's most successful recording artists of the late 1950s had his only Top 10 entry of this decade with a version of an old English folk song. In the US, the track was the B side of his minor hit 'A Little Dog Cried'. In the late 1970s, Rodgers managed a few small US country hits.

## RAY CHARLES
I CAN'T STOP LOVING YOU
*HMV*

See US entry (May).

# UNITED STATES
# JULY 1962

## CLAUDE KING
WOLVERTON MOUNTAIN
*Columbia*

The US's top country hit of 1962 was based on the true story of hillbilly Clifton Clowers, who kept suitors away from his daughter on a mountain in Arkansas. The song, composed by King and noted country composer Merle Kilgore, was the biggest hit of the Louisiana singer's 30 country chart entries. A tongue-in-cheek answer record, '(I'm The Girl On) Wolverton Mountain' by Jo-Ann Campbell, reached the Top 40. Clowers died in 1991 aged 100.

## JOE HENDERSON
SNAP YOUR FINGERS
*Todd*

This smooth and soulful Mississippi-born vocalist had his only noticeable hit with an instantly catchy finger-snapper on which he sounded remarkably like Brook Benton. Noted Nashville session musician Grady Martin composed the song with Alex Zanetis, and it had been recorded in 1959 by Ray Phillips. 'Snap Your Fingers' was a country hit by Dick Curless in 1971, Don Gibson in 1974 and topped that chart in 1987 by Ronnie Milsap. Henderson died in Nashville in 1966, aged only 36.

## JOANIE SOMMERS
JOHNNY GET ANGRY
*Warner*

This singer/actress from New York State paid her sole visit to the Top 40 with a cute pop item that is probably not too popular in the women's lib movement. Chart regulars Hal David and Sherman Edwards composed the song, which gave the singer of several Pepsi commercials her brief fling with chart fame. The hit inspired an answer record: 'Joanie Don't Be Angry' by Vinnie Monte.

## ORLONS
THE WAH-WATUSI
*Cameo*

In the early 1960s, Cameo Records had a knack of taking a regional dance craze and turning it into a national one. Following earlier successes with the Twist, the Pony and the Mashed Potato, staff writers Dave Appel and Kal Mann did the trick again with the Watusi. The prolific pair's 'The Wah-Watusi' gave the Philadelphia R&B vocal group, whose first two singles had attracted little attention, the biggest hit of their career.

## BRIAN HYLAND
SEALED WITH A KISS
*ABC Paramount*

▲ 3
⑩ 2
365/500

After a two-year absence, this teenage vocalist returned to the Top 10 with an enduring love ballad composed by Peter Udell and Gary Geld. His recording reached the UK Top 10 in both 1962 and 1975. An updated version by Jason Donovan in 1989 entered the UK chart at No 1.

## DEE DEE SHARP
GRAVY (FOR MY MASHED POTATOES)
*Cameo*

▲ 9
⑩ 2
—/500

What better way to top off a hit like 'Mashed Potato Time' than with a song called 'Gravy'? Cameo Records' regular writing team of Kal Mann and Dave Appell penned it for Sharp.

## PAT BOONE
SPEEDY GONZALES
*Dot*

▲ 6
⑩14•
—/500

The multi-million seller's last transatlantic Top 10 hit was a novelty penned by Buddy Kaye, David Hill and Ethel Lee. Boone's thirty-eighth US Top 40 entry was banned by many Mexican radio stations, who found it offensive. It was, however, a No 1 in such South American territories as Argentina, Peru and Uruguay. Incidentally, the female voice heard on the record belongs to Robin Ward, who had a Top 20 hit the following year with 'Wonderful Summer'.

## NEIL SEDAKA
BREAKING UP IS HARD TO DO
*RCA*

▲ 1
⑩ 5
125/500

Sedaka's first No 1 was an infectious up-tempo tune that he had based loosely on The Showmen's 'It Will Stand'. He was backed on the track by The Cookies, who shortly afterwards hit with 'Chains'. In 1975, the talented artist re-recorded the song as a ballad and it returned to the Top 10.

## RAY STEVENS
AHAB, THE ARAB
*Mercury*

▲ 5
⑩ 1
—/500

The humorous entertainer/singer/musician, who was born Ray Ragsdale in Georgia, had his biggest hit of the decade with a self-penned novelty. It inspired the answer record 'Ahab The Arab Ten Years Later' by Stan Ross.

# UNITED KINGDOM
# JULY 1962

## JIMMY JUSTICE
AIN'T THAT FUNNY
*Pye*

▲ 8
⑩ 2•
—/500

Foremost UK pop writer Johnny Worth wrote Justice's second successive Top 10 entry. His follow-up, a cover of King's 'Spanish Harlem', also reached the Top 20. Justice, one of the first of many UK acts to successfully record American R&B material, was often referred to as 'the UK's Ben E. King'.

## BOBBY VEE
SHARING YOU
*Liberty*

▲ 10
⑩ 6
—/500

The teaming of the young teen idol and youthful writers Carole King and Gerry Goffin again proved to be a winning combination and earned Vee his sixth UK Top 10 entry in 18 months.

## BRENDA LEE
HERE COMES THAT
FEELING
*Brunswick*

▲ 5
⑩ 3
—/500

Little Miss Dynamite had one of her top UK sellers with the Dorsey Burnette-composed B side of her US hit 'Everybody Loves Me But You'.

## EYDIE GORME
YES MY DARLING
DAUGHTER
*CBS*

▲ 10
⑩ 1•
—/500

The celebrated cabaret entertainer had her biggest UK hit with a revival of a song that Glenn Miller and Dinah Shore had made famous in the early 1940s. Astonishingly, the talented wife of Steve Lawrence failed to reach the Top 100 in her homeland with this swinging update.

## FRANK IFIELD
I REMEMBER YOU
*Columbia*

▲ 1
⑩ 1
3/500

Even though his first few singles had been virtually ignored, this English-born, Australian-raised singer became one of the era's biggest sellers. The turning point was his country-styled arrangement of a well-known wartime number, which included yodelling and a 'Waltzing Mathilda'-influenced harmonica phrase. The record sold over a million in the UK and crashed into the US Top 5. At the outset, producer Norrie Paramour thought Ifield had changed the song beyond recognition and did not want his name associated with it.

## CRAIG DOUGLAS
OUR FAVOURITE
MELODIES
*Columbia*

▲ 9
⑩ 7•
—/500

The popular singer-cum-actor's last Top 10 hit came before his twenty-first birthday. It was his rendition of 'Our Favourite Melodies', a US hit for Gary Criss, which contained title references to several current hits. The song came from the pens of Bob Elgin and Kay Rogers, who had co-written his earlier hit 'Hundred Pounds Of Clay'. Incidentally, later that year Douglas was supported on tour by newcomers The Beatles.

## PAT BOONE
SPEEDY GONZALES
*London American*

▲ 2
⑩ 12•
204/500

See US entry.

## CRICKETS
DON'T EVER CHANGE
*Liberty*

▲ 5
⑩ 4•
—/500

Buddy Holly's one-time backing band had their first Top 20 entry since he died with a song written by Carole King and Gerry Goffin. On this track, the Texas-based band included noted session singer Glen Campbell. In the US, the single failed to reach the Top 100.

# UNITED STATES
# AUGUST 1962

## LITTLE EVA
THE LOCO-MOTION
*Dimension*

Eva Boyd babysat for Carole King and Gerry Goffin and occasionally sang on the prolific duo's demos. When 'The Locomotion' (which she demoed) was rejected by Dee Dee Sharp, the writers launched their Dimension label with Eva's version. Interestingly, there was no dance until the single steamed up the chart, when Eva quickly invented the steps. The record returned to the UK Top 20 in 1972. The song topped the US chart again in 1974 by Grand Funk, and reappeared in the transatlantic Top 3 in 1988 by Kylie Minogue.

## RICHARD CHAMBERLAIN
THEME FROM *DR KILDARE* (THREE STARS WILL SHINE TONIGHT)
*MGM*

The photogenic star of the top-rated TV series *Dr Kildare* first hit the transatlantic Top 20 with a vocal version of the show's theme. He also reached the US Top 20 with a revival of 'All I Have To Do Is Dream' and the UK Top 20 with remakes of 'Love Me Tender' and 'Hi-Lili Hi-Lo'. Chamberlain's successful acting career continued long after his days as a pop idol were over.

## BARBARA LYNN
YOU'LL LOSE A GOOD THING
*Jamie*

A poem she had written about an old flame gave the 19-year-old Texas-based singer/guitarist (born Barbara Ozen) her sole Top 40 pop hit. This heartfelt R&B ballad was produced by Huey Meaux, as was tex-mex star Freddy Fender's 1976 country chart-topping interpretation.

## BOBBY DARIN
THINGS
*Atco*

The hugely popular performer climbed on the pop-country bandwagon with one of his own compositions. The song later made the country Top 40 by Anne Murray (1971) and Ronnie Dove (1975).

## RAY CHARLES
YOU DON'T KNOW ME
*ABC Paramount*

Many people felt that recording an album of C&W songs would be a big mistake for the top R&B act. However, *Modern Sounds In Country And Western Music* became the first No 1 LP by an R&B performer, and his interpretation of Eddy Arnold's self-composed 1956 hit almost made it two No 1 singles in succession from the LP. Incidentally, Mickey Gilley's version led the country list in 1981.

## DION
LITTLE DIANE
*Laurie*

Dion (born Dion DiMucci) was one of the most successful acts of the early 1960s. He added to his hit tally with another self-composed song that resembled his earlier successes.

## TOMMY ROE
SHEILA
*ABC Paramount*

Roe wrote 'Sheila' when he was 14 and first recorded it with his group The Satins in 1960, but at that time the Buddy Holly-influenced single had few takers. However, a re-recording in 1962 with producer Felton Jarvis turned the Georgia-born singer/songwriter into an international hit maker. Interestingly, later country hit maker

Jerry Reed played guitar on the 'Peggy Sue'-styled track, which was initially intended to be the B side.

## CLAUDINE CLARK
PARTY LIGHTS
*Chancellor*

▲ 5
⑩ 1•
—/500

This R&B singer from Georgia had a brief fling with fame thanks to her self-composed floor-filler about a party Mom would not allow her to attend. It was Clark's third single on Chancellor and was

originally planned as the B side to label owner Bob Marcucci's song 'Disappointed'. Follow-ups, including 'Walk Me Home From The Party', failed to shine.

## ELVIS PRESLEY
SHE'S NOT YOU
*RCA*

▲ 5
⑩ 27
—/500

The single that gave Presley his fourth UK No 1 in a row was written by the rock'n'roll dream team of Doc Pomus, Jerry Leiber and Mike Stoller.

# UNITED KINGDOM
# AUGUST 1962

## HELEN SHAPIRO
LITTLE MISS LONELY
*Columbia*

▲ 8
⑩ 5•
—/500

Before she reached 17, Shapiro notched up nine UK Top 40s, starred in a couple of films and headlined tours throughout Europe. Her last major hit was again written by John Schroeder and Mike Hawker. Over the next few months Shapiro toured the UK, supported by The Beatles, and recorded in Nashville with Elvis' backing group, The Jordanaires. Despite her age, however, she was soon deemed 'past it' and faded from the limelight.

## BERNARD CRIBBINS
RIGHT SAID FRED
*Parlophone*

▲ 10
⑩ 2•
—/500

While he was starting to work with The Beatles, George Martin produced this UK actor's second successive Top 10 entry. The song, which made fun of UK workmen and their supposed love of drinking tea, was, like its predecessor, written by Ted Dicks and Myles Rudge. Both of Cribbins' novelty hits were released in the US but, perhaps

not surprisingly, went nowhere. However, a UK group who named themselves after the track topped the transatlantic charts in the 1990s.

## SHADOWS
GUITAR TANGO
*Columbia*

▲ 4
⑩ 8
438/500

The group's first single since the departure of bassist Jet Harris was a French song which featured, for the first time on record, acoustic guitar work from Hank Marvin.

## BOBBY DARIN
THINGS
*London American*

▲ 2
⑩ 8
214/500

See US entry.

## BILLY FURY
ONCE UPON A DREAM
*Decca*

▲ 7
⑩ 6
—/500

Two of the UK's top producers, Norrie Paramor and Dick Rowe, composed this song for Fury's debut film *Play It Cool*.

## RONNIE CARROLL
ROSES ARE RED
*Philips*

Six years after he first charted, a cover version of the top US song by pop balladeer Carroll (born Ronald Cleghorn) outsold Bobby Vinton's original version in the UK. The Paul Evans-composed teen love lament presented the Irish singer and one-time impersonator with his biggest hit.

## BRIAN HYLAND
SEALED WITH A KISS
*HMV*

See US entry (July).

## NEIL SEDAKA
BREAKING UP IS HARD
TO DO
*RCA*

See US entry (July).

## CONNIE FRANCIS
VACATION
*MGM*

See US entry (September).

---

# UNITED STATES
# SEPTEMBER 1962

---

## CONNIE FRANCIS
VACATION
*MGM*

In the mid-1950s, that decade's top producer, Mitch Miller, rejected Francis saying 'She sounds like 50,000 other girl singers'. Fifty million records later, the first lady of pop and rock visited the Top 10 for the last time, with the first major hit she had helped compose. In 1977, a collection of her hits was the first LP by a female to head the UK charts.

## NAT 'KING' COLE
RAMBLIN' ROSE
*Capitol*

The multi-talented entertainer earned his biggest hit of the 1960s with a country-styled sing-along ballad. Noel and Joe Sherman composed both this and Paul Anka's current hit 'Eso Beso (That Kiss!)'.

## RICK NELSON
TEENAGE IDOL
*Imperial*

A song written for Bobby Vee added to this superstar's enviable hit tally. As it charted, the world's next major teenage idols, The Beatles, released their first single. Interestingly, top composer Barry Mann released a parody, 'Teenage Has Been'.

## FOUR SEASONS
SHERRY
*Vee Jay*

In 1956, RCA Records called The Four Lovers 'The Most Fantastic Group On Record'. Six years later the Frankie Valli-led act, now called The Four Seasons, had the first of an astonishing run of top US hits. The song was written by member Bob Gaudio in 15 minutes, and had briefly been called 'Terry', 'Peri', 'Jackie' and 'Cherie' before he settled on an alternative spelling of the latter. In 1975, Adrian Baker (who later joined the Four Seasons) took 'Sherry' back into the UK Top 10.

## BOOKER T. & THE MGs
GREEN ONIONS
*Stax*

▲ 3
🔟 1
367/500

This Memphis Group (hence the name MGs) evolved from the Mar-keys and was assembled by guitarist Steve Cropper and led by keyboard player Booker T. Jones. Their floor-filling first hit started life as 'Behave Yourself', but they thought the name of the B side, 'Green Onions', was too good to waste so they exchanged the titles. In the UK, the record did not hit until 1980, when it was included in the mod film *Quadrophenia*. The combo's follow-ups included 'Mo' Onions'.

## DICKEY LEE
PATCHES
*Smash*

▲ 6
🔟 1•
—/500

One of country music's most popular singers of the 1970s (born Dickey Lipscomb) had his biggest pop hit with a song penned by Barry Mann and Larry Kolber. Its success came soon after one of Lee's compositions 'She Thinks I Still Care' led the country list by George Jones. Lee had two more Top 20 singles in the early 1960s ('I Saw Linda Yesterday' and the eerie 'Laurie') while his No 1 country hit topped that chart again in 1974 by Anne Murray.

## DAVE 'BABY' CORTEZ
RINKY DINK
*Chess*

▲ 10
🔟 2•
—/500

Three years after keyboard player Cortez (born Dave Clowney) headed the list with 'The Happy Organ', he returned to the heights with another danceable R&B instrumental. Incidentally, the sax player on the track is later hit maker Jimmy Castor, who like Cortez had cut his musical teeth in doo-wop groups.

## CHRIS MONTEZ
LET'S DANCE
*Monogram*

▲ 4
🔟 1•
489/500

One of the best-known dance singles from the 1960s was this Latino rocker's biggest hit. Monogram label owner Jim Lee penned and produced the perennially popular track, which also re-entered the UK Top 10 in 1972. A re-recording of the song by Montez (born Chris Montanez) on Jamie in 1973 went virtually unnoticed.

## DUPREES
YOU BELONG TO ME
*Coed*

In the late 1950s, The Rivieras had some minor hits with big band-influenced, doo-wop-styled revivals of oldies. In the early 1960s, their label Coed repeated that formula on records by this Italian-American quintet from Jersey City. The ballad, which had been a transatlantic chart topper by Jo Stafford in 1952, was composed by country tunesmiths Pee Wee King, Redd Stewart and Chilton Price. It was the highest placed of the group's three Top 20 entries in the early years of the decade.

## MARY WELLS
YOU BEAT ME TO THE PUNCH
*Motown*

▲ 9
🔟 2
—/500

Perhaps not surprisingly, Wells was voted the US' Most Promising Female Singer in 1962. Her second Top 10 entry of the year was written by her producer Smokey Robinson. Gene Chandler charted with an answer record 'You Threw A Lucky Punch'.

## BOBBY 'BORIS' PICKETT & THE CRYPT KICKER
MONSTER MASH
*Garpax*

The all-time great Halloween hit was written and performed by a singer/actor from Massachusetts and featured his impersonation of horror film star Boris Karloff. In 1973, the record revisited the US Top 10 and hit in the UK for the first time (it was banned as 'offensive' in 1962). The novelty act's other releases, including 'Monster Holiday', 'Monster Swim', 'Monster Concert' and 'Monster Man Jam', were far from monster hits.

## BENT FABRIC
ALLEY CAT
*Atco*

A successful Danish pianist/band leader and record company head (born Bent Fabricius-Bjerre) had his only top US hit with a self-composed instrumental. To the surprise of many, this catchy MOR recording picked up the Grammy for 1962's Best Rock'n'Roll Recording. A vocal version by David Thorne also graced the Top 100.

# UNITED KINGDOM
# SEPTEMBER 1962

## ELVIS PRESLEY
SHE'S NOT YOU
*RCA*

See US entry (August).

## CLIFF RICHARD
IT'LL BE ME
*Columbia*

A rock'n'roll classic that Jerry Lee Lewis had released on the B side of 'Whole Lot of Shakin' Going On' in 1957 was the vehicle that conveyed Cliff into the Top 20 for the twentieth time in four years.

## DUANE EDDY
BALLAD OF PALADIN
*RCA*

'Mr Twangy Guitar' scored with the theme music from the Richard Boone TV western series *Have Gun, Will Travel* (which Boone co-wrote). Coincidentally, Eddy's first hit album in 1959 was entitled *Have 'Twangy' Guitar–Will Travel.*

## ADAM FAITH
DON'T THAT BEAT ALL
*Parlophone*

The last Les Vandyke composition that Faith took into the UK Top 10 coincided with the first release by his label-mates The Beatles. As it climbed the chart, his TV series *Adam Faith Sings Songs Old & New* was launched.

## TORNADOS
TELSTAR
*Decca*

The first single by a UK group to top the US chart was written and produced by Joe Meek. The Tornados were previously Meek's house band and had been Billy Fury's backing band on the road. The eerie organ-led instrumental, written to celebrate the launch of the first communications satellite, was the first of four consecutive Top 20 entries for the combo. Their re-recording in 1980 failed to get off the ground.

## TOMMY ROE
SHEILA
*HMV*

See US entry (August).

# UNITED STATES
# OCTOBER 1962

## JIMMY CLANTON
VENUS IN BLUE JEANS
*ACE*

This potent pop ditty was penned by Howard Greenfield and Jack Keller, who had earlier written chart toppers for Connie Francis. It was the pin-up from Louisiana's seventh and last Top 40 entry. In the UK, Mark Wynter had the hit version.

## FRANK IFIELD
I REMEMBER YOU
*Vee Jay*

See UK entry (July).

## CONTOURS
DO YOU LOVE ME
*Gordy*

Motown head Berry Gordy composed this epic floor-filler for The Temptations. When they were late for the session he cut it with The Contours, whose first three singles for his company had flopped. It was the first hit on Gordy and presented the Detroit sextet with their biggest seller. Amazingly, it returned to the Top 20 in 1988, after being heard in the film *Dirty Dancing*. The song became the Dave Clark Five's first UK hit and the only UK No 1 for Brian Poole & The Tremeloes.

## PETER, PAUL & MARY
IF I HAD A HAMMER
*Warner*

One of the top-selling acts of the 1960s had success with their rousing rendition of a traditional folk song that Pete Seeger and Lee Hays (of The Weavers) had amended and arranged. The single was taken from the trio's eponymous No 1 album. Less than a year later an up-tempo version by Trini Lopez was an even bigger hit.

## CRYSTALS
HE'S A REBEL
*UA*

When The Shirelles rejected this teen-targeted opus, composer Gene Pitney intended it for Vikki Carr. However, ace producer Phil Spector saw its potential, hurriedly cut it (in the same studio and at the same time as Carr) with LA session singers The Blossoms, and quickly released it as The Crystals (whose last two hits had reached the Top 20). As Spector expected, the supposed hit act's version outsold newcomer Carr's. It inspired the answer record 'He's A Yankee' by The Sweethearts.

## GENE PITNEY
ONLY LOVE CAN BREAK A HEART
*Musicor*

As his composition 'He's A Rebel' headed the chart by The Crystals, Pitney moved to No 2 with this Burt Bacharach and Hal David compostion.

## BRENDA LEE
ALL ALONE AM I
*Decca*

In the year that she was first voted World's Top Female Singer in the UK, Lee attained her first transatlantic Top 10 entry since 'Sweet Nothin's' with a memorable ballad by Greek composer Manos Hadjidakis.

## JOHNNY MATHIS
GINA
*Columbia*

The unmistakable vocalist, whose *Greatest Hits* album stayed on the chart for a record 10 years, reappeared in the Top 10 singles after a five-year absence. The song, which Johnny Janis had earlier recorded, was penned by regular hit writers Leon Carr and Paul Vance.

## UNITED KINGDOM
# OCTOBER 1962

**LITTLE EVA**
THE LOCOMOTION
*London American*

▲ 2
🔟 1•
212/500

See US entry (August).

**CAROLE KING**
IT MIGHT AS WELL RAIN
UNTIL SEPTEMBER
*London American*

▲ 3
🔟 1
368/500

The very successful 20-year-old tunesmith had her biggest UK hit as an artist with a self-composed teen love song she had originally intended for Bobby Vee. It would be a further ten years before New Yorker King (born Carole Klein) started her enviable string of US hits.

**RAY CHARLES**
YOU DON'T KNOW ME
*HMV*

▲ 9
🔟 3
—/500

See US entry (August).

**SHIRLEY BASSEY**
WHAT NOW MY LOVE
*Columbia*

▲ 8
🔟 8
—/500

'Et Maintenant' was the original title of this dramatic French ballad composed by Gilbert Becaud. In the mid-1960s the song entered the US Top 40 by Herb Alpert, Sonny & Cher and Mitch Ryder.

**NAT 'KING' COLE**
RAMBLIN' ROSE
*Capitol*

▲ 5
🔟 13
—/500

See US entry (September).

**MARK WYNTER**
VENUS IN BLUE JEANS
*Pye*

▲ 4
🔟 1
448/500

Clean-cut UK teen idol Wynter (born Terence Lewis) had the biggest of his four Top 20 hits with his interpretation of a Howard Greenfield and Jack Keller song that Jimmy Clanton had taken into the US Top 10.

**CHRIS MONTEZ**
LET'S DANCE
*London American*

▲ 2
🔟 1
198/500

See US entry (September).

**DEL SHANNON**
SWISS MAID
*London American*

▲ 2
🔟 5
203/500

Singer/songwriter Roger Miller's first UK success came with this regular chart entrant's interpretation of a country-yodelling opus that Miller had earlier recorded as 'Fair Swiss Maiden'.

# UNITED STATES
# NOVEMBER 1962

## FOUR SEASONS
BIG GIRLS DON'T CRY
*Vee Jay*

▲ 1
⑩ 2
15/500

A pop classic inspired by a line John Payne said in an old b-movie took the Frankie Valli-(born Francis Castelluccio) fronted group back to the top spot.

## CHUBBY CHECKER
LIMBO ROCK
*Parkway*

▲ 2
⑩ 7
207/500

The internationally famous Twister narrowly missed the top spot with a vocal version of a recent Top 40 hit by The Champs. Veteran session musician Billy Strange wrote the music and John Sheldon added the lyrics. Six months later Checker clicked with 'Let's Limbo Some More'.

## NEIL SEDAKA
NEXT DOOR TO AN ANGEL
*RCA*

▲ 5
⑩ 6
—/500

The durable pop performer had his last major success of the decade with another bouncy pop pearl penned with songwriting partner Howard Greenfield. In the mid-1970s, Sedaka returned and added three more Top 10s to his hit total.

## ELVIS PRESLEY
RETURN TO SENDER
*RCA*

▲ 2
⑩28
210/500

Elvis had his fifth UK No 1 in a row with a song composed by Otis Blackwell, who had penned Presley's earlier No 1s 'Don't Be Cruel' and 'All Shook Up'. It would be almost 18 months before another US act headed the UK chart.

## CHUBBY CHECKER
POPEYE (THE HITCHHIKER)
*Parkway*

▲ 10
⑩ 8•
—/500

The Popeye started in New Orleans and spread nationally when Checker hitched a ride on the dance's bandwagon. Kal Mann and Dave Appell penned the song, which like the record's A side, 'Limbo Rock', muscled its way into the Top 10, giving the singer his eighth Top 10 entry in two years. Incidentally, the Twist King returned to the Top 20 in 1988 with an update of 'The Twist' accompanied by rotund rappers The Fat Boys.

## MARCIE BLANE
BOBBY'S GIRL
*Seville*

▲ 3
⑩ 1•
285/500

Few women's lib supporters bought the 18-year-old New Yorker's only hit, but that didn't stop her debut single from passing the million sales mark. However, the record-buying public turned a deaf ear to her similarly slanted singles 'What Does A Girl Do', 'Why Can't I Get A Guy' and 'Bobby Did'.

## ORLONS
DON'T HANG UP
*Cameo*

▲ 4
⑩ 2
456/500

Composers Kal Mann and Dave Appell added to their hit list with a hooky R&B/pop item that gave the mixed quartet the second of five consecutive Top 20 entries.

## BOBBY RYDELL
THE CHA CHA CHA
*Cameo*

▲ 10
⑩ 5
—/500

The one-time member of Rocco & The Saints (as had been fellow Philadelphian teen idol Frankie Avalon) revived interest in the Latin dance the Cha Cha Cha, thanks to a catchy Kal Mann and Dave Appell song.

## DEE DEE SHARP
RIDE
*Cameo*

▲ 5
🔟 3
—/500

The ex-session singer was the top dance diva of 1962. Her third hit of the year was with a lively John Sheldon and David Leon composition.

---

## UNITED KINGDOM
# NOVEMBER 1962

---

## FRANK IFIELD
LOVESICK BLUES
*Columbia*

▲ 1
🔟 2
19/500

A song that had topped the US country chart for 16 weeks in 1949 by Hank Williams amassed over 200,000 advance orders for the pop-yodeller and quickly returned him to the summit.

## FOUR SEASONS
SHERRY
*Stateside*

▲ 8
🔟 1
—/500

See US entry (September).

## SUSAN MAUGHAN
BOBBY'S GIRL
*Philips*

▲ 3
🔟 1•
253/500

While she was still a singer with the Ray Ellington Quartet, Maughan also recorded as a solo artist, but her first three singles went nowhere. Her only hit was a cover version, 'Bobby's Girl', a hook-filled song that Marcie Blaine had charted with in the US. Despite being voted Top Female Singer in the UK in 1963, Maughan was unable to repeat this pop success and soon returned to the cabaret circuit.

## MARTY ROBBINS
DEVIL WOMAN
*CBS*

▲ 5
🔟 1•
—/500

During the 1950s, several songs that Robbins first recorded (including 'Singing The Blues', 'The Story

Of My Life', 'Stairway Of Love' and 'A White Sport Coat') were big UK hits for British acts. The tex-mex troubadour finally had a Top 10 UK hit of his own with a self-written song, which was also his sixth No 1 C&W hit in the US. It inspired several answer versions, including '(Don't Take Him From Me) Devil Woman' by Sherry Scott.

## DUANE EDDY
DANCE WITH THE GUITAR MAN
*RCA*

▲ 4
🔟 7
340/500

The addition of female vocal group The Rebelettes gave the guitar star his first transatlantic Top 20 entry since 'Pepe', and his last major UK hit until 1975. As usual, it was penned by Eddy and producer Lee Hazlewood, who later in the decade had hits as a vocalist in the company of Nancy Sinatra.

## ROLF HARRIS
SUN ARISE
*Columbia*

▲ 3
🔟 2
289/500

This self-composed aboriginal-styled single helped the unmistakable Australian entertainer briefly make the 'wobble board' a hit instrument on both sides of the Atlantic. He re-recorded it with top rave act 808 State in 1991.

# UNITED STATES
# DECEMBER 1962

## THE TIJUANA BRASS FEATURING HERB ALPERT
THE LONELY BULL
*A&M*

▲ 6
⑩ 1
—/500

Herb Alpert's first chart record was penned by his associate Sol Lake and originally titled 'Twinkle Star'. The single that introduced the world to Alpert's unique quasi-Mexican Ameriachi sound was cut in Alpert's garage for a reported $200. The trumpeter, who went on to sell over 45 million albums in all, had previously had some success as a writer and producer with acts like Sam Cooke and Jan & Dean.

## TORNADOS
TELSTAR
*London*

▲ 1
⑩ 1•
65/500

See UK entry (September).

## LITTLE ESTHER PHILLIPS
RELEASE ME
*Lenox*

▲ 8
⑩ 1•
—/500

In 1950, 14-year-old Little Esther (born Esther Mae Jones) first topped the R&B chart and country performer Eddie Miller recorded his composition 'Release Me'. Twelve years later, Esther's Dinah Washington-styled revival of that tune, produced by Lelan Rogers (brother of Kenny Rogers), became the biggest hit of her career. Engelbert Humperdinck made Phillips' arrangement of the song an international No 1 in 1967.

## STEVE LAWRENCE
GO AWAY LITTLE GIRL
*Columbia*

▲ 1
⑩ 4•
100/500

The enduringly popular balladeer gave Carole King and Gerry Goffin their fourth chart topper with his biggest hit single. The song, which the successful composers had originally written with the much

younger Bobby Vee in mind, also reached the Top 20 in 1966 by The Happenings and again led the list by teen icon Donny Osmond in 1971.

## RAY CHARLES
YOU ARE MY SUNSHINE
*ABC Paramount*

▲ 7
⑩ 8
—/500

A country tune that Tex Ritter and Gene Autry recorded 20 years earlier made it six successive Top 20 singles for the singer born Ray Charles Robinson. The B side, Hank Williams' song 'Your Cheating Heart', also attained a Top 40 position.

## DION
LOVE CAME TO ME
*Laurie*

▲ 10
⑩ 5
—/500

The singer's fifth Top 10 entry in succession was another infectious self-penned song which captured the feel and sound of his previous hits.

## BOB B. SOXX & THE BLUE JEANS
ZIP-A-DEE DOO-DAH
*Philles*

▲ 8
⑩ 1•
—/500

One of the year's most riveting revivals was this Phil Spector-produced R&B version of the classic children's song from the Walt Disney film *Song Of The South*. The unlikely named session group featured the vocals of Darlene Love, Fanita James (both from The Blossoms) and Bobby Sheen (who subsequently joined The Coasters).

## BROOK BENTON
HOTEL HAPPINESS
*Mercury*

▲ 3
⑩ 7
426/500

During his career, smooth R&B vocalist Benton had an enviable 49 US chart entries, none of which, astonishingly, cracked the UK Top 20. His last major hit of the 1960s came with a catchy Earl Shuman and Leon Carr composition.

# UNITED KINGDOM
# DECEMBER 1962

## ELVIS PRESLEY
RETURN TO SENDER
*RCA*

See US entry (November).

## CLIFF RICHARD
THE NEXT TIME/
BACHELOR BOY
*Columbia*

▲ 1
⑩18
44/500

Two songs from his film *Summer Holiday* shot the singer to the top spot for the sixth time. Buddy Kaye and Philip Springer composed the sentimental ballad on the A side, while Cliff and Bruce Welch penned the bouncy B side.

## BRENDA LEE
ROCKIN' AROUND THE
CHRISTMAS TREE
*Brunswick*

A track Brenda recorded in 1958 reached the US Top 20 in 1960 and the UK chart in 1962. This definitive Christmas rocker was composed by Johnny Marks, the person responsible for 'Rudolph The Red-Nosed Reindeer'. The song was a UK Top 3 hit for Kim Wilde & Mel Smith in 1987.

## SHADOWS
DANCE ON
*Columbia*

▲ 1
⑩ 9
158/500

As The Beatles' first chart topper entered, The Shadows clocked up their fourth No 1 with a toe-tapping instrumental penned for them by UK group The Avons. A vocal version by Kathy Kirby waltzed into the Top 20 in 1963.

# UNITED STATES
# JANUARY 1963

## LOU MONTE
PEPINO THE ITALIAN
MOUSE
*Reprise*

▲ 5
⑩ 1•
—/500

The veteran Italian/American entertainer, who had taken the multi-lingual 'Lazy Mary' into the Top 20 in 1958, had his biggest hit with a novelty written by Ray Allen and Wandra Merrell. Among his other recordings were the similarly slanted 'Pepino's Friend Pasqual (The Italian Pussy-Cat)', 'Pauluchhi, The Italian Parrot', 'Louis, The Italian Tarzan' and 'Domenic, The Italian Christmas Donkey'. He also released a series of tracks like 'Italian Hucklebuck', 'Italian Wallflower', 'Italian Jingle Bells' and 'Calypso Italiano' .

## EXCITERS
TELL HIM
*UA*

▲ 4
⑩ 1•
492/500

Jerry Leiber and Mike Stoller produced the New York group's biggest hit, which was composed by the multi-talented Bert Berns. The act, who were fronted by Brenda Reid and (her later husband) Herb Rooney, had several other Top 100 entries including the original version of 'Do-Wah-Diddy' and 'Get Him'. 'Tell Him', which Johnny Thunder had first recorded, was successfully covered in the UK by Billie Davis.

## BOBBY VEE
THE NIGHT HAS A
THOUSAND EYES
*Liberty*

▲ 3
⑩ 5
363/500

The teenage hit machine notched up his last Top 10 entry of the decade with a song that he featured in the UK pop movie *Just For Fun*. Thirty years later the singer, who had first come to the public's attention as Buddy Holly's replacement on the 'day the music died', was still packing in the crowds all around the world.

## MARY WELLS
TWO LOVERS
*Motown*

▲ 7
⑩ 3
—/500

Motown's hottest solo artist registered her third consecutive Top 10 entry with another outstanding Smokey Robinson-produced and written track. Later in her career, Wells recorded the similarly titled track 'Two Lovers History'.

## PAUL PETERSEN
MY DAD
*Colpix*

▲ 6
⑩ 1•
—/500

California born actor/singer Petersen was one of the original Mouseketeers and for eight years (1958–66) played Jeff Stone in TV's popular *Donna Reed Show*. He had the biggest of half a dozen hits with a moving Barry Mann and Cynthia Weil ballad that he sang on the show to his TV father, Carl Betz. In 1967 he became one of the first white acts signed to Motown – although his records on the soul label sold few. Petersen went on to become a successful paperback writer in the 1970s.

## PAUL & PAULA
HEY PAULA
*Philips*

▲ 1
⑩ 1
57/500

Student Ray Hildebrand was inspired to write this song by Annette's 1959 hit 'Tall Paul', and originally called it 'Paul & Paula'. He recorded it with his landlady's niece, Jill Jackson, and producer Major Bill Smith amended the title to make it similar to his previous hit, 'Hey Baby' by Bruce Channel. The single, which to begin with was released on Smith's Le Cam label as by Jill & Ray, was a Top 10 entry on both sides of the Atlantic. Included among the duo's subsequent releases were 'Dear Paula', 'It's All Over Paula' and 'Dear Paul'.

## ROOFTOP SINGERS
WALK RIGHT IN
*Vanguard*

One of the year's top transatlantic folk hits had been written and originally recorded by Gus Woods & The Jugstompers over 30 years before. The Rooftop Singers were formed by Erik Darling, a veteran of two of the 1950s leading folk groups, The Weavers and The Tarriers. The trio's follow-up, 'Tom Cat', also reached the US Top 20, but it was their last noticeable hit.

## RICK NELSON
IT'S UP TO YOU
*Imperial*

The popular star of the long-running TV series *The Adventures Of Ozzie And Harriet* scored his fifth Top 20 entry in a row with a song composed by Jerry Fuller – who had written Nelson's hits 'Travelin' Man' and 'Young World'.

# UNITED KINGDOM
# JANUARY 1963

## JOE BROWN & THE BRUVVERS
IT ONLY TOOK A MINUTE
*Piccadilly*

Successful American tunesmiths Mort Garson and Hal David composed the song that returned the happy-go-lucky cockney performer to the Top 10. Incidentally, in 1963 Brown retained his crown as Top UK Music Personality in the prestigious *NME* poll.

## MARK WYNTER
GO AWAY LITTLE GIRL
*Pye*

A Carole King and Gerry Goffin composition that Steve Lawrence had taken to the top in the US transported the teenaged singer/actor back to the heights. However, like so many other solo artists, his fan base eroded soon after the group boom started, and he moved into different show business areas.

## MAUREEN EVANS
LIKE I DO
*Oriole*

Frank Sinatra's daughter Nancy had the European hit with this song based on Ponchielli's 'Dance Of The Hours'. However, in the UK, the honours went to a Welsh vocalist, whose recording career started in 1958 with Woolworth's budget-priced cover-version label, Embassy. Helen Shapiro's mentor John Schroeder produced the single that gave Evans her only top seller. Among her other releases was the similarly titled 'Like You Used To Do'. Allan Sherman's 1963 novelty smash 'Hello Mudduh Hello Fadduh' was based on the same classical work.

## TORNADOS
GLOBETROTTER
*Decca*

The London-based group followed the million-selling 'Telstar' with another spacy instrumental written by producer Joe Meek. Later in the year, they had their final two Top 20 entries, 'Robot' and 'The Ice Cream Man'.

## JET HARRIS & TONY MEEHAN
DIAMONDS
*Decca*

▲ 1
⑩ 1
87/500

Ex-Shadows Harris and Meehan's first single together dethroned their old group's 'Dance On' (which had replaced their ex-boss Cliff Richard's 'The Next Time') at the top. Like The Shadows' first chart topper, 'Apache', this beat instrumental was composed by Jerry Lordan. 'Diamonds' was the first record by an instrumental duo to reach the summit. The single was voted Top Instrumental of 1963 by *MM*.

## MIKE BERRY
DON'T YOU THINK IT'S TIME
*HMV*

▲ 6
⑩ 1
—/500

Producer Joe Meek and composer Geoff Goddard (the team behind John Leyton's hits) helped give the talented Buddy Holly-influenced singer his biggest hit. Berry (born Michael Bourne), who became a successful actor, returned to the Top 10 in 1980 with a Chas Hodges-produced revival of 'The Sunshine Of Your Smile'. Hodges (later of Chas & Dave) was in Berry's band at the time of the first hit, as was Richie Blackmore (later of Deep Purple).

## KENNY LYNCH
UP ON THE ROOF
*HMV*

▲ 10
⑩ 1
—/500

Lynch, who has been one of the UK's best-loved all-round entertainers for 30 years, is one of the few recording artists of the rock era to receive an OBE from the Queen. His first big-selling single was his rendition of a Carole King and Gerry Goffin song which had been a US hit for The Drifters. As the record climbed, the London-born performer was supporting Helen Shapiro on tour, as were newcomers The Beatles.

## DEL SHANNON
LITTLE TOWN FLIRT
*London American*

▲ 4
⑩ 6
498/500

The singer, whose version of 'From Me To You' was the first Beatles composition to chart in the US, had his third transatlantic Top 20 entry with another of his own distinctive and punchy compositions.

## FRANK IFIELD
WAYWARD WIND
*Columbia*

▲ 1
⑩ 3
114/500

This record made Ifield the first British-based act to top the charts with three consecutive singles. Gogi Grant had originally taken it into the transatlantic Top 10 in 1956.

## CHRIS MONTEZ
SOME KINDA FUN
*London American*

▲ 10
⑩ 2
—/500

As this self-composed floor-filler slipped down the chart, Montez headlined a UK tour with The Beatles. Soon afterwards they copied his collar-less jacket look and made it their own.

# UNITED STATES
# FEBRUARY 1963

## JOHNNY THUNDER
LOOP DE LOOP
*Diamond*

▲ 4
⑩ 1•
—/500

Teddy Vann, one of the most talented, although little heralded, R&B 'backroom boys' of the early 1960s, penned and produced this winning version of the famous children's nursery rhyme. It was the only notable hit for the R&B vocalist from Florida, who had unsuccessfully released the original version of 'Tell Him' under his real name, Gil Hamilton. The follow-up, another nursery rhyme-based track, 'Ring Around The Rosey', disappeared without trace.

## DRIFTERS
UP ON THE ROOF
*Atlantic*

▲ 5
⑩ 3
—/500

The group, which had originally been formed by Clyde McPhatter in 1953, hit the heights with a Carole King and Gerry Goffin song, featuring the lead vocals of Rudy Lewis.

## FOUR SEASONS
WALK LIKE A MAN
*Vee Jay*

▲ 1
⑩ 3
90/500

Producer Bob Crewe and group member Bob Gaudio composed the pop trinket that took the instantly recognizable doo-wop-based vocal team to the top for the third successive time – a feat no other group had ever managed before.

## DION
RUBY BABY
*Columbia*

▲ 2
⑩ 6
292/500

The successful singer's first release on Columbia was an update of a Jerry Leiber and Mike Stoller song that had been a R&B hit for The Drifters in

1956. A version by Billy 'Crash' Craddock topped the country chart in 1974.

## MIRACLES
YOU'VE REALLY GOT A
HOLD ON ME
*Tamla*

▲ 8
⑩ 2
—/500

The soulful Detroit group delivered lead singer William 'Smokey' Robinson's classy ballad to the top of the R&B chart. It was one of several Motown copyrights recorded by The Beatles.

## CASCADES
RHYTHM OF THE RAIN
*Valiant*

▲ 3
⑩ 1•
282/500

John Gummoe, the leader of this smooth self-contained group from California, penned the haunting song that launched them into the transatlantic Top 10 for the only time. Their equally impressive follow-up 'Shy Girl'/'The Last Leaf' was only a minor hit, and the group's subsequent releases on several other labels went nowhere. In 1990, Australian teen idol Jason Donovan directed the timeless 'Rhythm Of The Rain' back into the UK Top 10.

## NED MILLER
FROM A JACK TO A KING
*Fabor*

▲ 6
⑩ 1•
—/500

This single narrowly missed the country chart when originally released in August 1957, and a cover by Jim Lowe almost reached the Top 100. However, when the Utah-born singer/song-writer's version was re-released five years later it was a huge US hit and came within an ace of reaching No 1 in the UK. Although he never returned to the pop Top 40, Miller had several other top country hits during the decade.

## BOBBY DARIN
YOU'RE THE REASON I'M
LIVING
*Capitol*

▲ 3
⑩ 8
327/500

The consistently best-selling artist had his first major hit on Capitol Records with a self-composed sing-along pop/country opus. Lamar Morris had a minor country hit with it in 1971.

## EYDIE GORME
BLAME IT ON THE BOSSA
NOVA
*Columbia*

▲ 7
⑩ 1•
—/500

Top composer Barry Mann added to his impressive hit tally with a bossa nova song that became the most successful single by the renowned night club entertainer from New York.

## REBELS
WILD WEEKEND
*Swan*

▲ 8
⑩ 1•
—/500

This rocking instrumental was the theme to top Buffalo DJ Tom Shannon's *The Wild Weekend Show*, and was first released in 1959 on the Mar-Lee label. Its late success surprised everyone, and chances are that there was a different line-up of group members on subsequent tracks such as 'Another Wild Weekend' and 'Monday Morning'. Their future singles were released as by the Rockin' Rebels – perhaps to save confusion with Duane Eddy's backing band.

# UNITED KINGDOM
# FEBRUARY 1963

## BEATLES
PLEASE PLEASE ME
*Parlophone*

▲ 2
⑩ 1
216/500

The rock era's most successful group debuted in the UK Top 10 with a tune that, according to John Lennon, was an attempt at writing a Roy Orbison song. It was a re-recording of a track they had cut at their initial EMI session the previous September. Soon after they returned from supporting Johnny & The Hurricanes in Germany, this single topped the *NME* chart. In the US, where the single was credited to The Beattles (sic), it went nowhere. When re-issued there a year later it reached the Top 3.

## SPRINGFIELDS
ISLAND OF DREAMS
*Philips*

▲ 5
⑩ 1
442/500

This pop/folk trio were voted Best UK Group in the two years prior to The Beatles' arrival on the scene. The innovative act, which featured lead vocalist Dusty Springfield, debuted in the Top 10 with their third Top 40 entry. 'Island Of Dreams' was an atmospheric and haunting song composed by Dusty's brother and fellow member Tom Springfield. This hit came shortly after they had become the first UK vocal group to reach the US Top 20 and the first UK act to enter the US country Top 20.

## FRANKIE VAUGHAN
LOOP DE LOOP
*Philips*

▲ 5
⑩ 10
—/500

In the US, Johnny Thunder's beat treatment of the well-loved children's classic entered the Top 5, but in the UK the honours went to this popular entertainer from Liverpool. A different arrangement of the song, 'Loo-Be-Loo' by session group The Chucks, also cracked the Top 40.

## BRENDA LEE
ALL ALONE AM I
*Brunswick*

See US entry (October 1962).

## KENNY BALL
SUKIYAKI
*Pye Jazz*

As British pop groups began to stake their claim on the charts, trad jazz quickly lost its foothold. One of the last hits of the genre was trumpeter/vocalist Ball's instrumental rendition of a top Japanese hit originally titled 'Ue O Muite Aruko'. This single's success brought attention to Kyu Sakamoto's original recording which, after borrowing Ball's catchier title, was a transatlantic smash the following year.

## BOBBY VEE
THE NIGHT HAS A
THOUSAND EYES
*Liberty*

See US entry (January).

## JOE BROWN &
## THE BRUVVERS
THAT'S WHAT LOVE
WILL DO
*Piccadilly*

The rise of the Liverpool groups did the cockney rocker no favours. His last Top 20 entry was written for him by Trevor Peacock (whose compositions included the US No 1 'Mrs Brown You've Got A Lovely Daughter'). In the US, this single and Bobby Goldsboro's cover vanished without trace. Brown, who had been a star before his record hits, remained a popular live attraction long after his sales peak.

## CLIFF RICHARD
SUMMER HOLIDAY
*Columbia*

Cliff had his second successive UK chart topper with an anthemic opus penned by Shadows Bruce Welch and Brian Bennett for his film *Summer Holiday*. He performed it on Ed Sullivan's popular US TV show – yet despite this, sales there were negligible.

# UNITED STATES
# MARCH 1963

## JOHNNY MATHIS
WHAT WILL MY MARY SAY
*Columbia*

Paul Vance, who composed the novelty No 1 'Itsy Bitsy Teenie Weenie Yellow Polka Dot Bikini', penned both of Mathis' US Top 10 hits in the 1960s. This was the last Top 10 entry for 15 years by the singer who has logged more chart albums than any American male singer apart from Frank Sinatra and Elvis Presley.

## RUBY & THE
## ROMANTICS
OUR DAY WILL COME
*Kapp*

When Ruby Nash joined male quartet The Supremes they renamed themselves Ruby & The Romantics and ear marked this bossa nova ballad as their debut disc. Writers Bob Hilliard and Mort Garson felt it was a hit and only let these unknowns record it on the understanding that if it flopped then the act's noted label-mate Jack Jones would cut it. The group's roller-rink organ-led version was the biggest of the Ohio quintet's hits. In 1975, Frankie Valli reached the Top 20 with the timeless tune.

## SKEETER DAVIS
THE END OF THE WORLD
*RCA*

▲ 2
⑩ 1
264/500

In 1953, Davis (born Mary Penick) had been in the duo the Davis Sisters, whose 'I Forgot More Than You'll Ever Know' topped the country chart soon after Davis' partner Betty Jack was killed in an automobile accident. Skeeter's biggest solo hit came with this poignant ballad about the loss of a loved one (having Betty Jack in mind when she cut it). The song, which Sylvia Dee penned after her father's death, returned to the UK Top 20 in 1990 by Sonia.

## CHIFFONS
HE'S SO FINE
*Laurie*

▲ 1
⑩ 1
40/500

A record many labels rejected for being 'too simple' took the female quartet from Brooklyn to the top. Fellow hit makers The Tokens produced it and handled backing vocals and instrumental chores on the track. Sadly, the 25-year-old composer Ronnie Mack died of Hodgkins disease shortly after this, his first hit, turned gold. Years later, Mack's heirs had another windfall when it was adjudged that George Harrison had subconsciously based his No 1 single 'My Sweet Lord' on the song. Interestingly, The Chiffons then recorded Harrison's hit, but it failed to arouse much interest.

## ORLONS
SOUTH STREET
*Cameo*

▲ 3
⑩ 3•
401/500

This was the third Mann & Appell song that The Orlons had taken into the Top 10 in less than nine months. The group, who included Rosetta Hightower, chalked up a handful of lesser hits before disbanding in 1968. Hightower relocated to the UK, even though the quartet had been strangers to the UK chart.

## ROY ORBISON
IN DREAMS
*Monument*

▲ 7
⑩ 6
—/500

The singer's singer toured the UK to promote this self-penned lost-love ballad. Supporting him were The Beatles and Gerry & The Pacemakers. He prophesied to the British press that both had the potential to be successful in the States.

## JACKIE WILSON
BABY WORKOUT
*Brunswick*

▲ 5
⑩ 5
—/500

After a relatively quiet sales period, the innovative and versatile vocalist hit with a brass-heavy contemporary dance track which he had composed with Alonzo Tucker.

## BILL PURSELL
OUR WINTER LOVE
*Columbia*

▲ 9
⑩ 1•
—/500

California-born pianist Pursell briefly found himself in the spotlight thanks to his recording of this John Cowell-composed instrumental, which had originally been titled 'Long Island Sound'. It came from an album of country-flavoured tracks he cut in Nashville with producer Grady Martin (composer of the recent Joe Henderson hit 'Snap Your Fingers'). The LP was arranged by Bill Justis, who had also tasted fleeting fame thanks to his earlier instrumental hit 'Raunchy'.

# UNITED KINGDOM
# MARCH 1963

## BILLY FURY
LIKE I'VE NEVER BEEN GONE
*Decca*

▲ 3
⑩ 7
356/500

Paul Hampton, who composed Ral Donner's 'You Don't Know What You've Got', wrote Fury's eleventh Top 20 hit in four years.

## ROOFTOP SINGERS
WALK RIGHT IN
*Fontana*

▲ 10
⑩ 1•
—/500

See US entry (January).

## PAUL & PAULA
HEY PAULA
*Philips*

▲ 8
⑩ 1
—/500

See US entry (January).

## SHADOWS
FOOT TAPPER
*Columbia*

▲ 1
⑩ 10
153/500

Member Bruce Welch wrote the group's fifth and last No 1 as well as the single it replaced at the top, Cliff Richard's 'Summer Holiday'. Both singles were featured in their film *Summer Holiday*. Surfing band The Challengers covered the record in the US.

## BILLIE DAVIS
TELL HIM
*Decca*

▲ 10
⑩ 1•
—/500

Six months after 'Will I What', a novelty duet with Mike Sarne, reached the Top 20, the singer from Surrey (born Carol Hedges) had her only major solo hit. The photogenic performer, who many regarded as the UK's first female R&B singer, scored with a striking cover version of the Exciters'

debut US hit. In 1974, teeny bop group Hello reintroduced the song to the UK Top 10.

## BACHELORS
CHARMAINE
*Decca*

▲ 6
⑩ 1
—/500

The Irish easy-listening trio notched up the first of a most impressive run of hits with their recycling of a late 1920s song which had been a transatlantic hit for Mantovani in 1951. Interestingly, the act, who had been recording for over two years with only minimal success, were all married.

## NED MILLER
FROM A JACK TO A KING
*London American*

▲ 2
⑩ 1•
206/500

See US entry (February).

## CASCADES
RHYTHM OF THE RAIN
*Warner*

▲ 5
⑩ 1•
—/500

See US entry (February).

## GERRY & THE PACEMAKERS
HOW DO YOU DO IT?
*Columbia*

▲ 1
⑩ 1
53/500

The second act signed by The Beatles' manager Brian Epstein became the first Merseybeat group to top the 'official' *Record Retailer* chart. The song that took them to No 1 had been written by Mitch Murray for Adam Faith, and was previously recorded (but not released) by The Beatles. The effervescent act, who were voted Best New Group of 1963, steered this single into the US Top 10 18 months later.

# UNITED STATES
# APRIL 1963

## ANDY WILLIAMS
CAN'T GET USED TO
LOSING YOU
*Columbia*

Doc Pomus and Mort Shuman, who had penned hits for such teen icons as Elvis Presley, Dion & The Belmonts and Fabian, composed the top MOR artist's biggest transatlantic hit of the decade.

## PAUL & PAULA
YOUNG LOVERS
*Philips*

The youthful Texans attained their second successive transatlantic Top 10 entry with a song that reportedly started life as part of the duo's initial hit, 'Hey Paula' (producer Major Bill Smith supposedly cut it from six minutes to three). The act's third release, 'First Quarrel', was their last Top 40 entry. Other recordings by Paul & Paula, as well as solos by both vocalists, failed to take them back to the top.

## LITTLE PEGGY MARCH
I WILL FOLLOW HIM
*RCA*

Shortly after her fifteenth birthday, March (born Margaret Battavio) became the youngest female ever to top the US charts. She hit the peak with a French song that Petula Clark had been successful with in Europe under its original title, 'Chariot'. The music was composed by Franck Pourcel and Paul Mauriat, who coincidentally both achieved instrumental US Top 10 hits in their own right. The diminutive vocalist, who amassed three US Top 40 hits before she was 16, relocated to Germany where she remained popular through-out the 1970s.

## PETER, PAUL & MARY
PUFF THE MAGIC DRAGON
*Warner*

In the late 1950s, student Lenny Lipton wrote a poem about lost childhood. Peter Yarrow later added music to it and, unbeknownst to the would-be poet, recorded it with his trio. Incidentally, Lipton, who had almost forgotten about Puff by the time of the hit, strongly denies that the song is drug related.

## DEE DEE SHARP
DO THE BIRD
*Cameo*

Miss Sharp flew into the Top 10 for the fourth time in a year with a dance-related record. This song, like her earlier hit 'Gravy', was written by the team of Kal Mann and Dave Appell. It was the last major success for the singer who married top producer Kenny Gamble in 1967.

## COOKIES
DON'T SAY NOTHIN'
(BAD ABOUT MY BABY)
*Dimension*

One of the busiest session groups of the early rock years had the biggest hit of their long career with a song penned by Gerry Goffin and Carole King. It was the act's second Top 20 hit in a row, following 'Chains', another Goffin and King composition, which The Beatles subsequently cut. The Cookies had been recording since the mid-1950s, with Ethel 'Earl-Jean' McCrae being the longest-standing member.

## CHANTAYS
PIPELINE
*Dot*

▲ 4
⑩ 1•
479/500

The first surf record to crack the transatlantic Top 20 was an instrumental written and performed by a quintet of California high school students. The track, which they had originally called 'Liberty's Whip', was released by the small surf-oriented Downey label and turned into a hit when Dot took over distribution. The teenage combo released several more singles, but as far as the charts were concerned they were wiped out.

## DRIFTERS
ON BROADWAY
*Atlantic*

▲ 9
⑩ 4
—/500

The durable group's last Top 10 hit featuring lead vocalist Rudy Lewis (who died in 1964) was

originally composed by Barry Mann and Cynthia Weil for The Cookies. 'On Broadway' returned to the Top 10 in 1978 by singer/guitarist George Benson. Incidentally, The Drifters' recording featured another noted guitarist, Phil Spector.

## MONGO SANTAMARIA
WATERMELON MAN
*Battle*

▲ 10
⑩ 1•
—/500

One of the best-known Latin percussionists of the era had a taste of pop fame with this compelling jazz-based Herbie Hancock composition. Before forming his own band, the Cuban-born musician had previously played in the bands of such noted musicians as Perez Prado, Ray Charles, Tito Puente and Cal Tjader. His re-recording of 'Watermelon Man' on Columbia in 1969 failed to make the grade.

---

# UNITED KINGDOM
# APRIL 1963

---

## RONNIE CARROLL
SAY WONDERFUL THINGS
*Philips*

▲ 6
⑩ 2•
—/500

Top producer and composer Norman Newell penned the UK's 1963 Eurovision Song Contest entry – it came fourth in the contest and gave the amiable Irish balladeer his last chart entry. Both Carroll's version and a cover by Patti Page were minor US hits.

## BUDDY HOLLY
BROWN EYED HANDSOME MAN
*Coral*

▲ 3
⑩ 4
395/500

The first of many R&B songs to crack the UK chart in 1963 had been recorded early in his career by the legendary rock singer/songwriter. His version of Chuck Berry's minor 1956 hit returned the late singer to the Top 10 for the first time in four years.

## TOMMY ROE
THE FOLK SINGER
*HMV*

▲ 4
⑩ 2
—/500

A song that composer Merle Kilgore based loosely on Johnny Cash's life was a far bigger hit in the UK for the Atlanta-born singer/songwriter than in his homeland. A few months later Roe was selected by The Beatles to appear on their first live US show.

## SPRINGFIELDS
SAY I WON'T BE THERE
*Philips*

▲ 5
⑩ 2•
—/500

Britain's most original and distinctive group before The Beatles disbanded soon after this memorable Tom Springfield song became their second Top 5 entry in a row. Unusually, all three members continued to be successful; Dusty Springfield (born Mary O'Brien) had numerous solo hits, Tom wrote many top sellers and Mike Hurst produced several chart records.

## ROY ORBISON
IN DREAMS
*London American*

▲ 6
⑩ 4
476/500

See US entry (March).

## BEATLES
FROM ME TO YOU
*Parlophone*

▲ 1
⑩ 2
10/500

The first Beatles song to top all the UK charts was also the first Lennon & McCartney composition to score Stateside – thanks to a cover by Del Shannon. When their version was re-promoted in 1964, it narrowly missed the US Top 40.

## FRANK IFIELD
NOBODY'S DARLIN' BUT MINE
*Columbia*

▲ 4
⑩ 4
475/500

A well-recorded country song, which had first been cut by its composer Jimmy Davis in the late 1940s, lengthened the Australian-raised pop/yodeller's enviable run of UK hits.

# UNITED STATES
# MAY 1963

## JIMMY SOUL
IF YOU WANNA BE HAPPY
*Spqr*

▲ 1
⑩ 1•
110/500

Frank Guida, who produced and wrote hits for Gary (U.S.) Bonds, was also behind this calypso-slanted R&B smash, which was based on the West Indian ode 'Ugly Women'. It was the second and last Top 40 entry for the vocalist born James McCleese in New York. Neither this song, nor its similarly themed (though far less successful) follow-up 'Treat 'Em Rough' are likely to make any feminist's Top 10.

## BEACH BOYS
SURFIN' U.S.A.
*Capitol*

▲ 3
⑩ 1
343/500

The first vocal surf single to reach the Top 10 was appropriately by the California combo who went on to become, arguably, the biggest-selling American group of the decade. They followed their self-composed debut Top 20 entry 'Surfin' Safari' with this rewrite, by leader Brian Wilson, of Chuck Berry's outstanding stomper 'Sweet Little

Sixteen'. The record entered the Top 40 again in 1974, and in 1977 teen star Leif Garrett's rendition reached the Top 20.

## SHIRELLES
FOOLISH LITTLE GIRL
*Scepter*

▲ 4
⑩ 6•
—/500

Howard Greenfield, who had penned several top hits for Connie Francis, composed this influential act's last major hit. In 1994, the ground-breaking girl group received the Pioneer Award from the R&B Foundation.

## KINGSTON TRIO
REVEREND MR BLACK
*Capitol*

▲ 8
⑩ 2•
—/500

This San Francisco-based trio were one of the top-selling album acts of the pre-Beatles years and are generally credited for the upsurge of interest in folk music in the decade. Billy Ed Wheeler composed their biggest hit since their No 1 'Tom Dooley' in 1958. It came from the act's sixteenth successive Top 20 album, *The Kingston Trio 16*.

## BRENDA LEE
LOSING YOU
*Decca*

One of the biggest-selling female singers of the 1960s clocked up her twelfth and last Top 10 hit while still in her teens. The transatlantic smash started life in France as 'Un Ange Est Renn' and had English lyrics added by Carl Sigman. The UK invasion of the States in 1964 did not spell an end to Lee's career – she amassed a further seven Top 20 entries over the next two years.

## AL MARTINO
I LOVE YOU BECAUSE
*Capitol*

One of the most successful country compositions of the 1950s reinstated the balladeer (born Al Cini in Philadelphia) into the Top 10 after an 11-year hiatus. It had originally been taken to the top of the C&W chart in 1950 by its blind composer Leon Payne, and it had been one of the first songs recorded by Elvis Presley. Interestingly, a version by Jim Reeves was one of the biggest sellers in the UK in 1964.

## LOU CHRISTIE
TWO FACES HAVE I
*Roulette*

After several small-selling singles released under various names, this distinctive vocalist (born Lugee Sacco) from Pennsylvania opened his Top 40 account with 'The Gipsy Cried'. Christie wrote this and its similar though even more profitable follow-up, 'Two Faces Have I', with mystic Twyla Herbert, who naturally foresaw their success.

## RAY CHARLES
TAKE THESE CHAINS
FROM MY HEART
*ABC Paramount*

Ten years after Hank Williams took this Fred Rose song to the top of the country chart, Ray Charles' distinctive interpretation turned it into a transatlantic Top 10 hit. Interestingly, Charles later recorded it with Williams' son, Hank Williams Jr.

## LESLEY GORE
IT'S MY PARTY
*Mercury*

Before Quincy Jones produced New Yorker Gore's version, both The Shirelles and the UK's teen pop queen Helen Shapiro had recorded 'It's My Party'. Phil Spector was also in the midst of cutting it with The Crystals when Gore's version was rushed out and quickly rocketed her to the top. This teen-targeted pop nugget was the first of eight US Top 20 hits for the 17-year-old and her only UK Top 10 entry.

## SAM COOKE
ANOTHER SATURDAY
NIGHT
*RCA*

A song he wrote in a London hotel room took the soul legend from Mississippi back into the transatlantic charts. In 1973, Cat Stevens' update of the soulful sing-along returned it to the Top 20 in both the US and the UK.

# UNITED KINGDOM
# MAY 1963

## ANDY WILLIAMS
CAN'T GET USED TO
LOSING YOU
*CBS*

▲ 2
⑩ 2
262/500

See US entry (April).

## JET HARRIS & TONY MEEHAN
SCARLETT O'HARA
*Decca*

▲ 2
⑩ 2
252/500

Bass player Harris and drummer Meehan returned with a Jerry Lordan composition which only The Beatles stopped from hitting the top. In the US, an easy-listening interpretation by polka king Lawrence Welk scraped into the bottom end of the chart.

## DEL SHANNON
TWO KINDS OF
TEARDROPS
*London American*

▲ 5
⑩ 7
—/500

As UK acts reclaimed the chart, the unmistakable American singer/songwriter scored his seventh UK Top 10 entry in two years. It would, however, be another two years before he returned, albeit briefly, to the same heights.

## BRENDA LEE
LOSING YOU
*Brunswick*

▲ 10
⑩ 6
—/500

See US entry.

## CLIFF RICHARD
LUCKY LIPS
*Columbia*

▲ 4
⑩ 20
487/500

In the year that he first replaced Elvis as World's Top Male Singer in the *NME* poll, Cliff's update of Ruth Brown's 1957 hit returned him to the US Top 100 after a four-year absence.

## BILLY J. KRAMER & THE DAKOTAS
DO YOU WANT TO KNOW
A SECRET
*Parlophone*

▲ 2
⑩ 1
230/500

Brian Epstein's third group followed the previous two at the top of the *NME* chart. Kramer (born William Ashton) said that Lennon & McCartney penned this song for him and added that he had been singing a slower version in his act for some time before The Beatles recorded it. In the US, The Beatles had the hit version.

## PAUL & PAULA
YOUNG LOVERS
*Philips*

▲ 9
⑩ 2•
—/500

See US entry (April).

## BILLY FURY
WHEN WILL YOU SAY I
LOVE YOU
*Decca*

▲ 3
⑩ 8
404/500

UK composer and failed singer Alan Fielding, who had written Fury's earlier Top 10 hit 'Last Night Was Made For Love', also penned this song, which kept the relative rock veteran Fury in the charts alongside many other Liverpudlians.

## WINK MARTINDALE
DECK OF CARDS
*London American*

▲ 5
⑩ 1•
455/500

When it was re-issued, US TV and radio personality Martindale (born Winston Conrad) marched his 1959 transatlantic Top 20 hit back into the UK chart. The monologue, which dealt with a soldier caught playing cards in church, was written and recorded by country performer T. Texas Tyler in the late 1940s. In 1973, both this single and a revival by Max Bygraves reached the UK Top 40.

# UNITED STATES
# JUNE 1963

## CRYSTALS
DA DOO RON RON
*Philles*

▲ 3
⑩ 2
402/500

After seeing two singles by The Blossoms chart under the name The Crystals, the real Crystals sang on a track that producer Phil Spector had earmarked for The Blossoms to record. It was a perfect example of Spector's unmistakable 'Wall of Sound' production technique. The ever-popular track also entered the UK Top 20 in 1974.

## DOVELLS
YOU CAN'T SIT DOWN
*Parkway*

▲ 3
⑩ 2•
376/500

A wild instrumental that R&B star Dee Clark had written as the introduction music to his stage act was turned into a Top 40 hit in 1961 by the Phil Upchurch Combo. When Kal Mann added lyrics, it transported The Dovells into the Top 40 for the fifth and last time. Lead singer Len Barry left shortly afterwards and had several hits on his own.

## KYU SAKAMOTO
SUKIYAKI
*Capitol*

▲ 1
⑩ 1•
72/500

Before becoming the only Japanese artist to have a big transatlantic hit, Sakamoto was already a major TV, film and recording star in his homeland. When his Japanese hit 'Ue O Muite Aruko' was released in the US, it was given the more easily pronounceable title that had earlier been coined for Kenny Ball's instrumental interpretation. In 1981, an English lyric version by Taste Of Honey sold over a million, and in 1995 R&B vocal group 4 PM delivered 'Sukiyaki' into the US Top 10 for the third time.

## BILL ANDERSON
STILL
*Decca*

▲ 8
⑩ 1•
—/500

In 1963, this distinctive and talented singer/songwriter was voted Top Male Artist and Top Songwriter by the Country Music Association, and 'Still' picked up the award for Record of the Year. In the UK it was a cover version by Karl Denver that made the Top 20. 'Still' was one of more than three dozen Top 10 country hits notched up by the performer known as 'Whispering Bill'. Incidentally, the South Carolina-born artist was still writing Top 10 county hits in 1995.

## NAT 'KING' COLE
THOSE LAZY-HAZY-CRAZY DAYS OF SUMMER
*Capitol*

▲ 6
⑩ 11•
—/500

The last US Top 10 hit for the critically acclaimed song stylist was a novelty sing-along pop piece composed by Hanse Carste and Charles Tobias. The influential entertainer, who had first recorded 27 years earlier, died from cancer in 1965. In the UK, he posthumously topped the album chart in 1978 and had a Top 10 single in 1988.

## BOBBY VINTON
BLUE ON BLUE
*Epic*

▲ 3
⑩ 2
386/500

Regular hit writer Burt Bacharach and Hal David composed this enduring ballad, which reinstalled the one-time leader of Dick Clark's touring band in the Top 10.

## BARBARA LEWIS
HELLO STRANGER
*Atlantic*

▲ 3
⑩ 1•
406/500

Michigan-born R&B singer Lewis penned the biggest of her three Top 20 hits. She was backed by doo-wop group The Dells, who later had several hits of their own. Lewis did not chart in the UK, but two songs she recorded first reached the Top 20 by The Searchers ('Someday We're Gonna Love Again') and Peter & Gordon ('Baby I'm Yours'). 'Hello Stranger' reappeared in the US Top 20 in 1975 by Yvonne Elliman, and Carrie Lucas took it into the R&B Top 20 in 1985.

## BOBBY DARIN
18 YELLOW ROSES
*Capitol*

▲ 10
⑩ 9
—/500

The multi-faceted singer/songwriter/actor's last major hit for three years was another of his own meritorious pop/country compositions.

## CHIFFONS
ONE FINE DAY
*Laurie*

▲ 6
⑩ 2
—/500

The Chiffons simply added their vocals to Carole King's demo of 'One Fine Day', and the result gave them a second successive Top 5 entry. Interestingly, King had planned the song for Little Eva, but her vocal did not suit the track. Astonishingly, in 1980, this sing-along pop gem returned to the Top 20 by Miss King herself.

## ESSEX
EASIER SAID THAN DONE
*Roulette*

▲ 1
⑩ 1•
146/500

William Linton was inspired by the sound of the teletype machines in his office to write the song that shipped his fellow US marines The Essex to the No 1 spot. The quintet, led by their only female member Anita Humes, were not keen on Linton's composition and recorded it as the B side to their own number 'Are You Going My Way'. However, it rocketed up the chart and their similar follow-up, 'A Walkin' Miracle', also entered the Top 20.

Staying at the top, though, proved to be easier said than done.

## LONNIE MACK
MEMPHIS
*Fraternity*

▲ 6
⑩ 1•
—/500

Critically acclaimed guitarist (born Lonnie McIntosh) from Indiana had the highest-ranked hit of his career with an instrumental update of a minor Chuck Berry hit. Later in the year both Berry's original version and Dave Berry's rendition reached the UK Top 20. In 1979, a re-issue of Mack's recording narrowly missed the UK Top 40.

## JAN & DEAN
SURF CITY
*Liberty*

▲ 1
⑩ 3
137/500

It is only fitting that the duo who helped lay the foundations of the surf vocal sound (with late 1950s hits like 'Baby Talk' and 'Jenny Lee'), should have the first No 1 surf hit. Jan (Berry) co-wrote the song with Brian Wilson. Beach Boy Wilson also sang backing vocals on the record, which extolled the virtues of the place where there were 'two girls for every boy'.

# UNITED KINGDOM
# JUNE 1963

## RAY CHARLES
TAKE THESE CHAINS
FROM MY HEART
*HMV*

▲ 5
⑩ 4•
436/500

See US entry (May).

## GERRY & THE PACEMAKERS
I LIKE IT
*Columbia*

▲ 1
⑩ 2
41/500

This Merseybeat band, fronted by Gerry Marsden, became the first act to reach No 1 with their initial two single releases. Like its predecessor, the song was written by tunesmith Mitch Murray. It had previously been recorded by the Dave Clark Five.

## FREDDIE & THE DREAMERS
IF YOU GOTTA MAKE A
FOOL OF SOMEBODY
*Columbia*

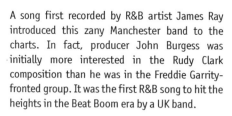
▲ 3
⑩ 1
394/500

A song first recorded by R&B artist James Ray introduced this zany Manchester band to the charts. In fact, producer John Burgess was initially more interested in the Rudy Clark composition than he was in the Freddie Garrity-fronted group. It was the first R&B song to hit the heights in the Beat Boom era by a UK band.

## SHADOWS
ATLANTIS
*Columbia*

▲ 2
⑩ 11
220/500

The combination of the UK's most successful instrumental act of all time and Jerry Lordan's catchy little composition almost gave this hit team a third No 1.

## BUDDY HOLLY
BO DIDDLEY
*Coral*

▲ 4
⑩ 5
—/500

Bo Diddley's self-penned theme song gave the legend from Lubbock, Texas, his second successive Top 5 entry. Even though he had died four years earlier, there is no doubt that Holly helped launch the R&B boom in the UK.

## ROY ORBISON
FALLING
*London American*

▲ 9
⑩ 5
—/500

The Texan with the dark glasses and the instantly recognizable soaring voice penned his sixth UK Top 20 entry of the decade, with a song that failed to crack the Top 20 in his homeland.

# UNITED STATES
# JULY 1963

## TYMES
SO MUCH IN LOVE
*Parkway*

This smooth soul quintet from Philadelphia made their chart debut with a stand-out semi-acappella song that incorporated the sound of waves and seabirds. The track was penned by lead singer George Willliams with producer Billy Jackson and arranger Roy Straigis. The group's 1974 re-recording went nowhere. However, in 1994 All-4-One reintroduced the winning ballad to the US Top 5.

## ROLF HARRIS
TIE ME KANGAROO
DOWN, SPORT
*Epic*

See UK entry (August 1960).

## SURFARIS
WIPE OUT
*Dot*

The most successful surf instrumental was composed and performed by a quintet of California high school students. The group quickly penned it in the studio as the B side to the Beach Boys-styled vocal 'Surfer Joe'. When Dot picked it up from the tiny Princess label, both sides charted. 'Wipe Out' (which featured drummer Ron Wilson) also entered the UK Top 5 and, astoundingly, returned to the US Top 20 in 1966. A vocal version by The Fat Boys and Beach Boys reached the transatlantic Top 20 in 1987.

## LITTLE STEVIE WONDER
FINGERTIPS (PT. 2)
*Tamla*

The first live recording to reach No 1 was also one of the most exciting of all time. It was the fourth single and first hit by the multi-talented

13-year-old. A studio version of 'Fingertips' was included on Wonder's second album, *The Jazz Soul Of Little Stevie*, while the seven-minute live cut was featured on his chart-topping third LP, *Little Stevie Wonder/The 12 Year Old Genius*. Astoundingly, the performer had to wait another 21 years for his first UK No 1.

## ELVIS PRESLEY
(YOU'RE THE) DEVIL IN
DISGUISE
*RCA*

The only single by an American artist to top the UK chart in 1963 was also Elvis' biggest hit of the year in his homeland. Incidentally, it was 11 months before another US act reached No 1 in the UK.

## MARVIN GAYE
PRIDE AND JOY
*Tamla*

After a lack-lustre career start, the Washington-born entertainer debuted in the Top 10 with his sixth solo single. The one-time member of doo-wop acts The Rainbows and The Marquees penned the R&B stomper with William 'Mickey' Stevenson and Norman Whitfield. He was backed on the single by fellow Top 10 newcomers Martha & The Vandellas.

## PETER, PAUL & MARY
BLOWIN' IN THE WIND
*Warner*

The first time Bob Dylan's name appeared on the transatlantic charts was as writer of this folk trio's version of 'Blowin' In The Wind'. Interestingly, some people question Dylan's authorship, saying he bought the song from Lorre Wyatt – the answer my friend is blowin' in the wind!

## DORIS TROY
JUST ONE LOOK
*Atlantic*

▲ 10
⑩ 1•
—/500

New Yorker Troy (born Doris Payne) wrote her only hit with Gregory Carroll, who had sung with the successful doo-wop groups The Four Buddies and The Orioles. In the UK, a lively cover by The Hollies

narrowly missed the top. Troy relocated to the UK in the late 1960s and became one of the most in-demand session singers. Among her later recordings were a disco version of this hit and 'Another Look'. A stage show based on Troy's life, *Mama I Want To Sing*, opened in the UK in 1995.

# UNITED KINGDOM
# JULY 1963

## FRANK IFIELD
CONFESSIN'
*Columbia*

▲ 1
⑩ 5
84/500

The Australian-raised singer achieved his fourth UK No 1 in a year with a song that Guy Lombardo and Rudy Vallee had helped popularize in 1930.

## JIM REEVES
WELCOME TO MY WORLD
*RCA*

▲ 6
⑩ 1
—/500

This easy-on-the-ear country vocalist from Texas had his third UK Top 20 single with a track that failed to crack the Top 100 pop chart in the US.

## LESLEY GORE
IT'S MY PARTY
*Mercury*

▲ 9
⑩ 1•
—/500

See US entry.

## ELVIS PRESLEY
DEVIL IN DISGUISE
*RCA*

See US entry.

## CRYSTALS
DA DOO RON RON
*London American*

See US entry.

## SEARCHERS
SWEETS FOR MY SWEET
*Pye*

▲ 1
⑩ 1
106/500

The Searchers originally cut this song as part of a self-produced demo album. When producer Tony Hatch re-recorded the track it became the fourth No 1 by a Liverpool-based band in four months. Incidentally, John Lennon described it as 'The best disc ever from a Liverpool group'. The song that introduced them to UK record buyers was penned by Pomus and Shuman and had been a US Top 20 entry in 1961 by The Drifters. In 1994 a reggae version by C.J. Lewis reached the UK Top 3.

## BRIAN POOLE & THE TREMELOES
TWIST AND SHOUT
*Decca*

In January 1962, Decca Records signed this Essex-based band in preference to The Beatles. The group, who owed as much to The Shadows and The Crickets as their Merseybeat rivals, finally charted 18 months later. The band's debut hit was based on The Beatles' interpretation of a song earlier recorded by American R&B acts Carla Thomas, the Top Notes and the Isley Brothers. 'Twist And Shout' also entered the UK Top 10 by Salt 'N' Pepa in 1988 and Chaka Démus & Pliers in 1994.

# UNITED STATES
# AUGUST 1963

## LESLEY GORE
JUDY'S TURN TO CRY
*Mercury*

▲ 5
⑩ 2
—/500

The sequel to 'It's My Party' followed its predecessor into the Top 5. It came from the pen of Beverly Ross, whose earlier hits included the even catchier Chordettes' hit 'Lollipop'.

## FOUR SEASONS
CANDY GIRL
*Vee Jay*

▲ 3
⑩ 4
378/500

The top-selling American vocal group of the decade added to their portfolio of pop hits with a song penned by Larry Santos. The B side 'Marlena' also went into the Top 40.

## KAI WINDING
MORE
*Verve*

▲ 8
⑩ 1•
—/500

This Danish-born jazz musician had the biggest-selling version of the much-recorded theme from the film *Mondo Cane*. Before scoring his only hit, the trombonist had played with top bands like Benny Goodman and Stan Kenton and had performed as a duo with J.J. Johnson. 'More' has now clocked up over five million plays on US radio, with Winding's interpretation accounting for a good proportion of them.

## ALLAN SHERMAN
HELLO MUDDUH, HELLO
FADDUH
*Warner*

▲ 2
⑩ 1•
303/500

Comedy scriptwriter and TV producer Sherman (born Allan Copelon) was one of the biggest-selling album artists of 1963. This humorous letter home from summer camp (set to the music of Ponchielli's 'Dance Of The Hours') came from the second of his three consecutive No 1 albums, *My*

*Son, The Celebrity*. An alternative version by Sherman in 1964 also reached the US Top 100.

## ANGELS
MY BOYFRIEND'S BACK
*Smash*

▲ 1
⑩ 1•
64/500

This New Jersey trio were the first white girl group to top the charts since the Fontane Sisters in early 1955. The song's publisher had earmarked it for The Shirelles, but the writers Robert Feldman, Jerry Goldstein and Richard Gottehrer insisted they produced it with The Angels. An answer record, 'Your Boyfriend's Back' by Bobby Comstock also entered the Top 100. A 1989 TV movie *My Boyfriend's Back* was loosely based on The Angels' story.

## RANDY & THE RAINBOWS
DENISE
*Rust*

▲ 10
⑩ 1•
—/500

A doo-wop quintet from Queens, New York, had five minutes of fame thanks to a perky song penned by friend Neil Levenson and produced by the talented Tokens. In 1978, Blondie made their chart debut with a female version entitled 'Denis'. As a 'thank you' to Blondie's leader, Debbie Harry, the reunited Randy & The Rainbows then re-recorded 'Denise' as 'Debbie'.

## TRINI LOPEZ
IF I HAD A HAMMER
*Reprise*

▲ 3
⑩ 1•
385/500

A year after Peter, Paul & Mary's rendition of this traditional folk opus reached the US Top 10, Texan Lopez turned it into an international dance hit. The one-time rockabilly performer, who was briefly a member of The Crickets, recorded the song live during his 18-month residency at

Hollywood's famous PJ's club. It came from the album *Trini Lopez At PJ's*, which was the first of the vocalist's seven successive Top 40 LPs.

## INEZ FOXX
MOCKINGBIRD
*Symbol*

▲ 7
⑩ 1•
—/500

Despite the solo label credit, Inez was actually part of a duo with her brother Charlie. They were one of the most soulful and popular live acts of the 1960s, and had their only Top 40 pop hit with an R&B rendition of an old children's nursery rhyme. Astonishingly, the act's best-known track took until 1969 to reach the UK Top 40. James Taylor and his wife Carly Simon's 1974 version entered the US Top 5.

---

# UNITED KINGDOM
# AUGUST 1963

---

## KYU SAKAMOTO
SUKIYAKI
*HMV*

▲ 6
⑩ 1•
—/500

See US entry (June).

## BILLY FURY
IN SUMMER
*Decca*

▲ 5
⑩ 9
—/500

UK vocal trio The Avons, who had earlier penned The Shadows' chart topper 'Dance On', composed the latest hit for the ever-popular performer. Incidentally, Fury sang it on the first-ever *Ready Steady Go* TV show.

## KENNY LYNCH
YOU CAN NEVER STOP ME
LOVING YOU
*HMV*

▲ 10
⑩ 2•
—/500

Ian Samwell, who had written several hits for Cliff Richard, co-wrote this infectious pop opus with Lynch. In the US, a cover version by Johnny Tillotson made the Top 20. Later in the decade, the talented singer/songwriter and TV personality penned hits for such acts as the Small Faces and Cilla Black.

## BILLY J. KRAMER & THE DAKOTAS
BAD TO ME
*Parlophone*

▲ 1
⑩ 2
98/500

This record topped the chart on the Liverpool-born lead singer's twentieth birthday. It was composed by John Lennon while on holiday in Spain with manager Brian Epstein. In the US, it started as the B side to 'Little Children', and when re-issued it reached the Top 10 in its own right.

## KEN THORNE & HIS ORCHESTRA
THEME FROM *THE LEGION'S LAST PATROL*
*HMV*

▲ 4
⑩ 1•
497/500

It took just five days after it was recorded for the ex-cathedral organist's version of the Italian movie theme to reach the shops. The keyboard player and arranger from Norwich notched up his only chart entry just before his fortieth birthday.

## SURFARIS
WIPE OUT
*London American*

▲ 5
⑩ 1•
—/500

See US entry (July).

## FREDDIE & THE DREAMERS
I'M TELLING YOU NOW
*Columbia*

▲ 3
⑩ 2
402/500

Their bespectacled gnome-like leader penned the group's biggest transatlantic hit with noted British songsmith Mitch Murray. Eighteen months after its UK success, the bouncy single shot the madcap band to the top in the US.

## JOHNNY KIDD & THE PIRATES
I'LL NEVER GET OVER YOU
*HMV*

▲ 4
⑩ 2•
433/500

After a relatively quiet sales period the influential British rock band hit with a Mersey-influenced song penned by Viscounts member Gordon Mills. The follow-up, another Mills composition, 'Hungry For Love', was the last Top 20 entry for the critically acclaimed band, whose charismatic singer died in an automobile accident in 1966.

## CARAVELLES
YOU DON'T HAVE TO BE A BABY TO CRY
*Decca*

▲ 6
⑩ 1•
—/500

On the week that The Beatles first catapulted into the US Top 20, this UK recording dropped out. The Caravelles were two teenage girls from London whose only claim to fame was their cute, breathy, Patience & Prudence-influenced interpretation of an Ernest Tubb country hit from 1950. The song came from the pen of the 1950's most successful tunesmith, Bob Merrill. The duo, who appeared on the first Beatles live show in the US, were unable to add to their hit tally on either side of the Atlantic.

## CLIFF RICHARD
IT'S ALL IN THE GAME
*Columbia*

▲ 2
⑩ 21
273/500

Five years after Tommy Edwards had taken this enduring ballad to the top on both sides of the Atlantic, it gave Cliff his biggest US hit of the decade. As it climbed the US Top 40, The Beatles made their US chart debut.

# UNITED STATES
# SEPTEMBER 1963

## BOBBY VINTON
BLUE VELVET
*Epic*

▲ 1
⑩ 3
60/500

A song that had charted for Tony Bennett in 1951 conveyed the pop balladeer from Pennsylvania to the summit. It took just two takes and was recorded in Nashville with top session musicians, including Floyd Cramer and Boots Randolph, but Vinton considered it too sweet and pretty to be a big hit. It finally entered the UK Top 10 in 1990, after being used in a skin cream commercial.

## MARTHA & THE VANDELLAS
HEAT WAVE
*Gordy*

▲ 4
⑩ 1
442/500

Motown's hottest songwriting team of Brian Holland, Lamont Dozier and Eddie Holland penned this R&B chart topper, which introduced the female trio to the Top 10. 'Heat Wave' was the third single from the act fronted by the composers' ex-secretary, Martha Reeves. An update by Linda Ronstadt in 1975 also reached the Top 5.

## MAJOR LANCE
THE MONKEY TIME
*Okeh*

▲ 8
⑩ 1
—/500

Although Chicago never replaced Detroit as the home of soul in the 1960s, there was a very successful Chicago soul sound masterminded by the multi-talented Curtis Mayfield. It was Mayfield who wrote and produced the single that introduced both Major Lance and the Monkey dance craze to the chart. 'The Monkey Time' was the first of six Top 40 hits for the Chicago-born singer, who had actually been recording to little effect since 1959.

## FREDDIE SCOTT
HEY, GIRL
*Colpix*

▲ 10
⑩ 1•
—/500

One of the less heralded but most soulful vocalists of the 1960s paid his only visit to the pop Top 20 with his smooth interpretation of a classy Gerry Goffin and Carole King ballad. The ex-doo-wop singer/songwriter from Rhode Island had many more worthy, though smaller-selling, singles in the 1960s. 'Hey Girl' later returned to the Top 40 by Bobby Vee in 1968 and Donny Osmond in 1972.

## CRYSTALS
THEN HE KISSED ME
*Philles*

▲ 6
⑩ 3
—/500

When people talk about the great girl group records of the 1960s, they have singles like this in mind. Jeff Barry, Ellie Greenwich and Phil Spector penned the pop/R&B nugget which gave The Crystals their third and last transatlantic Top 20 entry. A remake by The Beach Boys reached the UK Top 10 in 1967.

## BEACH BOYS
SURFER GIRL
*Capitol*

▲ 7
⑩ 2
—/500

The decade's most outstanding harmony vocal group had their first ballad hit with a beautiful Brian Wilson song written about a high school friend, Judy Bowles. It had been part of the band's repertoire since they were known as The Pendletones.

## JAYNETTS
SALLY, GO 'ROUND THE ROSES
*Tuff*

▲ 2
⑩ 1•
315/500

One of the most expensively produced and interesting left-field records of the decade gave the female R&B quartet from the Bronx their entry ticket to the 'One-Hit Wonders Hall of Fame'. Producer Abner Spector spent several days and many thousands of dollars recording this hypnotic track, whose ambiguous lyrics meant different things to different people.

## MIRACLES
MICKEY'S MONKEY
*Tamla*

▲ 8
⑩ 3
—/500

Motown's in-house writing team of Holland, Dozier and Holland penned this dance smash for the influential Detroit group, who barely put a foot wrong during the decade.

## GARNET MIMMS & THE ENCHANTERS
CRY BABY
*UA*

▲ 4
⑩ 1•
465/500

Arguably the first really soulful single to crack the pop Top 10 came from a mixed vocal group, whose gospel background was evident on this outstanding single. The West Virginia native Mimms' quartet, who recorded some of the most outstanding soul sides in the 1960s, chalked up a further three Top 40 entries before fading from view. In 1971, the Bert Berns-penned R&B classic was included on Janis Joplin's No 1 LP *Pearl*.

## RONETTES
BE MY BABY
*Philles*

▲ 2
⑩ 1•
290/500

Whenever 1960s girl groups are discussed The Ronettes' name is certain to crop up. The trio, fronted by the easily recognizable Ronnie Bennett (later Spector), epitomized the genre, and their unmistakable Phil Spector-produced singles are among the era's best-remembered recordings. This family act achieved five consecutive Top 40 hits, the biggest of which entered the Top 3 on both sides of the Atlantic. The song, composed by

Phil Spector, Jeff Barry and Ellie Greenwich, was taken back into the Top 20 in 1970 by Andy Kim.

### TYMES
WONDERFUL! WONDERFUL!
*Parkway*

▲ 7
⑩ 2•
—/500

The group scored their second successive Top 10 entry with an update of a Ben Raleigh and Sherman Edwards ballad that Johnny Mathis had taken into the Top 20 in 1957. The act achieved a couple more US Top 20 hits over the next ten years, and in 1974 topped the UK chart with 'Ms Grace'.

# UNITED KINGDOM
# SEPTEMBER 1963

### BEATLES
SHE LOVES YOU
*Parlophone*

▲ 1
⑩ 3
1/500

With over 300,000 advance orders, 'She Loves You' broke the record for UK singles. The final home sales tally for this genuine pop gem were over 1.6 million copies. Although ignored in the US at the time, it topped the chart there six months afterwards.

### HEINZ
JUST LIKE EDDIE
*Decca*

▲ 5
⑩ 1•
—/500

This photogenic ex-member of the chart-topping Tornadoes had the biggest of his four UK Top 40 hits with a tribute to the late American rock star Eddie Cochran. Heinz (born Heinz Burt) was discovered by Joe Meek, who produced the track. The song was written by Geoff Goddard, whose earlier successes included 'Tribute To Buddy Holly'.

### STEVE LAWRENCE & EYDIE GORME
I WANT TO STAY HERE
*CBS*

▲ 3
⑩ 1•
420/500

The ever-popular American night-club act were more successful in the UK than the US with their recording of a song written by another well-known married couple, Carole King and Gerry Goffin. The composers had earlier penned Lawrence's most successful single, 'Go Away Little Girl'.

### JET HARRIS & TONY MEEHAN
APPLEJACK
*Decca*

▲ 4
⑩ 3•
—/500

The duo introduced their third and last single on the first *Ready Steady Go* TV show. Like its predecessors, this Johnny Worth composition reached the Top 5. Soon afterwards Harris (and hit-making girlfriend Billie Davis) were involved in a car crash, which virtually ended his recording career. Meehan then formed his own group and later went back into production, working with such artists as Roger Daltrey.

### BRIAN POOLE & THE TREMELOES
DO YOU LOVE ME
*Decca*

▲ 1
⑩ 2
68/500

Their sixth single was the biggest of Poole's eight UK Top 40 hits. It was a diluted version of a Berry Gordy composition that had been a major US hit for The Contours. The single reportedly topped the chart in more than a dozen countries.

## TRINI LOPEZ
IF I HAD A HAMMER
*Reprise*

▲ 4
⑩ 1•
411/500

See US entry (August).

## CRYSTALS
THEN HE KISSED ME
*London American*

▲ 2
⑩ 2•
247/500

See US entry.

## BUDDY HOLLY
WISHING
*Coral*

▲ 10
⑩ 6•
—/500

Amazingly, the innovative and influential singer/songwriter had his most successful chart spell four years after his death in February 1959. This dreamy ballad, written with one-time singing partner Bob Montgomery, was his third consecutive UK Top 10 entry. In the US, Holly's only solo Top 10 entry had been in 1957.

# UNITED STATES
# OCTOBER 1963

## JIMMY GILMER & THE FIREBALLS
SUGAR SHACK
*Dot*

▲ 1
⑩ 1
17/500

Before Chicago-born Gilmer joined them, The Fireballs had already stacked up three Top 40 instrumental hits in their own right and played on several UK hits by Buddy Holly. The band's biggest seller, and its equally cute Top 20 follow-up 'Daisy Petal Pickin', were both penned by Keith McCormack. All the group's hits were produced by Norman Petty, who also produced McCormack's Top 10 band, The String-A-Longs.

## RAY CHARLES
BUSTED
*ABC Paramount*

▲ 4
⑩ 10
446/500

Soon after Johnny Cash had a country hit with this Harlan Howard composition, the innovative R&B singer/songwriter/band leader and pianist transported it into the transatlantic Top 20.

## ROY ORBISON
MEAN WOMAN BLUES
*Monument*

▲ 5
⑩ 7
—/500

The one-time Sun Records artist clicked with a song previously made famous by two other ex-Sun singers, Elvis Presley and Jerry Lee Lewis. On the UK chart it was listed as a double-sided hit with 'Blue Bayou'.

## DION DI MUCI
DONNA THE
PRIMA DONNA
*Columbia*

▲ 6
⑩ 7
—/500

Dion (who now added his surname) teamed up again with singer/songwriter Ernie Maresca to create another outstanding, if not too original, good-time rock hit. On this and his other Columbia hits he was backed by vocal group The Wanderers. The record inspired the answer single 'Dion, My Dion' by Donna Prima.

## NINO TEMPO & APRIL STEVENS
DEEP PURPLE
*Atco*

▲ 1
⑩ 1•
173/500

When she was only 15, April (born Carol Lo Tempio) had her first Top 10 entry with a revival of 'I'm In Love Again'. Her biggest hit came when she teamed with brother Nino (a noted sax session player) on a unique interpretation of the Mitchell Parish and Peter De Rose standard. They recorded it in 15 minutes and at the outset their producer/label owner Ahmet Ertegun did not consider it worthy of release. In 1976 Donny & Marie Osmond's similar treatment also attained a Top 20 position.

## PETER, PAUL & MARY
DON'T THINK TWICE IT'S ALL RIGHT
*Warner*

▲ 9
⑩ 4
—/500

Not only was this the New York trio's third Top 10 single in succession, it was also the second penned by Bob Dylan. It came from the act's third album *In The Wind,* which held the top spot as their self-titled debut album stood at No 2.

## VILLAGE STOMPERS
WASHINGTON SQUARE
*Epic*

▲ 2
⑩ 1•
265/500

This Dixieland jazz band's only major hit was an instrumental named after a park in the middle of Greenwich Village – the area of New York that gave the combo their name. Perhaps surprisingly, the Village Stomper's similarly titled album, which included trad versions of many recent hits, also reached the Top 5.

# UNITED KINGDOM
# OCTOBER 1963

## SHADOWS
SHINDIG
*Columbia*

▲ 6
⑩ 12
—/500

Britain's most imitated group before The Beatles ended their run of 12 consecutive Top 10 entries with an instrumental composed by members Hank Marvin and Bruce Welch.

## ROY ORBISON
BLUE BAYOU/MEAN WOMAN BLUES
*London American*

▲ 3
⑩ 6
263/500

Unlike their American cousins, UK audiences preferred the Orbison-penned 'Blue Bayou' to his revival of the 1950s rock classic. The song finally entered the US Top 10 in 1977 when recorded by Linda Ronstadt.

## ADAM FAITH
THE FIRST TIME
*Parlophone*

▲ 5
⑩ 11•
—/500

Despite its title, this contemporary Chris Andrews composition was the last Top 10 entry for the early 1960s teen icon, who was now joined on record by The Roulettes. Incidentally, in the US his only Top 40 entry came in 1965 with 'It's Alright'. Faith subsequently went into management and production and helped the careers of acts such as Sandie Shaw, Leo Sayer and Roger Daltrey.

## GERRY & THE PACEMAKERS
### YOU'LL NEVER WALK ALONE
*Columbia*

This revival of the show-stopping song from the 1945 Rodgers and Hammerstein musical *Carousel* lifted the Liverpool lads to the top spot for the third time in six months. It would be over 20 years before another act achieved three No 1s with their first three releases. In 1985, a recording of this anthemic ballad by The Crowd (which featured the Pacemaker's leader Gerry Marsden) also headed the UK chart.

## TOMMY ROE
### EVERYBODY
*HMV*

See US entry (November).

## SHIRLEY BASSEY
### I (WHO HAVE NOTHING)
*Columbia*

The internationally celebrated entertainer's last big seller of the decade was her UK-targeted treatment of a US hit by Ben E. King. The emotional ballad started life in Italy as 'Uno Dei Tanti' and Jerry Leiber and Mike Stoller added the English lyrics.

## FOURMOST
### HELLO LITTLE GIRL
*Parlophone*

Brian Epstein managed this quirky quartet, changed their name from the Four Mosts and signed them to Parlophone. He also arranged for Lennon & McCartney to supply songs for the group's first two singles. The cheerful 'Hello Little Girl', which The Beatles often performed in their early days, had originally been pencilled in as the follow-up to Gerry & The Pacemakers' debut hit, 'How Do You Do It'.

## CHUCK BERRY
### LET IT ROCK/MEMPHIS TENNESSEE
*Pye International*

Berry, one of the all-time great rockers of the 1950s, was arguably the most influential artist of the year. His music helped launch both the R&B boom in the UK and the surf music craze back in the US. His compositions charted by such diverse acts as The Beach Boys, The Rolling Stones, Buddy Holly, Lonnie Mack and Johnny Rivers. Berry's first UK Top 10 entry coupled two 1950s recordings that had previously been B sides. A cover version of 'Memphis Tennessee' by Dave Berry simultaneously reached the Top 20.

## SEARCHERS
### SUGAR AND SPICE
*Pye*

Producer Tony Hatch penned the Liverpool quartet's second successive Top 3 entry. It was the only British-written Top 10 entry for the act who, unlike most of their contemporaries, were regarded as having an American vocal sound.

# UNITED STATES
# NOVEMBER 1963

### SKEETER DAVIS
I CAN'T STAY MAD AT YOU
*RCA*

Gerry Goffin and Carole King composed this perky pop song which gave the easy-to-recognize country singer from Kentucky her fourth pop Top 40 entry. The record was one of over 40 country hits notched up by the singer with the child-like vocal quality.

### IMPRESSIONS
IT'S ALL RIGHT
*ABC Paramount*

The group, whose 1958 single 'For Your Precious Love' (featuring lead vocalist Jerry Butler) was arguably the first soul hit, reached the Top 20 for the third time. Like their top 1961 hit 'Gypsy Woman', the ground-breaking 'It's All Right' was penned by the act's multi-talented leader Curtis Mayfield – the person most responsible for the successful Chicago soul sound.

### LOS INDIOS TABAJARAS
MARIA ELENA
*RCA*

One of the most unexpected hits of the decade came from two sons of a Brazilian Indian chieftain. Natalicio and Antenor Lima, who were raised in the jungle town of Ceara, had a one-off transatlantic hit with a melodious instrumental remake of a Mexican tune that Jimmy Dorsey & His Orchestra (featuring vocalist Bob Eberly) had taken to the top in 1941.

### DALE & GRACE
I'M LEAVING IT UP TO YOU
*Montel*

When Dale Houston's solo version of Don & Dewey's 1956 R&B hit did not work out, producer/label owner Sam Montel recruited

teenager Grace Broussard to record it with him. Their version became the fourth single by a duo to top the US chart in 1963. The single stood at No 1 on the day President Kennedy died, and coincidentally the duo were among the crowd watching the Presidential motorcade in Dallas that day. In 1974, Donny and Marie Osmond's revival reached the transatlantic Top 5.

### ELVIS PRESLEY
BOSSA NOVA BABY
*RCA*

Elvis boarded the bossa nova bandwagon with a version of a Jerry Leiber and Mike Stoller floor-filler that had previously been recorded by Tippie & The Clovers. Incidentally, this song taken from his film *Fun In Acapulco* was his smallest UK hit since 1956.

### LESLEY GORE
SHE'S A FOOL
*Mercury*

America's hottest new teen sensation added to her hits with a song penned by Ben Raleigh and Mark Barkan. Between them, the writers had written top sellers for acts like Connie Francis, Adam Wade, Eddie Fisher and Johnny Mathis.

### TOMMY ROE
EVERYBODY
*ABC Paramount*

A song he wrote on the plane back to the US, after headlining a UK tour with The Beatles, gave the performer from Georgia his second transatlantic Top 10 hit. In 1976 a re-recording on Monument sold relatively few copies.

### BOBBY BARE
500 MILES AWAY FROM
HOME
*RCA*

In 1958, Bare's voice was heard on Bill Parson's million-selling novelty rocker 'All American Boy'. The singer/songwriter's biggest hit under his own name came with his adaptation of an old folk favourite '500 Miles'. It was the third of 70 singles that the performer put into the country charts.

### SINGING NUN (SOEUR SOURIRE)
DOMINIQUE
*Philips*

The first female singer to hold down the top spot on the singles and album charts simultaneously was a Belgian nun known as Soeur Sourire (born Jeanine Deckers). 'Dominique', a self-penned ode to the founder of the Dominican order, rocketed her into one-hit wonderland. A Hollywood version of the Singing Nun's life story starring Debbie Reynolds was filmed in 1966. After a problematical life she committed suicide in 1985 – two years after her rockier re-recording of 'Dominique' vanished without trace.

### DIXIEBELLES
(DOWN AT) PAPA JOE'S
*SS7*

This trio of session singers from Memphis had two successful Top 20 hits in the US. Bill Justis signed the female act to the label and noted session pianist Jerry Smith composed the song and played on the record. Their equally infectious if somewhat dated follow-up, 'Southtown USA', was one of the first of many hits penned by Billy Sherrill, who became one of the most renowned country producer/songwriters.

# UNITED KINGDOM
# NOVEMBER 1963

### RONETTES
BE MY BABY
*London American*

See US entry (September).

### CLIFF RICHARD
DON'T TALK TO HIM
*Columbia*

Soon after replacing Elvis as the World's Top Male Singer in the *NME* poll, Cliff clocked up his fourth Top 5 hit of the year with a song he composed with Bruce Welch.

### KATHY KIRBY
SECRET LOVE
*Decca*

One of the UK's best-known pre-war bandleaders, Ambrose, discovered and managed the Marilyn Monroe look-a-like songstress, who had four successive Top 20 entries in nine months. Her most lucrative release was an update of a chart-topping ballad from Doris Day's 1954 movie *Calamity Jane*.

### BILLY J. KRAMER & THE DAKOTAS
I'LL KEEP YOU SATISFIED
*Parlophone*

The group voted Best Newcomers of 1963 collected their third consecutive UK Top 5 entry –

all of which were composed by Lennon & McCartney. As the record climbed, Kramer became the first UK beat boom act to visit the US.

## FREDDIE & THE DREAMERS
YOU WERE MADE FOR ME
*Columbia*

▲ 3
⑩ 3
303/500

Only Lennon & McCartney had more UK hits in 1963 than songwriter Mitch Murray, who composed the energetic act's third successive Top 5 entry. Eighteen months later the catchy single narrowly missed entering the US Top 20.

## LOS INDIOS TABAJARAS
MARIA ELENA
*RCA*

▲ 5
⑩ 1•
—/500

See US entry.

# UNITED STATES
# DECEMBER 1963

## KINGSMEN
LOUIE LOUIE
*Wand*

▲ 2
⑩ 1
216/500

Richard Berry wrote and recorded this West Indian-influenced, Latin-laced rock epic in 1956. Oregon quintet The Kingsmen based their ground-breaking garage version on a later, more manic, interpretation by the Fabulous Wailers. The low-budget muzzy track was helped on its way by an FBI investigation into its suspected obscene lyrics. Lead vocalist Jack Ely left after the hit and cut 'Louie Louie 66' and 'Louie Go Home'. 'Louie Louie' became one of the most recorded and best-loved songs of the rock era.

## CARAVELLES
YOU DON'T HAVE TO BE A BABY TO CRY
*Smash*

▲ 3
⑩ 1•
427/500

See UK entry (August).

## BEACH BOYS
BE TRUE TO YOUR SCHOOL
*Capitol*

▲ 6
⑩ 3
—/500

Female vocal group The Honeys joined the surf superstars on this Brian Wilson-penned high school anthem. For the third time in a row, both sides of their single reached the Top 40. A year after the hit Wilson wed Honeys member Marilyn Rovell.

## RUFUS THOMAS
WALKING THE DOG
*ABC*

▲ 10
⑩ 1•
—/500

Veteran R&B DJ and performer Thomas walked four successive 'dog' discs into the Top 100. The most successful was a self-penned stomper that The Rolling Stones recorded on their first album. The entertainer, whose daughter Carla was notching up pop hits before him, also scored with songs which mentioned a bear cat, a chicken and a penguin in the titles.

## LENNY WELCH
SINCE I FELL FOR YOU
*Cadence*

▲ 4
⑩ 1•
440/500

One of the most recorded R&B ballads gave this Asbury Park-born, MOR-oriented singer the biggest of his seven US chart entries in the decade. The song was written and originally released by band leader/vocalist Buddy Johnson in 1947. Welch, who had been recording with little success since 1958, based his interpretation on the Harptones 1954 version.

## DION DI MUCI
DRIP DROP
*Columbia*

▲ 6
⑩ 8
—/500

For the second time in a year the singer/songwriter successfully revived a previous Jerry Leiber and Mike Stoller hit that had charted in the mid-1950s by The Drifters. It was his twentieth Top 40 entry and his last Top 10 single for five years.

## BOBBY VINTON
THERE I'VE SAID IT AGAIN
*Epic*

▲ 1
⑩ 4
43/500

A song that Vaughn Monroe had taken to the top in 1945 became Vinton's second successive No 1. Recorded in just one take, it was the last US chart topper before The Beatles monopolized the summit.

## MURMAIDS
POPSICLES AND ICICLES
*Chattahoochee*

▲ 3
⑩ 1•
360/500

David Gates (later of Bread) had his first taste of success as the composer of this clean-cut LA teen trio's only chart entry. The act, which included sisters Carol and Terry Fischer, were produced by the eccentric Kim Fowley. Soon after recording the cute, if silly, song they headed for college and obscurity.

## BOBBY RYDELL
FORGET HIM
*Cameo*

▲ 4
⑩ 6•
473/500

Rydell registered the last of 18 US Top 40 entries with a song written and produced in London by Tony Hatch. As with many other American acts, the British invasion almost destroyed his fan following. He boarded The Beatles bandwagon by cutting Lennon & McCartney's 'A World Without Love' but Peter & Gordon's version easily outsold his.

## JOHNNY TILLOTSON
TALK BACK TREMBLING LIPS
*MGM*

▲ 7
⑩ 4•
—/500

The pop/country artist had the last of his six Top 20 singles with a commercial cover version of a superior John D. Loudermilk song, which Ernest Ashworth had taken to the top of the country chart. Like many other American solo acts, Tillotson's sales slumped when the British began to monopolize the US airwaves.

# UNITED KINGDOM
# DECEMBER 1963

## DAVE CLARK FIVE
GLAD ALL OVER
*Columbia*

▲ 1
⑩ 1
57/500

The first UK group to crack the US charts after The Beatles were this London-based quintet. The act's initial hit came with their third release on their third label. It was a bass drum-heavy stomper composed by Clark and the quintet's keyboard-playing vocalist Mike Smith, which sold almost a million in the UK alone. To the group's annoyance, Epic Records in the US erred by describing the single as 'The Mersey Sound with the Liverpool beat'.

## DUSTY SPRINGFIELD
I ONLY WANT TO
BE WITH YOU
*Philips*

▲ 4
⑩ 1
338/500

Dusty's debut solo single was the first song ever heard on UK TV's longest-running music show, *Top of The Pops*. The ex-lead vocalist of The Springfields took this Mike Hawker and Ivor Raymonde foot-tapper into the transatlantic Top 20. The contagious composition also reached the charts on both sides of the Atlantic by the Bay City Rollers in 1976, The Tourists (with Annie Lennox) in 1979 and Samantha Fox in 1989.

## BEATLES
I WANT TO HOLD
YOUR HAND
*Parlophone*

▲ 1
⑩ 4
26/500

This was the single that started the UK invasion of the US charts. In the UK, it sold over a million in a record three days and replaced the group's 'She Loves You' at the top. The Beatles aimed the single at the US and their aim was true – thanks partly to a massive promotional push, the single rocketed to No 1. It is the biggest-selling UK single of all time, with world sales of over 15 million.

## SINGING NUN
DOMINIQUE
*Philips*

▲ 7
⑩ 1•
—/500

See US entry (November).

## GENE PITNEY
TWENTY-FOUR HOURS
FROM TULSA
*Stax*

▲ 4
⑩ 1
458/500

The one-time leader of doo-wop group The Embers was one of the most successful American artists in the UK in the Swinging Sixties. This memorable song was penned by Burt Bacharach and Hal David, who had also written three of Pitney's other eight US hits to date.

# UNITED STATES
# JANUARY 1964

## MARTHA & THE VANDELLAS
QUICKSAND
*Gordy*

▲ 8
🔟 2
—/500

The trio, who started by singing backing vocals for Marvin Gaye, scored their second successive Top 10 entry with another up-tempo Holland, Dozier & Holland R&B gem.

## SHIRLEY ELLIS
THE NITTY GRITTY
*Congress*

▲ 8
🔟 1
—/500

When the gospel-rooted New Yorker got down to the real nitty gritty she racked up three Top 10 entries in less than 15 months. All of her big hits were written by her husband/manager Lincoln Chase, who had previously penned R&B crossover hits 'Such A Night' and 'Jim Dandy' and the English lyric to the 1961 chart topper 'Wonderland By Night'. The singer, who had also recorded as Shirley Elliston, followed this single with the less rewarding '(That's) What The Nitty Gritty Is'.

## JOEY POWERS
MIDNIGHT MARY
*Amy*

▲ 10
🔟 1•
—/500

Fame was fleeting for the one-time wrestling coach at Ohio State University, his only best-seller being a semi-suggestive song written by regular chart visitor Ben Raleigh and Artie Wayne. The unlikely named Lorna Dune released an answer record, 'Midnight Joey'.

## TRASHMEN
SURFIN' BIRD
*Garrett*

▲ 4
🔟 1•
482/500

If proof was needed that it is not necessary to be a good vocalist to have a hit, then listen to this top-notch garage rock band from Minneapolis/St Paul.

The group, whom many consider aptly named, were fronted by Dal Winslow, whose gravelly voice you either love or hate. Both this hit and their Top 40 follow-up 'Bird Dance Beat' were based on earlier R&B hits by the much underrated Rivingtons.

## RIP CHORDS
HEY LITTLE COBRA
*Columbia*

▲ 4
🔟 1•
447/500

One of the biggest hot rod hits came from a LA-based session group that included Beach Boy Bruce Johnson and Doris Day's talented son Terry Melcher. The most popular of the act's five chart entries was composed by Carol Connors (born Annette Kleinbard), who had been a member of Phil Spector's first hit act, The Teddy Bears.

## MARKETTS
OUT OF LIMITS
*Warner*

▲ 3
🔟 1•
416/500

This West Coast session group achieved their biggest hit with an instrumental based on the theme from the popular TV series *Outer Limits* (they had to amend the title when threatened with a lawsuit). At times the combo, whose 'Surfer's Stomp' was the first surf-titled hit, included Leon Russell, Jim Gordon and Glen Campbell. They were assembled from the same pool of musicians as B. Bumble & The Stingers and The Routers.

## JAN & DEAN
DRAG CITY
*Liberty*

▲ 10
🔟 4
—/500

When drag racing became more hip than surfing, the Los Angeles duo changed their allegiance from 'Surf City' to 'Drag City'. They later offered musical tickets to 'Fun City' and 'Folk City', but few journeyed with them then.

## BEATLES
I WANT TO HOLD YOUR HAND
*Capitol*

▲ 1
🔟 1
5/500

The single that introduced The Beatles to the US broke down the long-standing barriers that had prevented most UK records from scoring Stateside. See also UK entry (December 1963).

## MAJOR LANCE
UM, UM, UM, UM, UM, UM
*Okeh*

▲ 5
🔟 2•
—/500

Curtis Mayfield wrote and produced the single that gave the R&B vocalist the third of his four consecutive Top 20 entries. In the UK, this undeniably commercial opus transported Wayne Fontana & The Mindbenders into the Top 20 for the first time. Lance, whose many other recordings failed to sustain his popularity, died in 1994 from heart failure.

# UNITED KINGDOM
# JANUARY 1964

## SWINGING BLUE JEANS
HIPPY HIPPY SHAKE
*HMV*

▲ 2
🔟 1
242/500

In the film *The World Of Suzie Wong*, the star, Nancy Kwan, often prefaced her sentences with 'For goodness' sake'. This phrase inspired Latin rocker Chan Romero to pen 'Hippy Hippy Shake'. Four years later, long-time Merseyside favourites The Swinging Blue Jeans, who had first introduced The Beatles to Liverpool's Cavern Club, had their biggest hit with a lively remake of it. The group's version also reached the US Top 40 – a feat Romero had failed to achieve.

## HOLLIES
STAY
*Parlophone*

▲ 8
🔟 1
—/500

One of most successful acts ever to come from Manchester earned the second of 21 successive Top 20 entries with 'Stay'. It was an updated version of a song which had been taken to the top of the US chart in 1960 by composer Maurice Williams & The Zodiacs. Unlike many other British groups, The Hollies were not instantly accepted in the US. The big hits only came after they curtailed their cover versions and concentrated on original material.

## BIG DEE IRWIN
SWINGING ON A STAR
*Colpix*

▲ 7
🔟 1•
—/500

The rotund American R&B performer (born Defosca Ervin) had his only major hit with a beat revival of an Oscar-winning song composed for the Bing Crosby movie *Going My Way*. The one-time leader of hit doo-wop group The Pastels was accompanied on the track by hit maker Little Eva. Interestingly, on Crosby's chart-topping 1944 recording he was joined by a youthful Andy Williams. Irwin subsequently released several noteworthy soul singles which the public ignored.

## SEARCHERS
NEEDLES AND PINS
*Pye*

▲ 1
🔟 3
81/500

Jackie DeShannon first recorded the Sonny Bono (of Sonny & Cher fame) composition which gave the unmistakable quartet their biggest transatlantic hit. However, The Searchers learnt it from Cliff Bennett & The Rebel Rousers' (whose bass player Frank Allen subsequently joined The Searchers) live rendition. Smokie shipped this superior pop song back into the UK Top 10 in 1977.

## BRENDA LEE
AS USUAL
*Brunswick*

| ▲ 5 |
| ⑩ 7• |
| —/500 |

As usual, the young superstar had a top seller with this Alex Zanetis-composed ballad. Soon afterwards, she became one of the first American acts to board the British bandwagon. Her last transatlantic Top 20 hit, 'Is It True', was produced in the UK by Mickie Most and featured guitarist Jimmy Page.

## GERRY & THE PACEMAKERS
I'M THE ONE
*Columbia*

| ▲ 2 |
| ⑩ 4 |
| 272/500 |

After three No 1 singles, this record-breaking Merseybeat act narrowly missed the top spot with a song penned by lead singer Gerry Marsden.

# UNITED STATES
# FEBRUARY 1964

## LESLEY GORE
YOU DON'T OWN ME
*Mercury*

| ▲ 2 |
| ⑩ 4• |
| 309/500 |

As Beatlemania took hold, the 17-year-old vocalist had the last of four successive Top 5 entries. John Madara composed this noteworthy song with ex-Danny & The Juniors member David White. Later in her career, Gore recorded for such labels as Motown and A&M, but by then her fan base had all but dissolved.

## DIONNE WARWICK
ANYONE WHO HAD A HEART
*Scepter*

| ▲ 8 |
| ⑩ 1 |
| —/500 |

One of the decade's biggest-selling female singers started her recording career as a session vocalist, and frequently cut song demos for Burt Bacharach. It was this celebrated composer who penned and produced the majority of her 20 Top 40 entries in the 1960s. In the UK, a cover version of the heartfelt ballad by Cilla Black topped the chart.

## RICK NELSON
FOR YOU
*Decca*

| ▲ 6 |
| ⑩17 |
| —/500 |

Soon after Decca paid $1 million for his contract, Nelson notched up his last major hit of the decade with a beat rendition of the 1930 song 'For You'. It was composed by Al Dubin and Joe Burke, whose other hits included 'Tip-Toe Through The Tulips'. Nelson returned briefly to the Top 10 in 1972 with the highly touted 'Garden Party', which name-dropped several of the one-time teenage idol's 1960s hits.

## BEATLES
SHE LOVES YOU
*Swan*

| ▲ 1 |
| ⑩ 2 |
| 55/500 |

This classic pop single replaced the group's ground-breaking 'I Want To Hold Your Hand' at the top. See also UK entry (September 1963).

## AL HIRT
JAVA
*RCA*

| ▲ 4 |
| ⑩ 1• |
| 435/500 |

The bearded New Orleans-born Dixieland trumpeter had nine US Top 40 albums during the 1960s. His biggest single was named after a famous racehorse and had originally been released on

Hirt's label, RCA, by its composer Allen Toussaint (writer of the 1961 topper 'Mother-In-Law') under the name Tousan. It came from Hirt's album *Honey In The Horn,* which held the No 3 place on the chart behind The Beatles' first two LPs.

## TAMS
WHAT KIND OF FOOL (DO YOU THINK I AM)
*ABC*

One of the pioneering beach music acts had their sole US Top 40 hit with a song composed by fellow Atlanta resident Ray Whitley and produced by later chart regular Rick Hall. In 1971, the soulful Joe Pope-fronted quintet's 1964 version of Whitley's 'Hey Girl Don't Bother Me' topped the UK chart when re-released there.

## FOUR SEASONS
DAWN (GO AWAY)
*Philips*

A track recorded in December 1963 (which, coincidentally, was the title of the group's last chart topper) gave the Four Seasons their first hit on Philips and their fifth Top 5 single in 18 months.

## RIVIERAS
CALIFORNIA SUN
*Riviera*

A high school band from Indiana had their day in the sun with a quickly recorded, sped-up version of a good-time song that R&B performer Joe Jones had charted with in 1961. Vocalist Marty

Fortson left the group shortly after they cut their only hit, and the sextet (who should not be confused with the 1950s doo-wop act of the same name) disbanded after a few disappointing follow-ups.

## DIANE RENAY
NAVY BLUE
*20th Century*

This vocalist from Philadelphia (born Diane Kushner) sailed into the Top 40 with two consecutive singles, 'Navy Blue' and 'Kiss Me Sailor', before sinking without trace. The single was written by singer/songwriter Eddie Rambeau (who charted the next year with 'Concrete And Clay') and produced by the Four Seasons' mentor Bob Crewe.

## BEATLES
PLEASE PLEASE ME
*Vee Jay*

On 14 March 1964 this single completed the treble for The Beatles – it was the first time an act had simultaneously held the top three places in the US chart. See also UK entry (February 1963).

## DALE & GRACE
STOP AND THINK IT OVER
*Montel*

This duo from Louisiana made it two Top 10 entries in a row with a song penned by Jake Graffagnino. Not long afterwards, Dale & Grace stopped and thought it over and decided to go their separate ways.

# UNITED KINGDOM
# FEBRUARY 1964

**FRANK IFIELD**
DON'T BLAME ME
*Columbia*

▲ 8
⑩ 6•
—/500

The singer, who specialized in giving pop/country treatments to standards, had his last major success with a Dorothy Fields and Jimmy McHugh song that had been written for the 1933 movie *Dinner At Eight*. For a year, Ifield's sales had been virtually unaffected by the rise of the beat groups; however, his days as a chart regular were now coming to an end.

**BACHELORS**
DIANE
*Decca*

▲ 1
⑩ 2
143/500

The Dublin trio's first two Top 10 entries, 'Charmaine' and 'Diane', were written by Lew Pollack and Erno Rapee in 1927. This was the first record by an Irish group to head the UK chart and the first to reach the US Top 10.

**MANFRED MANN**
5-4-3-2-1
*HMV*

▲ 5
⑩ 1
—/500

South African keyboard player Mann (born Michael Lubowitz) led the most jazz-influenced of the British R&B bands. After two small-selling singles, they made their chart debut with a self-composed number that was used as the theme for the top-rated UK pop TV show *Ready Steady Go*. In the US, noted jazz label Prestige released the single, but it vanished without trace.

**MERSEYBEATS**
I THINK OF YOU
*Fontana*

▲ 5
⑩ 1•
—/500

They may have had one of the corniest names, but The Merseybeats were one of the most innovative UK acts of the era. The quartet, who specialized in ballads rather than beat, reached the Top 20 with

two successive singles penned by Peter Lee Stirling (aka Daniel Boone), 'I Think Of You' and 'Don't Turn Around'.

**CILLA BLACK**
ANYONE WHO HAD A HEART
*Parlophone*

▲ 1
⑩ 1
74/500

Manager Brian Epstein's first female client hit the top with her second UK release. It was her interpretation of Dionne Warwick's debut US Top 10 hit, composed by Burt Bacharach and Hal David. This emotionally charged single, which almost passed the million sales barrier in the UK alone, headed the first all-UK Top 10 singles chart.

**CLIFF RICHARD**
I'M THE LONELY ONE
*Columbia*

▲ 8
⑩23
—/500

Britain's most successful male vocalist had success with a song composed by Gordon Mills, who later managed Cliff's biggest rivals for that title, Tom Jones and Engelbert Humperdinck.

**DAVE CLARK FIVE**
BITS AND PIECES
*Columbia*

▲ 2
⑩ 2
270/500

The combo amassed over 250,000 advance orders in the UK for their second stomper. This self-composed rocker joined 'Glad All Over' in the US Top 10.

**BRIAN POOLE & THE TREMELOES**
CANDY MAN
*Decca*

▲ 6
⑩ 3
—/500

One of the most successful groups from the south of England charted with a Fred Neil composition, which Roy Orbison had earlier released on the B side of 'Crying'.

# UNITED STATES
# MARCH 1964

## BEACH BOYS
FUN, FUN, FUN
*Capitol*

▲ 5
⑩ 4
—/500

Undaunted by the arrival of The Beatles, this innovative all-American family group continued to write their own chapter in rock history with a Brian Wilson-penned summertime smash.

## BOBBY GOLDSBORO
SEE THE FUNNY LITTLE CLOWN
*UA*

▲ 9
⑩ 1
—/500

As his first major hit was breaking, the singer/songwriter and guitarist was working as a member of Roy Orbison's backing band. This self-composed song was produced by Jack Gold and was one of 19 US chart entries by the Florida-born performer through the 1960s.

## AL MARTINO
I LOVE YOU MORE AND MORE EVERY DAY
*Capitol*

▲ 9
⑩ 3•
—/500

One of the decade's most successful MOR artists hit the heights with a ballad composed by the noted Nashville session pianist Don Robertson. In 1973, a version by Sonny James reached the country Top 10.

## BEATLES
TWIST AND SHOUT
*Tollie*

▲ 2
⑩ 4
250/500

In their homeland, this track was released on an EP which charted alongside a similarly styled version by Brian Poole & The Tremeloes in the *NME* Top 5. In the US, it joined three other Beatles singles already in the Top 4!

## LOUIS ARMSTRONG
HELLO, DOLLY!
*Kapp*

▲ 1
⑩ 1•
51/500

'Satchmo' is the oldest artist to ever head the US or UK charts. At the age of 63, he ended The Beatles' run of three consecutive No 1s with his Grammy-winning interpretation of the title song from Jerry Herman's Broadway musical. The unmistakable gravel-voiced jazz trumpeter and entertainer also topped the album charts with *Hello Dolly*. In 1969, the internationally renowned ambassador of American music sang 'Hello Dolly' to Barbra Streisand in the film version of the musical.

## TERRY STAFFORD
SUSPICION
*Crusader*

▲ 3
⑩ 1•
354/500

A Doc Pomus and Mort Shuman song that Elvis Presley had recorded on the 1962 album *Pot Luck* gave this Presley-esque performer from Oklahoma his biggest hit. When Presley's version was released, on the B side of his mid-table hit 'Kiss Me Quick', it was too late to slow down the progress of Stafford's carefully cloned cover.

## BOBBY VINTON
MY HEART BELONGS TO ONLY YOU
*Epic*

▲ 9
⑩ 5
—/500

The top-selling song stylist had his fourth successive Top 10 entry with a winning ballad that June Christy had clicked with in 1953.

## DAVE CLARK FIVE
GLAD ALL OVER
*Epic*

▲ 6
⑩ 1
—/500

See UK entry (December 1963).

# UNITED KINGDOM
# MARCH 1964

## BILLY J. KRAMER & THE DAKOTAS
LITTLE CHILDREN
*Parlophone*

▲ 1
🔟 4
120/500

Mort Shuman, who penned many outstanding rock hits, composed this popular band's biggest US hit. It was the first non-Lennon & McCartney single they released.

## ROLLING STONES
NOT FADE AWAY
*Decca*

▲ 3
🔟 1
348/500

After charting with cover versions of songs first recorded by Chuck Berry and The Beatles, the UK's most exciting R&B band debuted in the Top 10 with a Bo Diddley-styled update of an earlier Crickets B side. Buddy Holly had penned the rebellious quintet's first US Top 100 entry with his producer Norman Petty.

## HOLLIES
JUST ONE LOOK
*Parlophone*

▲ 2
🔟 2
284/500

Their treatment of Doris Troy's 1963 US hit was the fourth consecutive cover of an R&B song to crack the chart for the Manchester group. When re-issued three years later, it almost entered the US Top 40.

## EDEN KANE
BOYS CRY
*Fontana*

▲ 8
🔟 5•
—/500

The rise of beat groups put the brakes on Kane's career. However, before the stylish performer boarded the bus to chart oblivion, he recruited a group of his own, The Downbeats, and together they charted with a memorable song written by Buddy Kaye and Tommy Scott. Soon afterwards, the singer relocated to Australia, before moving on to Los Angeles where he worked in real estate.

## KATHY KIRBY
LET ME GO, LOVER
*Decca*

▲ 10
🔟 2•
—/500

The youthful cabaret entertainer earned her second successive Top 10 entry with another mid-1950s hit. The song, which started life as the temperance tune 'Let Me Go Devil', had been a 1955 hit in the UK for Teresa Brewer, Joan Weber, Dean Martin and Ruby Murray. Incidentally, the photogenic Kirby was voted Top UK Female Singer in the 1963 *NME* poll.

## JIM REEVES
I LOVE YOU BECAUSE
*RCA*

▲ 5
🔟 2
208/500

'Gentleman' Jim spent 47 weeks in the UK chart with his revival of the romantic 1950 Leon Payne/Ernest Tubb country ballad. The song had been a Top 10 hit in the US a year earlier by Al Martino.

## BEATLES
CAN'T BUY ME LOVE
*Parlophone*

▲ 1
🔟 5
96/500

With unprecedented advance orders of over two million in the US and one million in the UK, this single topped the US charts in an unprecedented two weeks – a record not bettered until 1995.

## GENE PITNEY
THAT GIRL BELONGS TO YESTERDAY
*UA*

▲ 8
🔟 2
—/500

The success of this hit composed by Rolling Stones members Mick Jagger and Keith Richard encouraged them to release their own songs on the A sides of Stones' singles.

## BACHELORS
I BELIEVE
*Decca*

▲ 2
⑩ 3
207/500

A song that Frankie Laine had topped the UK chart with for 18 weeks in 1953 added to the sweet harmony trio's stockpile of hits. A version by Robson Green and Jerome Flynn headed the UK chart in 1995.

# UNITED STATES
# APRIL 1964

## BEATLES
CAN'T BUY ME LOVE
*Capitol*

▲ 1
⑩ 5
48/500

The record-shattering group's third successive US No 1 completed an all-Beatles US Top 5! At times the quartet had an unprecedented 14 singles in the Top 100 and accounted for 60 per cent of all record sales in the US! See also UK entry (March).

## BETTY EVERETT
SHOOP SHOOP SONG
(IT'S IN HIS KISS)
*Vee Jay*

▲ 6
⑩ 1
—/500

Seven years after her recording debut, this Mississippi soul singer had the biggest solo hit of her career with a hook-filled Rudy Clark song, which had earlier been released by Merry Clayton. In the UK, it finally reached the Top 40 in 1968, and an update by Cher in 1991 topped the chart.

## SERENDIPITY SINGERS
DON'T LET THE RAIN
COME DOWN (CROOKED
LITTLE MAN)
*Philips*

▲ 6
⑩ 1•
—/500

Rockabilly singer/songwriter Ersel Hickey composed this nine-piece pop/folk outfit's biggest hit. The group, who had formed at the University of Colorado, also piloted their eponymous debut

LP into the Top 20. Despite much campus and club work, the New Christy Minstrels-styled entourage only managed one more Top 40 entry, the novelty 'Beans In My Ears'.

## BEATLES
DO YOU WANT TO KNOW
A SECRET
*Vee Jay*

▲ 2
⑩ 6
312/500

A song that John Lennon initially intended George Harrison to sing went to the heights in the UK by Billy J. Kramer & The Dakotas. However, in the US it was The Beatles' original recording that grabbed all the sales.

## JAN & DEAN
DEAD MAN'S CURVE
*Liberty*

▲ 8
⑩ 5
—/500

This disaster record gave the ground-breaking duo their fourth consecutive Top 20 entry. Ironically, in 1966 co-writer Jan (Berry) was critically injured in an automobile accident similar to the one described in the song. Jan & Dean's 1978 TV biopic was named after this hit.

## DAVE CLARK FIVE
BITS AND PIECES
*Epic*

▲ 4
⑩ 2
477/500

See UK entry (February).

## MARY WELLS
MY GUY
*Motown*

▲ 1
⑩ 4•
109/500

Smokey Robinson's classic song gave Motown its first US chart topper and its first major UK hit. 'My Guy' was also Wells' last single for the label before heading to 20th Century and relative obscurity. Interestingly, she toured the UK with The Beatles in 1964 and was voted Top Female Singer in Britain. In 1972, the record re-entered the UK Top 20. The singer, who in total notched up 12 US Top 40 entries, died of cancer in 1992 aged 49.

# UNITED KINGDOM
# APRIL 1964

## PETER & GORDON
A WORLD WITHOUT LOVE
*Columbia*

▲ 1
⑩ 1
137/500

School friends Peter Asher and Gordon Waller's recording career had a fairytale start when their debut disc became a transatlantic No 1. The song, which pop idol Bobby Rydell covered unsuccessfully in the US, had previously been rejected by Billy J. Kramer. It was the eighth UK No 1 composed by Lennon & McCartney in 14 months, and the fifth US No 1 they had penned in just 22 weeks!

## APPLEJACKS
TELL ME WHEN
*Decca*

▲ 7
⑩ 1•
—/500

This youthful sextet from Birmingham (which included two Sunday school teachers) had two Top 20 entries in succession. The clean-cut act's highest-placed hit was a bouncy pop jewel composed by two of the decade's most eminent UK songsmiths, Geoff Stevens and Les Reed. Their other major hit came with the little-known Lennon & McCartney composition 'Like Dreamers Do'. (The American hit-making Applejacks on Cameo are a different act.)

## MILLIE
MY BOY LOLLIPOP
*Fontana*

▲ 2
⑩ 1•
236/500

Effervescent 17-year-old Jamaican vocalist Millie (known as Millie Small in the US) had the biggest-selling blue beat hit with a song that had few takers when first released in 1956. Even though her cute rendition was not too dissimilar to that of Barbie Gaie's original recording, Millie took it into the runner-up position on both sides of the Atlantic. 'My Boy Lollipop', which was written by one-time Cadillacs member Bobby Spencer, returned to the UK Top 10 in 1982 by 2-tone band Bad Manners.

## SEARCHERS
DON'T THROW YOUR
LOVE AWAY
*Pye*

▲ 1
⑩ 4
146/500

One-hit wonder instrumentalist Kokomo (real name Jimmy Wisner) composed this group's second successive No 1. The song had started life as the B side of an Orlons single.

# UNITED STATES
# MAY 1964

## FOUR SEASONS
RONNIE
*Philips*

This unmistakable vocal combo added to their hit list with another potent Bob Gaudio and Bob Crewe composition.

## DANNY WILLIAMS
WHITE ON WHITE
*UA*

After his run of UK bestsellers had ended, South African song stylist Williams had his only major US hit with a romantic ballad from the pens of Bernice Ross and Lor Crane.

## BEATLES
LOVE ME DO
*Tollie*

Amazingly, The Beatles' first release, which had only been a mid-table UK hit in 1962, gave the Fab Four their fourth US No 1 in four months. Unlike the earlier UK release, the US single featured Andy White and not Ringo on drums.

## ROY ORBISON
IT'S OVER
*Monument*

In the UK, this powerful self-penned lost-love lament became the first American record to reach No 1 for almost a year. 'It's Over' was later included on separate *Greatest Hits* collections which topped the UK charts in 1975 and 1988.

## DIXIE CUPS
CHAPEL OF LOVE
*Red Bird*

A female R&B trio from New Orleans, who had been discovered by Joe Jones (of 'You Talk Too Much' fame), directed the first release on Jerry Leiber and Mike Stoller's label Red Bird to the top. Ellie Greenwich, Jeff Barry and Phil Spector penned this simplistic pop masterpiece, and the former two produced it. Spector, incidentally, had earlier cut it with his protégés The Ronettes. Interestingly, the Dixie Cups were not too enamoured at first with the song that put them on the musical map.

## RAY CHARLES SINGERS
LOVE ME WITH ALL
YOUR HEART
*Command*

Surprisingly, at the height of Beatlemania, this MOR singing group had a million seller with an English version of the Italian song 'Cuando Calienta El Sol'. It was the first major hit for the veteran vocal team led by conductor/arranger Charles (born Charles Offenberg). The Emmy-winning ensemble were previously best known on both sides of the Atlantic as the backing singers on Perry Como' successful TV show.

## REFLECTIONS
(JUST LIKE)
ROMEO & JULIET
*Golden World*

One of the last doo-wop-influenced acts to chart in the 1960s were also one of the only white acts on the Detroit R&B label Golden World. A Freddie Gorman (composer of 'Please Mr Postman') song, that the vocal harmony outfit considered to be a frivolous throwaway, gave them their only noticeable hit. The public did not particularly like the similar-sounding follow-ups 'Like Columbus Did' and 'Like Adam & Eve', but the group's mid-table single 'Poor Man's Son' was big in the UK when covered by the Rockin' Berries.

## PETER & GORDON
A WORLD WITHOUT LOVE
*Capitol*

▲ 1
🔟 1
179/500

See UK entry (April).

## BILLY J. KRAMER & THE DAKOTAS
LITTLE CHILDREN
*Imperial*

▲ 7
🔟 1
—/500

See UK entry (March).

## DIONNE WARWICK
WALK ON BY
*Scepter*

▲ 6
🔟 2
—/500

This easy-listening/R&B song stylist had her first transatlantic Top 10 entry with a enduring lost-love ballad composed by Burt Bacharach and Hal David. Isaac Hayes brought it back into the Top 40 in 1969, and in 1990 a dance version by Sybil strolled into the UK Top 10.

# UNITED KINGDOM
# MAY 1964

## GERRY & THE PACEMAKERS
DON'T LET THE SUN CATCH YOU CRYING
*Columbia*

▲ 6
🔟 5
—/500

The Liverpool group's fifth consecutive UK Top 10 entry started their run of US hits. Lead singer Gerry Marsden penned the song, which was first released by Louise Cordet.

## DORIS DAY
MOVE OVER DARLING
*CBS*

One of the most popular film stars and recording artists of the 1950s had a UK-only hit with the title tune from her latest movie. The film was co-produced by her husband Marty Melcher and the song part-written by their son Terry. In 1983 another singing actress, Tracey Ullman, returned the semi-suggestive song to the UK Top 10.

## MOJOS
EVERYTHING'S ALRIGHT
*Decca*

This youthful Liverpool quintet's second single was one of the year's most original and interesting UK R&B-styled releases. The infectious self-composed 'Everything's Alright' was the first of

three successive Top 40 entries for the group, who disbanded in 1966. Lead singer Stu James (Stuart Slater) went on to become one of the UK music industry's top executives.

## MIGIL FIVE
MOCKINGBIRD HILL
*Pye*

Transatlantic hit maker Kenny Ball helped these London-based one-time jazz musicians secure a recording deal with his label Pye. The band's commercial success centred around their second single, a blue-eyed blue beat re-tread of the 1951 smash 'Mockingbird Hill'. The follow-up, a similarly styled revival of a 1947 No 1, 'Near You', was the act's last chart entry.

## FOUR PENNIES
JULIET
*Philips*

This talented Lancashire quartet were the only chart-topping UK band in 1964 not to score Stateside. Their second single, 'Juliet', which was initially intended to be the B side, was the first and biggest of the act's four UK Top 20 entries. In 1976, the group re-formed and re-recorded the haunting self-penned ballad. This time, however, 'Juliet' earned them few pennies.

## DIONNE WARWICK
WALK ON BY
*Pye International*

▲ 9
⑩ 1
—/500

See US entry.

## ROY ORBISON
IT'S OVER
*London American*

▲ 1
⑩ 7
60/500

See US entry.

## CLIFF RICHARD
CONSTANTLY
*Columbia*

▲ 4
⑩24
486/500

'L'edera' was the original title of the song that gave the UK's most consistent Top 10 entrant his biggest hit of 1964. It was the first Italian composition he had released as an A side and one of his few recordings to date without The Shadows.

## FOURMOST
A LITTLE LOVING
*Parlophone*

▲ 6
⑩ 2•
—/500

This archetypal Merseybeat band chalked up half a dozen UK Top 40 entries from 1963–65. Their third consecutive Top 20 entry was composed by Russell Alquist. As the record climbed the chart, the zany outfit started an eight-month residency at the world-famous London Palladium. In 1965, the group faded, alongside the musical style that made them famous.

## CILLA BLACK
YOU'RE MY WORLD
*Parlophone*

▲ 1
⑩ 2
59/500

Carl Sigman, composer of No 1 hits 'Answer Me', 'The Day The Rains Came Down' and It's All In The Game', wrote the English lyrics to this Italian ballad which gave Black her second successive chart topper. In the US the song was her only Top 40 entry, and in 1977 Helen Reddy took it into the Top 20.

## SHADOWS
THE RISE & FALL OF
FLINGEL BUNT
*Columbia*

▲ 5
⑩13
—/500

This self-penned single was voted Top Instrumental Record of the Year in the *MM* poll. Incidentally, despite the rise of many other UK groups in the US, all The Shadows' releases fell by the wayside there.

## CHUCK BERRY
NO PARTICULAR PLACE
TO GO
*Pye International*

▲ 3
⑩ 2
472/500

See US entry (July 1964).

# UNITED STATES
# JUNE 1964

## BEATLES
PS I LOVE YOU
*Tollie*

Surprisingly, the moptops' eighth Top 10 entry in five months was the B side of their first single 'Love Me Do', which had been recorded at the group's first EMI session in September 1962.

## BARBRA STREISAND
PEOPLE
*Columbia*

One of the world's most successful and popular performers made her singles chart debut with a show-stopping song from her Broadway musical *Funny Girl*. The ever-popular ballad was composed by Jule Styne and top 1950s tunesmith Bob Merrill, and this vocalist's rendition of it won the multi-talented New Yorker a Grammy for Best Female Performance. The track came from Streisand's fourth Top 10 album in a year, *Funny Girl*. A version by R&B group The Tymes reached the Top 40 in 1968.

## BEACH BOYS
I GET AROUND
*Capitol*

A year after his song 'Surf City' topped the chart by Jan & Dean, Brian Wilson's ground-breaking group collected their first No 1 with one of his pop gems. This stand-out single also intoduced the unmistakable band to the UK Top 10.

## MILLIE SMALL
MY BOY LOLLIPOP
*Smash*

See UK entry (April).

## GERRY & THE PACEMAKERS
DON'T LET THE SUN CATCH YOU CRYING
*Laurie*

See UK entry (May).

## BACHELORS
DIANE
*London*

See UK entry (February).

## JOHNNY RIVERS
MEMPHIS
*Imperial*

This talented rock star from New York (born Johnny Ramistella) had been recording for eight years on numerous labels before he debuted on the chart. The track that started his impressive run of hits was his live version (cut at the Whisky A Go-Go in LA) of a well-known Chuck Berry composition. Only a year before, 'Memphis' had reached the US Top 10 for guitarist Lonnie Mack and climbed into the UK Top 20 by both Berry himself and Dave Berry.

## BILLY J. KRAMER & THE DAKOTAS
BAD TO ME
*Imperial*

See UK entry (August 1963).

# UNITED KINGDOM
# JUNE 1964

## BRIAN POOLE & THE TREMELOES
SOMEONE SOMEONE
*Decca*

▲ 2
⑩ 4•
248/500

A sentimental ballad, which had been first recorded by The Crickets, gave Poole his last Top 10 hit. It was co-written by Vi Petty, and her husband Norman (The Crickets' producer) played piano on this Mike Smith-produced track. A re-recording by Poole in 1983 went nowhere.

## HOLLIES
HERE I GO AGAIN
*Parlophone*

▲ 4
⑩ 3
—/500

Mort Shuman, composer of some of the greatest hits of the early rock era, teamed with UK songwriter Clive Westlake and produced this punchy pop opus which kept The Hollies on a UK hit roll.

## MARY WELLS
MY GUY
*Stateside*

▲ 5
⑩ 1•
—/500

See US entry (April).

## LULU & THE LUVVERS
SHOUT
*Decca*

▲ 7
⑩ 1•
—/500

This effervescent 15-year-old who, at the outset, was tagged 'Scotland's answer to Brenda Lee', shot up the charts with her debut disc. It was a spirited, if carefully cloned, revival of an Isley Brothers R&B classic from 1959 which Joey Dee & The Starliters had transported into the US Top 10 in 1962. In the US, Lulu's single reached the bottom of the Top 100 in both 1964 and 1967. Interestingly, when the sales of her 1986 re-recording were combined with sales of the original version, 'Shout' re-entered the UK Top 10.

## LOUIS ARMSTRONG
HELLO, DOLLY!
*London American*

▲ 4
⑩ 3
—/500

See US entry (March).

## BACHELORS
RAMONA
*Decca*

▲ 4
⑩ 4
—/500

For the third time the easy-on-the-ear Irish trio hit the Top 10 with a song written before they were born. This time it was a hum-able number that Gene Austin had taken to the top in 1928.

## SWINGING BLUE JEANS
YOU'RE NO GOOD
*HMV*

▲ 3
⑩ 2•
454/500

One of the first, if not one of the most original Merseybeat bands, had the last of three Top 20 entries with their cover of a Clint Ballard Jr composition that Betty Everett had recorded earlier. The song was taken to the top of the US chart in 1975 by Linda Ronstadt. In 1995, a reggae revival by Aswad went into the UK Top 40.

## DAVE CLARK FIVE
CAN'T YOU SEE THAT SHE'S MINE
*Columbia*

▲ 10
⑩ 3
—/500

The mod-dressed combo clocked up their third successive transatlantic Top 10 hit with another Dave Clark and Mike Smith composition. They performed it on the first of the band's record 12 appearances on Ed Sullivan's top-rated US TV Show.

# UNITED STATES
# JULY 1964

## FOUR SEASONS
RAG DOLL
*Philips*

America's hottest group had their biggest UK hit of the decade with the single that rushed them to the top of the US chart for the fourth time in two years. The B side 'Silence is Golden' became a transatlantic hit in 1967 when recycled by The Tremeloes.

## DAVE CLARK FIVE
CAN'T YOU SEE THAT SHE'S MINE
*Epic*

See UK entry (June).

## STAN GETZ/ASTRUD GILBERTO
THE GIRL FROM IPANEMA
*Verve*

This perennial poll-winning jazz saxophonist from Philadelphia had two Top 20 bossa nova hits in the 1960s, both of which were composed by noted Brazilian Antonio Carlos Jobim. Getz teamed with Brazilian vocalist Astrid Gilberto on the single, which was voted Record of the Year at the Grammy awards. Its parent album, *Getz/Gilberto* (which featured Astrid's guitar-playing husband Joao Gilberto), earned the Grammy for Album of the Year.

## CHUCK BERRY
NO PARTICULAR PLACE TO GO
*Chess*

The legendary singer, songwriter and guitarist had his first transatlantic Top 10 entry with a memorable rock gem that was cut from the same cloth as his 1957 hit 'School Day'. No one was particularly surprised when Berry was one of the first acts placed in the Rock and Roll Hall of Fame when it was launched in 1988.

## JAN & DEAN
THE LITTLE OLD LADY (FROM PASADENA)
*Liberty*

A TV sketch by comedian Jack Benny inspired Roger Christian to compose this song about a hot-rod granny who knew how to shut them down. It was one of 15 Top 40 hits recorded by the influential vocal duo before Jan's accident halted their career in 1966.

## ROGER MILLER
DANG ME
*Smash*

In the early 1960s this Nashville-based singer/songwriter wrote pop chart entries for such acts as Andy Williams and Del Shannon. As a recording artist, the Texan performer had several years of small-selling singles before finally making the big time with a self-penned crossover country novelty. Miller won the Grammy for Best New Country Artist, and 'Dang Me' picked up the trophy for Best Country Single and Best Country Song. 1950s hit makers Teresa Brewer and Ruby Wright released answer records entitled 'Dern Ya'.

## IMPRESSIONS
KEEP ON PUSHING
*ABC Paramount*

One of the first socially aware soul songs gave the Chicago R&B trio, fronted by singer/songwriter and producer Curtis Mayfield, their fourth consecutive Top 20 single.

## BEATLES
A HARD DAY'S NIGHT
*Capitol*

See UK entry.

## DUSTY SPRINGFIELD
WISHIN' AND HOPIN'
*Philips*

As The Merseybeats' version of this Bacharach & David beat ballad climbed the UK chart, Springfield's rendition was scoring Stateside. For the record books, American Dionne Warwick released the song before either of the UK acts.

# UNITED KINGDOM
# JULY 1964

## P.J. PROBY
HOLD ME
*Decca*

British fame came to the Houston-born vocalist after he relocated to the UK and adopted a *Tom Jones* (the film, not the singer) image – complete with eighteenth-century pony tail. Proby (born James Marcus Smith), whose career was now guided by UK pop TV producer Jack Good, had his first hit with a cleverly arranged beat reworking of a song which had originally been popular in 1933. 'Hold Me' was also a minor hit in the US, where his many previous recordings had failed to create any interest.

## ANIMALS
HOUSE OF THE RISING SUN
*Columbia*

The Animals' second single topped the trans-atlantic charts and made them the first UK group to reach the summit Stateside since The Beatles. They knew the old blues song from Josh White's recording, but based their keyboard-driven arrangement on Bob Dylan's recent version. It was the first of many Top 10s for producer Mickie Most and, at over four minutes, was the longest No 1 yet. The single, which took just 20 minutes to record, returned to the UK Top 20 in 1982.

## PETER & GORDON
NOBODY I KNOW
*Columbia*

One of the decade's most successful recording duos scored their second successive transatlantic Top 20 entry with a song composed by John Lennon & Paul McCartney (who was then dating Peter's actress sister Jane Asher).

## ROLLING STONES
IT'S ALL OVER NOW
*Decca*

Britain's most popular R&B band had their first UK chart topper with a version of a song originally released by soul group The Valentinos and composed by member Bobby Womack. The Stones recorded it in the legendary Chess Records studio in Chicago.

## JIM REEVES
I WON'T FORGET YOU
*RCA*

Even though his US success was now confined to the country field, Jim Reeves was one of the biggest-selling pop acts in the UK. This ironically titled Harlan Howard ballad was in the UK Top 10 when the singer died in a plane crash.

## ELVIS PRESLEY
KISSIN' COUSINS
*RCA*

Fred Wise, who penned such Presley songs as 'Wooden Heart' and 'Fame And Fortune', composed the title tune from a movie in which the King played twins. It peaked at No 12 in his homeland – his smallest US hit single to date.

## BEATLES
A HARD DAY'S NIGHT
*Parlophone*

Both the soundtrack album to the group's first movie *A Hard Day's Night* and the title song quickly rocketed The Beatles to the top spot on both sides of the Atlantic. In the US, the album sold a million in a record four days!

## DUSTY SPRINGFIELD
I JUST DON'T KNOW WHAT TO DO WITH MYSELF
*Philips*

The soulful vocalist, born Mary O'Brien, registered her third UK Top 20 single in succession with an emotionally heart-wrenching Burt Bacharach and Hal David ballad. The top composers had penned the song for Tommy Hunt (ex-lead singer of doo-wop group The Flamingos).

## CLIFF RICHARD
ON THE BEACH
*Columbia*

Shortly before he headed off to Nashville to record, Cliff added to his staggering hit tally with a song from his film *Wonderful Life*. He penned the bouncy summer ode with Shadows Bruce Welch and Hank Marvin.

## BARRON KNIGHTS
CALL UP THE GROUPS
*Columbia*

During their long career this humorous UK quintet had many top-selling records. They specialized in parodying current pop groups – as The Four Preps had done previously in the US. The Barron Knights' first hit, which concerned the drafting of groups into the services, was an anglicized version of the Four Preps' 1962 US chart entry, 'The Big Draft'.

## MANFRED MANN
DO WAH DIDDY DIDDY
*HMV*

The well-respected British R&B band's biggest hit was also their first cover version. The song, penned by Jeff Barry and Ellie Greenwich (who had written the similarly titled ' Da Doo Ron Ron'), was originally recorded as 'Do Wah Diddy' by R&B act The Exciters. Mann's more commercial rendition topped the chart on both sides of the Atlantic.

# UNITED STATES
# AUGUST 1964

## DEAN MARTIN
EVERYBODY LOVES SOMEBODY
*Reprise*

▲ 1
⑩ 4
147/500

A song that Reprise label owner Frank Sinatra had recorded in 1948 reinstalled the legendary entertainer in the Top 10 after six years away. One-time rock star Jimmy Bowen produced this MOR jewel and co-writer Ken Lane was the musical director. When 'Dino' hosted his own long-running TV series in 1965, this transatlantic smash hit was used as his theme.

## SUPREMES
WHERE DID OUR LOVE GO
*Motown*

▲ 1
⑩ 1
95/500

This female R&B trio from Detroit were the US's most frequent visitors to the No 1 position during the decade. Two years and a handful of minor hits after their chart debut, they first cracked the Top 20 with a pop/R&B gem that is regarded as one of the era's major musical milestones. The hook-laden Holland, Dozier & Holland composition had earlier been rejected by The Marvellettes. In 1972, Donnie Elbert re-introduced it to the transatlantic Top 20.

## DRIFTERS
UNDER THE BOARDWALK
*Atlantic*

▲ 4
⑩ 5•
448/500

Johnny Moore, who had sung lead on the group's mid-1950s hits such as 'Ruby Baby' and 'Adorable', fronted them on their version of this compelling Arthur Resnick and Kenny Young composition. When The Drifters' US hits dried up, they relocated to the UK where they were very successful in the 1970s. In 1988, they were inducted into the Rock and Roll Hall of Fame alongside The Beatles and Beach Boys.

## JELLY BEANS
I WANNA LOVE HIM SO BAD
*Red Bird*

▲ 9
⑩ 1•
—/500

The mixed R&B quartet from Jersey City had a 'girl group'-sounding smash with this song composed by regular hit writers Jeff Barry and Ellie Greenwich. The noted songwriters also wrote the act's only other chart entry, 'Baby Be Mine'.

## BOBBY FREEMAN
C'MON AND SWIM
*Autumn*

▲ 5
⑩ 2•
—/500

Six years after his self-penned gold disc 'Do You Wanna Dance', the underrated rock'n'roll star from San Francisco returned to the Top 10 with another dance track. 'C'mon And Swim' was the single that introduced the public to the short-lived Swim dance craze. Freeman's producer Sly Stone (later a successful recording star) wrote the million seller. The follow-up 'S-W-I-M', also written by Stone, was only a minor hit and was the last of his nine US-only chart entries.

## ANIMALS
HOUSE OF THE RISING SUN
*MGM*

▲ 1
⑩ 1
89/500

See UK entry (July).

## DAVE CLARK FIVE
BECAUSE
*Epic*

▲ 3
⑩ 4
414/500

The transatlantic teen idols from London had their first ballad hit with a song penned by members Clark and Mike Smith. It was one of a staggering seven singles they released in 1964 that reached the US Top 20.

## VENTURES
WALK-DON'T RUN '64
*Dolton*

The guitar-based combo returned to the Top 10 with a surfin' styled update of their 1960 debut hit. Incidentally, it was coupled with a cover of The Dakotas' UK hit 'The Cruel Sea'. Thirteen years later, 'Walk Don't Run '77' failed to crack the Top 100.

## GERRY & THE PACEMAKERS
HOW DO YOU DO IT?
*Laurie*

See UK entry (March 1963).

## NEWBEATS
BREAD AND BUTTER
*Hickory*

When recording duo Dean & Marc joined with soloist Larry Henley they formed one of the most recognizable new acts of 1964. The shrill-sounding Nashville-based pop/rock trio had an instant transatlantic Top 20 hit with their anthemic debut single. It was the first of three US Top 20 hits for the unmistakable falsetto-led vocal team. Incidentally, lead vocalist Henley later penned the acclaimed MOR ballad 'Wind Beneath My Wings'.

---

# UNITED KINGDOM
# AUGUST 1964

---

## NASHVILLE TEENS
TOBACCO ROAD
*Decca*

Despite the group's name, this combo were neither from Nashville nor teenagers. Nevertheless, the Surrey-based sextet, who were one of the most interesting of the new UK rock bands, directed their debut disc into the transatlantic Top 20. They hit with a Mickie Most-produced version of John D. Loudermilk's composition 'Tobacco Road', that had earlier proved less fruitful for such acts as Frank Ifield and Lou Rawls.

## BEACH BOYS
I GET AROUND
*Capitol*

See US entry (June).

## BILLY FURY
IT'S ONLY MAKE BELIEVE
*Decca*

Along with Cliff Richard, Fury was the only pre-Beatles rock star who still frequently hit the heights. His latest hit was his rendition of the Conway Twitty classic from 1958.

## HONEYCOMBS
HAVE I THE RIGHT?
*Pye*

Producer Joe Meek, who always felt that the Dave Clark Five had borrowed his thumping bass drum sound, now used it to good effect on The Honeycombs' debut disc. The result gave the group, who featured female drummer Annie 'Honey' Lantree, their sole transatlantic Top 10 entry. The song was written for them by managers Ken Howard and Howard Blaikley, who subsequently penned many hits for The Herd and Dave Dee, Dozy, Beaky, Mick & Tich. An updated version by the Dead End Kids in 1977 also reached the UK Top 10.

## BILLY J. KRAMER & THE DAKOTAS
### FROM A WINDOW
*Parlophone*

▲ 10
🔟 5•
—/500

One of the most successful acts of the beat boom era had the last of five consecutive George Martin-produced UK Top 10 entries with a song written for them by Lennon & McCartney. 'From A Window' was also the fourth and last US Top 40 entry for the group, who disbanded in 1968.

## KINKS
### YOU REALLY GOT ME
*Pye*

▲ 1
🔟 1
145/500

After two heavily hyped flops, and tours supporting the Dave Clark Five, The Hollies and The Beatles, this London-based quartet commenced their rise to stardom with a single generally regarded as one of British rock's finest moments. American Shel Talmy produced the 'Louie Louie'-influenced single, which the group's talented front man Ray Davies penned. The record rocketed into the transatlantic Top 10 and started the act's enviable run of hits. In 1978, 'You Really Got Me' introduced another legendary rock act, Van Halen, to the Top 40.

## CILLA BLACK
### IT'S FOR YOU
*Parlophone*

▲ 7
🔟 3
—/500

The Liverpudlian lass (born Priscilla White) with the refreshing girl-next-door image added to her hit list with a song composed by her famous label-mates John Lennon and Paul McCartney.

# UNITED STATES
# SEPTEMBER 1964

## RONNY & THE DAYTONAS
### GTO
*Mala*

▲ 4
🔟 1•
468/500

Nashville's best-known hot-rod music hit makers were a session act which included noted singer/songwriters Buzz Cason and Bobby Russell. The most successful of their five US chart records was produced by Bill 'Raunchy' Justis. It was composed by lead singer John Buck Wilkin, whose mother Marijohn had penned Top 10 hits for Stonewall Jackson and Jimmy Dean.

## SHANGRI-LAS
### REMEMBER (WALKIN' IN THE SAND)
*Red Bird*

▲ 5
🔟 1
—/500

Two pairs of New York sisters made up the most successful white female group of the mid-1960s. The first of their six US Top 40 singles was a haunting lost-love lament written by producer George 'Shadow' Morton. The sound of seagulls and waves, combined with the teenager's plaintive vocals, helped create one of the era's most memorable pop singles.

## ROY ORBISON
### OH PRETTY WOMAN
*Monument*

▲ 1
🔟 9
59/500

The most successful American star in the UK during the beat boom achieved his only transatlantic chart topper with a bouncy song that he composed with Bill Dees. It was a Top 20 hit for Van Halen in 1982, and rappers 2 Live Crew recorded a parody version in 1989.

## MANFRED MANN
### DO WAH DIDDY DIDDY
*Ascot*

▲ 1
🔟 1
105/500

See UK entry (July).

## MARTHA & THE VANDELLAS
DANCING IN THE STREET
*Gordy*

▲ 2
⑩ 3
281/500

A song Marvin Gaye and Mickey Stevenson wrote for Kim Weston, and which was rejected by Mary Wells, became a club classic by this Detroit trio. Five years later the perennially popular track took them into the UK Top 10 for the only time. In 1985, a Mick Jagger and David Bowie revival also attained a transatlantic Top 10 placing.

## GENE PITNEY
IT HURTS TO BE IN LOVE
*Musicor*

▲ 7
⑩ 3
—/500

The singer/songwriter who had penned the hits 'Rubber Ball' and 'Hello Mary Lou' reached the US Top 40 for the ninth time with a Howard Greenfield and Helen Miller composition.

## FOUR SEASONS
SAVE IT FOR ME
*Philips*

▲ 10
⑩ 8
—/500

Following their usual pattern, producer Bob Crewe penned this hit with group member Bob Gaudio. The track was extracted from the quartet's fourth Top 10 album, *Rag Doll*.

# UNITED KINGDOM
# SEPTEMBER 1964

## DAVE BERRY
THE CRYING GAME
*Decca*

▲ 5
⑩ 1
—/500

One of the era's most imaginative performers (born Dave Grundy) followed three Top 40 cover versions with a Geoff Stevens' composition which initially had not impressed him. In the US, Brenda Lee had a minor hit with it a year later in 1965. In 1993, Boy George placed the plaintive song into the transatlantic Top 40, and Berry's original recording charted in the US on the soundtrack album from the film *The Crying Game*.

## BACHELORS
I WOULDN'T TRADE YOU FOR THE WORLD
*Decca*

▲ 4
⑩ 5
391/500

For the first time, the clean-cut trio clicked with a song written in the 1960s, their third transatlantic chart entry being partly penned by noted Texas producer Major Bill Smith.

## HERMAN'S HERMITS
I'M INTO SOMETHING GOOD
*Columbia*

▲ 1
⑩ 1
118/500

Sixteen-year-old Peter Noone fronted the Manchester group, who ranked alongside The Beatles and Dave Clark Five as the most popular British act in the US during the mid-1960s. The band's first release, a compelling Carole King and Gerry Goffin composition, was their biggest UK hit. Even though The Cookies' lead singer Earl-Jean had taken the song into the US chart just a few months earlier, the Hermits' interpretation also opened the quintet's Top 20 account Stateside. In 1989, Noone's solo re-recording went unnoticed on both sides of the Atlantic.

## FOUR SEASONS
RAG DOLL
*Philips*

▲ 2
⑩ 2
286/500

See US entry (July).

## MARIANNE FAITHFULL
AS TEARS GO BY
*Decca*

▲ 9
⑩ 1
—/500

Six months before they penned a hit for themselves, Rolling Stones Mick Jagger and Keith Richard composed this haunting ballad for the photogenic 16-year-old. The virginal-voiced, folk-flavoured vocalist was discovered by the Stones' manager Andrew Loog Oldham and later became Jagger's regular girlfriend. The prolific Stones' front man considers this early effort to be one of the best songs he has ever written.

## SUPREMES
WHERE DID OUR LOVE GO
*Stateside*

▲ 3
⑩ 1
309/500

See US entry (August).

## ROY ORBISON
OH PRETTY WOMAN
*London American*

▲ 1
⑩ 8
76/500

See US entry.

---

# UNITED STATES
# OCTOBER 1964

---

## GALE GARNETT
WE'LL SING IN THE SUNSHINE
*RCA*

▲ 4
⑩ 1•
436/500

As an actress, this New Zealand-born performer appeared in such well-known TV series as *Bonanza* and *Hawaiian Eye*. As a vocalist, her debut album *My Kind Of Folk Songs* narrowly missed the Top 40, and this self-written sing-along feminist anthem earned Garnett the Grammy for Best Folk Recording. However, her time in the sunshine was short and she was soon on her way to obscurity.

## J. FRANK WILSON & THE CAVALIERS
LAST KISS
*Josie*

▲ 2
⑩ 1•
234/500

In the UK, this touching tale of death in an automobile accident was deemed in 'bad taste' and received no noticeable airplay. In the US, the original 1962 version by blue-eyed soul shouter Wayne Cochran got little play outside his home state, Georgia. However, this later version (which first appeared on the Le Cam and Tamara labels) gave J. Frank Wilson's Texan sextet their first and last major hit. A re-recording by the act in 1969

went nowhere, but the group's 1973 version dented the bottom of the US chart.

## CHAD & JEREMY
A SUMMER SONG
*World Artists*

▲ 7
⑩ 1•
—/500

Even though these upper-class heroes from Britain sold few records in the UK, the duo's 'Oxford sound' earned them seven US Top 40 entries. The folk-styled pair, who wisely relocated to the US, had their biggest hit with a soft rocker co-written by Chad (Stuart). When the screaming stopped, the ex-drama school students moved on to acting with reasonable success.

## BEACH BOYS
WHEN I GROW UP
(TO BE A MAN)
*Capitol*

▲ 9
⑩ 6
—/500

The unique and influential group added to their stockpile of smashes with another particularly effective Brian Wilson song. The track was featured on the quintet's seventh successive Top 20 LP, *The Beach Boys Today!*.

## BETTY EVERETT & JERRY BUTLER
LET IT BE ME
*Vee Jay*

Two of Vee Jay Record's top R&B stars teamed to remake a French composition (originally titled 'Je t'Appartiens') that the Everly Brothers had taken into the Top 10 in 1960. This enduring ballad later reached the Top 40 in 1969 by Glen Campbell and Bobbie Gentry and in 1982 by Willie Nelson.

## SUPREMES
BABY LOVE
*Motown*

The top trio had their only transatlantic No 1 with a Holland, Dozier & Holland composition. The single was the first record by a female group to head the UK charts. This gem of the girl group genre returned to the UK Top 20 in 1974.

## HONEYCOMBS
HAVE I THE RIGHT?
*Interphon*

See UK entry (August).

## HONDELLS
LITTLE HONDA
*Mercury*

A cover of a Brian Wilson ode to the popular Japanese motorbike gave this session group from Southern California their only major hit. Ritchie Burns fronted the act, who were the brainchild of noted surf/hot rod backroom boy Gary Usher. The Beach Boys' original version (taken from the album *All Summer Long*), which was released after The Hondells, stalled in the lower reaches of the chart. These session-surfers appeared in several movies before finally driving off into the sunset.

## ROGER MILLER
CHUG-A-LUG
*Smash*

The noted Nashville singer/songwriter had his second successive Top 10 pop entry and third country Top 10 hit with another of his unique self-composed country novelties.

---

# UNITED KINGDOM
# OCTOBER 1964

---

## JULIE ROGERS
THE WEDDING
*Mercury*

'La Novia', which with Fred Jay's English lyric became 'The Wedding', is one of few internationally known Argentinian songs. It originally charted Stateside in 1958 by June Valli, and gave Londoner Rogers (born Julie Rolls) her only major hit. It was the first record by a UK female to reach the transatlantic Top 10 in the beat boom era. The single had become a must-play at weddings and is reported to have sold seven million copies. Her less rewarding follow-ups included another well-loved betrothal ballad, 'Hawaiian Wedding Song'.

## P.J. PROBY
TOGETHER
*Decca*

The charismatic American performer, voted the year's Best Newcomer in the *MM* poll, registered in the chart with a rousing revival of a 1928 song that Connie Francis had taken into the transatlantic Top 10 in 1961.

## SEARCHERS
WHEN YOU WALK IN
THE ROOM
*Pye*

For the second time, the critically lauded group reached the Top 10 with a sing-along song originally recorded by its composer Jackie DeShannon. In 1995, an updated interpretation by Pam Tillis topped the country chart.

## ANIMALS
I'M CRYING
*Columbia*

Arguably the most authentic-sounding British R&B band reappeared in the transatlantic Top 20 with a song composed by keyboard-playing leader Alan Price and their gruff-voiced front man Eric Burdon.

## HOLLIES
WE'RE THROUGH
*Parlophone*

The Everly Brothers-influenced quintet, whose name was inspired by Buddy Holly and whose first two singles were covers of songs recorded previously by The Coasters, clocked up their first self-penned hit.

## SANDIE SHAW
(THERE'S) ALWAYS
SOMETHING THERE
TO REMIND ME
*Pye*

Burt Bacharach and Hal David composed the first major hits for both Cilla Black and fellow UK pop princess Sandie Shaw, who was discovered by early 1960s star Adam Faith. The latter's second single, a Tony Hatch-produced cover of a minor US hit by R&B performer Lou Johnson, rocketed her to the top. This meritorious lost-love song charted several times Stateside, the biggest hit being by UK techno duo Naked Eyes in 1983. In 1995, rave act Tin Tin Out transported the ever-popular tune back into the UK Top 20.

## MATT MONRO
WALK AWAY
*Parlophone*

Top UK songsmith Don Black wrote the English lyric to leading German composer Udo Jergens' composition 'Warum Nur Warum', which returned the headlining MOR vocalist to the transatlantic Top 40.

## HENRY MANCINI & HIS ORCHESTRA
HOW SOON
*RCA*

This internationally renowned composer/ arranger/conductor and orchestra leader had eight US Top 10 LPs to his credit before scoring his only major UK hit single. Surprisingly, the self-composed theme for TV's *Richard Boone Show* did not reach the US Top 100.

## CLIFF RICHARD
THE TWELFTH OF NEVER
*Columbia*

An outstanding love ballad that Johnny Mathis had hit with in the US seven years earlier now hit in his homeland for the UK's most consistent hitmaker. In 1973, Donny Osmond had the only transatlantic Top 10 entry with this enduring composition.

## CLIFF BENNETT & THE REBEL ROUSERS
ONE WAY LOVE
*Parlophone*

One of the most exciting pre-Beatles bands in the UK had their first excursion into the charts courtesy of a Bert Berns and Jerry Ragovoy composition that The Drifters had taken just outside the US Top 40 earlier in the year.

# UNITED STATES
# NOVEMBER 1964

## SHANGRI-LAS
### LEADER OF THE PACK
*Red Bird*

▲ 1
⑩ 2
198/500

George 'Shadow' Morton, Jeff Barry and Ellie Greenwich wrote and produced this internationally acclaimed 'death disc'. The single, which is said to have sold over seven million, features 16-year-old lead vocalist Mary Weiss and, reportedly, the piano playing of the even younger Billy Joel. The record, which includes motorcycle noises, reached the UK Top 20 in three separate years: 1965, 1972 and 1976. A humorous answer version, 'Leader Of The Laundromat' by The Detergents, also made the US Top 20.

## JAY & THE AMERICANS
### COME A LITTLE
### BIT CLOSER
*UA*

▲ 3
⑩ 2
415/500

A lively Latin-based Tommy Boyce and Bobby Hart-composed pop opus, which the Four Coins had previously recorded, gave the chart regulars their highest-ranked hit.

## DEAN MARTIN
### THE DOOR IS STILL OPEN
### TO MY HEART
*Reprise*

▲ 6
⑩ 5
248/500

The late R&B star Chuck Willis composed the song which lifted the ever-popular veteran balladeer/actor (born Dino Crocetti) into the Top 10 for the second time in succession.

## ZOMBIES
### SHE'S NOT THERE
*Parrot*

▲ 2
⑩ 1
248/500

One of the year's most haunting songs rushed this UK group to the runner-up position in the US, even though it failed to crack the Top 10 in their homeland. 'She's Not There' was written by the

quintet's talented keyboard player Rod Argent. A remake by lead singer Colin Blunstone (under the name Neil MacArthur) returned it to the UK chart in 1970, and in 1977 Santana put it back in the transatlantic lists.

## LORNE GREENE
### RINGO
*RCA*

▲ 1
⑩ 1•
184/500

Thanks to his starring role as Ben Cartwright in the internationally popular TV series *Bonanza*, this Canadian-born actor became one of the world's best-known TV stars. He recorded several tracks for RCA before the cowboy saga about Johnny Ringo briefly thrust him into the pop spotlight. Unlike Greene, composers Don Robertson and Hal Blair were no strangers to the chart.

## KINKS
### YOU REALLY GOT ME
*Reprise*

▲ 7
⑩ 1
—/500

See UK entry (August).

## ROLLING STONES
### TIME IS ON MY SIDE
*London*

▲ 6
⑩ 1
—/500

The UK's No 1 rebels finally cracked the US Top 20 with a carefully cloned cover version of a Jerry Ragovoy song, previously recorded by R&B star Irma Thomas. They launched it on their controversial first appearance on the *Ed Sullivan Show*.

## BOBBY VINTON
### MR LONELY
*Epic*

▲ 1
⑩ 6
138/500

A song that the regular hit maker had recorded in 1962 (at the same session as 'Roses Are Red') gave him his fourth and final chart topper. Incidentally, an earlier version of this composition by cabaret star Buddy Greco attracted few buyers.

## JOHNNY RIVERS
MOUNTAIN OF LOVE
*Imperial*

▲ 9
⑩ 2
—/500

A rockabilly song, which its composer Harold Dorman had taken into the Top 40 in 1960, returned this Louisiana-raised rocker to the heights. 'Mountain Of Love', which had reached runner-up position on the country list in 1963 by David Houston, topped that chart in 1982 by Charley Pride.

---

# UNITED KINGDOM
# NOVEMBER 1964

---

## MANFRED MANN
SHA LA LA
*HMV*

▲ 3
⑩ 3
—/466

As usual, Paul Jones (born Paul Pond) handled the vocal chores on the popular group's second successive transatlantic Top 20 hit. The song had previously been recorded by The Shirelles.

## SUPREMES
BABY LOVE
*Stateside*

▲ 1
⑩ 2
131/500

See US entry (October).

## ROCKIN' BERRIES
HE'S IN TOWN
*Piccadilly*

▲ 3
⑩ 1
456/500

After a few unrewarding releases, this Birmingham-based band charted with their rendition of a Carole King and Gerry Goffin composition that The Tokens had scored with Stateside. It was the biggest hit of the entertaining live act's long career.

## KINKS
ALL DAY AND ALL OF THE NIGHT
*Pye*

▲ 2
⑩ 2
332/500

This riff-laden rock masterpiece returned the instantly recognizable group into the transatlantic Top 10 and helped lay the foundations of the heavy metal guitar sound. Few can doubt that the record inspired The Doors' 1968 US chart topper, 'Hello I Love You'. A version by The Stranglers also reached the UK Top 10 in 1988.

## WAYNE FONTANA & THE MINDBENDERS
UM UM UM UM UM UM
*Fontana*

▲ 5
⑩ 1
—/500

It was fifth time lucky for the photogenic Fontana (born Glyn Ellis) and the Manchester-based rock band who had named themselves after a 1963 Dirk Bogarde film. After four small-selling singles, they hit the heights with a repetitively titled Curtis Mayfield composition that had given Major Lance his biggest US hit.

## NASHVILLE TEENS
GOOGLE EYE
*Decca*

▲ 10
⑩ 2•
—/500

This visually striking combo made it two UK Top 10 hits in a row with a song about a catfish. Like their previous hit, it was composed by noted Nashville tunesmith John D. Loudermilk and produced by Mickie Most.

## HELMUT ZACHARIAS ORCHESTRA
TOKYO MELODY
*Polydor*

▲ 9
⑩ 1•
—/500

The theme music from the Tokyo Olympic Games earned this German orchestra leader and violinist a silver disc in the UK. Coincidentally, his only US hit, 'When The White Lilacs Bloom Again', came in 1956 – the year of the Melbourne Olympics. Perhaps, not surprisingly, the veteran's subsequent releases included 'Mexico Melody' (1968), 'Munich Melody' (1972) and 'Moscow Melody' (1980).

## PRETTY THINGS
DON'T BRING ME DOWN
*Fontana*

It was claimed that Pretty Thing Phil May was the longest-haired man in the UK. Even so, the group (named after a Bo Diddley song), who made the Stones seem clean cut, smart and musically polished, strung together three consecutive UK Top 40 singles. Their biggest hit met with resistance at certain US radio stations due to the line 'I laid her on the ground'. The R&B band's 1968 album *SF Sorrow* is generally regarded as the first rock opera.

## ROLLING STONES
LITTLE RED ROOSTER
*Decca*

Willie Dixon, one of the premiere blues composers, penned the only UK chart topper by the Stones not to be released in the US. Howlin' Wolf and Sam Cooke were among the US recording artists who cut the song earlier.

## GENE PITNEY
I'M GONNA BE STRONG
*Stateside*

See US entry (December).

## JIM REEVES
THERE'S A HEARTACHE
FOLLOWING ME
*RCA*

Shortly after the internationally successful country singer died, eight of his albums simultaneously entered the UK Top 20. He also added another major hit to his collection with a country ballad that was not released as a single in the US.

## PETULA CLARK
DOWNTOWN
*Pye*

The first UK single by a female artist to top the US charts since 1952 was composed by Clark's producer Tony Hatch. It went on to win the Grammy for Best Rock and Roll Record. Her disco re-recording in 1976 went nowhere. However, a remix of the original track reinstalled Petula in the UK Top 10 in 1988.

## DUSTY SPRINGFIELD
LOSING YOU
*Philips*

Soon after being voted Top UK Female Singer in the *NME* poll, the striking-looking singer hit with a song co-written by Tom Springfield. Incidentally, both Dusty and Tom had previously been in the *NME* poll-winning group The Springfields.

# UNITED STATES
# DECEMBER 1964

## SUPREMES
COME SEE ABOUT ME
*Motown*

▲ 1
🔟 3
91/500

The trio's tenth Motown single became their third chart topper in a row. Like its two predecessors, it was composed for them by another winning trio, Eddie Holland, Lamont Dozier and Brian Holland.

## GENE PITNEY
I'M GONNA BE STRONG
*Musicor*

▲ 9
🔟 4•
—/500

A dramatic Barry Mann and Cynthia Weill ballad that Frankie Laine had earlier recorded gave the frequent hit maker his only transatlantic Top 10 entry. An update of the song also reached the UK Top 40 in 1995 by Cyndi Lauper.

## BEATLES
I FEEL FINE
*Capitol*

▲ 1
🔟 10
96/500

See UK entry.

## BEACH BOYS
DANCE, DANCE, DANCE
*Capitol*

▲ 8
🔟 7
—/500

One of the most consistently successful American acts of the decade registered their seventh successive Top 10 entry with a memorable song written by Brian and Carl Wilson.

## LITTLE ANTHONY &
## THE IMPERIALS
GOIN' OUT OF MY HEAD
*DCP*

▲ 6
🔟 2
—/500

After a four-year chart absence, one of the most popular and distinctive doo-wop ensembles of the late 1950s returned to string together a run of five Top 40 hits in succession. All of these singles were produced and co-written by fellow 1950s hit maker Teddy Randazzo. The Lettermen re-installed the song in the Top 10 in 1968, and Frank Sinatra had a minor hit with it a year later.

## BEATLES
SHE'S A WOMAN
*Capitol*

▲ 4
🔟 11
—/500

The B side of 'I Feel Fine' entered the US Top 5 in its own right. It crowned an absolutely amazing year for the group; in less than 12 months they had put a record-shattering 30 singles and 11 albums into the US chart!

## LARKS
THE JERK
*Money*

▲ 7
🔟 1•
—/500

Don Julian first tasted success in the mid-1950s when 'Heaven And Paradise' by his doo-wop outfit The Meadowlarks created a stir. After a few quiet years he returned with his new group, The Larks, and had another brief fling with fame, thanks to a self-composed dance song which introduced record buyers to one of the year's hottest dance crazes, the Jerk. Subsequent singles such as 'Soul Jerk' and 'Mickey's East Coast Jerk' generated little interest.

# UNITED KINGDOM
# DECEMBER 1964

## BEATLES
### I FEEL FINE
*Parlophone*

▲ 1
⑩ 7
39/500

The Beatles ended the first year of the UK invasion with this innovative single topping the chart on both sides of the Atlantic. 'I Feel Fine', which opened with the (claimed) first use of feedback guitar, amassed advance orders of over 750,000 in the UK.

## VAL DOONICAN
### WALK TALL
*Decca*

▲ 3
⑩ 1
325/500

At the height of the beat boom, smooth Irish pop/country performer Doonican had a string of easy-listening hits in the UK. His first chart success came with a breezy song written by Nashville tunesmith Don Wayne, which was a US country hit for Faron Young.

## ROY ORBISON
### PRETTY PAPER
*London American*

▲ 6
⑩ 9
—/500

The singer who, more than anyone else, kept the stars and stripes flying on the UK chart, clicked with a seasonal Willie Nelson song which had been recorded in Orbison's pre-hit days.

## FREDDIE &
## THE DREAMERS
### I UNDERSTAND
*Columbia*

▲ 5
⑩ 4•
—/500

The unique Manchester band visited the Top 20 for the sixth and last time with a revival of the G-Clef's 1961 hit. Amazingly, as their UK chart career ended, the agile act finally took off in the US. In America the group's stage routine even created a short-lived dance craze, the Freddie. Both this zany combo and dance king Chubby Checker charted with Freddie records.

## BACHELORS
### NO ARMS COULD EVER HOLD YOU
*Decca*

▲ 8
⑩ 6
—/500

Soon after appearing in a Royal Variety Performance, The Bachelors notched up their fifth consecutive UK Top 10 entry with a song that Pat Boone had taken into the US Top 40 in 1955.

## CLIFF RICHARD
### I COULD EASILY FALL
*Columbia*

▲ 6
⑩ 27
—/500

His backing band The Shadows penned Cliff's fifth Top 10 entry of the year. It was featured in his musical show *Aladdin And His Wonderful Lamp*.

## P.J. PROBY
### SOMEWHERE
*Liberty*

▲ 6
⑩ 3
—/500

The controversial pop idol made it three Top 10 hits in just seven months with a Billy Eckstine-styled reworking of a show-stopping song from the huge hit musical *West Side Story*.

# UNITED STATES
# JANUARY 1965

## SEARCHERS
LOVE POTION
NUMBER NINE
*Kapp*

A track that was not released as a single in the UK gave the noted Merseyside act the biggest of their three US Top 20 hits. The novelty rocker was originally written in 1959 by Jerry Leiber and Mike Stoller for The Clovers.

## IMPRESSIONS
AMEN
*ABC Paramount*

This gospel-based soul single was the seventh of 14 Top 40 entries by the R&B vocal trio in the 1960s. Despite US success, they failed to make their first impression on the UK chart until 1975, five years after the act's talented leader Curtis Mayfield had gone solo. The Impressions were inducted into the Rock and Roll Hall of Fame in 1991.

## JULIE ROGERS
THE WEDDING
*Mercury*

See UK entry (October).

## PETULA CLARK
DOWNTOWN
*Warner*

See UK entry (November).

## RIGHTEOUS BROTHERS
YOU'VE LOST THAT
LOVIN' FEELIN'
*Philles*

This is one of the definitive pop records and arguably the highlight of producer Phil Spector's amazing career. Barry Mann, Cynthia Weil and Spector loosley based the timeless song (which

has amassed over five million US radio plays) on the Four Tops' hit 'Baby I Need Your Loving'. In the US, subsequent versions by Dionne Warwick in 1969 and Hall & Oats in 1980 also reached the Top 20. Incidentally, both the Righteous Brothers and member Bill Medley later re-recorded the transatlantic chart topper.

## MARVIN GAYE
HOW SWEET IT IS TO BE
LOVED BY YOU
*Tamla*

Motown's best-known staff writers Eddie Holland, Lamont Dozier and Brian Holland composed the ex-session drummer's ninth Top 40 entry. The song also entered the Top 20 in 1966 by Jr Walker and in 1975 by James Taylor.

## DEL SHANNON
KEEP SEARCHIN'(WE'LL
FOLLOW THE SUN)
*Amy*

The influential singer from Michigan returned to the US Top 10 after a three-year absence, during which time he notched up a handful of UK chart entries. 'Keep Searchin' was his last major transatlantic success as a vocalist, although he arranged Smith's Top 5 entry 'Baby It's You' in 1969 and produced Brian Hyland's Top 5 single 'Gypsy Woman' in 1970.

## SHIRLEY ELLIS
THE NAME GAME
*Congress*

A catchy tongue-twisting novelty song penned with her husband Lincoln Chase returned the one-time Apollo Theatre talent-show winner back into the Top 10.

## JOE TEX
HOLD WHAT YOU'VE GOT
*Dial*

▲ 5
⑩ 1
—/500

Tex, one of the most recognizable R&B stars of the 1960s, had his first major pop hit with his twenty-ninth single, which was released ten years after he started recording. Interestingly, this self-composed chart debut, which showcased Tex's half-preaching half-singing style, was the first hit recorded at Muscle Shoals. This unique performer from Texas (born Joseph Arrington Jr) was one of the era's biggest-selling R&B acts and earned himself the tag 'Soul Brother No 2'.

## GARY LEWIS & THE PLAYBOYS
THIS DIAMOND RING
*Liberty*

▲ 1
⑩ 1
119/500

One of the first American groups to find fame after the British invasion scored the first of many hits with a song previously rejected by both Bobby Vee and The Drifters. Vee's regular producer Snuff Garrett was behind the desk, and several top-line session musicians and singers were used on the track. It was co-written by Al Kooper (founder member of Blood, Sweat & Tears) and had earlier been recorded by R&B singer Sammy Ambrose. Wendy Hill cut an answer version, '(Gary Please Don't Sell) My Diamond Ring'.

## KINKS
ALL DAY AND ALL OF THE NIGHT
*Reprise*

▲ 7
⑩ 2
—/500

See UK entry (November).

# UNITED KINGDOM
# JANUARY 1965

## GEORGIE FAME
YEH YEH
*Columbia*

▲ 1
⑩ 1
149/500

Before this song gave the critically acclaimed singer and pianist his first taste of fame, it had been recorded by co-writer John Hendricks (as part of Lambert, Hendricks & Ross) and Cuban percussionist Mongo Santamaria. Fame (born Clive Powell), one of the leading lights of the early UK R&B movement, initially considered it 'too jazzy' for commercial release. Nonetheless, his Tony Palmer-produced version topped the UK chart and only narrowly missed the US Top 20. In 1985, Matt Bianco's updated rendition also reached the UK Top 20.

## TWINKLE
TERRY
*Decca*

▲ 4
⑩ 1•
464/500

The first UK female in the rock era to write her own hit was Twinkle (born Lynn Ripley and now Lynn Rogers). At the age of 17 she rode into the Top 10 with a song about her supposed biker boyfriend Terry, which became the UK's best-known home-grown death disc of the 1960s. Twinkle receives more respect than many other 'little stars' even though follow-ups such as 'Tommy' and 'Poor Old Johnny' were chart flops, as was her 1978 re-recording of 'Terry'.

## SANDIE SHAW
GIRL DON'T COME
*Pye*

▲ 3
⑩ 2
410/500

This teenaged pop vocalist (born Sandra Goodrich) from Essex had the first of many memorable Chris Andrews-written and produced hits with a noteworthy song that had started out as the B side of another Andrews' composition, 'I'd Be Far Better Off Without You'.

## MOODY BLUES
GO NOW!
*Decca*

▲ 1
⑩ 1
168/500

For their second single this Birmingham-based R&B quintet recorded a faithful cover of a song co-written by ex-doo-wopper Larry Banks, and originally sung by his wife Bessie Banks. The group's less intense version (with lead vocals by Denny Laine – later of Wings) entered the transatlantic Top 10 but was the act's only major hit of the decade. However, after a few personnel changes and a shift to a more innovative classic rock style, the band went on to become one of the top-selling acts of the era.

## GERRY & THE PACEMAKERS
FERRY ACROSS THE MERSEY
*Columbia*

▲ 8
⑩ 6•
—/500

The group who epitomised Merseybeat achieved their third and last transatlantic Top 10 entry with the self-penned theme tune from the act's debut movie. Gerry Marsden, who left the Pacemakers in 1967, has remained a popular entertainment figure in the UK. In 1989 he sang on a chart-topping re-recording of this song, which raised money for the Hillsborough Football Ground disaster fund.

## SOUNDS ORCHESTRAL
CAST YOUR FATE TO THE WIND
*Piccadilly*

▲ 5
⑩ 1•
—/500

Producer/songwriter John Schroeder (best-known for his work with Helen Shapiro) wanted to produce an orchestral sound that would appeal to adults and teenagers. With help from noted pianist and arranger Johnny Pearson (who headed the *Top Of The Pops* orchestra for many years), he formed this session orchestra. Their first single, a revival of jazz pianist Vince Guaraldi's self-composed 1963 US Top 40 entry, reached the Top 10 on both sides of the Atlantic. It was fated to be the act's only major hit.

## CILLA BLACK
YOU'VE LOST THAT LOVIN' FEELIN'
*Parlophone*

▲ 2
⑩ 4
430/500

Producer George Martin's brave decision to cover the Righteous Brothers stunning US hit almost paid off. However, the Phil Spector-produced original just pipped Cilla's emotional version at the post.

## RIGHTEOUS BROTHERS
YOU'VE LOST THAT LOVIN' FEELIN'
*London American*

▲ 1
⑩ 1
5/500

This is the only single to reach the UK Top 10 on three separate occasions (1965, 1969, 1990). See also US entry.

## MANFRED MANN
COME TOMORROW
*HMV*

▲ 4
⑩ 4
—/500

In 1961, American Marie Knight first recorded the dramatic R&B ballad that gave the acclaimed London-based band their third UK Top 5 entry in succession.

## KINKS
TIRED OF WAITING FOR YOU
*Pye*

▲ 1
⑩ 3
183/500

Thanks in part to an appearance on the US TV show *Shindig*, this melodic Ray Davies song shipped the UK quartet into the Top 10 for the third successive time.

# UNITED STATES
# FEBRUARY 1965

## TEMPTATIONS
MY GIRL
*Gordy*

▲ 1
⑩ 1
159/500

Soul music's No 1 group were not an overnight success; their eleventh Motown release was the quintet's first Top 10 entry. This perennially popular song was written (for The Miracles) and produced by Smokey Robinson and Ronald White, and like Robinson's similarly titled 'My Guy' it topped the US chart. In the UK, Otis Redding's rendition grabbed the lion's share of sales and The Temptations' version only cracked the Top 10 in 1992, after being heard in the movie of the same name.

## SAM COOKE
SHAKE
*RCA*

▲ 7
⑩ 5•
—/500

The first release after his death took the all-time great R&B performer into the Top 10 for the last time in the US. Surprisingly, just weeks after he was inducted into the Rock and Roll Hall of Fame in 1986, he had his biggest UK hit with 'Wonderful World' – a track that had reached the US Top 20 way back in 1960.

## KINGSMEN
THE JOLLY GREEN GIANT
*Wand*

▲ 4
⑩ 2•
493/500

A novelty song that the Oregon combo cut purely for fun was the last of their three Top 20 entries. Lead vocalist Lynn Easton penned the lyric about the well-known TV commercial cartoon character, and the music was taken from The Olympics' 1960 hit 'Big Boy Pete'. The Kingsmen's subsequent less rewarding releases included 'Little Green Thing'.

## PETER & GORDON
I GO TO PIECES
*Capitol*

▲ 9
⑩ 2
—/500

Despite its chart failure in the UK, the popular soft rock duo had their fourth US Top 20 single with a Del Shannon composition that The Searchers had earlier rejected.

## AD LIBS
THE BOY FROM NEW YORK CITY
*Blue Cat*

▲ 8
⑩ 1•
—/500

The Newark-based R&B quartet fronted by Mary Ann Thomas recorded for a handful of labels, but their only noticeable hit came with a up-tempo tune written by close friend John T. Taylor. The single was produced by the chart-making team of Jerry Leiber and Mike Stoller and was on the composers' Blue Cat label. The song first charted in the UK in 1978 by doo-wop revivalists The Darts and scored again in the US in 1981 by Manhattan Transfer.

## ZOMBIES
TELL HER NO
*Parrot*

▲ 6
⑩ 2
—/500

Colin Blunstone's choir boy-like vocal interpretation of a magnetic Rod Argent song helped give the group from Hertfordshire their second successive US Top 10 entry. Astoundingly, in the act's homeland, this Zombies single had little very life in it.

## ROGER MILLER
KING OF THE ROAD
*Smash*

▲ 4
⑩ 3
413/500

The humorous country performer had the highest-placed hit of his career with a self-written song about the joys of hobo life. Astoundingly, it earned the Grammy for Best Rock'n'Roll Single. An answer version, 'Queen Of The House' by Jody Miller, also entered the Top 20 and won a Grammy. In the UK Miller's record reached No 1, and in 1990 The Proclaimers placed 'King Of The Road' back in the Top 10.

# UNITED KINGDOM
# FEBRUARY 1965

## DEL SHANNON
KEEP SEARCHIN' (WE'LL
FOLLOW THE SUN)
*Stateside*

▲ 3
⑩ 8•
446/500

See US entry (January).

## SEEKERS
I'LL NEVER FIND
ANOTHER YOU
*Columbia*

▲ 1
⑩ 1
112/500

After successful pop/folk trio The Springfields disbanded, member Tom Springfield, who had penned their biggest hits, produced and wrote a long string of top international sellers for this Australian quartet. It was the first single by an Australian act to head the UK chart. Not only did the record also reach the US Top 5, but a version in 1967 by Sonny James headed the country lists.

## VAL DOONICAN
THE SPECIAL YEARS
*Decca*

▲ 7
⑩ 2
—/500

Noted Nashville tunesmith and now top music business executive Martha Sharp composed the song that took the easy-going UK MOR/country singer into the Top 10 for the second successive time.

## THEM
BABY PLEASE DON'T GO
*Decca*

▲ 10
⑩ 1
—/500

Van Morrison fronted this raw and rebellious Irish R&B band, and top US songwriter Bert Berns handled production chores on both of the group's hits. In the UK, they made their chart debut with an updated version of an R&B standard that Morrison learned from John Lee Hooker's version. In the US, it was the Morrison-composed B side 'Gloria' that clicked. The latter song became a must-play for every US garage rock band and in 1966 a recording by the Shadows of Knight reached the Top 10.

## WAYNE FONTANA & THE MINDBENDERS
GAME OF LOVE
*Fontana*

▲ 2
⑩ 2•
351/500

Top American composer Clint Ballard Jr composed this memorable song, which reached runner-up spot in the group's homeland and went one better across the Atlantic. For the record books, it was the second of three consecutive US No 1 singles by bands from Manchester. Later in the year, Fontana (voted Best New Singer of 1965) split from The Mindbenders, with both acts then adding to their hit tallies.

## ANIMALS
DON'T LET ME BE
MISUNDERSTOOD
*Columbia*

▲ 3
🔟 3
452/500

Soon after returning from a successful first US tour, the Newcastle-based quintet entered the transatlantic Top 20 for the third time in a row with their interpretation of a recent Nina Simone single.

## IVY LEAGUE
FUNNY HOW LOVE
CAN BE
*Piccadilly*

▲ 8
🔟 1
—/500

This smooth-sounding, close-harmony vocal trio included top session singers and songwriters John Carter and Ken Lewis. The duo, who penned both of the act's Top 10 entries, also wrote hits in the 1960s for such notables as Herman's Hermits, Manfred Mann, Mary Hopkin and Brenda Lee.

## JIM REEVES
IT HURTS SO MUCH
*RCA*

▲ 8
🔟 5
—/500

The late country performer notched up his fourth Top 10 entry in a row with a ballad composed by singer/songwriter Bonnie Guitar. Despite its UK success, it was not released as a single in the US.

## TOM JONES
IT'S NOT UNUSUAL
*Decca*

▲ 1
🔟 1
165/500

Welshman Jones (born Thomas Woodward) was the first UK solo artist to win a Grammy for Best New Artist. The song that introduced him to the top 10 on both sides of the Atlantic was composed by his manager Gordon Mills and Les Reed with Sandie Shaw in mind. Jones' perennially popular recording, which featured lead guitar work from Jimmy Page, reappeared in the UK Top 20 in 1987.

# UNITED STATES
# MARCH 1965

## BEATLES
EIGHT DAYS A WEEK
*Capitol*

▲ 1
🔟 12
170/500

The Beatles' seventh US chart topper in a year was the first UK single to head the US lists that was not even released in the UK. At home, it was included on the LP *Beatles For Sale*, while in the US it could be found on the album *Beatles VI*.

## JEWEL AKENS
THE BIRDS AND THE BEES
*Era*

▲ 3
🔟 1•
361/500

A much-recorded Texas pop/R&B singer, who in the 1950s was a member of the Four Dots (their backing musicians reportedly included guitarist Eddie Cochran), Akens had his only noticeable hit with a bouncy teen-love opus about the facts of life penned by his label head Herb Newman, whose erstwhile compositions included the chart-topping 'The Wayward Wind'. The similar-sounding follow-up 'Georgie Porgie' fared less well.

## GERRY & THE PACEMAKERS
FERRY ACROSS THE
MERSEY
*Laurie*

▲ 6
🔟 3•
—/500

See UK entry (January).

## SUPREMES
STOP! IN THE NAME
OF LOVE
*Motown*

▲ 1
⑩ 4
122/500

As usual, Brian Holland and Lamont Dozier produced and wrote (with Eddie Holland) the single which made this Detroit girl group the first act to have four successive US No 1s. In 1983, fellow 1960s hit makers The Hollies returned it to the US Top 40.

## HERMAN'S HERMITS
CAN'T YOU HEAR MY
HEARTBEAT
*MGM*

▲ 2
⑩ 1
302/500

The B side of the clean-cut UK band's version of 'Silhouettes' gave the burgeoning teen idols the first of their 11 Mickie Most-produced US Top 10 entries. Ivy League members John Carter and Ken Lewis composed the potent pop ditty, which US group Goldie & The Gingerbreads guided into the UK Top 40.

## LITTLE ANTHONY &
## THE IMPERIALS
HURT SO BAD
*DCP*

▲ 10
⑩ 3•
—/500

This outstanding R&B vocal group, fronted by falsetto vocalist Anthony Gourdine, continued

their string of dramatic ballad hits with 'Hurt So Bad'. Producer Teddy Randazzo penned it with Bobby Wilding and Bobby Hart (later a writer for The Monkees). In 1969, The Lettermen lifted the song back into the Top 20 and in 1980 Linda Ronstadt's interpretation climbed into the Top 10.

## SHIRLEY BASSEY
GOLDFINGER
*UA*

▲ 8
⑩ 1•
—/500

The British vocalist, who had first played Las Vegas in 1957 when aged 20, had her only major US hit with the title song from the popular movie. 'Goldfinger' was composed by English writers John Barry, Anthony Newley and Leslie Bricusse and was one of three James Bond themes Bassey recorded. Astonishingly, in the UK, where she was a chart regular, this single missed the Top 20.

## JR WALKER &
## THE ALL STARS
SHOTGUN
*Soul*

▲ 4
⑩ 1
455/500

One of Motown's most recognizable acts was fronted by saxophonist/singer Walker (born Autry DeWalt II) from Arkansas. The group's first and biggest hit came with an innovative self-composed dance track that Walker added his vocals to when the proposed singer did not show up at the session.

# UNITED KINGDOM
# MARCH 1965

## HERMAN'S HERMITS
SILHOUETTES
*Columbia*

▲ 3
⑩ 2
381/500

The Manchester pop quintet had their first trans-atlantic Top 10 entry with an update of a stand-out Bob Crewe and Frank Slay song that had earned The Rays a gold disc in 1957. Cliff Richard reinstalled 'Silhouettes' in the UK Top 10 in 1990.

## GENE PITNEY
I MUST BE SEEING THINGS
*Stateside*

▲ 6
⑩ 4
—/500

The multi-talented vocalist, who was voted Top Male Singer in the UK in 1965, registered the biggest of his 17 UK hits in the 1960s with an emotive ballad co-written by Al Kooper (later leader of Blood, Sweat & Tears).

## MARIANNE FAITHFULL
COME AND STAY WITH ME
*Decca*

The London-born, convent-educated daughter of an Austrian baroness had her biggest UK hit with a Jackie DeShannon composition. It was the third time in a year that a song first cut by DeShannon had reached the UK Top 10 – the others were 'Needles And Pins' and 'When You Walk In The Room'.

## SANDIE SHAW
I'LL STOP AT NOTHING
*Pye*

Chris Andrews originally composed this catchy song for Adam Faith, but was only too happy when it became the bare-footed singer's third consecutive Top 5 entry.

## ROLLING STONES
THE LAST TIME
*Decca*

For the first time, the Stones had a UK hit with a self-composed song (although some may detect a resemblance to 'Maybe The Last Time' by the Staple Singers).'The Last Time' was also the group's first transatlantic Top 10 entry.

## HOLLIES
YES I WILL
*Parlophone*

Hit machine Gerry Goffin composed the instantly recognizable Manchester group's sixth successive UK Top 20 entry. The Monkees later recorded the song as 'I'll Be True To You'.

## SEARCHERS
GOODBYE MY LOVE
*Pye*

One of the best-regarded and most successful UK bands of the mid-1960s paid their last visit to the UK Top 10 with a dirge-like R&B song that Jimmy Hughes had first recorded. The group, who relied heavily on cover versions, are widely considered to be one of the seminal folk/rock acts.

## UNIT 4 PLUS 2
CONCRETE AND CLAY
*Decca*

This hypnotic Latin-laced track was one of the year's most original and outstanding pop singles. It was the Hertfordshire sextet's third single and by far their most memorable recording. In the US, the UK band took the self-composed hit into the Top 40, where it joined a closely mirrored rendition by Eddie Rambeau. In 1976, American Randy Edelman brought the song back to the UK Top 20.

## CLIFF RICHARD
THE MINUTE YOU'RE GONE
*Columbia*

Elvis' backing group The Jordanaires backed Cliff on this Nashville-recorded track. The song, which had been a top country hit for Sonny James, was Cliff's first UK No 1 for two years and was the last of a staggering run of 26 successive Top 10 entries!

# UNITED STATES
# APRIL 1965

## FREDDIE & THE DREAMERS
I'M TELLING YOU NOW
*Tower*

See UK entry (August 1963).

## MARTHA & THE VANDELLAS
NOWHERE TO RUN
*Gordy*

In the UK, this outstanding Holland, Dozier & Holland dance track, which had been one of the first releases on the Tamla Motown label, charted in 1965, 1969 and 1988.

## VIC DANA
RED ROSES FOR A BLUE LADY
*Dolton*

Three versions of an old-school love ballad penned by Sid Tepper and Roy Bennett in the late 1940s reached the US Top 40 in 1965. Perhaps surprisingly, both previous chart topper Bert Kaempfert and Vegas superstar Wayne Newton's interpretations were outpaced by Vic Dana's version. In total, the New York-born balladeer, who had earlier fronted The Fleetwoods (when Gary Troxel went into the Navy), had 13 US-only chart entries in the decade.

## WAYNE FONTANA & THE MINDBENDERS
GAME OF LOVE
*Fontana*

See UK entry (February).

## PETULA CLARK
I KNOW A PLACE
*Warner*

Tony Hatch was inspired to write this ode to night life in London's 100 Club. Ten years after her first UK hit, the single gave Clark her second of 15 US Top 40 entries in a row.

## KINKS
TIRED OF WAITING FOR YOU
*Reprise*

See UK entry (January).

## SHIRLEY ELLIS
THE CLAPPING SONG
*Congress*

Noted R&B composer Lincoln Chase penned his wife's second successive Top 10 entry which, like its predecessor 'The Name Game', was a danceable novelty item. In the UK, the song gave Ellis her only major hit, and in 1982 it returned to the Top 20 by the Belle Stars.

## MOODY BLUES
GO NOW!
*London*

See UK entry (January).

## HERMAN'S HERMITS
MRS BROWN YOU'VE GOT A LOVELY DAUGHTER
*MGM*

Their version of a dated novelty song, which had originally been sung by actor Tom Courtenay in the 1963 UK TV play *The Lads*, amassed an amazing 600,000 advance orders. The single, which was not deemed suitable for release in the act's homeland, entered the Hot 100 at No 12 (a record) and inspired a slew of answer versions. It was a tune the group sang frequently on stage in their early days, and they recorded it as a throwaway album filler in just one take.

## SEEKERS
I'LL NEVER FIND
ANOTHER YOU
*Capitol*

See UK entry (February).

## HERMAN'S HERMITS
SILHOUETTES
*MGM*

See UK entry (March).

# UNITED KINGDOM
# APRIL 1965

## YARDBIRDS
FOR YOUR LOVE
*Columbia*

To begin with, The Yardbirds were regarded as Stones clones and their repertoire also relied heavily on US R&B and blues material. After two small-selling R&B singles the group recorded a blatantly commercial song that Graham Gouldman had written for his own band, The Mockingbirds. Guitarist Eric Clapton left soon after the single's release, but that did not stop it giving the act its first transatlantic Top 10 entry.

## DONOVAN
CATCH THE WIND
*Pye*

Controversy surrounded the launch of this folk singer/songwriter, who was at first considered by many to be a pale imitation of Bob Dylan. Nevertheless, his self-written debut disc came in to the UK chart a week before Dylan's first hit, thanks in no small part to his unprecedented three consecutive appearances on TV's *Ready Steady Go*. The Ivor Novello Award-winning song also transported the Scottish teenager into the US Top 40.

## THEM
HERE COMES THE NIGHT
*Decca*

Ireland's first major R&B band had their biggest transatlantic hit with a song composed by producer Bert Berns. Incidentally, Lulu had earlier charted with 'Here Comes The Night', although she recorded her version after Them. This influential group disbanded in 1966, when lead singer Van Morrison launched his successful solo career.

## WHO
I CAN'T EXPLAIN
*Brunswick*

One of rock music's most original, innovative and influential acts charted with their first single as The Who (they previously had a release as the High Numbers). Also heard on the London group's ground-breaking single were session guitarist Jimmy Page and backing vocalists the Ivy League. This track, like the vast majority of the image-conscious mod band's later recordings, was composed by member Pete Townshend.

### SUPREMES
STOP! IN THE NAME
OF LOVE
*Tamla Motown*

See US entry (March).

### BOB DYLAN
TIMES THEY ARE
A-CHANGIN'
*CBS*

On the week he debuted in the Top 10 singles, the legendary singer/songwriter's second album, *The Freewheelin' Bob Dylan*, topped the UK list almost a year after it first charted. The LP was the first by an act other than The Beatles or Rolling Stones to reach No 1 for over two years! During the chart run of this ground-breaking protest song the revolutionary performer embarked on his first UK tour. Incidentally, a well-timed, if phoney, folk feud with Donovan did no harm to either act's record sales.

### BEATLES
TICKET TO RIDE
*Parlophone*

Not unexpectedly, The Beatles' run of transatlantic No 1s continued with the first single released from their second film, *Help*. Unexpectedly, during its chart stay it was announced that the group were to receive MBEs from the Queen.

### DAVE BERRY
LITTLE THINGS
*Decca*

This slinky, tongue-in-cheek performer from Sheffield had the UK hit with a jaunty song that composer Bobby Goldsboro had taken into the US Top 20.

### ROGER MILLER
KING OF THE ROAD
*Philips*

See US entry (February).

# UNITED STATES
# MAY 1965

### GARY LEWIS & THE PLAYBOYS
COUNT ME IN
*Liberty*

On 8 May the only US single in the US Top 10 was this West Coast group's bouncy version of a song written by ex-Cricket Glen D. Hardin. 'Count Me In' inspired the answer record 'I'll Count You In' by Little Jona Jaye.

### ROLLING STONES
THE LAST TIME
*London*

See UK entry (March).

### BEATLES
TICKET TO RIDE
*Capitol*

See UK entry (April).

### SOUNDS ORCHESTRAL
CAST YOUR FATE TO
THE WIND
*Parkway*

See UK entry (January).

## BEACH BOYS
HELP ME, RHONDA
*Capitol*

The much-imitated group returned to the top with another bona fide Brian Wilson-penned gem. For the record books, Daryl Dragon (the Captain of Captain & Tennille) and Sun rockabilly star Billy Lee Riley played on the track.

## MARVIN GAYE
I'LL BE DOGGONE
*Tamla*

Smokey Robinson produced and co-wrote this funky R&B track, which helped the seminal soul singer establish himself as a regular visitor to the Top 10.

## RIGHTEOUS BROTHERS
JUST ONCE IN MY LIFE
*Philles*

The outstanding blue-eyed soul duo, who had first recorded together in 1962, followed a transatlantic No 1 hit with another critically acclaimed Phil Spector production. Spector penned the dramatic ballad with Gerry Goffin and Carole King.

## SAM THE SHAM & THE PHARAOHS
WOOLLY BULLY
*MGM*

This Texas garage rock band, fronted by the bearded, turban-wearing singer/songwriter Domingo 'Sam' Samudio, were one of the first American groups to chart on both sides of the Atlantic after the UK invasion. The hard-hitting song was the act's second release on the XL label (it was picked up by MGM), and it came within a whisker of topping the US list. Coincidentally, the combo's last chart entry was another woolly waxing, 'Black Sheep'.

## SUPREMES
BACK IN MY ARMS AGAIN
*Motown*

Shortly before this high-flying pop/R&B trio from Detroit opened successfully at New York's premier adult night-spot, The Copacabana, they registered a record fifth No 1 in a row.

## ELVIS PRESLEY
CRYING IN THE CHAPEL
*RCA*

After a two-year absence, the King reappeared in the transatlantic Top 10 with a revival of a song penned by Artie Glenn, which his teenage son Darrell had taken into the Top 10 in 1953. Interestingly, Presley's version was recorded at the same session as 'Surrender' in 1960.

## BEAU BRUMMELS
JUST A LITTLE
*Autumn*

One of the America's earliest answers to the British group invasion first cracked the Top 20 in February 1965 with 'Laugh, Laugh'. These Beatle-influenced San Francisco rockers were produced by Sylvester Stewart (later Sly of Sly & The Family Stone). Member Ron Elliott penned both their Top 20 entries and Sal Valentino handled lead vocal chores.

## TOM JONES
IT'S NOT UNUSUAL
*Parrot*

See UK entry (February).

# UNITED KINGDOM
# MAY 1965

## BARRON KNIGHTS
POP GO THE WORKERS
*Columbia*

Britain's premier musical jesters returned to the Top 10 with another humorous collection of pop parodies, including ones of The Bachelors and Supremes. The group, who added a little light relief to the UK music scene, failed to chart Stateside during the decade.

## ANIMALS
BRING IT ON HOME TO ME
*Columbia*

A song that its composer Sam Cooke conveyed into the US Top 20 in 1962 continued this band's enviable run of transatlantic hits. In the US, Eddie Floyd had a Top 20 entry with it in 1968. A remake by Rod Stewart reached the UK Top 10 in 1974, and Mickey Gilley's 1976 recording topped the country chart.

## SEEKERS
A WORLD OF OUR OWN
*Columbia*

This Tom Springfield-written and produced track gave the commercial folk foursome their second successive transatlantic Top 20 entry. In 1968, Sonny James steered the memorable song to No 1 in the country chart (he also topped that chart with the group's previous hit 'I'll Never Find Another You').

## PETER & GORDON
TRUE LOVE WAYS
*Columbia*

A tender ballad that had been a minor UK hit for composer Buddy Holly in 1960 returned this easy-listening/pop duo to the transatlantic Top 20. 'True Love Ways' topped the country chart in 1980 by Mickey Gilley and in 1983 it entered the UK Top 10 by courtesy of Cliff Richard.

## JACKIE TRENT
WHERE ARE YOU NOW (MY LOVE)
*Pye*

This little-heralded singer/songwriter was the most successful female UK composer of the decade. Together with her producer Tony Hatch (whom she married in 1967), she penned not only her chart-topping ballad but also a string of international hits for Petula Clark. Incidentally, the Staffordshire singer's smash gave producer Hatch his fifth UK No 1 in less than two years.

## BOB DYLAN
SUBTERRANEAN HOMESICK BLUES
*CBS*

The most talked-about American recording artist of the moment fared better in the UK with this Chuck Berry-influenced single than in his homeland. It came from the album *Bringing It All Back Home* which, in the UK, replaced his previous LP at the top.

## MARIANNE FAITHFULL
THIS LITTLE BIRD
*Decca*

One of 1965's leading ladies had her third major hit with a lilting John D. Loudermilk composition. It was the Nashville songwriter's third UK Top 10 entry in a year, the other two being recorded by the Nashville Teens, whose version of 'This Little Bird' was easily outpaced by Faithfull's vulnerable vocal interpretation.

## HERMAN'S HERMITS
WONDERFUL WORLD
*Columbia*

▲ 7
⑩ 3
—/500

Herb Alpert co-wrote this top-notch teen tune with Sam Cooke, whose version had been a major US hit in 1960. Herman's interpretation joined two other singles by the Manchester marvels in the US Top 20. In 1986, a re-issue of Cooke's original recording reached the UK Top 3.

## ROCKIN' BERRIES
POOR MAN'S SON
*Piccadilly*

▲ 5
⑩ 2•
—/500

This entertaining UK outfit notched up their last notable bestseller with a closely cloned cover of a US Top 10 single by The Reflections. When the hits stopped, the group continued to be a draw on the club circuit thanks to their unique blend of humour and music.

## SANDIE SHAW
LONG LIVE LOVE
*Pye*

▲ 1
⑩ 4
102/500

Even though she performed this catchy Chris Andrews-composed UK chart topper on the *Ed Sullivan Show*, the fashion-conscious young performer still did not break into the US market.

## SHIRLEY ELLIS
THE CLAPPING SONG
*London American*

▲ 6
⑩ 1•
—/500

See US entry (April).

# UNITED STATES
# JUNE 1965

## FOUR TOPS
I CAN'T HELP MYSELF
*Motown*

▲ 1
⑩ 1
82/500

Nine years after their first release, the legendary Detroit R&B quartet debuted in the US Top 10 with a song penned by celebrated producers, Holland, Dozier & Holland. This definitive Motown track was the top R&B single of 1965. In the UK, despite a successful Brian Epstein-promoted tour, it did not crack the Top 10 until 1970. A remake by Donnie Elbert in 1972 reached the transatlantic Top 40.

## BYRDS
MR TAMBOURINE MAN
*Columbia*

▲ 1
⑩ 1
178/500

The Byrds' version of this Bob Dylan composition was the record that put folk/rock on the musical map. It was also the first single by an US group to top the UK charts in almost four years. On the ground-breaking track, noted surf-producer Terry Melcher tried to combined the sounds of The Beach Boys, The Beatles and Dylan. Interestingly, Jim McGuinn was the only member of the legendary West Coast act who actually played on it.

## ROGER MILLER
ENGINE ENGINE
*Smash*

▲ 7
⑩ 4
—/500

One of the decade's most popular country entertainers collected his fourth Top 10 entry in less than a year with a self-penned train song. As usual, this crossover hit was produced by the one-time child vocal prodigy, Jerry Kennedy.

## HERMAN'S HERMITS
WONDERFUL WORLD
*MGM*

▲ 4
⑩ 4
499/500

See UK entry (May).

## YARDBIRDS
FOR YOUR LOVE
*Epic*

▲ 6
⑩ 1
—/500

See UK entry (April).

## PATTI PAGE
HUSH, HUSH SWEET
CHARLOTTE
*Columbia*

▲ 8
⑩14•
—/500

One of the US's most popular female singers and best-known TV celebrities of the 1950s clocked up the last of her two dozen Top 10 entries with the title song of an award-winning Bette Davis movie. Frank DeVol and Mack David penned it, and it was Al Martino who sang it over the film's credits. Page, known as 'The Singing Rage', was born Clara Fowler in Muskogee, Oklahoma, and pioneered the use of multi-track vocals on record.

## ROLLING STONES
(I CAN'T GET NO)
SATISFACTION
*London*

▲ 1
⑩ 3
34/500

See UK entry (September).

## JOHNNY RIVERS
SEVENTH SON
*Imperial*

▲ 7
⑩ 3
—/500

A Willie Dixon-penned blues/R&B standard became the fifth Top 20 entry in succession for the singer who was given his stage name by 'Mr Rock And Roll', DJ Alan Freed. Among stand-out earlier recordings of the song were ones by such acts as Muddy Waters, Willie Mabon and Mose Allison.

# UNITED KINGDOM
# JUNE 1965

## BURT BACHARACH
TRAINS AND BOATS
AND PLANES
*London American*

▲ 4
⑩ 1•
—/500

This Kansas City-born composer/conductor and arranger was arguably the US's most successful songsmith of the rock era. He had his only hit as a recording artist with a potent pop ditty which also became a chart vehicle for Billy J. Kramer & The Dakotas. In the US, Bacharach's treatment was overlooked, but his protégé Dionne Warwick whisked it into the Top 40 in 1966.

## ELVIS PRESLEY
CRYING IN THE CHAPEL
*RCA*

▲ 1
⑩33
144/500

See US entry (May).

## EVERLY BROTHERS
THE PRICE OF LOVE
*Warner*

▲ 2
⑩13•
277/500

At the height of the British group craze, the duo who had influenced many of the top UK acts returned to the heights with a self-penned song that failed to chart in their homeland. In all the UK music polls the brothers were voted third top group of 1965 behind The Beatles and The Rolling Stones.

## HOLLIES
I'M ALIVE
*Parlophone*

▲ 1
⑩ 6
75/500

Clint Ballard, who penned the chart-topping 'Good Timing' (by Jimmy Jones), composed this highly touted group's first No 1. He had written it for Wayne Fontana & The Mindbenders, who had recently taken his 'Game Of Love' to the top of the US chart. Amazingly, it was The Hollies' last UK No 1 for 23 years.

### BACHELORS
MARIE
*Decca*

The most successful UK MOR act in the beat boom era were The Bachelors, who added to their transatlantic Top 20 total with a melodic interpretation of a late 1920s number composed by Irving Berlin.

### DONOVAN
COLOURS
*Pye*

The singer tagged 'the UK's Bob Dylan' scored his second Top 5 single in a row with another of his wistful compositions. Coincidentally, as the record was charting Donovan appeared at the prestigious Newport Folk Festival with Dylan.

### KINKS
SET ME FREE
*Pye*

A song leader Ray Davies had written for Cilla Black returned the innovative group to the heights in their homeland. Its release coincided with the act's debut US tour, which ended with them receiving a four-year live ban after missing some performances.

### GENE PITNEY
LOOKING THROUGH THE
EYES OF LOVE
*Stateside*

Pitney was arguably the most consistently successful US artist in the UK during the beat boom. He added to his hit tally with a compelling Barry Mann and Cynthia Weill composition that the Partridge Family re-introduced to the transatlantic Top 40 in 1973.

---

# UNITED STATES
# JULY 1965

---

### BARBARA MASON
YES, I'M READY
*Artic*

This 17-year-old soul singer from Philadelphia had the biggest of her seven R&B Top 20 entries with a seductive self-written song. In 1980, her updated rendition, 'Yes, I'm Ready '80', failed to ignite interest, but a version by Teri DeSario and KC reached runner-up slot in the US pop chart.

### JACKIE DeSHANNON
WHAT THE WORLD
NEEDS NOW IS LOVE
*Imperial*

After seeing songs that she had first recorded chart for The Searchers and Marianne Faithfull,

DeShannon finally had a hit of her own. This plea for world peace was penned by Burt Bacharach and Hal David, who produced her single in Nashville. DeShannon, who had toured the US with The Beatles in 1964, had been recording with little success under various names since 1959. DJ Tom Clay's moving 1971 rendition of the stand-out song also entered the Top 10.

### JAY & THE AMERICANS
CARA MIA
*UA*

Their pop version of a big ballad that British vocalist David Whitfield (with Mantovani's Orchestra) had taken into the Top 10 in 1954 lifted the New York group into the Top 5 for the third time.

## IAN WHITCOMB
YOU TURN ME ON
*Tower*

▲ 8
⑩ 1•
—/500

A wild fun-filled retro rocker, which Whitcomb recorded as an album filler, gave the singer/songwriter from Surrey a major US hit. Oddly, this few-holds-barred single, which several US stations banned, turned on few record buyers in his homeland. When future releases proved less fruitful, Whitcomb reverted to production (working with such celebrities as Mae West and Goldie Horn), and has also written critically acclaimed books on the history of music.

## HERMAN'S HERMITS
I'M HENRY VIII I AM
*MGM*

▲ 1
⑩ 5
196/500

Manchester's top teen idols reached No 1 for the second time in three months with a novelty number that started life in pre-World War I British music halls. Like their previous chart topper, this single was considered 'too British' to merit a UK release. Interestingly, in the UK, hit maker Joe Brown's 1961 recording of the song had few takers.

## TOM JONES
WHAT'S NEW PUSSYCAT?
*Parrot*

▲ 3
⑩ 2
393/500

Burt Bacharach and Hal David composed the title song from the madcap Peter Sellers and Woody Allen movie, which nearly gave the powerful vocalist his second transatlantic Top 10 entry in six months.

## GARY LEWIS & THE PLAYBOYS
SAVE YOUR HEART FOR ME
*Liberty*

▲ 2
⑩ 3
339/500

A Gary Geld and Peter Udell song took the quintet, fronted by the son of top comedian Jerry Lewis, back up the charts. It had previously been the B side of Brian Hyland's 1963 hit 'I'm Afraid To Go Home'.

## DAVE CLARK FIVE
I LIKE IT LIKE THAT
*Epic*

▲ 7
⑩ 5
—/500

In 1961 composer Chris Kenner had narrowly missed the top with his original version of this contagious R&B classic, which now added to the London combo's stockpile of US hits.

# UNITED KINGDOM
# JULY 1965

## WHO
ANYWAY ANYHOW ANYWHERE
*Brunswick*

▲ 10
⑩ 2
—/500

The group who, more than anyone, personified the British mod movement, stretched the boundaries of pop with another unconventional Pete Townshend-penned single. This feedback-filled track was used as the theme for *Ready Steady Go*.

## YARDBIRDS
HEART FULL OF SOUL
*Columbia*

▲ 2
⑩ 2
300/500

One of the most successful groups of 1965 had their second transatlantic Top 10 entry in a row with a Graham Gouldman composition. In the UK, the similarly named Byrds stopped them from scoring a possible No 1.

## PETER & GORDON
TO KNOW YOU IS TO
LOVE YOU
*Columbia*

▲ 5
🔟 4•
—/500

Peter & Gordon, one of the most popular crowd pleasers of the period, added to their collection of transatlantic charters with a revival of Phil Spector's first hit song. Bobby Vinton returned this outstanding romantic ballad to the Top 40 in 1969.

## BYRDS
MR TAMBOURINE MAN
*CBS*

▲ 1
🔟 1
134/500

See US entry (June).

## LULU
LEAVE A LITTLE LOVE
*Decca*

▲ 8
🔟 2
—/500

The Scottish teenager, voted Best Newcomer of 1964, came runner-up in the Brighton Song Festival (Kenny Lynch won with 'I'll Stay By You') with this noteworthy Les Reed composition.

## IVY LEAGUE
TOSSING AND TURNING
*Piccadilly*

▲ 3
🔟 2•
399/500

One of the most polished British vocal groups of the 1960s had their highest-ranked hit with a song composed by Birmingham-born members John Carter (real name John Shakespeare) and Ken Lewis (real name James Hawker). Carter and Lewis left in 1966 to concentrate on song writing.

## DUSTY SPRINGFIELD
IN THE MIDDLE OF
NOWHERE
*Philips*

▲ 8
🔟 4
—/500

Buddy Kaye, who penned such pop novelties as 'A You're Adorable' and 'Speedy Gonzales', composed this equally commercial song. Like most of Dusty's hits, it was produced by Johnny Franz.

## FORTUNES
YOU'VE GOT YOUR
TROUBLES
*Decca*

▲ 2
🔟 1
298/500

This clean-cut vocal harmony act's fifth release was their first and biggest hit. The instantly infectious sing-along song also introduced writers Roger Greenaway and Roger Cook to the transatlantic Top 10. In the UK, only 'Help' from The Beatles halted the single's progress to the very top.

## BEATLES
HELP!
*Parlophone*

▲ 1
🔟 9
80/500

As the title song from the world's most popular group's second film headed the UK charts, they started their third US tour in front of a record crowd of 55,600 at New York's Shea Stadium.

## ANIMALS
WE GOTTA GET OUT OF
THIS PLACE
*Columbia*

▲ 2
🔟 5
335/500

The short-haired UK band achieved their fourth transatlantic Top 20 entry in a year with a rebellious song that composers Barry Mann and Cynthia Weil had intended for the Righteous Brothers. Lead singer Eric Burdon re-recorded it with Katrina & The Waves in 1990.

## JOAN BAEZ
THERE BUT FOR FORTUNE
*Fontana*

▲ 8
🔟 1
—/500

Despite the fact that her version of this thought-provoking Phil Ochs composition was her only hit single of the decade, folk music's leading lady was no stranger to the transatlantic album charts. The track came from the politically active New Yorker's fifth US Top 20 LP, *Joan Baez/5*, which was one of the vocalist's three UK Top 10 albums in 1965.

# UNITED STATES
# AUGUST 1965

## SONNY & CHER
I GOT YOU BABE
*Atco*

▲ 1
⑩ 1
113/500

This way-out, hippie-dressed married couple were the world's most talked-about new act of 1965. The one-time Phil Spector session singers topped the transatlantic charts with a Sonny (Bono) composition that is often called the first hippie anthem. To begin with, Atlantic felt that the track which gave the label their first UK No 1 should have been the B side. Sonny's composition also headed the UK chart 20 years later by UB40.

## PATTY DUKE
DON'T JUST STAND THERE
*UA*

▲ 8
⑩ 1•
—/500

In 1962, when she was only 14, the New York-born actress/singer became the youngest person to win an Oscar for her role in *The Miracle Worker*. She was given her own TV series in 1963 and two years later achieved a couple of Top 40 singles. Duke's biggest hit came with a Lor Crane and Bernice Ross (writers of 'White On White') song that had earlier been recorded by The Five Chords. Incidentally, she subsequently headed the Screen Actors Guild.

## RIGHTEOUS BROTHERS
UNCHAINED MELODY
*Philles*

▲ 4
⑩ 3
459/500

'Unchained Melody' is one of the most remarkable songs of the rock era. In 1955, three versions of the film theme reached the Top 10 on both sides of the Atlantic. Added to this, the Righteous Brothers' timeless interpretation was a transatlantic Top 20 hit in both 1965 and 1990 (in the US in 1990, both their original recording and a new version by the duo made the Top 20!). In 1995, a closely cloned cover by Robson Green and Jerome Flynn sold almost two million in the UK.

## FOUR TOPS
IT'S THE SAME OLD SONG
*Motown*

▲ 5
⑩ 2
—/500

Ironically, this single bore a marked resemblance to the foursome's previous release, 'I Can't Help Myself'. A 1971 version by The Weathermen (aka Jonathan King) took the song into the UK Top 20 for the only time.

## BEACH BOYS
CALIFORNIA GIRLS
*Capitol*

▲ 3
⑩ 9ʰ
410/500

One of the great all-time summer songs continued the Beach Boys' phenomenal US chart run. Amazingly, in the UK this single, and their previous No 1 'Help Me Rhonda', only managed mid-table placings. A revival by David Lee Roth in 1985 also reached the US Top 5.

## BILLY JOE ROYAL
DOWN IN THE BOONDOCKS
*Columbia*

▲ 9
⑩ 1•
—/500

Joe South penned the 'wrong side of the tracks' opus which took the distinctive singer on the first of his four visits to the US Top 40 in the 1960s. The song was a Top 40 country hit for Penny DeHaven in 1969 and fellow Georgia boy Freddy Weller in 1970. After a relatively quiet recording period, Royal became a frequent visitor to the country charts himself in the late 1980s.

## BEATLES
HELP!
*Capitol*

▲ 1
⑩ 14
101/500

See UK entry (July).

## BOB DYLAN
LIKE A ROLLING STONE
*Columbia*

This extraordinary singer/songwriter from Minnesota (born Robert Zimmerman) finally cracked the US Top 20 with a six-minute track that is universally regarded as a milestone in rock music.

## MEL CARTER
HOLD ME THRILL ME KISS ME
*Imperial*

Updating oldies was this Cincinnati-born balladeer's speciality. The biggest of his handful of US chart entries came with his version of Karen Chandler's 1952 Top 10 entry, which its composer

Harry Noble had recorded first. The one-time award-winning gospel singer later moved into the acting field with some success. In 1994, Gloria Estefan brought the song back into the UK Top 20.

## JAMES BROWN
PAPA'S GOT A BRAND NEW BAG
*King*

Nine years after his R&B chart debut, the 'hardest working man in show business' debuted in the pop Top 10 with his twenty-fourth Top 100 entry. The renowned Georgia-born entertainer, known as 'Soul Brother No 1', registered with an innovative self-composed R&B stomper that is rightfully regarded as a classic of 1960s soul. Brown's protégé Anna King recorded an answer version, 'Mama's Got A Bag Of Her Own'.

---

# UNITED KINGDOM
# AUGUST 1965

---

## DAVE CLARK FIVE
CATCH US IF YOU CAN
*Columbia*

This was the title song from the group's first starring film (it was retitled *Having A Wild Weekend* in the US). One-time movie stunt man Clark composed it with the quintet's guitarist Lenny Davidson.

## JONATHAN KING
EVERYONE'S GONE TO THE MOON
*Decca*

One of the great characters of the British pop music scene scored his only transatlantic Top 20 entry with a wistful song that he had written 'as a take-off of Bob Dylan'. The well-educated

London-born entrepreneur was one of the most successful producers in the UK during the 1970s (when he also personally had hits under several pseudonyms). It was the ever-controversial King who first recorded such acts as Genesis, The Bay City Rollers and 10cc.

## BILLY FURY
IN THOUGHTS OF YOU
*Decca*

Fury's five-year reign as a Top 10 regular ended with a song composed by UK writers Geoff Morrow and Chris Arnold (who later wrote for Elvis Presley and Barry Manilow). After a long dry spell, this major UK rock figure returned to notch up a couple of minor hits in the early 1980s. He died from heart failure aged 41 in 1983.

## MARIANNE FAITHFULL
SUMMER NIGHTS
*Decca*

▲ 10
⑩ 4•
—/500

In her first year of recording, Faithfull notched up four consecutive UK Top 10 and US Top 40 singles. Nevertheless, 'Summer Nights' was to be her last notable hit. Since the mid-1960s, this distinctive and controversial vocalist has maintained a sizeable cult following on both sides of the Atlantic.

## SONNY & CHER
I GOT YOU BABE
*Atlantic*

▲ 1
⑩ 1
122/500

See US entry.

## HORST JANKOWSKI
A WALK IN THE BLACK FOREST
*Mercury*

▲ 3
⑩ 1•
297/500

One of the year's biggest left-field transatlantic Top 20 hits was a bouncy piano instrumental originally called 'Eine Schwarzwaldfahrt', which was performed by a poll-winning German musician. The multi-instrumentalist, who had worked with such international stars as Ella Fitzgerald and Miles Davis, also earned a US gold record for his album *Genius Of Jankowski*. His long-forgotten follow-ups included 'Black Forest Holiday'.

## MARCELLO MINERBI
ZORBA'S DANCE
*Durium*

▲ 6
⑩ 1•
—/500

Italian orchestra leader Minerbi had a one-off UK hit with the music from the dance scene in the Oscar-winning Anthony Quinn movie *Zorba The Greek*. In the US, Herb Alpert & The Tijuana Brass had the Top 20 version of the film's title song. Both these works came from the pen of noted Greek composer Mikis Theodorakis, whose orchestra recorded them on the film's successful soundtrack album.

## BYRDS
ALL I REALLY WANT TO DO
*CBS*

▲ 4
⑩ 2•
—/500

This pioneering West Coast folk/rock band's treatment of a memorable Bob Dylan song battled with Cher's version on both sides of the Atlantic. In the US, Cher out-pointed them, but in the UK, where their live shows had only been coolly received, they had the top-selling version.

## SHADOWS
DON'T MAKE MY BABY BLUE
*Columbia*

▲ 10
⑩ 14
—/500

The ground-breaking UK instrumental band's last Top 10 entry of the decade came with a vocal version of a Barry Mann and Cynthia Weill song that charted earlier in the US by Frankie Laine. The Shadows, who continued to add to their hit tallies in the 1970s, 1980s and 1990s, have a chart span unmatched by any other UK group.

# UNITED STATES
# SEPTEMBER 1965

## WE FIVE
YOU WERE ON MY MIND
*A&M*

Mike Stewart, the brother of Kingston Trio member John Stewart, was in the California-based folk/pop quintet who are best remembered for their version of this winning Sylvia Fricker composition. In the UK, the song introduced Crispian St Peters to the chart.

## BARRY McGUIRE
EVE OF DESTRUCTION
*Dunhill*

Despite bans on many stations, this hard-hitting protest record was one of the year's biggest transatlantic successes. It was the only major solo hit for the rough-edged vocalist, who had co-written and sung lead on the New Christy Minstrels' 1963 Top 20 entry 'Green Green'. The song was composed by P.F. Sloan and Steve Barri and inspired many answer versions, including Top 40 entry 'Dawn Of Correction' by The Spokesmen.

## TURTLES
IT AIN'T ME BABE
*White Whale*

This West Coast group, who first recorded as The Crossfires, found success by dint of a song that Johnny Cash and June Carter had charted with on both sides of the Atlantic earlier in the year. Interestingly, before they cut the noteworthy Bob Dylan composition the pop/folk quintet had rejected the chart-topping 'Eve Of Destruction'.

## RAMSEY LEWIS TRIO
THE 'IN' CROWD
*Argo*

Pianist Lewis and his trio were the most popular jazz act on the singles chart in the mid-1960s, and

they had a string of bestsellers with jazzy instrumental interpretations of current R&B and pop hits. The biggest of the combo's three Top 20 entries was a toe-tapping treatment of a recent transatlantic chart entry by Dobie Gray; their interpretation earned them the Grammy for Top Jazz Instrumental. Only The Beatles' album *Help* prevented the trio's *The 'In' Crowd* LP from heading the charts.

## DAVE CLARK FIVE
CATCH US IF YOU CAN
*Epic*

See UK entry (August).

## McCOYS
HANG ON SLOOPY
*Bang*

A song that charted in 1964 by The Vibrations (under the title 'My Girl Sloppy') introduced the youthful band to the transatlantic Top 10. Hit makers The Strangeloves intended to record it themselves, but instead added The McCoys' vocals to their existing backing track. This infectious Bert Berns and Wes Farrell song also reached the US Top 20 in 1965 by the Ramsey Lewis Trio. Interestingly, a 1975 revival by McCoys' member Rick Derringer was a minor hit.

## YARDBIRDS
HEART FULL OF SOUL
*Epic*

See UK entry (July).

## SONNY
LAUGH AT ME
*Atco*

▲ 10
⑩ 1•
—/500

This 30-year-old singer/songwriter and A&R man from Detroit (born Salvatore Bono) had the only major solo hit of his long career with his

self-penned plea for understanding. Some may have laughed at Sonny's appearance, but he laughed all the way to the bank. He also showed that an old hippy can make good when he was elected Mayor of Palm Springs in 1988.

# UNITED KINGDOM
# SEPTEMBER 1965

## ROLLING STONES
(I CAN'T GET NO)
SATISFACTION
*Decca*

▲ 1
⑩ 5
127/500

One of the all-time great rock singles was recorded and first released in the US. This legendary Jagger and Richards-composed teen anthem gave the universally acclaimed quintet their fourth UK No 1 in a row and their first US chart topper. Interestingly, the single's instantly recognizable opening riff was inspired by the Martha & The Vandella's hit 'Dancing In The Street' – a song front man Mick Jagger recorded with David Bowie 20 years later.

## WALKER BROTHERS
MAKE IT EASY ON
YOURSELF
*Philips*

▲ 1
⑩ 1
147/500

Their third release after relocating to the UK gave this photogenic, but unrelated, Los Angeles trio the first of three successive UK Top 3 hits. Chart regulars Burt Bacharach and Hal David composed the lost-love lament that took them to the top. The trio's single also graced the Top 20 in the US, bettering the chart performance of the original 1962 recording by R&B balladeer Jerry Butler. The group became instant teen idols in the UK and were consequently voted Brightest Hope of 1965 in the *MM* poll.

## BOB DYLAN
LIKE A ROLLING STONE
*CBS*

▲ 4
⑩ 3
492/500

See US entry.

## KINKS
SEE MY FRIENDS
*Pye*

▲ 10
⑩ 5
—/500

One of the most popular UK bands scored their sixth UK Top 20 single in a year with another perceptive song from the pen of prolific front man Ray Davies.

## CHER
ALL I REALLY WANT
TO DO
*Liberty*

On both sides of the Atlantic, Cher (born Cherilyn Sakisian LaPierre) clicked with her interpretation of this superior Bob Dylan song. In the US it was bigger than the version by recent chart toppers The Byrds. Her album of the same name also entered the transatlantic Top 20.

## SONNY
LAUGH AT ME
*Atlantic*

See US entry.

## HOLLIES
LOOK THROUGH ANY
WINDOW
*Parlophone*

▲ 4
⑩ 7
490/500

The influential act's seventh successive UK Top 10 single was the first of several Hollies' hits composed for them by fellow Manchester resident Graham Gouldman (later of 10cc). This potent pop ditty also launched them into the US Top 10 for the first time.

## KEN DODD
TEARS
*Columbia*

▲ 1
⑩ 2
7/500

A song Rudy Vallee made popular in 1931, sold over a million copies in the UK by this popular entertainer. 'Tears' was the UK's top single in 1965 – the year the comedian/singer was voted Top Show Business Personality.

## BARRY MCGUIRE
EVE OF DESTRUCTION
*RCA*

▲ 3
⑩ 1•
346/500

See US entry.

# UNITED STATES
# OCTOBER 1965

## BEATLES
YESTERDAY
*Capitol*

▲ 1
⑩ 15
62/500

Paul McCartney was the only Beatle who appeared on the tenth US chart-topping single accredited to the group. The song, which McCartney originally called 'Scrambled Eggs', has been recorded by thousands of different artists and has received an unprecedented six million plays on US radio. In their homeland Matt Monro had the 1965 hit, while The Beatles' version did not crack the Top 10 until 1976.

## ROY HEAD & THE TRAITS
TREAT HER RIGHT
*Back Beat*

▲ 2
⑩ 1•
328/500

If it had not have been for The Beatles unstoppable single 'Yesterday', this soulful Texas-born entertainer would have topped the charts with his self-composed stomper. It was the only major pop hit for the rubber-legged performer, who ten years later began a string of country successes.

## FORTUNES
YOU'VE GOT YOUR
TROUBLES
*Press*

▲ 7
⑩ 1•
—/500

See UK entry (July).

## SONNY & CHER
BABY DON'T GO
*Reprise*

▲ 8
⑩ 2
—/500

A track that the year's hottest new act had recorded in 1964 as Caesar & Cleo joined three of their other singles in the UK and US charts.

## LOVIN' SPOONFUL
DO YOU BELIEVE IN MAGIC
*Kama Sutra*

▲ 9
⑩ 1
—/500

One of the decade's most successful US groups placed their first seven releases in the Top 10. This debut hit was an infectious jug band-influenced folk/rock song composed by lead vocalist and autoharp player John Sebastian. Teen idol Shaun Cassidy's 1978 revival also reached the Top 40.

## TOYS
A LOVER'S CONCERTO
*Dynovoice*

▲ 2
⑩ 1•
296/500

Only The Beatles and Stones halted the chart progress of this female R&B trio's first hit. The single, which was based on Bach's 'Minuet In G', also climbed into the UK Top 5. Soon after their hit, tone-deaf singer Mrs Miller charted with the song. The New York group's next release, 'Attack', followed it into the US Top 20, but subsequent releases, including the similar 'My Love Sonata', fared less well.

## GENTRYS
KEEP ON DANCING
*MGM*

▲ 4
⑩ 1•
—/500

Noted Memphis producer/composer Chips Moman was behind the desk on these Tennessee teenagers' only major hit. The song, which was quickly cut as a throwaway B side, had originally been released by another local act, The Avantis, on Chess in 1963. In the UK, the stomping 'Keep On Dancing' gave The Bay City Rollers their first chart entry in 1971. WWF fans may be interested to note that Gentrys' member Jimmy Hart now manages Hulk Hogan.

## HERMAN'S HERMITS
JUST A LITTLE BIT BETTER
*MGM*

▲ 7
⑩ 6
—/500

The act that headed Billboard's survey of US hit singles artists for 1965 clocked up their sixth Top 10 entry of the year. The song was written by Kenny Young, who coincidentally had recorded an answer version to the group's first chart topper entitled 'Mrs Green's Ugly Daughter'.

## ROLLING STONES
GET OFF OF MY CLOUD
*London*

▲ 1
⑩ 4
152/500

See UK entry (November).

## GARY LEWIS & THE PLAYBOYS
EVERYBODY LOVES A CLOWN
*Liberty*

▲ 4
⑩ 4
—/500

Lead singer Lewis (born Gary Levitch) co-wrote the popular Hollywood-based combo's latest million seller with producer Snuff Garrett and their regular arranger Leon Russell. It was also the title track to the act's third album.

## BOB DYLAN
POSITIVELY 4TH STREET
*Columbia*

▲ 7
⑩ 2
—/500

The performer whose nasal vocal style redefined the word 'singer', continued his move from cult hero to commercial superstar with another self-composed folk-rock favourite.

## VOGUES
YOU'RE THE ONE
*Co & Ce*

▲ 4
⑩ 1
—/500

A song that Petula Clark had released on her *I Know A Place* album opened the chart account for this smooth harmony vocal group from Pennsylvania. Their recording of Tony Hatch's catchy composition was picked up by Co & Ce from the even smaller Blue Star label.

## LEN BARRY
1-2-3
*Decca*

▲ 2
⑩ 1•
277/500

The ex-leader of The Dovells (born Leonard Borisoff) had a transatlantic Top 3 single with this up-tempo blue-eyed soul gem that he co-wrote with John Madara and David White (ex Danny & The Juniors). Interestingly, among the numbers he later recorded with less success was '4-5-6'.

# UNITED KINGDOM
# OCTOBER 1965

## MANFRED MANN
IF YOU GOTTA GO, GO NOW
*HMV*

▲ 2
⑩ 5
312/500

During the decade the celebrated quintet chalked up three UK Top 10 entries written by Bob Dylan. The first was a suggestive song which lead singer Paul Jones handled convincingly.

## NINI ROSSO
IL SILENZIO
*Durium*

▲ 8
⑩ 1•
—/500

Italian trumpet star Rosso had his only UK chart entry with an instrumental that earned the first European Common Market gold disc (it reputedly sold over five million copies). The song, which he based on 'The Last Post' was covered in the US by hit maker Al Hirt. Interestingly, a year earlier a theme Rosso had written and originally recorded, 'The Legion's Last Patrol', had been a UK Top 10 entry by Ken Thorne.

## ANDY WILLIAMS
ALMOST THERE
*CBS*

▲ 2
⑩ 3
271/500

Despite a relatively poor showing Stateside, a song that the popular TV show host performed in the movie *I'd Rather Be Rich*, almost made it to the top in the UK.

## McCOYS
HANG ON SLOOPY
*Immediate*

▲ 5
⑩ 1•
—/500

See US entry (September).

## SANDIE SHAW
MESSAGE UNDERSTOOD
*Pye*

▲ 6
⑩ 5
—/500

As the model-like entertainer was voted Top UK Female Singer of 1965 she logged up her fifth consecutive Top 10 entry with another catchy Chris Andrews song.

## DUSTY SPRINGFIELD
SOME OF YOUR LOVIN'
*Philips*

▲ 8
⑩ 5
—/500

The first UK vocalist voted World's Top Female Singer in the *NME* poll continued her string of UK hits with a Carole King and Gerry Goffin beat ballad. She was backed on the soulful single by US session singers Doris Troy and Madeleine Bell.

## YARDBIRDS
EVIL HEARTED YOU/
STILL I'M SAD
*Columbia*

▲ 3
⑩ 3
451/500

This pioneering band's most innovative release to date coupled a Graham Gouldman song with a ground-breaking opus that included a Gregorian chant. In the US, 'Still I'm Sad' was the B side of the group's third Top 20 entry, 'I'm A Man'.

## HEDGEHOPPERS ANONYMOUS
IT'S GOOD NEWS WEEK
*Decca*

▲ 5
⑩ 1•
—/500

Jonathan King composed and produced the sarcastic semi-protest song that briefly transported this group of RAF servicemen to the heights. Cleverly combining a message with a catchy chorus, it almost jetted the high-flying quintet into the US Top 40 as well. Although it was the first of many hit productions for King, all the band's later releases failed to take off.

## CHRIS ANDREWS
YESTERDAY MAN
*Decca*

▲ 3
⑩ 1•
375/500

One of the UK's most successful songwriters of the 1960s had a major hit of his own with an engaging European-sounding foot stomper. The man who wrote many hits for Adam Faith and Sandie Shaw topped the German chart with this million-selling single. Voted second Best Newcomer of the Year in the *NME* poll, he managed one more Top 20 entry before he became a yesterday man.

## FORTUNES
HERE IT COMES AGAIN
*Decca*

▲ 4
⑩ 2
—/500

Top songsmiths Les Reed and Barry Mason composed The Fortunes' second successive UK Top 10 entry. In the US, the record's progress was harmed when they were refused a TV permit and had to cancel several shows. Unlike most beat boom acts, Dame Fortune continued to smile on the group in the 1970s, when they added a couple more hits to their transatlantic totals.

## MATT MONRO
YESTERDAY
*Parlophone*

▲ 8
⑩ 5•
—/500

The ballad-singing chart regular had the UK hit single with this Lennon & McCartney masterpiece (The Beatles' version was not released then as a single in their homeland). However, it was the last major success for the singer, who died in 1984.

---

# UNITED STATES

# NOVEMBER 1965

---

## FONTELLA BASS
RESCUE ME
*Checker*

▲ 4
⑩ 1•
467/500

One of the best-remembered soul singles of the mid-1960s gave this St Louis-born singer her only major hit. The Motown-influenced song was composed by Chess Record's staff writers Carl Smith and Raynard Miner. A re-recording by Bass in 1980 failed to rescue her from relative obscurity.

## HERB ALPERT & THE TIJUANA BRASS
A TASTE OF HONEY
*A&M*

▲ 7
⑩ 2
—/500

The top instrumental combo's Mexican-styled treatment of jazz composer/arranger Bobby Scott's 'A Taste Of Honey' picked up three Grammy awards, including Record of the Year in 1965. It was written for the 1962 Broadway musical of the same name. In the UK, the song was a hit for Acker Bilk in 1963 and later that year was recorded by The Beatles.

## SUPREMES
I HEAR A SYMPHONY
*Motown*

▲ 1
⑩ 6
157/500

This supreme 1960s girl group returned to the top with the title song of their third Top 10 album. Like all the trio's previous hits, the Holland, Dozier & Holland team wrote and produced 'I Hear A Symphony' and Diana Ross sang lead.

## FOUR SEASONS
LET'S HANG ON!
*Philips*

▲ 3
⑩ 9
256/500

One of the decade's bona fide pop classics gave the quartet their fifth transatlantic Top 20 entry. The song also reached the UK Top 20 by The Darts in 1980 and Barry Manilow in 1981. In 1995, lead singer Frankie Valli re-recorded it with Manhattan Transfer.

## MARVIN GAYE
AIN'T THAT PECULIAR
*Tamla*

▲ 8
⑩ 4
—/500

The Miracles composed the outstanding vocalist's third Top 10 single of the year, and their leader Smokey Robinson produced the track. In 1975, Diamond Reo narrowly missed the Top 40 with the song.

## BYRDS
TURN! TURN! TURN!
*Columbia*

▲ 1
⑩ 2•
71/500

The Byrds played a pivotal role in 1960s music. Their second chart topper was a memorable song that folk pioneer Pete Seeger had adapted from a bible passage in the Book of Ecclesiastes. The group (and its off-shoots), who laid the groundwork for both folk/rock and country/rock music, were rightfully added to the Rock and Roll Hall of Fame in 1991.

## JAMES BROWN
I GOT YOU (I FEEL GOOD)
*King*

▲ 3
⑩ 2
336/500

R&B's most influential and imitated performer registered his biggest hit with a self-composed soul masterpiece which Yvonne Fair had earlier released as 'I Found You'. It was the first of many million sellers recorded at the Criteria studio in Miami.

## SILKIE
YOU'VE GOT TO HIDE
YOUR LOVE AWAY
*Fontana*

▲ 10
⑩ 1•
—/500

John Lennon and Paul McCartney wrote and co-produced British folk group Silkie's only hit, and Paul and George Harrison played on the track. Surprisingly, this Brian Epstein-managed quartet's version of the song from The Beatles' *Help* album was only a mid-table charter in their homeland.

# UNITED KINGDOM
# NOVEMBER 1965

## ROLLING STONES
GET OFF OF MY CLOUD
*Decca*

▲ 1
⑩ 6
119/500

The world's No 2 group had their fifth UK No 1 single in succession with another outstanding self-penned rocker. In the US, where they were in the midst of a very profitable tour, it also reached the top rung.

## ANIMALS
IT'S MY LIFE
*Columbia*

▲ 7
⑩ 6
—/500

The celebrated UK band clocked up their sixth successive UK Top 10 entry with a rebellious offering composed by Roger Atkins (who subsequently wrote with Neil Sedaka and Ron 'The Archies' Dante).

## SEEKERS
THE CARNIVAL IS OVER
*Columbia*

▲ 1
⑩ 3
42/500

Distinctive vocalist Judith Durham fronted the pop/folk foursome who sold over a million copies of this haunting Tom Springfield song in the UK alone. For the record books, The Seekers spent more weeks in the UK chart in 1965 than any other act.

## WHO
MY GENERATION
*Brunswick*

▲ 2
⑩ 3
251/500

The band, who seemed hell bent on breaking every rule of pop music, had their biggest UK hit with a rebellious song that became an anthem for their generation. Writer Pete Townshend later called the track 'The only successful social statement I've ever made'.

## LEN BARRY
I-2-3
*Brunswick*

▲ 3
⑩ 1
308/500

See US entry (October).

## BOB DYLAN
POSITIVELY 4TH STREET
*CBS*

▲ 8
⑩ 4
—/500

See US entry (October).

## CLIFF RICHARD
WIND ME UP (LET ME GO)
*Columbia*

▲ 2
⑩ 29
209/500

Buddy Holly's ex-singing partner Bob Montgomery co-wrote this track, which was produced in Nashville by Billy Sherrill (who later produced many country hits by acts such as Tammy Wynette and George Jones).

# UNITED STATES
# DECEMBER 1965

## SHANGRI-LAS
I CAN NEVER GO HOME ANYMORE
*Red Bird*

▲ 6
⑩ 3•
—/500

This easily recognizable young vocal quartet had their last major hit with a melodramatic tear-jerker written by talented producer George 'Shadow' Morton. The quartet never charted in the US after 1966, and by the mid-1970s members Marge and Mary Ann Ganser had died.

## DAVE CLARK FIVE
OVER AND OVER
*Epic*

▲ 1
⑩ 7
199/500

The popular UK band scored their sole US No 1 with an update of the B side of Bobby Day's 1958 US smash 'Rock-in Robin'. Amazingly, in Britian this stomping single failed to crack the Top 40.

## DEAN MARTIN
I WILL
*Reprise*

▲ 10
⑩ 6•
—/500

This venerable Las Vegas regular had his seventh US Top 40 hit in 14 months with a song that previously charted in the US by Vic Dana and in the UK by Billy Fury. R&B singer Ruby Winters took the melodic ballad into the UK Top 10 in 1977.

## EDDY ARNOLD
MAKE THE WORLD GO AWAY
*RCA*

▲ 6
⑩ 1•
—/500

No singer in history has had more country chart entries than the 'Tennessee Plowboy'. His only transatlantic Top 10 hit came with his seventeenth country No 1. The song was written by Hank Cochran and had charted in 1963 by both Ray

Price and Timi Yuro. Donny and Marie Osmond brought it back into the transatlantic lists in 1975. Less than a year after this hit, Arnold was elected into the prestigious Country Music Hall of Fame.

## ROGER MILLER
ENGLAND SWINGS
*Smash*

The award-winning country singer/songwriter's last major pop hit returned him to the Top 20 on both sides of the Atlantic. This ode to swinging Britain was one of ten US Top 40s notched up by the Texan in the 1960s. Miller, who remained a leading country artist in the 1970s, died of cancer in 1992.

## MCCOYS
FEVER
*Bang*

This teenage band from Indiana had their second Top 10 entry in a row with a Feldman, Goldstein & Gottehrer (The Strangeloves) produced remake of a song that was hot in the 1950s by Little Willie John and Peggy Lee. Intriguingly, the B side, 'Sorrow', was a UK Top 5 entry for The Merseys in 1966 and David Bowie in 1973. Oft-recorded 'Fever' was a UK Top 10 hit in 1993 by Madonna.

## SIMON & GARFUNKEL
THE SOUNDS OF SILENCE
*Columbia*

One of the decade's biggest-selling acts had their first major hit eight years after debuting on the chart as Tom & Jerry. The pair originally recorded this thought-provoking Paul Simon song as part of the acoustic album *Wednesday Morning, 3 AM*. The duo had already split when, without their permission, rock guitar (played by Vinnie Bell of The Ramrods) and drums were added to the track and the resulting single started Simon & Garfunkel's enviable run of hits. In the UK, The Bachelors' interpretation easily outsold the original version.

## RIGHTEOUS BROTHERS
EBB TIDE
*Philles*

After their revival of R&B singer Roy Hamilton's 'Unchained Melody' turned to gold, the blue-eyed soul duo piloted another Hamilton hit (first recorded by its composer Robert Maxwell) from the mid-1950s up the US charts. In the UK, it reached the Top 3 in 1990.

# UNITED KINGDOM
# DECEMBER 1965

## TOYS
A LOVER'S CONCERTO
*Stateside*

See US entry (October).

## GENE PITNEY
PRINCESS IN RAGS
*Stateside*

Helen Miller, who had composed his earlier US chart hit 'It Hurts To be In Love', penned Pitney's latest UK Top 10 entry which, like his previous few singles, was more successful in the UK than in the US.

## BEATLES
DAY TRIPPER/WE CAN
WORK IT OUT
*Parlophone*

▲ 1
⑩ 10
35/500

In the US, both sides of the group's first double-sided UK No 1 hit entered the Top 5. The Vontastics' treatment of 'Day Tripper' reached the R&B Top 10, while Stevie Wonder's interpretation of 'We Can Work It Out' climbed into the US Top 20 in 1971.

## KEN DODD
THE RIVER
*Columbia*

▲ 3
⑩ 3
293/500

The Liverpool-born family entertainer's English lyric version of the Italian MOR song 'Le Colline Sono In Fioro' joined his chart-topping 'Tears' in the Top 10.

## P.J. PROBY
MARIA
*Liberty*

▲ 8
⑩ 4•
—/500

Proby's first Top 10 hit after a headline-grabbing, trouser-splitting incident on stage was his unique rendition of the well-known love song from West Side Story. 'Maria' was his sixth and last UK Top 20 single. The American-born vocalist's only US Top 40 entry came in 1967 with 'Niki Hoeky'.

## WALKER BROTHERS
MY SHIP IS COMING IN
*Philips*

▲ 3
⑩ 2
322/500

This instantly recognizable American trio was one of the UK's most popular recording acts in the mid-1960s. Their third Top 20 single was originally released by R&B vocalist Jimmy Radcliffe.

## FOUR SEASONS
LET'S HANG ON!
*Philips*

▲ 4
⑩ 3
427/500

See US entry (November).

# UNITED STATES
# JANUARY 1966

## BEATLES
WE CAN WORK IT OUT
*Capitol*

▲ 1
⑩ 16
85/500

See UK entry (December 1965).

## GARY LEWIS & THE PLAYBOYS
SHE'S JUST MY STYLE
*Liberty*

▲ 3
⑩ 5
403/500

A sing-along song co-written by Lewis, producer Snuff Garrett and arranger Leon Russell was the group's fifth Top 5 single from their first five releases. The singing drummer may not have been one of the decade's greatest vocalists, but he was one of the era's most popular front men in the US.

## STATLER BROTHERS
FLOWERS ON THE WALL
*Columbia*

▲ 4
⑩ 1•
—/500

For many years this Virginia vocal harmony quartet were the No 1 group in country music – their highly individual self-penned songs and unique vocal blend set them apart from the rest. The award-winning foursome, who put almost 50 records into the country Top 20, had their only major pop hit with a cleverly composed Grammy-winning country classic.

## VOGUES
FIVE O'CLOCK WORLD
*Co & Ce*

▲ 4
⑩ 2
428/500

The easy-on-the-ear vocal team had their second Top 5 entry in succession with a toe-tapping Allen Reynolds' composition. Reynolds went on to produce scores of country hits, including Garth Brooks' amazing run of multi-platinum albums and Hal Ketchum's 1992 country Top 20 revival of this song.

## BEATLES
DAY TRIPPER
*Capitol*

▲ 5
⑩ 17
—/500

See UK entry (December 1965).

## MIKE DOUGLAS
THE MEN IN MY LITTLE GIRL'S LIFE
*Epic*

▲ 6
⑩ 1•
—/500

In the late 1960s Chicago-born Douglas was America's No 1 daytime TV celebrity. His sole hit in the rock era came with a schmaltzy dad-to-daughter ode. It was not his first taste of fame, as he had been lead vocalist on such late 1940s Kay Kyser hits as 'Old Buttermilk Sky' and 'The Old-Lamplighter', songs which had charted in the 1960s for Bill Black's Combo and The Browns.

## ROLLING STONES
AS TEARS GO BY
*London*

▲ 6
⑩ 5
—/500

A melodic Jagger & Richard ballad, which had been a transatlantic Top 40 hit in 1964 for Marianne Faithfull, gave the controversial outfit their fifth US Top 20 entry in a year.

## T-BONES
NO MATTER WHAT SHAPE (YOUR STOMACH'S IN)
*Liberty*

▲ 3
⑩ 1•
379/500

One of the most successful TV jingles of the mid-1960s was turned into a hit by studio musicians assembled by producer Joe Saraceno. The instrumental track, which was used in an ad for Alka Seltzer, was composed by New Yorker Sascha Burland whose own studio act The Nutty Squirrels were scoring with 'Uh! Oh!' when the decade started. The nucleus of the T-Bones later became hit-making trio Hamilton, Joe Frank and Reynolds.

## HERMAN'S HERMITS
A MUST TO AVOID
*MGM*

See UK entry.

## LOVIN' SPOONFUL
YOU DIDN'T HAVE TO BE
SO NICE
*Kama Sutra*

This good-time rock quartet (named after a line in blues man Mississippi John Hurt's 'Coffee Blues') quickly returned to the Top 10 with a winning song composed by Steve Boone and John Sebastian.

## BEACH BOYS
BARBARA ANN
*Capitol*

Their rousing remake of The Regents' 1961 hit conveyed the consistent US chart entrants into the transatlantic Top 10 for the second time. Adding vocal support on the track were Jan &

Dean and later star Glen Campbell (who himself was briefly a member of the group).

## PETULA CLARK
MY LOVE
*Warner*

See UK entry (February).

## MITCH RYDER & THE DETROIT WHEELS
JENNY TAKE A RIDE!
*New Voice*

This white Detroit-based combo had the first of five Top 40 entries with a track that cleverly combined two rock/R&B favorites, Little Richard's 'Jenny Jenny' and the Ma Rainey/Chuck Willis standard 'C.C. Rider'. It was the fourth single by Ryder's (born William Levise Jr) band, who had recorded as Billy Lee & The Rivieras before noted producer Bob Crewe changed their name. Ryder's 1971 retread of this hit had relatively few takers.

# UNITED KINGDOM
# JANUARY 1966

## SPENCER DAVIS GROUP
KEEP ON RUNNIN'
*Fontana*

Seventeen-year-old singer/pianist Steve Winwood fronted this R&B band, who were led by Welshman Spencer Davis. The critically acclaimed group, whose first four releases had all been R&B cover versions, raced to No 1 with a catchy song penned by ska star Jackie Edwards.

## BARRON KNIGHTS
MERRIE GENTLE POPS
*Columbia*

The quirky quintet's last Top 20 entry of the decade was another of their trademark parody

singles. On this one, recent hits by such as The Rolling Stones, Marianne Faithfull and The Hollies were given the typical Barron Knights treatment.

## KINKS
TILL THE END OF THE DAY
*Pye*

As this instantly recognizable Ray Davies work continued the act's run of UK Top 20 entries, his clever composition 'A Well Respected Man' (a US-only single) took the quartet into the US Top 20.

## HERMAN'S HERMITS
A MUST TO AVOID
*Columbia*

▲ 6
⑩ 4
—/500

Noted West Coast composers Steve Barri and P.F. Sloan wrote this memorable song, which was heard in the record-breaking band's first starring film *Hold On*.

## HERB ALPERT
SPANISH FLEA
*Pye International*

▲ 3
⑩ 1
276/500

The most successful instrumental act of the 1960s first charted in the UK with a catchy toe-tapper written by band member Julius Wechter (who also led another popular A&M outfit, the Baja Marimba Band).

## OVERLANDERS
MICHELLE
*Pye*

▲ 1
⑩ 1•
142/500

The first UK one-hit wonders of 1966 were a quintet who had been recording with little success since 1961. Their timely Tony Hatch-produced treatment of the acclaimed bilingual Beatles ballad topped the UK lists just three weeks after its release. A version by UK duo David & Jonathan (aka Roger Greenaway and Roger Cook) grabbed the honours with the Grammy-winning song in the US.

## CRISPIAN ST PETERS
YOU WERE ON MY MIND
*Decca*

▲ 2
⑩ 1
310/500

Not only did his cover of We Five's US Top 10 hit almost head the UK chart, but this Kent vocalist's (born Peter Smith) version also reinstated the song in the US Top 40.

---

# UNITED STATES

# FEBRUARY 1966

---

## LOU CHRISTIE
LIGHTNIN' STRIKES
*MGM*

▲ 1
⑩ 2
195/500

MGM did not see the potential of this song, and released it only under pressure from Christie and manager Bob Marcucci (who had earlier handled Frankie Avalon and Fabian). It was produced by Charles Calello (who frequently worked with the Four Seasons) and, like much of Christie's vocal work, it had a Frankie Valli feel. In 1994, the single logged its millionth play on US radio.

## RAY CHARLES
CRYING TIME
*ABC Paramount*

▲ 6
⑩ 11•
—/500

This outstanding performer won a Grammy (Best R&B Recording) for his heartfelt rendition of a song penned and released by country superstar Buck Owens. The influential singer, whose chart entries have spanned six decades, was one of the first acts inducted into the Rock and Roll Hall of Fame. In 1987 he deservedly received a Lifetime Grammy Award.

## STEVIE WONDER
UPTIGHT (EVERYTHING'S ALRIGHT)
*Tamla*

After almost three years of mid-table US hits, the talented vocalist/multi-instrumentalist achieved his first transatlantic Top 20 entry with this up-tempo self-composed soul anthem. Incidentally, Bill Cosby based his biggest-selling single, 'Little Ole Man' (1967), on it.

## SUPREMES
MY WORLD IS EMPTY WITHOUT YOU
*Motown*

For the first time in their career, the influential, platinum-plated trio had a Top 10 single that did not reach No 1. The song returned to the US charts in 1969 by José Feliciano.

## MARVELETTES
DON'T MESS WITH BILL
*Tamla*

Bill 'Smokey' Robinson composed and produced the ground-breaking Motown act's first major hit for four years – it also proved to be the ladies' last Top 10 entry. The group, who went through various personnel changes in their long career, were still recording in 1992 with original members Gladys Horton and Wanda Young. In 1995, they were awarded a Pioneer Award by the R&B Foundation.

## NANCY SINATRA
THESE BOOTS ARE MADE FOR WALKIN'
*Reprise*

After more than a dozen small-selling singles, Frank Sinatra's oldest child finally had a hit with this feminist-slanted foot stomper. The unforgettable transatlantic topper was composed for her by producer Lee Hazlewood, who had previously co-written a string of instrumental chart entries with Duane Eddy. Interestingly, the New Jersey-born vocalist had been the subject of her father's 1945 song hit 'Nancy (With The Laughing Face)'.

## SGT BARRY SADLER
THE BALLAD OF THE GREEN BERETS
*RCA*

Surprisingly, the US's top single of 1966 was written and recorded by a Vietnam veteran as a tribute to his fellow Green Berets (the nickname of the US Special Forces). The single (which at first was intended only for the armed services) headed the chart, as did his album of similarly themed patriotic songs. An answer version, 'He Wore The Green Beret' by Nancy Ames also marched into the US Top 100. The singing/songwriting soldier's future assaults on the chart made far less headway.

## MAMAS & THE PAPAS
CALIFORNIA DREAMIN'
*Dunhill*

When recent chart topper Barry McGuire recorded this haunting and melodic John and Michelle Phillips song on his *This Precious Time* album, he was backed by composers' group The Mamas & The Papas. The New York quartet replaced McGuire's vocal with their own unique harmonies and the resulting track gave them a dream career start.

## BOB LIND
ELUSIVE BUTTERFLY
*World Pacific*

This folk-oriented singer/songwriter from Baltimore had a transatlantic Top 5 entry with his very first release (in the UK a cover by Val Doonican also joined it). Within a short time Lind's songs had been recorded by such notables as Cher, Marianne Faithfull, Nancy Sinatra and The Turtles. Nevertheless, despite this creditable career start he found future hits as elusive as that butterfly, and turned his hand to writing plays and stories.

## FOUR SEASONS
WORKING MY WAY BACK TO YOU
*Philips*

Sandy Linzer and Denny Randell, who penned 'Let's Hang On', composed another top hit for the group whose span of chart entries now exceeds 38 years (1956–1995). A rework by The Spinners in 1980 took the song into the transatlantic Top 3.

# UNITED KINGDOM
# FEBRUARY 1966

## CILLA BLACK
LOVE'S JUST A BROKEN HEART
*Parlophone*

UK singer/songwriter Kenny Lynch composed Black's sixth successive Top 20 entry with leading US tunesmith Mort Shuman. The hit came soon after she appeared with The Beatles on Ed Sullivan's top-rated US TV show.

## NANCY SINATRA
THESE BOOTS ARE MADE FOR WALKIN'
*Reprise*

See US entry.

## MINDBENDERS
A GROOVY KIND OF LOVE
*Fontana*

The talented Manchester band had a transatlantic No 2 with a Carole Bayer Sager and Toni Wine composition, which had earlier been recorded by Patti Labelle & The Blue Belles. In 1988, Phil Collins went one better and took this renowned pop opus to the top on both sides of the Atlantic. The Mindbenders later evolved into hit makers Hotlegs and then 10cc.

## PINKERTON'S ASSORTED COLOURS
MIRROR MIRROR
*Decca*

Guitarist Tony Newman penned the bouncy song that gave this visually unique Warwickshire quintet their sole hit. The group, whose name was inspired by the colourful stage outfits they wore, were fronted by amplified autoharp player Sam 'Pinkerton' Kemp. In 1969 the combo successfully toured the US as the Flying Machine.

## LEN BARRY
LIKE A BABY
*Brunswick*

Blue-eyed soul singer Barry's similar-sounding follow-up to '1-2-3' was more popular in the UK than his homeland. It was, however, to be his last major hit as a vocalist, although he has since written several successful soul and dance records.

## ROLLING STONES
19TH NERVOUS BREAKDOWN
*Decca*

Coincidentally, the single that ended the gold-getting quintet's run of five UK No 1s held the runner-up position for three weeks on both sides of the Atlantic.

## SANDIE SHAW
TOMORROW
*Pye*

The singer who arguably personified the UK look of the 1960s more than any other had her highest-placed hit of 1966 with the fifth Chris Andrews-composed Top 10 entry of her career.

## PETULA CLARK
MY LOVE
*Pye*

This accessible and inviting Tony Hatch composition gave the internationally successful singer/actress her second US No 1 – the first time a UK female artist had achieved the feat. The track was recorded in the US and written by her producer on a flight over from the UK.

## SMALL FACES
SHA LA LA LA LEE
*Decca*

▲ 3
⑩ 1
393/500

Among the would-be mod gods only the Small Faces threatened to take The Who's throne. The photogenic London foursome's second Top 20 single was the first of their four Top 10 entries in 1966. The bubblegum rock song was co-written by US hit machine Mort Shuman and popular British entertainer Kenny Lynch.

## BEACH BOYS
BARBARA ANN
*Capitol*

▲ 3
⑩ 2
401/500

See US entry (January).

# UNITED STATES
# MARCH 1966

## HERMAN'S HERMITS
LISTEN PEOPLE
*MGM*

▲ 3
⑩ 8
449/500

This was one of the hugely popular British act's six US Top 10 hits that did not dent the UK chart (it was the B side to 'You Won't Be Leaving'). Written by fellow Manchester native Graham Gouldman, 'Listen People' was featured in the film *Where The Boys Meet The Girls*.

## ROLLING STONES
19TH NERVOUS
BREAKDOWN
*London*

▲ 2
⑩ 6
293/500

See UK entry (February).

## BEATLES
NOWHERE MAN
*Capitol*

▲ 3
⑩ 18
397/500

After nine consecutive No 1s on Capitol, The Beatles only managed a Top 3 hit with this Lennon & McCartney composition. In the UK, the track was only available on their album *Rubber Soul*.

## BOBBY FULLER FOUR
I FOUGHT THE LAW
*Mustang*

▲ 9
⑩ 1•
—/500

Once again, a group hit with a song previously recorded as a Crickets' B side. This time it was a quartet from Buddy Holly's home state, Texas, who had earlier released several small sellers on a handful of minor labels. Fuller's biggest seller was his fifth Mustang release – a noteworthy composition by Cricket Sonny Curtis, which punk band The Clash clicked with in the UK in 1988. Sadly, Fuller was found dead in his car just months after this debut hit – his death is still a mystery to the law.

## SIMON & GARFUNKEL
HOMEWARD BOUND
*Columbia*

▲ 5
⑩ 2
—/500

Paul Simon penned this lilting ballad while in a homesick mood during a UK folk club tour in the days before fame found him. It became the first of many transatlantic Top 10 entries for the folk-rock duo.

## LOVIN' SPOONFUL
DAYDREAM
*Kama Sutra*

| ▲ 2 |
| 🔟 3 |
| 298/500 |

These New York moptops' first transatlantic Top 10 entry was a particularly effective summer song written by lead singer John Sebastian. Their album of the same name also reached the Top 10 in the US and the UK.

## RIGHTEOUS BROTHERS
(YOU'RE MY) SOUL AND
INSPIRATION
*Verve*

| ▲ 1 |
| 🔟 5 |
| 67/500 |

A song Barry Mann and Cynthia Weil considered too similar to their earlier composition for the Righteous Brothers, 'You've Lost That Lovin' Feelin', returned the soulful duo to the top. It was the duo's first release on MGM after a $1 million move from Phil Spector's Philles label. Bill Medley produced the track, which gave his duo their fifth Top 5 hit in succession. In 1994, Medley re-recorded the song with another noted Spector protégé, Darlene Love.

# UNITED KINGDOM
# MARCH 1966

## GENE PITNEY
BACKSTAGE
*Stateside*

| ▲ 4 |
| 🔟 7 |
| —/500 |

As he successfully toured the UK, this dramatic beat ballad gave the transatlantic superstar his seventh UK Top 10 entry in less than two years.

## EDDY ARNOLD
MAKE THE WORLD
GO AWAY
*RCA*

| ▲ 8 |
| 🔟 1• |
| —/500 |

See US entry (December).

## HOLLIES
I CAN'T LET GO
*Parlophone*

| ▲ 2 |
| 🔟 8 |
| 357/500 |

A Chip Taylor song that Evie Sands had recorded previously narrowly missed the top spot by one of the decade's most popular UK acts. Interestingly, a couple of months later The Troggs took another Taylor tune, 'Wild Thing', into the runner-up position.

## WALKER BROTHERS
THE SUN AIN'T GONNA
SHINE (ANYMORE)
*Philips*

For the second time in six months the popular US trio reached No 1 in the UK with a dramatic lost-love ballad. This song, which also returned them to the US Top 20, was composed by Bob Crewe and Bob Gaudio and had previously been recorded by Frankie Valli.

## YARDBIRDS
SHAPES OF THINGS
*Columbia*

This legendary band's last release before session guitarist Jimmy Page joined them was an innovative self-penned psychedelic rock track. It completed a run of four successive UK Top 3 hits.

## KINKS
DEDICATED FOLLOWER OF
FASHION
*Pye*

This tongue-in-cheek ode to trendy UK young men kept the unique London foursome in fashion. It was another composition by the group's quintessential English singer/songwriter Ray Davies.

## BOB LIND
ELUSIVE BUTTERFLY
*Fontana*

See US entry (February).

---

# UNITED STATES
# APRIL 1966

---

## CHER
BANG BANG (MY BABY
SHOT ME DOWN)
*Imperial*

Only the Righteous Brothers (for whom she used to sing backing vocals) stopped Cher from reaching the top in the US. She finally reached No 1 there five years later, while in the UK the ever-popular vocalist had to wait until 1991.

## GARY LEWIS &
## THE PLAYBOYS
SURE GONNA MISS HER
*Liberty*

Bobby Russell composed the latest in a long line of US-only hits by the West Coast band, who had few rivals in the teen popularity stakes. This track features stand-out guitar playing from noted session musician Tommy Tedesco.

## JOHNNY RIVERS
SECRET AGENT MAN
*Imperial*

P.F. Sloan and Steve Barri, who composed the controversial 1965 No 1 'Eve Of Destruction', wrote Rivers' biggest hit for two years. It was the theme song from the British-made TV series *Secret Agent Man* (known as *Danger Man* in the UK).

## B.J. THOMAS &
## THE TRIUMPHS
I'M SO LONESOME I
COULD CRY
*Scepter*

Oklahoma-born singer Thomas and his group had their debut chart entry with a pop update of a song that its composer, country legend Hank Williams, had earlier made famous. At his father's suggestion, B.J. recorded it on an album for the tiny Pacemaker label. When it started to pick up airplay, Scepter took over distribution. Interestingly, Thomas became a regular country hit maker himself in the late 1970s.

## OUTSIDERS
TIME WON'T LET ME
*Capitol*

Their guitarist Tom King co-wrote the biggest of the Cleveland combo's four 1966 US Top 40 entries. The British-influenced quartet's lead vocalist Sonny Geraci later fronted Climax, whose 'Precious And Few' also entered the Top 10 in 1972.

## YOUNG RASCALS
GOOD LOVIN'
*Atlantic*

▲ 1
⑩ 1
177/500

R&B group The Olympics had a minor hit with this stomping Rudy Clark and Arthur Resnick composition a year before it rushed the Young Rascals to the top. The song had been a frequent feature in the New York quartet's live act for many months (member Felix Cavaliere was a big fan of The Olympics) before they recorded it as their second Atlantic single.

## PAUL REVERE & THE RAIDERS
KICKS
*Columbia*

▲ 4
⑩ 1
431/500

Surprisingly, one of the US's most successful groups of the late 1960s first charted in 1961 with an instrumental, and had to wait until their seventeenth single before finally cracking the Top 10. This photogenic quartet, who wore revolutionary war uniforms on stage, scored with an early anti-drug song composed by frequent chart visitors Barry Mann and Cynthia Weil.

## BEACH BOYS
SLOOP JOHN B
*Capitol*

▲ 3
⑩ 11
408/500

Brian Wilson's adaptation of a West Indian shanty from the 1920s sailed up the charts on both sides of the Atlantic. Incidentally, Lonnie Donegan's arrangement of the song had been a UK hit in 1960.

## MAMAS & THE PAPAS
MONDAY MONDAY
*Dunhill*

▲ 1
⑩ 2
97/500

A song that three of the quartet disliked (only composer John Phillips and producer Lou Adler saw its potential) was the acclaimed West Coast vocal group's only No 1 single. This Grammy-winning single came from their chart-topping debut album, *If You Can Believe Your Eyes And Ears*.

## HERMAN'S HERMITS
LEANING ON THE LAMP POST
*MGM*

▲ 9
⑩ 9
—/500

This gold-plated group notched up their ninth consecutive US Top 10 entry in just 15 months with a song made famous in the UK in 1937 by the popular entertainer George Formby. The band sang it in the movie *Hold On*.

# UNITED KINGDOM
# APRIL 1966

## VAL DOONICAN
ELUSIVE BUTTERFLY
*Decca*

▲ 5
⑩ 3
—/500

The easy-on-the-ear Irish vocalist's interpretation of 'Elusive Butterfly' joined Bob Lind's original version in the UK Top 5. Doonican sang it on his very popular TV series, which was not too dissimilar from the US show hosted by the equally relaxed and casually dressed Andy Williams.

## SPENCER DAVIS GROUP
SOMEBODY HELP ME
*Fontana*

▲ 1
⑩ 2
161/500

For the second time within three months, this highly regarded Birmingham band topped the UK chart with an infectious song composed by ska performer Jackie Edwards.

## DAVE DEE, DOZY, BEAKY, MICK & TICH
HOLD TIGHT
*Fontana*

▲ 4
⑩ 1
435/500

The UK's most successful new group of 1966 had the first of ten Top 20 entries in a row with a song penned by their managers Ken Howard and Alan Blaikley. This foot-stomping opus, which owed something to the Routers' US hit 'Let's Go', was adopted as an anthem by football fans.

## BACHELORS
THE SOUND OF SILENCE
*Decca*

▲ 3
⑩ 8•
390/500

In the UK, the hit version of Simon & Garfunkel's US No 1 was by the Dublin group who had been chart regulars for over three years. It was one of the few contemporary songs the trio recorded. Their last Top 20 entry came a year later with a revival of another old standard, 'Marta'.

## WHO
SUBSTITUTE
*Reaction*

▲ 5
⑩ 4
—/500

The quartet, who set as many fashion trends as musical ones, reached the UK Top 10 for the fourth time in a row with this self-penned single. Nevertheless, in the US, most record buyers still greeted their name with 'who?'. 'Substitute' revisited the UK Top 10 in 1976.

## DUSTY SPRINGFIELD
YOU DON'T HAVE TO SAY YOU LOVE ME
*Philips*

▲ 1
⑩ 6
171/500

This was the critically acclaimed vocalist's only No 1 single and her first transatlantic Top 10 entry. It was an intense and dramatic Italian song which,

under the title 'Io Che No Vivo Senza Ta', had won the prestigious San Remo Song Festival in 1965. A later recording by Elvis Presley also reached the transatlantic Top 20 in 1970.

## CHER
BANG BANG (MY BABY SHOT ME DOWN)
*Liberty*

▲ 3
⑩ 2
432/500

See US entry.

## ALAN PRICE SET
I PUT A SPELL ON YOU
*Decca*

▲ 9
⑩ 1
—/500

A year after his arrangement of 'House Of The Rising Sun' had taken The Animals to the top, the group's keyboard player left the act, which he had originally formed as The Alan Price Combo. The first hit with his new band came with their second single, a particularly effective retread of a song written and originally recorded by the outrageous R&B performer Screamin' Jay Hawkins.

## CRISPIAN ST PETERS
PIED PIPER
*Decca*

▲ 5
⑩ 2•
—/500

A pop/folk song penned by Artie Kornfeld and Steve Duboff, and originally recorded by the writers under the name The Changin' Times, guided the UK vocalist into the transatlantic Top 10 for the only time. Unlike the subject of the song, few people followed St Peters' musical lead after this single.

## MANFRED MANN
PRETTY FLAMINGO
*HMV*

▲ 1
⑩ 6
123/500

The widely touted quintet's second chart topper was their last hit single to feature vocalist Paul Jones, and the first to include short-lived bass player Jack Bruce (he left to form Cream). Mark Barkan wrote the song, which Tommy Vann had recorded previously.

## LOVIN' SPOONFUL
DAYDREAM
*Pye International*

See US entry (March).

## CILLA BLACK
ALFIE
*Parlophone*

In the UK, this distinctive songstress had the hit version of Bacharach & David's oft-recorded film theme. However, in the US, Cher escorted 'Alfie' into the Top 40, and in the following year Dionne Warwick (whose 'Anyone Who Had A Heart' Cilla had earlier covered) had a Top 20 entry with it.

---

# UNITED STATES
# MAY 1966

---

## BOB DYLAN
RAINY DAY WOMEN #12 & 35
*Columbia*

The singer who, more than anyone else, broke the stranglehold of UK acts on the chart, clocked up his third transatlantic Top 10 entry in nine months. This top-notch folk/rock track came from his critically acclaimed double album *Blonde On Blonde*.

## SHADOWS OF KNIGHT
GLORIA
*Dunwich*

One of the great garage rock records of the decade was an explosive version of a Van Morrison song which had originally been released by the composer's group, Them. The single briefly catapulted this stomping Chicago combo into the spotlight. In 1969, lead singer Jim Sohns, and a new bubblegum-oriented line-up of the Shadows of Knight, recycled 'Gloria' to little effect.

## NANCY SINATRA
HOW DOES THAT GRAB YOU DARLIN'
*Reprise*

Like her previous chart-topping single, this transatlantic Top 20 entry was composed by the vocalist's talented producer Lee Hazlewood. She re-recorded both of her first two hits in 1973 on RCA.

## DIONNE WARWICK
MESSAGE TO MICHAEL
*Scepter*

One of the most covered recording acts of the era returned to the Top 10 after a two-year absence with a Bacharach and David composition that Lou Johnson had released earlier as 'Message To Martha'. The song had also hit the UK Top 20 in 1964 by Adam Faith.

## PERCY SLEDGE
WHEN A MAN LOVES A WOMAN
*Atlantic*

Few records better epitomize the soulful sixties than the single that gave this Alabama-born vocalist the first of his four Top 20 hits. Although not given composer credits, Sledge says he penned the heartbreak dirge with his band members Calvin Lewis and Andrew Wright. This emotion-drenched recording entered the UK Top 5 in both 1967 and 1987. An equally impassioned update by Michael Bolton also reached the transatlantic Top 10 in 1991.

## MINDBENDERS
A GROOVY KIND OF LOVE
*Fontana*

▲ 2
⑩ 1•
318/500

See UK entry (February).

## SUPREMES
LOVE IS LIKE AN ITCHING
IN MY HEART
*Motown*

▲ 9
⑩ 8
—/500

The consistently enjoyable threesome, who had amassed six No 1s in just 15 months, only managed a relatively minor hit with this infectious Holland, Dozier & Holland song. In the UK, it was their second successive single to miss the chart altogether.

## ROLLING STONES
PAINT IT BLACK
*London*

▲ 1
⑩ 7
149/500

See UK entry.

## SIMON & GARFUNKEL
I AM A ROCK
*Columbia*

▲ 3
⑩ 3
370/500

This unmistakable folk/rock duo chalked up their third US Top 5 entry in a row with another well-crafted Paul Simon song that he had first recorded as a solo in 1964.

## LOVIN' SPOONFUL
DID YOU EVER HAVE TO
MAKE UP YOUR MIND
*Kama Sutra*

▲ 2
⑩ 4
314/500

A song John Sebastian had written a couple of years earlier (about two sisters that he knew) was one of five Top 10 singles that Lovin' Spoonful charted in 1966.

## JAMES BROWN
IT'S A MAN'S MAN'S
MAN'S WORLD
*King*

▲ 8
⑩ 3
—/500

Soon after his successful UK debut, the legendary soul star scored his first UK Top 20 entry with an intense self-penned soul ballad, which also rocketed him to the top of the R&B chart for the third time in a year.

# UNITED KINGDOM
# MAY 1966

## BEACH BOYS
SLOOP JOHN B
*Capitol*

▲ 2
⑩ 3
269/500

See US entry (April).

## SIMON & GARFUNKEL
HOMEWARD BOUND
*CBS*

▲ 9
⑩ 1
—/500

See US entry (March).

## ROY 'C'
SHOTGUN WEDDING
*Island*

▲ 6
⑩ 1
—/500

In the US, this hypnotic self-penned track reached the R&B Top 20 but failed to make the Top 100 – the title probably deterred many pop radio stations. However, on the other side of the Atlantic the semi-controversial track shot into the Top 10 in both 1965 and 1973. Among the US artist's later overlooked recordings was 'The Wedding Is Over'. A revival of 'Shotgun Wedding' by Rod Stewart narrowly missed the UK Top 20 in 1993.

## TROGGS
WILD THING
*Fontana*

▲ 2
⑩ 1
326/500

One of the UK's most successful groups of the late 1960s steered their second single to the top of the US chart (where, because of legal problems, it appeared on two labels). This Hampshire band's raw rock track sold over five million copies. 'Wild Thing', which became one of pop music's best-loved and most recorded songs, was written by Chip Taylor especially for New York band Jordan Christopher & The Wild Ones. It was taken back into the US Top 20 by Senator Bobby in 1967 and Fanny in 1974.

## ROLLING STONES
PAINT IT BLACK
*Decca*

▲ 1
⑩ 8
187/500

A memorable, if somewhat macabre, sitar-led single transported the Stones back to the top of the transatlantic charts – in the UK it was their last No 1 for two years. Curiously, the Indian-influenced single returned to the top of the Dutch Top 10 in 1990.

## MERSEYS
SORROW
*Fontana*

▲ 4
⑩ 1•
473/500

Ex-Merseybeats Tony Crane and Billy Kinsley had their sole hit as The Merseys with a Bob Feldman, Gerry Goldstein and Richard Gottehrer (US chart act The Strangeloves) composition. The song was first cut by The McCoys on the B side of 'Fever'. In 1973 a revival of the song by David Bowie also went into the Top 5.

## BOB DYLAN
RAINY DAY WOMEN
NOS 12 & 35
*CBS*

▲ 7
⑩ 5
—/500

See US entry.

## FRANK SINATRA
STRANGERS IN
THE NIGHT
*Reprise*

▲ 1
⑩ 7
45/500

See US entry (June).

## MAMAS & THE PAPAS
MONDAY MONDAY
*RCA*

▲ 3
⑩ 1
364/500

See US entry (April).

## SMALL FACES
HEY GIRL
*Decca*

▲ 10
⑩ 2
—/500

This was the first of many self-composed hits by the cherubic-looking London quartet, which was fronted by one-time child-actor and solo singer Steve Marriott.

# UNITED STATES
# JUNE 1966

## GARY LEWIS & THE PLAYBOYS
GREEN GRASS
*Liberty*

▲ 8
🔟 7•
—/500

Shortly before Lewis was drafted into the army, his group notched up a record seventh successive Top 10 entry with their seventh single release. Roger Cook and Roger Greenaway's composition was one of the highlights of the act's US summer tour with Herman's Hermits. It would appear that Lewis' two years in the services hastened the end of the act's chart career.

## FRANK SINATRA
STRANGERS IN THE NIGHT
*Reprise*

▲ 1
🔟 6
187/500

One of the twentieth century's most acclaimed artists had his only transatlantic chart-topping single with a ballad written for a little-heralded Hollywood film, *A Man Could Get Killed*. This multi-Grammy-winning record was produced by Jimmy Bowen and arranged by Ernie Freeman, both of whom, incidentally, had last reached the Top 20 as artists in 1957. The song gave German composer Bert Kaempfert his second No 1 of the decade on both sides of the Atlantic.

## ROBERT PARKER
BAREFOOTIN'
*Nola*

▲ 7
🔟 1•
—/500

Many of the biggest New Orleans recorded hits of the 1950s and 1960s featured Parker, whose mellow saxophone can be heard on tracks by such diverse acts as Jimmy Clanton and Fats Domino. He had 15 minutes in the spotlight courtesy of a toe-tapping self-written dance track, which for a while had people barefootin' on both sides of the Atlantic. Among the veteran musician's other soul – or should that be sole – singles were 'Happy Feet' and 'Tip Toe'.

## CAPITOLS
COOL JERK
*Karen*

▲ 7
🔟 1•
—/500

The Jerk was one of the mid-1960s most popular dance crazes. This Detroit trio kept it hot with an infectious track written by member Don Storball. The group, whose later, less successful, singles included the similar 'Cool Pearl' and 'Cool Jerk '68', were renamed the 3 Caps in the UK to avoid confusion with an Irish showband.

## CYRKLE
RED RUBBER BALL
*Columbia*

▲ 2
🔟 1•
306/500

Manager Brian Epstein's first American band are primarily remembered for their interpretation of this bouncy folk favourite penned by Paul Simon and Bruce Woodley (of The Seekers). Coincidentally, the only act that stood between the record and the top spot were Epstein's first signing, The Beatles. The Pennsylvania group, who supported The Beatles on their last US tour, split up soon after Esptein's death in 1967.

## BEATLES
PAPERBACK WRITER
*Capitol*

▲ 1
🔟 19
168/500

See UK entry.

## DUSTY SPRINGFIELD
YOU DON'T HAVE TO
SAY YOU LOVE ME
*Philips*

▲ 4
⑩ 2
472/500

See UK entry (April).

## CHIFFONS
SWEET TALKIN' GUY
*Laurie*

▲ 10
⑩ 3•
—/500

After a three-year absence, the New York quartet returned to the heights with a pop/dance classic that eventually entered the UK Top 10 six years later.

# UNITED KINGDOM
# JUNE 1966

## KEN DODD
PROMISES
*Columbia*

▲ 6
⑩ 4•
—/500

This popular comedian must have been tickled pink when he registered his third Top 10 entry in a row. The song, based on Beethoven's Pathetique Sonata, was written by Tom Springfield and Dodd's producer Norman Newell. In 1982, the Queen presented the balladeer with an OBE.

## PERCY SLEDGE
WHEN A MAN LOVES A
WOMAN
*Atlantic*

▲ 4
⑩ 1
474/500

See US entry (May).

## ANIMALS
DON'T BRING ME DOWN
*Decca*

▲ 6
⑩ 7
—/500

Carole King and Gerry Goffin composed the widely acclaimed group's fifth and last transatlantic Top 20 entry. After a summer tour of the US with Herman's Hermits, the influential act disbanded.

## BEATLES
PAPERBACK WRITER
*Parlophone*

▲ 1
⑩ 11
162/500

Soon after their final UK live show (*NME* Poll Winners' Concert) The Beatles collected their tenth UK No 1 in a row with this Paul McCartney-penned song. Curiously, in the UK they replaced Frank Sinatra at the top, while in the US he replaced them.

## YARDBIRDS
OVER UNDER SIDEWAYS
DOWN
*Columbia*

▲ 10
⑩ 5•
—/500

The group that played a pivotal role in rock scored their fourth transatlantic Top 20 entry with another self-composed psychedelic piece. The quintet, who pioneered many technical innovations and helped lay the foundations for heavy metal, disbanded in 1968 when Jimmy Page formed the New Yardbirds (who evolved into Led Zeppelin). The Yardbirds were elected into the Rock and Roll Hall of Fame in 1992.

## KINKS
SUNNY AFTERNOON
*Pye*

▲ 1
⑩ 8
128/500

The well-respected group's third UK chart topper was also their last major US hit of the decade. Like all the act's successes, this telling snapshot of English life came from the pen of leader Ray Davies.

## CILLA BLACK
DON'T ANSWER ME
*Parlophone*

Two years after the Italian song 'You're My World' had given her a chart topper, Cilla again turned to that country for a hit. This time it was the composition 'Ti Vedo Uscuiri', with English lyrics from Peter Callandar, that did the trick.

## IKE & TINA TURNER
RIVER DEEP MOUNTAIN HIGH
*London American*

Phil Spector considered this epic recording to be

one of his finest productions, and soon after its relative failure in the US he closed his label and went into semi-retirement. The single, which finally introduced the UK public to Tina Turner's outstanding voice, was penned by Spector, Jeff Barry and Ellie Greenwich. The classic track, which cost a then staggering $22,000 to produce, returned to the UK Top 40 in 1969. Two years later a version by The Four Tops and The Supremes put the song into the transatlantic Top 20.

# UNITED STATES
# JULY 1966

## TOMMY JAMES & THE SHONDELLS
HANKY PANKY
*Roulette*

Top composers Jeff Barry and Ellie Greenwich penned this simplistic song as a throwaway B side for their own single (as The Raindrops) 'That Boy John' in 1963. A few months later James cut the song for the tiny Snap label. Amazingly, two years afterwards, when Roulette took over distribution, the amateurishly recorded track topped the US chart. A song that Barry described as' terrible' launched the career of one of the US's biggest singles acts of the late 1960s.

## TROGGS
WILD THING
*Fontana and Atco*

See UK entry (May).

## SYNDICATE OF SOUND
LITTLE GIRL
*Bell*

Group members Don Baskin and Bob Gonzalez composed the garage rock classic that shot this San Jose quintet into the spotlight. The crudely recorded cut was originally released on the small Hush label and became a US hit when Bell picked up the rights. Unfortunately, the group's future more polished productions failed to ignite much interest.

## ASSOCIATION
ALONG COMES MARY
*Valiant*

One of the US's most successful acts of the late 1960s debuted on the chart with their third single. Although it reputedly had no drug connotations, the song ran into trouble when it was suspected that 'Mary' meant marijuana. The track came from the group's Top 5 album, *And Then... Along Comes The Association*. The LP was recorded at a small studio owned by early 1960s hit maker Gary Paxton of Hollywood Argyles, Bobby 'Boris' Pickett and Skip & Flip fame.

### SAM THE SHAM & THE PHARAOHS
LIL' RED RIDING HOOD
*MGM*

▲ 2
⑩ 2•
246/500

For the second time, the colourful Texas rock band reached the runner-up place in the US chart. This time it was with a semi-novelty produced by Stan Kesler. MGM also released an answer record to the act's last noticeable hit, 'Hey There Big Bad Wolf' by The Sham-Ettes.

### PAUL REVERE & THE RAIDERS
HUNGRY
*Columbia*

▲ 6
⑩ 2
—/500

The teen idols from Oregon quickly returned to the top rungs with a hard-rocking Mann and Weil song. It came from their second gold album *Midnight Ride*.

### CRISPIAN ST PETERS
THE PIED PIPER
*Jamie*

▲ 4
⑩ 1•
496/500

See UK entry (April).

### MAMAS & THE PAPAS
I SAW HER AGAIN
*Dunhill*

▲ 5
⑩ 3
—/500

This laid-back West Coast harmony quartet clocked up a second successive transatlantic Top 20 entry with a song composed by their two male members, John Phillips and Denny Doherty.

### TOMMY ROE
SWEET PEA
*ABC Paramount*

▲ 8
⑩ 3
—/500

Soon after he completed a two-year spell in the army, Roe reappeared in the Top 10 with a self-composed bubblegum-oriented tune that some thought had a hidden meaning.

### LOVIN' SPOONFUL
SUMMER IN THE CITY
*Kama Sutra*

▲ 1
⑩ 5
107/500

The US's top group of 1966 had their sole No 1 with a song that conjured up a picture of a sun-baked city (complete with traffic noises). This transatlantic smash started life as a poem written by lead singer John Sebastian's brother Mark.

### ROLLING STONES
MOTHERS LITTLE HELPER
*London*

▲ 8
⑩ 8
—/500

In their homeland this track was only available on the *Aftermath* album. However, in the US, it gave the celebrated group their ninth Top 20 single in succession. The B side, 'Lady Jane', also climbed into the US Top 40.

### RAY CONNIFF & THE SINGERS
SOMEWHERE, MY LOVE
*Columbia*

▲ 9
⑩ 1•
—/500

One of the biggest-selling and most distinctive album acts of the 1960s had his only major single hit with Lara's Theme from the film *Dr Zhivago*. It was the title song from the internationally renowned arranger's nineteenth US Top 20 album. In the UK, where the 'Ray Conniff sound' was equally popular, a cover version by the Mike Sammes Singers snatched the chart honours.

# UNITED KINGDOM
# JULY 1966

### GENE PITNEY
NOBODY NEEDS YOUR
LOVE
*Stateside*

Singer/songwriter Randy Newman's first major hit came courtesy of Pitney, who was one of the decade's most popular solo performers. Surprisingly, this single failed to crack the US Top 100.

### HOLLIES
BUS STOP
*Parlophone*

Three years after they debuted on the UK chart, the distinctive Manchester quintet scored their first transatlantic Top 10 hit with a song penned for them by Graham Gouldman. It was the group's first track featuring new bass player Bernie Calvert.

### DAVE DEE, DOZY, BEAKY, MICK & TICH
HIDEAWAY
*Fontana*

This quirkily named Salisbury-based quintet, who spent more weeks on the UK chart in 1966 than any other act, returned to the Top 10 with another Ken Howard and Alan Blaikley composition.

### GEORGIE FAME
GET AWAY
*Columbia*

A catchy song that the Lancashire-born R&B- and jazz-influenced performer had written as a jingle for petrol gave him his second No 1 single. He was backed on both chart toppers by his quintet The Blue Flames.

### PETULA CLARK
I COULDN'T LIVE WITHOUT
YOUR LOVE
*Pye*

The most successful UK female singer in the US during the Swinging Sixties added to her transatlantic Top 10 tally with a song composed by producer Tony Hatch and his wife Jackie Trent.

### CHRIS FARLOWE
OUT OF TIME
*Immediate*

Ex-skiffle group leader Farlowe (born John Deighton) was one of the UK's best exponents of R&B in the early 1960s. The craggy-voiced vocalist released a handful of noteworthy singles before his version of a stand-out Jagger & Richard song (from *Aftermath*) topped the chart. This critically acclaimed performer, voted Best Newcomer in the *RM*, never collected another major hit.

### LOS BRAVOS
BLACK IS BLACK
*Decca*

Top Spanish group Mike & The Runaways hit the transatlantic Top 10 with their first release under the name Los Bravos. The Motown-like sing-along pop classic was produced by noted A&R man/composer Ivor Raymonde, and was written by Englishmen Tony Hayes and Steve Wadey. French disco team La Belle Epoque returned the song to the runner-up position in the UK in 1977.

### ELVIS PRESLEY
LOVE LETTERS
*RCA*

Readers of the UK pop paper *RM* voted Presley's Ketty Lester-influenced remake of Dick Haymes' 1945 hit as Record of the Year.

## TROGGS
WITH A GIRL LIKE YOU
*Fontana*

Lead singer Reg Presley (born Reginald Ball) composed the stomping song that gave the refreshingly unsophisticated quartet their only UK No 1. In the US, where it had previously been released as the B side of the group's chart-topping Atco label version of 'Wild Thing', it obviously fared less well.

## CHRIS MONTEZ
THE MORE I SEE YOU
*Pye International*

After three years away, the Ritchie Valens-influenced vocalist reappeared on the scene with an easy-on-the-ear update of a song from Dick Haymes' 1945 film *Diamond Horseshoe*. The Herb Alpert-produced record reached the transatlantic Top 20 and was the last major hit by Montez.

## DUSTY SPRINGFIELD
GOIN' BACK
*Philips*

▲ 10
⑩ 7
—/500

This perennially popular Goffin & King ballad clicked as the chart regular launched her UK TV series, *Dusty*. A year later The Byrds took the song into the US Top 100, and in 1994 Springfield's re-issued single was a minor UK hit.

---

# UNITED STATES
# AUGUST 1966

---

## NAPOLEON XIV
THEY'RE COMING TO
TAKE ME AWAY HA-HAAA!
*Warner*

▲ 3
⑩ 1•
495/500

This madman's monologue was the strangest transatlantic hit of the 1960s. Engineer-cum-successful MOR songsmith Jerry Samuels recorded the odd ode, which told of waiting to be taken to the funny farm by 'nice young men in their clean white coats'. The track, which was coupled with the A side played backwards(!), cost $15 to record and sold half a million copies in its first week. Not unexpectedly, mental health organisations did not see the funny side of it and soon had it taken off most radio playlists.

## BOBBY HEBB
SUNNY
*Philips*

A song he wrote after the violent deaths of his brother Hal (of doo-wop group The Marigolds) and President Kennedy gave this pop/R&B performer from Nashville his biggest hit. In the UK, both Hebb's single and a cover by Georgie Fame reached the Top 20. However, Hebb's time in the sun was brief and subsequent records like 'Sunny 76' and 'My Pretty Sunshine' failed to make the Grammy-winning composer hot again.

## HAPPENINGS
SEE YOU IN SEPTEMBER
*B.T. Puppy*

For their fourth release, this New Jersey vocal harmony group revived a teen-love song that The Tempos had taken into the Top 40 in 1959. It was the first of four 'oldies' that the somewhat dated quartet placed in the Top 20. All the act's hits were recorded under the watchful eye of the multi-talented Tokens.

### PETULA CLARK
I COULDN'T LIVE WITHOUT
YOUR LOVE
*Warner*

See UK entry (July).

### DONOVAN
SUNSHINE SUPERMAN
*Epic*

See UK entry (December).

### SUPREMES
YOU CAN'T HURRY LOVE
*Motown*

After a relatively quiet sales year, The Supremes bounced back and achieved their biggest transatlantic hit since 'Where Did Our Love Go'. On the R&B chart, the single made a record-breaking jump from 22 to 1. In 1983, Phil Collins returned this commercially compelling song to the transatlantic Top 10.

### BEATLES
YELLOW SUBMARINE
*Capitol*

See UK entry.

### BILLY STEWART
SUMMERTIME
*Chess*

One of the most individual soul singers of the 1960s had his biggest hit with a stunning version of the much-recorded Gershwin classic, which no doubt had the composer turning in his grave. The 'Fat Boy', who was discovered in the mid-1950s by Bo Diddley, died in an automobile accident in 1970. He is also fondly remembered for such self-penned soul classics as 'Sitting In The Park' and 'I Do Love You'.

# UNITED KINGDOM
# AUGUST 1966

### DAVE BERRY
MAMA
*Decca*

A song that B.J. Thomas had recently taken into the US Top 40 became the last of Berry's seven UK Top 40 entries. This unique performer, who is best remembered for his suggestive, peek-a-boo stage movements, influenced several later acts, including 1970s chart regular Alvin Stardust.

### BEACH BOYS
GOD ONLY KNOWS
*Capitol*

This is arguably the most outstanding track from The Beach Boys' universally acclaimed *Pet Sounds* album. It is a splendid showcase for the group's trademark harmonies. Astonishingly, in the US it was tucked away on the B side of 'Wouldn't It Be Nice'.

### BEATLES
YELLOW SUBMARINE/
ELEANOR RIGBY
*Parlophone*

The last of the record-shattering quartet's eleven consecutive UK chart toppers was their first hit sung by drummer Ringo Starr. It was a double A side in the UK, the coupling being an intriguing story song which Paul McCartney confided was originally entitled 'Miss Daisy Hawkins'.

### LOVIN' SPOONFUL
SUMMER IN THE CITY
*Kama Sutra*

See US entry (July).

### CLIFF RICHARD
VISIONS
*Columbia*

This memorable ballad (recorded without The Shadows) was one of the musical highlights of a relatively disappointing chart year for Cliff. The song was subsequently used as the closing theme for his TV series.

### NAPOLEON XIV
THEY'RE COMING TO TAKE ME AWAY HA-HAAA!
*Warner*

See US entry.

### SMALL FACES
ALL OR NOTHING
*Decca*

Group members Steve Marriott and Ronnie Lane composed the single that gave the highly touted teen idols their biggest UK hit. Despite the band's status in the UK, the record did nothing in the US. A 1989 solo version by Marriott was a non-starter on both sides of the Atlantic.

### DAVID & JONATHAN
LOVERS OF THE WORLD UNITE
*Columbia*

Top British songwriters Roger Cook and Roger Greenaway had two UK Top 20 hits under the pseudonym David & Jonathan. The first, a George Martin-produced cover of The Beatles' ballad 'Michelle', also cracked the US Top 20. Their biggest UK seller was a bouncy self-written pop pearl that The Vogues covered in the US.

# UNITED STATES
# SEPTEMBER 1966

### WILSON PICKETT
LAND OF 1,000 DANCES
*Atlantic*

R&B singer/songwriter Chris Kenner based this club classic on an old gospel favourite, 'Children Go Where I Send You', and his original recording was a minor hit in 1963. Two years later, when garage rockers Cannibal & The Headhunters added the 'Na Na Na Na Na' refrain, the song went into the Top 40. However, it took the Alabama-born soul superstar Wilson Pickett to turn it into gold. The much-recorded opus was also incorporated into Ini Kamoze's 1994 million seller, 'Here Comes The Hotstepper'.

### LEE DORSEY
WORKING IN THE COAL MINE
*Amy*

The one-time boxer and garage mechanic took this soul song into the Top 10 on both sides of the Atlantic. New Orleans' best-known backroom boy, Allen Toussaint, wrote and produced it.

### STEVIE WONDER
BLOWIN' IN THE WIND
*Tamla*

The first R&B artist to take a Bob Dylan song into the Top 10 was the multi-talented 16-year-old performer from Detroit. In 1963, the protest song had reached the Top 3 by Peter, Paul & Mary.

## HOLLIES
BUS STOP
*Imperial*

▲ 5
⑩ 1
—/500

See UK entry (July).

## SANDPIPERS
GUANTANAMERA
*A&M*

▲ 9
⑩ 1•
—/500

After a few minor sellers as The Grads, this LA trio had the first and biggest of their three Top 40 entries with their debut release as The Sandpipers. The easy-listening act transported the multi-lingual single into the Top 10 on both sides of the Atlantic, and the album of the same name also graced the US Top 20.

## ASSOCIATION
CHERISH
*Valiant*

▲ 1
⑩ 2
112/500

A stand-out soft rock song that lead singer Terry Kirkman penned in half an hour whisked the West Coast outfit to the top. In 1971, this classy composition gave teen idol David Cassidy his only transatlantic Top 10 entry.

## BEACH BOYS
WOULDN'T IT BE NICE
*Capitol*

▲ 8
⑩12
—/500

The group's unmistakable harmonies were to the fore on this classic pop gem and its superb B side, 'God Only Knows', which only narrowly missed the top slot in the UK.

## TEMPTATIONS
BEAUTY IS ONLY
SKIN DEEP
*Gordy*

▲ 3
⑩ 2
458/500

Producer Norman Whitfield penned this instantly infectious song with Eddie Holland. It was Whitfield's first major hit with the Detroit-based group and was their first Top 20 entry in the UK.

## LOS BRAVOS
BLACK IS BLACK
*Parrot*

▲ 4
⑩ 1•
—/500

See UK entry (July).

## ? (QUESTION MARK) & THE MYSTERIANS
96 TEARS
*Cameo*

▲ 1
⑩ 1ª
141/500

At the time that this top-notch garage rock track headed the US chart the identity of the vocalist was a mystery. It later came to light that the Farfisa organ-led stomper was sung by its youthful composer Rudy Martinez. As proof of the group's punk credentials, the Michigan-based quintet from Mexico recorded the track in a converted front room, and it was initially released on the small Texas indie label Pa-Go-Go. The song (originally called 'Too Many Teardrops') finally climbed into the UK Top 20 in 1990 by The Stranglers.

## FOUR TOPS
REACH OUT I'LL
BE THERE
*Motown*

▲ 1
⑩ 3
140/500

This timeless pop/soul classic gave the acclaimed group the only transatlantic No 1 of their long and very successful career. A Stock, Aitken & Waterman remix in 1988 also reached the UK Top 20. A disco-slanted recording of the Holland, Dozier & Holland gem hit the UK Top 20 in 1975 by Gloria Gaynor.

# UNITED KINGDOM
# SEPTEMBER 1966

### ROY ORBISON
TOO SOON TO KNOW
*London American*

One of the decade's most successful artists paid his last visit to the UK Top 10 in the 1960s with a minor US hit composed by country singer Don Gibson. Shortly after Orbison's death in 1988, his composition 'You Got It' returned this perennially popular entertainer to the transatlantic Top 10.

### JIM REEVES
DISTANT DRUMS
*RCA*

Two years after Reeves' death, a song that Roy Orbison had released earlier gave the velvet-voiced country crooner his only UK No 1. It made composer Cindy Walker the first woman to compose a UK chart topper on her own. 'Distant Drums' was one of Reeves' 21 UK Top 40 entries and one of his 11 US country No 1s.

### LEE DORSEY
WORKING IN THE COAL
MINE
*Stateside*

See US entry.

### CLIFF BENNETT & THE
### REBEL ROUSERS
GOT TO GET YOU
INTO MY LIFE
*Parlophone*

The UK hit of this Beatles song was by a band that played the Hamburg clubs at the same time as the 'Fab Four'. It was the highest-ranking record by the powerful vocalist and his rocking band (who named themselves after Duane Eddy's first hit). In the US, The Beatles' original version gave them their last Top 10 entry in 1976, and two years later Earth, Wind & Fire took the song back there.

### MANFRED MANN
JUST LIKE A WOMAN
*Fontana*

The top-selling quintet's eighth Top 20 hit in just over two years was their first on Fontana. It was also the first featuring vocalist Mike D'Abo and the first produced by ex-Springfields member Mike Hurst. In the US, Bob Dylan's original version garnered the most sales.

### WHO
I'M A BOY
*Reaction*

Soon after causing riots at the annual Windsor Jazz Festival, The Who had their second UK No 2 hit. Surprisingly, the group never topped the chart on either side of the Atlantic.

### SONNY & CHER
LITTLE MAN
*Atlantic*

This internationally acclaimed duo scored their fifth UK Top 20 single in a year with a Sonny-penned single that headed the chart in Holland.

### SUPREMES
YOU CAN'T HURRY LOVE
*Tamla Motown*

See US entry (August).

# UNITED STATES
# OCTOBER 1966

## NEIL DIAMOND
CHERRY CHERRY
*Bang*

▲ 6
⑩ 1
—/500

A year after first tasting success as composer of Jay & The American's hit 'Sunday And Me', New Yorker Diamond (born Noah Kaminsky) opened his chart account as an artist. 'Cherry Cherry' was the first of many bestsellers by the legendary singer/songwriter, who has since amassed more than 30 US gold albums (18 of which also turned platinum). In 1973, a live version by Diamond also made the Top 40.

## MONKEES
LAST TRAIN TO CLARKSVILLE
*Colgems*

▲ 1
⑩ 1
153/500

In 1967 The Beatles were toppled as world's No 1 recording act by this carefully chosen foursome, whose fame owed more than a little to their TV series. Two weeks after The Beatles' last live show, NBC TV's Beatle-influenced series, *The Monkees*, was launched in the US. Less than two months later the group's debut disc reached the summit. Like many of the quartet's tracks, the catchy song was written and produced by Tommy Boyce and Bobby Hart, and top-notch LA session musicians handled the instrumental chores.

## COUNT FIVE
PSYCHOTIC REACTION
*Double Shot*

▲ 5
⑩ 1•
—/500

Kenn Ellner fronted the vampire-garbed garage rock group from San José, who recorded one of the first successful psychedelic singles. However, this ground-breaking self-composed song proved to be the California teen band's only hit.

## FOUR SEASONS
I'VE GOT YOU UNDER MY SKIN
*Philips*

▲ 9
⑩ 11
—/500

Their unique interpretation of Cole Porter's 1936 Academy Award-winning song continued the unmistakable group's run of hits. This single was the quartet's last UK Top 20 entry for nine years.

## LEFT BANKE
WALK AWAY RENEE
*Smash*

▲ 5
⑩ 1•
—/500

Baroque-rock found a place in the Top 10 courtesy of this New York quintet's debut hit. The track was recorded at a studio owned by the harmony vocal group's keyboard player Michael Brown (born Michael Lookofsky), who was inspired to write 'Walk Away Renee' by Renee Fladen, a girlfriend of another Left Banke member. The Four Tops' Motown treatment of it entered the transatlantic Top 20 in 1968.

## JIMMY RUFFIN
WHAT BECOMES OF THE BROKENHEARTED
*Soul*

▲ 7
⑩ 1
—/500

Five years after he first recorded for Motown, this soulful singer (whose brother David Ruffin was in The Temptations) had his first and biggest-selling hit. In the UK, not only did the Mississippi-born performer's debut smash reach the Top 10 again in 1974, but the song also became a Top 20 entry for Dave Stewart in 1980.

## JOHNNY RIVERS
POOR SIDE OF TOWN
*Imperial*

▲ 1
⑩ 5
171/500

One of the US's most popular recording stars of the decade had his only No 1 with his first self-composed single (he wrote it with long-time producer Lou Adler). Joe Stampley, also from Louisiana, lifted the song into the country Top 20 in 1983.

### HERMAN'S HERMITS
DANDY
*MGM*

▲ 5
⑩ 10
—/500

The last of the group's dozen successive UK Top 20 entries was written by The Kinks main man, Ray Davies. The track was included on Herman's sixth Top 20 album, *There's A Kind Of Hush All Over The World*.

### ERIC BURDON & THE ANIMALS
SEE SEE RIDER
*MGM*

▲ 10
⑩ 2
—/500

Burdon's new line-up of Animals had instant US success with a song first recorded 40 years earlier by Ma Rainey. This time-honoured blues number

had reached the Top 10 earlier in the year as part of the medley 'Jenny Take A Ride!' by Mitch Ryder & The Detroit Wheels.

### TOMMY ROE
HOORAY FOR HAZEL
*ABC*

▲ 6
⑩ 4
—/500

Roe's fourth self-composed Top 10 entry of the decade was with a captivating bubblegum-flavoured pop song. It was, incidentally, his fourth US chart hit to date that contained a girl's name.

### ROLLING STONES
HAVE YOU SEEN YOUR MOTHER, BABY, STANDING IN THE SHADOWS?
*London*

▲ 9
⑩ 9
—/500

See UK entry.

# UNITED KINGDOM
# OCTOBER 1966

### DAVE DEE, DOZY, BEAKY, MICK & TICH
BEND IT
*Fontana*

▲ 2
⑩ 3
292/500

Although its *double entendre* lyrics earned it numerous bans around the world, this Greek-sounding single added to the flashy yet fashionably dressed fivesome's already impressive collection of UK hits.

### NEW VAUDEVILLE BAND
WINCHESTER CATHEDRAL
*Fontana*

▲ 4
⑩ 1
444/500

Top songwriter Geoff Stephens was the master-mind behind one of the decade's biggest-selling novelties. He wrote, produced and sang lead on

this single, which topped the US chart and sold more copies there during 1966 than any other UK record. Astoundingly, the Temperance Seven-influenced track won the Grammy for Best Contemporary Rock & Roll Recording. The song has since been recorded by over 400 artists, including Frank Sinatra.

### SEEKERS
WALK WITH ME
*Columbia*

▲ 10
⑩ 4
—/500

One of the most consistently successful and easily recognizable groups in the UK during the mid-1960s clicked with another song composed by their producer Tom Springfield.

## ROLLING STONES
HAVE YOU SEEN YOUR
MOTHER, BABY, STANDING
IN THE SHADOWS?
*Decca*

Many people were shocked when the controversial quintet dressed in drag to promote their third transatlantic Top 10 entry of the year. For the record, it was the Stones' lowest UK chart hit since 1963.

## DUSTY SPRINGFIELD
ALL I SEE IS YOU
*Philips*

American tunesmith Ben Weisman teamed with the UK's Clive Westlake on the song that gave the 1960s superstar her third transatlantic Top 20 single.

## SANDPIPERS
GUANTANAMERA
*Pye International*

See US entry (September).

## TROGGS
I CAN'T CONTROL MYSELF
*Page One*

The mixture of sex, Troggs and rock'n'roll proved a winning concoction in the group's homeland,

where this controversial single gave the influential quartet their third Top 3 single of the year.

## FOUR TOPS
REACH OUT I'LL
BE THERE
*Tamla Motown*

See US entry (September).

## HOLLIES
STOP STOP STOP
*Parlophone*

For the only time in their long career The Hollies had two US Top 10 singles in a row. 'Stop Stop Stop', which unusually featured a six-string banjo, was composed by members Alan Clarke, Graham Nash and Tony Hicks.

## HERMAN'S HERMITS
NO MILK TODAY
*Columbia*

Chart regular Graham Gouldman composed this top-selling UK quintet's biggest UK hit of 1966. In the US, the track was relegated to the B side of 'There's A Kind Of Hush'.

# UNITED STATES
# NOVEMBER 1966

## BOBBY DARIN
IF I WERE A CARPENTER
*Atlantic*

The accomplished entertainer's last transatlantic Top 20 single was his rendition of the much-recorded folk song penned by singer/songwriter Tim Hardin. Coincidentally, Hardin's only hit came three years later with Darin's composition 'Simple Song Of Freedom'. Darin, who had been the first person to win the Grammy for Best New Artist, died in 1973. He was posthumously inducted into the Rock and Roll Hall of Fame in 1990.

## BEACH BOYS
GOOD VIBRATIONS
*Capitol*

Many people consider this single to be one of the few truly outstanding recordings of the rock era. Producer/composer Brian Wilson spent six months working on the track, during which time he utilized four major studios. He used 90 hours of studio time and ran up record bills of $50,000. The resulting track – a mini masterpiece – rightfully topped the transatlantic charts.

## NEW VAUDEVILLE BAND
WINCHESTER CATHEDRAL
*Fontana*

See UK entry (October).

## SUPREMES
YOU KEEP ME HANGIN' ON
*Motown*

This internationally acclaimed threesome clocked up their fifth transatlantic Top 10 entry with yet another captivating Holland, Dozier & Holland composition. In 1987, Kim Wilde shipped the song back into the Top 10 in both the UK and the US.

## MITCH RYDER & THE DETROIT WHEELS
DEVIL WITH A BLUE DRESS ON & GOOD GOLLY MISS MOLLY
*New Voice*

A return to the format of rock medleys proved beneficial to Ryder and his entourage. This time he combined songs that had previously hit for Shorty Long and Little Richard.

## JAMES & BOBBY PURIFY
I'M YOUR PUPPET
*Bell*

Two cousins from Florida had the first and biggest of four US Top 40 entries with a song that composer Dan Penn had released a year earlier. Curiously, the soulful duo recorded it on two separate occasions with two different producers. Their hit version, produced in Muscle Shoals by Rick Hall, finally reached the UK Top 20 ten years after its US chart run.

## LOVIN' SPOONFUL
RAIN ON THE ROOF
*Kama Sutra*

As the popular East Coast band toured the US, they added to their record-breaking run of Top 10 hits with another noteworthy self-composed song. The single was included on the act's third Top 10 LP, *Hums Of The Lovin' Spoonful*.

## PETER & GORDON
LADY GODIVA
*Capitol*

From 1964–66, these middle-class heroes notched up eight US and six UK Top 20 singles. The pair's last transatlantic Top 20 entry was a novelty-slanted pop song composed by Mike Leander (who co-wrote most of Gary Glitter's 1970s hits). The duo went their own ways in 1967. Peter (Asher) became a Grammy-winning producer working with such acts as Linda Ronstadt and James Taylor.

## DONOVAN
MELLOW YELLOW
*Epic*

See UK entry (February 1967).

## ROGER WILLIAMS
BORN FREE
*Kapp*

America's top-selling solo pianist of the rock era had his biggest hit single of the 1960s with the theme from the movie *Born Free*. 'Born Free' was also the title track on the Omaha musician's (born Louis Weertz) fourteenth Top 20 album.

# UNITED KINGDOM
# NOVEMBER 1966

## PAUL JONES
HIGH TIME
*HMV*

Manfred Mann's ex-lead vocalist, who was born Paul Pond in Portsmouth, was instantly successful as a soloist in his homeland. His first single was part-written by Mike Leander, who co-wrote and produced a string of hits by Gary Glitter in the 1970s.

## CLIFF RICHARD
TIME DRAGS BY
*Columbia*

The Shadows composed this noteworthy pop song for Cliff's film *Finders Keepers*. The group also wrote the music for his show *Cinderella*, which opened at the London Palladium as the single climbed the chart.

## MANFRED MANN
SEMI-DETACHED
SUBURBAN MR JAMES
*Fontana*

British tunesmiths Geoff Stevens and John Carter composed the song as 'Semi-Detached Suburban Mr Jones', but, understandably, the group amended the title to avoid confusion with their recently departed lead singer, Paul Jones.

## BEACH BOYS
GOOD VIBRATIONS
*Capitol*

As the record hit, the act replaced The Beatles as World's Best Group in British music paper polls. This classic track returned to the UK Top 20 in 1976. See also US entry.

## SPENCER DAVIS GROUP
GIMME SOME LOVING
*Fontana*

A remix of the band's first self-penned single gave the act, voted Best New Group of 1966 in the *NME* poll, their first and biggest US Top 40 hit.

## LEE DORSEY
HOLY COW
*Stateside*

Allen Toussaint wrote and produced the record that steered this New Orleans-born entertainer into the US Top 40 for the fifth (and last) time. The single was also the popular live performer's biggest UK hit.

## BOBBY DARIN
IF I WERE A CARPENTER
*Atlantic*

See US entry.

## TOM JONES
GREEN GREEN GRASS
OF HOME
*Decca*

After a relatively quiet sales period, this magnetic performer sold over a million copies in the UK alone of a song that Porter Wagoner had earlier taken into the country Top 5. The classic Curly Putnam composition had been inspired by a scene in the ground-breaking 1950 film *The Asphalt Jungle*.

## VAL DOONICAN
WHAT WOULD I BE
*Decca*

Singer Jackie Trent, who had headed the chart the previous year with 'Where Are You Now', penned this top-selling MOR artists' highest-placed hit single.

---

## UNITED STATES

# DECEMBER 1966

---

## HOLLIES
STOP STOP STOP
*Imperial*

See UK entry (October).

## MARTHA & THE VANDELLAS
I'M READY FOR LOVE
*Gordy*

A song that The Supremes had rejected increased this trio's impressive chart inventory and became the fourth Holland, Dozier & Holland composition that they had taken into the Top 10.

## FRANK SINATRA
THAT'S LIFE
*Reprise*

This legendary entertainer, who has amassed more Top 10 albums than any other solo artist, had his last major solo hit single in the US with an atmospheric song recorded two years earlier by R&B/jazz vocalist O.C. Smith.

## MONKEES
I'M A BELIEVER
*Colgems*

With advance orders of over a million, this record rocketed to No 1 in the US. Thanks to the launch of their TV series in the UK, the Anglo-American foursome hit the top there with Neil Diamond's winning song. In the UK, a 1995 remake by EMF with Reeves & Mortimer reached the Top 3.

## NANCY SINATRA
SUGAR TOWN
*Reprise*

In 1967, the one-time wife of 1950s teen idol Tommy Sands had Top 20 duet hits with both Lee Hazlewood and her famous father Frank. Her third and last solo transatlantic Top 10 entry was composed and produced by Hazlewood.

## STEVIE WONDER
A PLACE IN THE SUN
*Tamla*

The well-respected performer attained his fourth

successive Top 20 entry with an MOR-slanted ballad by Ronald Miller. An Italian vocal version by Wonder also sold well in parts of the world.

## ROYAL GUARDSMEN
SNOOPY VS THE
RED BARON
*Laurie*

For four weeks running, only the unstoppable Monkees prevented this Florida pop sextet from topping the US charts with their debut hit. The group's follow-up, 'The Return Of The Red Baron', also marched into the US Top 20. However, later Snoopy-related novelties, including 'Snoopy For President', 'Snoopy's Christmas' and 'Snoopy Vs The Black Knight', were less rewarding. The record was the second transatlantic Top 20 entry for Phil Gernhard, who had earlier produced 'Stay' by Maurice Williams.

## TEMPTATIONS
(I KNOW) I'M LOSING YOU
*Gordy*

The popular quintet topped the R&B chart for a fourth consecutive time with a memorable Norman Whitfield and Eddie Holland composition. In 1970, Motown's white rock act Rare Earth returned the song to the Top 10.

## AARON NEVILLE
TELL IT LIKE IT IS
*Par-Lo*

One of the most lauded vocalists of the rock era had his first and biggest solo hit with a soulful ballad which topped the R&B chart for five weeks. The New Orleans song stylist's single was co-written by Lee Diamond from noted Louisiana band The Upsetters. Rock band Heart took the song back into the Top 10 in 1981. In the 1990s, this veteran of several 1950s groups grabbed a couple of Grammy awards for duets performed with Linda Ronstadt and Trisha Yearwood.

## PAUL REVERE & THE RAIDERS
GOOD THING
*Columbia*

Producer Terry Melcher composed the teen idols' fifth Top 20 entry in succession with the group's front men Mark Lindsay and Paul Revere, whose faces adorned many teen magazines at the time.

# UNITED KINGDOM
# DECEMBER 1966

## SMALL FACES
MY MIND'S EYE
*Decca*

This mod-dressed quartet scored their fourth Top 10 entry in a row with a self-composed opus that borrowed bits of its melody from a carol entitled 'Angels From The Realms Of Glory'.

## GENE PITNEY
JUST ONE SMILE
*Stateside*

Singer/songwriter Randy Newman composed the pop single that gave Pitney his seventh successive UK Top 10 entry. Newman had also written Pitney's previous hit, 'Nobody Needs Your Love'.

## SEEKERS
MORNINGTOWN RIDE
*Columbia*

For four weeks this popular Australian act held the runner-up spot with composer Malvina Reynold's infectious folk song. It was included on *Best Of The Seekers,* the first album by a non-British or American artist to top the UK charts.

## EASYBEATS
FRIDAY ON MY MIND
*UA*

The first Australian-based rock group to crack the international charts were a quintet who found brief transatlantic fame after relocating to Britain. The record that launched them into the Top 20 on both sides of the Atlantic was a weekend-welcoming winner composed by members George Young and Harry Vanda. After they disbanded, that duo became eminent producers and writers for acts such as one of the better-known Aussie bands AC/DC (which included two of Scottish-born Young's younger brothers).

## KINKS
DEAD END STREET
*Pye*

As usual, this influential group's ever-controversial lead singer Ray Davies penned the lyrically superior pop song that gave them their third Top 5 entry of the year.

## SUPREMES
YOU KEEP ME
HANGIN' ON
*Tamla Motown*

See US entry (November).

## JIMMY RUFFIN
WHAT BECOMES OF THE
BROKEN HEARTED
*Tamla Motown*

See US entry (October).

## DONOVAN
SUNSHINE SUPERMAN
*Pye*

Donovan Leitch's first Mickie Most-produced single was the biggest hit of his career. Due to contractual problems, 'Sunshine Superman' was released in the UK three months after it had topped the US chart.

## DAVE DEE, DOZY, BEAKY, MICK & TICH
SAVE ME
*Fontana*

Dave Dee (born Dave Harman) and his oddly named group reached the Top 10 for the fourth time in a row with another innovative pop single produced by American Steve Rowland.

## ELVIS PRESLEY
IF EVERY DAY WAS
LIKE CHRISTMAS
*RCA*

The biggest-selling soloist of the twentieth century had his last Top 10 entry for two and a half years with a seasonal song penned by his bodyguard and buddy Red West.

# UNITED STATES
# JANUARY 1967

## MAMAS & THE PAPAS
WORDS OF LOVE
*Dunhill*

▲ 5
⑩ 4
—/500

One of the most celebrated West Coast groups of the 1960s revisited the Top 10 with a song composed by member John Phillips. The track was included on the foursome's fourth consecutive Top 5 LP, *Farewell To The First Golden Era.*

## FOUR TOPS
STANDING IN THE
SHADOWS OF LOVE
*Motown*

▲ 6
⑩ 4
—/500

The Levi Stubbs-fronted foursome achieved their eighth US Top 40 hit in a row with another song written by the production team of Holland, Dozier & Holland.

## SEEKERS
GEORGY GIRL
*Capitol*

▲ 2
⑩ 2•
244/500

See UK entry.

## LOVIN' SPOONFUL
NASHVILLE CATS
*Kama Sutra*

▲ 8
⑩ 7
—/500

Few acts have equalled the Lovin' Spoonful's record of seven US Top 10 entries in less than 18 months. Nevertheless, before the end of 1968 the group's talented leader John Sebastian had gone solo. Their last Top 10 entry was a tribute to the faceless Nashville musicians who made that Tennessee town one of the major music centres of the world.

## FOUR SEASONS
TELL IT TO THE RAIN
*Philips*

▲ 10
⑩ 12
—/500

As this single added to the Seasons' stockpile of hits, the group were also scoring under the name the Wonder Who, and their lead singer Frankie Valli was charting as a soloist.

## BUCKINGHAMS
KIND OF A DRAG
*USA*

▲ 1
⑩ 1
143/500

Their fourth release on the local USA label was the Chicago rock quintet's first and biggest hit. It was composed by members of fellow Chicago band The Mob, Jim Holvay and Gary Beisher. Incidentally, this successful English-sounding band (who coined their name to make themselves appear more British) never charted across the Atlantic.

## BLUES MAGOOS
(WE AIN'T GOT)
NOTHIN' YET
*Mercury*

▲ 5
⑩ 1•
—/500

After several small-selling singles, the ground-breaking New York band had their only major hit with a self-composed psychedelic rock gem. The quintet, who previously called themselves the Bloos Magoos, were fronted by Peppy Castro (born Emil Thielman). As the group's concept album *Psychedelic Lollipop* was charting, they toured the US with Herman's Hermits and The Who.

# UNITED KINGDOM
# JANUARY 1967

## WHO
HAPPY JACK
*Reaction*

▲ 3
⑩ 6
439/500

The Who were not instantly successful in the US. The group's first Top 40 entry there, 'Happy Jack', charted soon after they performed their guitar-wrecking act live in the States.

## CLIFF RICHARD
IN THE COUNTRY
*Columbia*

▲ 6
⑩32
—/500

This bouncy Shadows-penned paean to country life was the most successful of the songs from Cliff's long running musical *Cinderella*.

## MONKEES
I'M A BELIEVER
*RCA*

▲ 1
⑩ 1
46/500

See US entry (December).

## TROGGS
ANY WAY THAT YOU WANT ME
*Page One*

▲ 8
⑩ 4
—/500

American Chip Taylor, who penned the group's biggest hit 'Wild Thing', composed the seldom subtle band's fourth Top 10 single in a row.

## MOVE
NIGHT OF FEAR
*Deram*

▲ 2
⑩ 1
354/500

Singer/songwriter Roy Wood and lead vocalist Carl Wayne fronted this innovative and often controversial quintet, which was composed of youthful veterans of the Birmingham beat scene. Wood penned their Denny Cordell-produced debut disc, which heavily featured a riff taken from Tchaikovsky's '1812 Overture'.

## FOUR TOPS
STANDING IN THE SHADOWS OF LOVE
*Tamla Motown*

▲ 6
⑩ 2
—/500

See US entry.

## CAT STEVENS
MATTHEW AND SON
*Deram*

▲ 2
⑩ 1
341/500

One of the late 1960's most innovative and commercial pop artists metamorphosed into one of the world's biggest-selling singer/songwriters in the 1970s. Initially, Londoner Stevens' (born Steven Georgiou) success was limited to the UK, where only The Monkees prevented his first hit from topping the chart.

## ROLLING STONES
LET'S SPEND THE NIGHT TOGETHER/ RUBY TUESDAY
*Decca*

▲ 3
⑩10
431/500

The Stones' first double-sided UK hit coupled a controversial rock classic with a melodic and memorable ballad. In the US 'Ruby Tuesday' topped the chart, while the other side was only a mid-table entry. Melanie's recording of 'Ruby Tuesday' reached the UK Top 10 in 1970.

## JIMI HENDRIX EXPERIENCE
HEY JOE
*Polydor*

▲ 6
⑩ 1
—/500

Without doubt, this revolutionary singer/guitarist was one of the rock era's most important and influential performers. To improve his chances of finding success, the Seattle-born artist relocated to the UK. He first charted with a unique treatment of a song taken into the US Top 40 by The Leaves in 1966.

# UNITED STATES
# FEBRUARY 1967

## KEITH
98.6
*Mercury*

Teenager James 'Keith' Keefer from Philadelphia clocked up three US Top 40 entries in sixth months. His hottest hit came with a bouncy George Fischoff and Tony Powers-penned pop item on which he was backed by The Tokens. In the UK, the record outsold a cover by The Bystanders and entered the Top 40. Keith's career was curtailed when he was drafted into the services.

## ROLLING STONES
RUBY TUESDAY
*London*

See UK entry (January).

## SUPREMES
LOVE IS HERE AND NOW YOU'RE GONE
*Motown*

The group, who first recorded as The Primettes on the small Lupine label, scored another chart topper with a haunting song penned by long-time producers Holland, Dozier & Holland. It was their first hit to include a spoken section from Diana Ross.

## SONNY & CHER
THE BEAT GOES ON
*Atco*

Sonny Bono's anthemic composition gave the most successful man-and-wife recording duo of all time their sixth US Top 20 entry in 18 months.

## SPENCER DAVIS GROUP
GIMME SOME LOVIN'
*UA*

See UK entry.

## CASINOS
THEN YOU CAN TELL ME GOODBYE
*Fraternity*

Country composer John D. Loudermilk wrote the memorable song that put this clean-cut nine-man group from Cincinnati into the rock history books. The ensemble, led by Gene Hughes, had released several singles before their version of the retro-sounding ballad paid off for them. They later recorded other country compositions, but Dame Fortune never smiled on them again. Johnny Nash had earlier cut the song, which reached the country Top 5 in 1968 by Eddy Arnold and in 1976 by Glen Campbell.

## JOHNNY RIVERS
BABY I NEED YOUR LOVIN'
*Imperial*

As the first hit on his own label Soul City ('Go Where You Wanna Go' by 5th Dimension) climbed into the Top 20, Rivers added to his chart score with an update of the Four Tops' 1964 classic.

# UNITED KINGDOM
# FEBRUARY 1967

## PAUL JONES
I'VE BEEN A BAD BAD BOY
*HMV*

Mike Leander composed this ex-Manfred Mann vocalist's second UK Top 5 entry in a row. It was the last major hit for the talented performer, who subsequently achieved a measure of success in both the acting and radio DJ fields.

## PETULA CLARK
THIS IS MY SONG
*Pye*

The pop/MOR star reached the summit with her last Top 10 hit of the decade. The track was recorded in the US with leading US arranger Ernie Freeman. Movie legend Charlie Chaplin penned the song for the Marlon Brando and Sophie Loren film *A Countess From Hong Kong*. It made the 70-something silent movie star the oldest person to write a million seller.

## SPENCER DAVIS GROUP
I'M A MAN
*Fontana*

Distinctive lead vocalist Steve Winwood and producer Jimmy Miller composed the internationally acclaimed act's fifth successive UK Top 20 entry, which was also their second US Top 10 single in a row. In 1970, a version by US group Chicago entered the UK Top 10. Winwood left soon after 'I'm A Man' clicked to form Traffic, and the Spencer Davis Group's hits halted.

## NANCY SINATRA
SUGAR TOWN
*Reprise*

See US entry.

## ENGELBERT HUMPERDINCK
RELEASE ME (AND LET ME LOVE AGAIN)
*Decca*

Eight years after his debut disc, this Indian-born entertainer (real name Arnold Dorsey) notched up the first of many transatlantic successes with the second release under his new stage name. The song was a country standard which composer Eddie Miller had first released in 1950. However, it was Esther Phillips' 1962 recording that Humperdinck's version was based on. The single was on the UK charts for a record 56 weeks and sold over a million copies on both sides of the Atlantic.

## ROYAL GUARDSMEN
SNOOPY VS THE RED BARON
*Stateside*

See US entry (December 1966).

## TREMELOES
HERE COMES MY BABY
*CBS*

When Brian Poole left the group in 1966, most people assumed his hits would continue and that The Tremeloes would fade into obscurity. In reality it was the other way around. After a couple of poor sellers, The Tremeloes started an impressive run of chart entries with their version of a catchy Cat Stevens composition.

## BEATLES
PENNY LANE/
STRAWBERRY FIELDS
FOREVER
*Parlophone*

▲ 2
⑩ 13
280/500

Liverpool's finest act clocked up their third doubled-sided chart topper with two songs about their home town. In 1984, Yoko Ono presented the Strawberry Fields home with a donation of £250,000 on behalf of her late husband, John Lennon.

## NEW VAUDEVILLE BAND
PEEK-A-BOO
*Fontana*

▲ 7
⑩ 2•
—/500

Geoff Stevens, the mastermind behind this top-selling novelty band, co-wrote the second of their three Top 20 singles with Ivy League member John Carter.

## DONOVAN
MELLOW YELLOW
*Pye*

▲ 8
⑩ 4
—/500

This archetypal flower child spent three weeks in the runner-up position in the US with a self-composed song that featured Paul McCartney whispering backing vocals. Interestingly, the track was arranged by John Paul Jones, who later found fame in Led Zeppelin.

# UNITED STATES
# MARCH 1967

## MITCH RYDER & THE DETROIT WHEELS
SOCK IT TO ME–BABY!
*New Voice*

▲ 6
⑩ 3•
—/500

Larry Brown (who later wrote pop classics like 'Tie A Yellow Ribbon Round The Ole Oak Tree') and the combo's celebrated producer Bob Crewe penned the influential act's last major hit. Interestingly, it was their first Top 10 single that was not a medley. Ryder, who left the group shortly afterwards, never rode back to the upper reaches of the chart.

## BEATLES
PENNY LANE
*Capitol*

▲ 1
⑩ 21
206/500

See UK entry (February).

## TURTLES
HAPPY TOGETHER
*White Whale*

▲ 1
⑩ 2
54/500

One of the year's catchiest compositions was written by Garry Bonner and Alan Gordon and had been put together with Frank Sinatra in mind. Curiously, numerous acts, including The Happenings and The Vogues, rejected the song before The Turtles took it to the top.

## ED AMES
MY CUP RUNNETH OVER
*RCA*

▲ 8
⑩ 1•
—/500

Nineteen years after first recording as part of the successful Ames Brothers, this balladeer from Massachusetts (born Ed Urick) had his biggest solo single with a show-stopping song from the musical *I Do, I Do, I Do*. His eponymous album transported him into the Top 10 for the only time.

## MAMAS & THE PAPAS
DEDICATED TO THE
ONE I LOVE
*Dunhill*

▲ 2
⑩ 5
304/500

A song written and originally recorded by doo-wop quintet the Five Royales kept the hippy harmony team hot on both sides of the Atlantic. It was their fifth US Top 10 entry in a year.

## HERMAN'S HERMITS
THERE'S A KIND OF HUSH
*MGM*

▲ 4
⑩11•
—/500

See UK entry.

## BUFFALO SPRINGFIELD
FOR WHAT IT'S WORTH
(STOP, HEY WHAT'S
THAT SOUND)
*Atco*

▲ 7
⑩ 1•
—/500

One of the most influential groups of the late 1960s included noteworthies Stephen Stills, Neil Young and Jim Messina. The folk/rock band, who named themselves after a brand of steamroller, had their only major hit with their second single. The politically slanted song was composed by Stills after witnessing a confrontation between police and youths on Sunset Strip in Los Angeles. The volatile act folded a year later, with members then forming Crosby, Still, Nash & Young and Poco.

# UNITED KINGDOM
# MARCH 1967

## VINCE HILL
EDELWEISS
*Columbia*

▲ 2
⑩ 1•
259/500

In the early 1960s, when much of the music on UK radio was live, few people were heard more often than this amiable MOR vocalist. The one-time member of UK group The Raindrops (along with Jackie Lee and hit composer Johnny Worth) had seven Top 40 entries in the late 1960s. His biggest seller was his interpretation of the well-loved song from the Rodgers & Hammerstein musical *The Sound Of Music*.

## HOLLIES
ON A CAROUSEL
*Parlophone*

▲ 4
⑩ 11
—/500

The Manchester quintet, whose harmony vocals were to influence numerous later groups, continued to add to their stockpile of trans-atlantic single smashes with another self-composed pop gem.

## HERMAN'S HERMITS
THERE'S A KIND OF HUSH
*Columbia*

▲ 7
⑩ 6
—/500

Noted UK tunesmiths Geoff Stevens and Les Reed composed the superior soft-rock song that became the Manchester teeny bop idols' fourth and final transatlantic Top 10 entry. 'There's A Kind of Hush' revisited the transatlantic charts in 1976 by The Carpenters.

## SEEKERS
GEORGY GIRL
*Columbia*

▲ 3
⑩ 6•
460/500

Soon after this title song from a Lynn Redgrave movie gave the group their biggest US hit, lead singer Judith Durham left for a solo career. The quartet's mentor Tom Springfield produced the track, which he co-wrote with actor/singer Jim Dale. Member Keith Potger formed the chart-making New Seekers in 1970, and the original Seekers re-united in 1993 for successful tours of the UK and Australia.

## TOM JONES
DETROIT CITY
*Decca*

▲ 8
⑩ 3
—/500

The UK's foremost cabaret entertainer had the first of four Top 10 entries in 1967 with a sad song that country singer Bobby Bare had taken into the US Top 20 in 1963.

## ALAN PRICE SET
SIMON SMITH & HIS
AMAZING DANCING BEAR
*Decca*

▲ 4
⑩ 2
—/500

Although it sold few copies in the US, Alan Price was right to cover this good-time Randy Newman novelty, as it gave the ex-Animal the first of his two consecutive Top 5 entries in the UK.

## WHISTLING JACK SMITH
I WAS KAISER BILL'S
BATMAN
*Deram*

▲ 5
⑩ 1•
—/500

Successful songwriting team Roger Greenaway and Roger Cook composed this infectious little opus, which reached the Top 20 on both sides of the Atlantic. Members of the noted British vocal team The Mike Sammes Singers handled the actual whistling chores, but for promotional purposes Billy Moeller (brother of Unit 4 + 2 singer Tom Moeller) fronted the record. The fictitious act's forgettable follow-up was 'I Was Bizet's Carmen'.

## HARRY SECOMBE
THIS IS MY SONG
*Philips*

▲ 2
⑩ 1•
320/500

For more than 15 years this Welsh-born comedian/singer had been one of the UK's most popular radio and TV entertainers. His last and biggest-selling UK Top 20 entry came with his rendition of the theme from the film *A Countess From Hong Kong* – a ballad that earlier in the year had topped the chart by Petula Clark. Coincidentally, both Secombe and the song's composer Charlie Chaplin were later knighted by the Queen.

---

# UNITED STATES
# APRIL 1967

---

## FOUR TOPS
BERNADETTE
*Motown*

▲ 4
⑩ 5
—/500

Thanks in no small part to producers Holland, Dozier & Holland, The Four Tops clocked up their third transatlantic Top 10 single in six months. 'Bernadette' was included on the quartet's first US Top 20 album, *Reach Out*.

## PETULA CLARK
THIS IS MY SONG
*Warner*

▲ 3
⑩ 5
411/500

See UK entry (February).

## BEATLES
STRAWBERRY FIELDS
FOREVER
*Capitol*

▲ 8
⑩ 22
—/500

See UK entry (February).

## NANCY & FRANK SINATRA
SOMETHIN' STUPID
*Reprise*

▲ 1
⑩ 8
41/500

In less than 15 months, Frank and daughter Nancy not only scored solo transatlantic chart toppers but also achieved one together with a captivating

MOR song written by C. Carson Parks. This early example of eight-track recording was co-produced by Jimmy Bowen and Lee Hazlewood. Surprisingly, a follow-up by the duo, 'Feelin' Kinda Sunday', went virtually unnoticed.

## FIVE AMERICANS
WESTERN UNION
*Abnak*

Early rock'n'roll star Dale Hawkins produced all of the Dallas-based band's four US Top 40 entries. The quintet's biggest-selling single was co-written by group members Cliff Goldsmith and John Durrill (who wrote Cher's 1974 chart topper 'Dark Lady').

## TOMMY JAMES & THE SHONDELLS
I THINK WE'RE ALONE NOW
*Roulette*

This Pittsburgh band, fronted by Ohio native James (born Thomas Jackson), had their biggest hit of 1967 with a song penned by producers Ritchie Cordell and Bo Gentry. A reworking by Tiffany in 1986 topped the transatlantic charts.

## MONKEES
A LITTLE BIT ME, A LITTLE BIT YOU
*Colgems*

Only British-born Davy Jones appeared on the internationally successful act's third gold record in a row. It is rumoured that composer Neil Diamond helped out on backing vocals.

## ARETHA FRANKLIN
I NEVER LOVED A MAN (THE WAY I LOVE YOU)
*Atlantic*

Eleven years after her first recording and five years after her chart debut, the 'Queen Of Soul' had her first major hit. Atlantic, unlike Franklin's

previous label, Columbia, aimed the performer's records solidly at the R&B market, and the results made the unmistakable vocalist the hottest female singles act of the late 1960s. This superior slice of southern soul was composed by Ronnie Shannon and produced in Muscle Shoals, Alabama. Franklin's album of the same name was only kept from the top by *More Of The Monkees*.

## MARTHA & THE VANDELLAS
JIMMY MACK
*Gordy*

The well-respected female trio scored their second R&B chart topper with another jewel from the Holland, Dozier & Holland songbook. This record also returned to the UK Top 40 in 1970. The group, who disbanded before the end of the 1960s, were inducted into the Rock and Roll Hall of Fame in 1995.

## ARTHUR CONLEY
SWEET SOUL MUSIC
*Atco*

Otis Redding produced and co-wrote the song that introduced the Atlanta-born soul singer/songwriter to the transatlantic Top 10. This name-dropping opus was based on an earlier Sam Cooke album track entitled 'Yeah Man'. Conley, who earlier recorded on Redding's Jotis label, collected a few more chart singles in the late 1960s, but a sound-alike 1972 single, 'More Sweet Soul Music', sold few copies.

## SUPREMES
THE HAPPENING
*Motown*

Noted composer/conductor and arranger Frank DeVol composed this film theme with the golden girls' regular writers Holland, Dozier & Holland. It completed the superstars' second run of four successive US No 1s.

# UNITED KINGDOM
# APRIL 1967

## SANDIE SHAW
PUPPET ON A STRING
*Pye*

▲ 1
⑩ 7
50/500

After a run of minor hits, Shaw's rendition of this bouncy Phil Coulter and Bill Martin composition won the Eurovision Song Contest for the UK. The four million-selling single also made Shaw the first female to notch up three UK No 1s – a feat only bettered in 1987 by Madonna.

## NANCY & FRANK SINATRA
SOMETHIN' STUPID
*Reprise*

▲ 1
⑩ 8
97/500

See US entry.

## MONKEES
A LITTLE BIT ME,
A LITTLE BIT YOU
*RCA*

▲ 3
⑩ 2
412/500

See US entry.

## MANFRED MANN
HA HA SAID THE CLOWN
*Fontana*

▲ 4
⑩ 9
—/500

In the late 1960s UK songwriter Tony Hazzard composed a handful of Top 10 hits, the first of which gave these chart regulars their highest-placed single of the year.

## CLIFF RICHARD
IT'S ALL OVER
*Columbia*

▲ 9
⑩33
—/500

A song composed by Don Everly and originally recorded by the Everly Brothers continued Cliff's almost unprecedented run of UK hits. Coincidentally, the UK superstar subsequently released a couple of successful singles with Don's brother Phil.

## JIMI HENDRIX EXPERIENCE
PURPLE HAZE
*Track*

▲ 3
⑩ 2
428/500

The ground-breaking performer, who re-wrote the book of rock guitar playing, had his first self-composed hit with a track that is regarded as one of psychedelic music's finest moments.

## FOUR TOPS
BERNADETTE
*Tamla Motown*

▲ 8
⑩ 3
—/500

See US entry.

## CAT STEVENS
I'M GONNA GET ME A GUN
*Deram*

▲ 6
⑩ 2
—/500

Shortly before he was voted Most Promising Singer of 1967 in the *RM* poll, this classy pop performer collected his second UK-only Top 10 entry of the year with a self-penned song. Stevens then had a couple of quiet sales years before he burst on to the international record scene with both barrels blasting in the early 1970s.

## MOVE
I CAN HEAR THE
GRASS GROW
*Deram*

▲ 5
⑩ 2
—/500

The innovative and controversial Birmingham band were one of the most popular UK acts of the late 1960s. Group member Roy Wood penned this psychedelic-influenced single.

## MAMAS & THE PAPAS
DEDICATED TO THE
ONE I LOVE
*RCA*

▲ 2
⑩ 2
241/500

See US entry (March).

# UNITED STATES
# MAY 1967

## BUCKINGHAMS
DON'T YOU CARE
*Columbia*

Before finding international fame for his work with Chicago and Blood, Sweat & Tears, James William Guercio produced The Buckingham's biggest Columbia hits. Like their previous chart topper, 'Kind Of A Drag', this noteworthy track was written by Jim Holvay and Gary Beisber from the group The Mob.

## PEACHES & HERB
CLOSE YOUR EYES
*Date*

This sweet soul duo from Washington DC amassed five US-only Top 40 singles in the late 1960s, the majority of which were revivals of songs from the 1950s. Their biggest hit was a top-notch romantic doo-wop ballad which had been taken up the R&B charts in 1955 by the Five Keys. Surprisingly, the duo (albeit, with a new Peaches) notched up a couple of transatlantic charters at the end of the 1970s.

## DAVE CLARK FIVE
YOU GOT WHAT IT TAKES
*Epic*

One of the most renowned acts of the 1960s clocked up the last of 14 Top 20 singles with a Berry Gordy composition that had been a transatlantic hit in 1960 by Marv Johnson. The track was taken from their seventh successive US Top 40 LP. As the next decade dawned the group folded, and Clark went on to become a top music business entrepreneur.

## SPENCER DAVIS GROUP
I'M A MAN
*UA*

See UK entry (February).

## YOUNG RASCALS
GROOVIN'
*Atlantic*

Their fourth self-penned single returned the acclaimed quartet to the top spot. Initially, Atlantic did not want to release the classic summertime pop/R&B opus, which became the act's only transatlantic Top 10 entry. An instrumental interpretation by Booker T. & The MG's also graced the Top 40 a few months later.

## HAPPENINGS
I GOT RHYTHM
*BT Puppy*

For the third time in nine months the easy-listening/pop vocal group reached the Top 20 with a reworking of an old favourite. This time it was a George & Ira Gershwin standard that had first been performed by Ethel Merman in the 1930 musical *Girl Crazy*. The quartet's follow-up, the even older Al Jolson classic 'My Mammy', was their last noticeable hit.

## ARETHA FRANKLIN
RESPECT
*Atlantic*

Aretha amassed an amazing 14 Top 20 singles from 1967–69. The most successful of these was her unique interpretation of Otis Redding's self-penned Top 40 hit from 1965. Franklin's Grammy-winning single introduced her to the UK charts and was the Top R&B Single of the Year.

## ENGELBERT HUMPERDINCK
RELEASE ME (AND LET ME LOVE AGAIN)
*Parrot*

See UK entry (February).

## PAUL REVERE & THE RAIDERS
HIM OR ME – WHAT'S IT GONNA BE
*Columbia*

Vocalist Mark Lindsay and Doris Day's son Terry Melcher composed the popular quintet's fourth US Top 10 single in a year. In total, the photogenic group amassed 10 US Top 20 singles and four Top 10 LPs in the 1960s. Surprisingly, the act, named after a hero of the Revolutionary War against the British, never made their mark on the UK charts.

## MAMAS & THE PAPAS
CREEQUE ALLEY
*Dunhill*

John and Michelle Phillips penned this autobio-graphical opus, which became the internationally renowned quartet's fourth and last transatlantic Top 20 entry. The unmistakable team, who topped the bill at the 1967 Monterey Pop Festival, disbanded in 1968.

## NEIL DIAMOND
GIRL, YOU'LL BE A WOMAN SOON
*Bang*

The talented and instantly recognizable pop singer's fourth consecutive Top 20 entry was another of his noteworthy compositions. In 1994, Urge Overkill's updated version was a transatlantic chart entry.

# UNITED KINGDOM
# MAY 1967

## TOM JONES
FUNNY FAMILIAR FORGOTTEN FEELING
*Decca*

'F' words abounded on the international sex symbol's third consecutive country cover record. Don Gibson had scored on the country chart with the song earlier in the year. Interestingly, ten years later Jones started his own impressive run of US country hits.

## LULU
THE BOAT THAT I ROW
*Columbia*

Composer Neil Diamond's second simultaneous UK Top 10 entry was with the first Lulu hit produced by Mickie Most. The track was her first release for the EMI group (who had rejected her earlier).

## TREMELOES
SILENCE IS GOLDEN
*CBS*

The Tremeloes' version of a melodic Bob Crewe and Bob Gaudio song, which had been recorded previously by the Four Seasons, gave the British group their biggest transatlantic hit. It became the act's second successive Top 20 entry in the US. A 1984 retread sold few copies.

## WHO
PICTURES OF LILY
*Track*

As 'Pictures Of Lily' slowly climbed the US Top 100, the boundary-stretching British band appeared at the Monterey Pop Festival and toured the US with Herman's Hermits. In the UK, it extended their run of Top 10 hits to seven.

## DUBLINERS
SEVEN DRUNKEN NIGHTS
*Major Minor*

In 1967, the popular Irish folk band had two Top 20 singles and a couple of Top 20 albums in the UK. Their biggest-selling single was a rousing rendition of a traditional drinking song which came from the act's album *A Drop Of The Hard Stuff*. Amazingly, the crowd-pulling group returned to the Top 10 27 years later in the company of The Pogues.

## KINKS
WATERLOO SUNSET
*Pye*

Londoner Ray Davies painted a musical portrait of life south of the Thames in a wistful and low-key gem. This skilful pop lyricist had originally written it as 'Liverpool Sunset'; however, he quickly re-located the song after The Beatles released their eulogy to life in Liverpool, 'Penny Lane'.

## BEACH BOYS
THEN I KISSED HER
*Capitol*

The innovative multi-platinum act's fifth UK Top 5 single in succession was a unique interpretation of a 1963 hit by The Crystals. The track was not released as a single in the group's homeland.

## JIMI HENDRIX EXPERIENCE
THE WIND CRIES MARY
*Track*

Another self-composed rock classic gave the godfather of heavy metal his third UK Top 10 entry in five months. It came from the platinum album *Are You Experienced?* which took a record 59 weeks on the US chart to reach the Top 5.

# UNITED STATES
# JUNE 1967

## JEFFERSON AIRPLANE
SOMEBODY TO LOVE

*RCA*

The first of the new wave of San Francisco rock bands to crack the singles Top 10 did so with their fifth single, a magnetic song penned by lead vocalist Grace Slick's brother-in-law, Darby Slick, which Grace had also recorded with her previous group, Great Society. The track came from the act's acclaimed Top 3 album, *Surrealistic Pillow*.

## TEMPTATIONS
ALL I NEED
*Gordy*

This highly touted R&B group registered another winner with a song written for them by Eddie

Holland, Frank Wilson and R. Dean Taylor. It was one of four top hits on their third Top 10 album *With A Lot O' Soul*.

## TURTLES
SHE'D RATHER BE WITH ME
*White Whale*

Like their chart-topping 'Happy Together', the Los Angeles group's biggest transatlantic hit was also composed by Garry Bonner and Alan Gordon, who had been in Columbia's little-noticed group The Magicians.

## MUSIC EXPLOSION
LITTLE BIT O' SOUL
*Laurie*

▲ 2
⑩ 1•
221/500

Producers Jerry Kasenetz and Jeff Katz chalked up the first of many hits with this early example of bubblegum pop. Ivy League members John Carter and Ken Lewis composed the catchy pop tune that shot the quintet into the spotlight. It was the only noteworthy release by the Ohio outfit, who disbanded soon afterwards.

## ASSOCIATION
WINDY
*Warner*

▲ 1
⑩ 3
32/500

A song that teenager Ruthann Friedman composed about a hippie acquaintance of hers from San Francisco took her friends The Association to the top for the second time in nine months.

## TOMMY JAMES & THE SHONDELLS
MIRAGE
*Roulette*

▲ 10
⑩ 3
—/500

James, who was the US's most successful male artist in 1967, reached the Top 10 for the second time in four months with songs produced and written by Ritchie Cordell and Bo Gentry.

## SCOTT MCKENZIE
SAN FRANCISCO (BE SURE TO WEAR FLOWERS IN YOUR HAIR)
*Ode*

▲ 4
⑩ 1•
469/500

One of the biggest hits from the 'summer of love' was written and co-produced by Mamas & Papas member John Phillips, who had earlier sung in The Journeymen with McKenzie (born Philip Blondheim). This hippy anthem topped the UK chart and sold a reported seven million copies worldwide. However, fame was fleeting for the bearded, bead-wearing vocalist, whose recording career faded with the flowers he wore, although in 1988 he returned as co-writer of the Beach Boys' million-selling 'Kokomo'.

## FRANKIE VALLI
CAN'T TAKE MY EYES OFF YOU
*Philips*

▲ 2
⑩ 1
223/500

The falsetto-voiced leader of the Four Seasons had his highest-placed solo hit of the decade with a classy pop ballad composed by fellow group member Bob Gaudio and producer Bob Crewe. The Lettermen reinstated the song in the US Top 10 in 1968. In the UK, Andy Williams' interpretation also entered the Top 10 in 1968, and the Boys Town Gang followed suit in 1982.

## SPANKY & OUR GANG
SUNDAY WILL NEVER BE THE SAME
*Mercury*

▲ 9
⑩ 1•
—/500

Elaine 'Spanky' McFarlane fronted this Chicago pop/folk quintet who were cast in The Mamas & The Papas mould. They amassed five consecutive US-only Top 40 hits, the biggest being their rendition of a Terry Cashman and Gene Pistilli song that The Mamas & The Papas had rejected. When the latter re-formed in the early 1980s, Spanky was recruited to take the place of Mama Cass.

## GRASS ROOTS
LET'S LIVE FOR TODAY
*Dunhill*

▲ 8
⑩ 1
—/500

Initially, producer/songwriters Steve Barri and P.F. Sloan were the nucleus of Grass Roots and sang on the act's first two chart singles. However, they were too busy to tour and brought in San Francisco group 13th Floor to take their place. The new Grass Roots added a further 13 US Top 40 entries by 1972, the first of which was an Americanized treatment of a song that had been an Italian hit for The Rokes.

# UNITED KINGDOM
# JUNE 1967

## PROCOL HARUM
A WHITER SHADE OF PALE
*Deram*

▲ 1
⑩ 1
23/500

In the UK, one of the top hits of the 'summer of love' was a haunting surreal song based on Bach's Suite No 3 in D Major. The record, which also transported the Southend-based band into the US Top 5, was composed by keyboard player Gary Booker and lyricist/poet Keith Reid. Generally regarded as one of pop music's finest moments, this single re-entered the UK Top 20 in 1972, and in total sold over six million copies. Annie Lennox' 1995 rendition also reached the UK Top 20.

## ENGELBERT HUMPERDINCK
THERE GOES MY EVERYTHING
*Decca*

▲ 2
⑩ 2
202/500

Amazingly, the UK's Top 3 chart hits of 1967 were all recorded by Humperdinck. The popular balladeer's second smash was a revival of a Dallas Frazier song that Jack Greene had taken to the top of the country list in 1966.

## SUPREMES
THE HAPPENING
*Tamla Motown*

▲ 6
⑩ 6
—/500

See US entry (April).

## ARTHUR CONLEY
SWEET SOUL MUSIC
*Atlantic*

▲ 7
⑩ 1•
—/500

See US entry (April).

## HOLLIES
CARRIE-ANNE
*Parlophone*

▲ 3
⑩12
422/500

The celebrated act's second run of five successive UK Top 10 singles ended with another outstanding group-composed pop opus. As it entered the US Top 10, The Hollies were on tour there with The Turtles.

## DAVE DEE, DOZY, BEAKY, MICK & TICH
OKAY!
*Fontana*

▲ 4
⑩ 5
—/500

This theatrical and experimental British pop quintet put another anthemic foot-stomping Howard and Blaikley ditty into the Top 10. Lead guitarist Ian 'Tich' Amey played balalaika on the track.

## TRAFFIC
PAPER SUN
*Island*

▲ 5
⑩ 1
—/500

When singer/songwriter and keyboard player Steve Winwood left the Spencer Davis Group he formed pioneering progressive rock band Traffic, who were instantly successful. The album-oriented act kick started their career with a song written by Winwood and fellow group member Jim Capaldi.

# UNITED STATES
# JULY 1967

## EVERY MOTHERS' SON
COME ON DOWN TO MY
BOAT
*MGM*

As the act's name implies, this New York quintet were a clean-cut crew who would have made any 1960s mum proud. Their only Top 40 success came with a bubblegum-oriented opus co-written by producer Wes Farrell and previously recorded by Rare Breed. The group fell out with Farrell soon after their boat came in and never sailed back into the Top 40.

## PETULA CLARK
DON'T SLEEP IN THE
SUBWAY
*Warner*

The British pop vocalist, who had been voted Top Female Singer in the US in 1966, added to her transatlantic Top 20 tally with another infectious Tony Hatch and Jackie Trent song. During her 50-year show business career Clark has sold over 30 million records.

## 5TH DIMENSION
UP UP & AWAY
*Soul City*

Talented singer/songwriter Jim Webb originally composed this instantly infectious song for a film about hot air balloons. The film was never completed, but that did not stop the Fifth Dimension's recording from transporting the mixed quintet into the Top 20 for the second time that year. Rock star Johnny Rivers produced the single, which appeared on his own label, Soul City. In the UK, a US cover by the Johnny Mann singers hit the heights. Coincidentally, both Fifth Dimension and Mann earned Grammy Awards for their versions.

## JOHNNY RIVERS
THE TRACKS OF
MY TEARS
*Imperial*

Though little known outside the US, this singer/songwriter/producer took his tenth trip into the US Top 20 with an update of a Miracles hit from 1965. The track was included on his sixth Top 40 LP of the decade, *Rewind*. A later update of the Smokey Robinson composition reached the Top 40 in 1976 by Linda Ronstadt.

## DOORS
LIGHT MY FIRE
*Elektra*

Jim Morrison, one of rock's most controversial and talented figures, fronted the LA quartet who topped the chart with their self-penned second single. The track was taken from the act's eponymous debut album, which only *Sgt Pepper* stopped from reaching No 1. A year later, José Feliciano's reworking of this classic went into the transatlantic Top 10. Amazingly, The Doors' original recording was only a hit in the UK in 1991 (when the legendary group's bio-pic was released).

## FOUR SEASONS
C'MON MARIANNE
*Philips*

With the exception of The Beatles, The Four Seasons were arguably the top vocal group of the 1960s. Their twenty-fifth Top 40 entry was penned by Larry Brown, who was responsible for several of Dawn's (named after a Four Seasons hit) biggest sellers in the 1970s. The Four Seasons, who left an indelible mark on the pop scene, were inducted into the Rock and Roll Hall of Fame in 1990. In 1976, Donny Osmond re-introduced the infectious song to the Top 40.

## PROCOL HARUM
A WHITER SHADE
OF PALE
*Deram*

▲ 5
🔟 1•
—/500

See UK entry (June).

## STEVIE WONDER
I WAS MADE TO
LOVE HER
*Tamla*

▲ 2
🔟 5
257/500

Henry Cosby, who had co-written Wonder's chart-topping debut, 'Fingertips', wrote this memorable slice of soul with the talented teenage entertainer. The single also introduced the vocalist to the UK Top 10.

## BUCKINGHAMS
MERCY, MERCY, MERCY
*Columbia*

▲ 5
🔟 3•
—/500

Well-respected jazz pianist Joe Zawinul (noted for his work with Miles Davis and Weather Report) co-wrote the third of this Chicago rock act's five Top

20 entries in 1967. Zawinul had also played on the original Top 20 version by saxophonist Cannonball Adderley's quintet earlier in the year. Despite their tremendous chart start, The Buckinghams sold few records in 1968 and disbanded before the decade's end.

## JEFFERSON AIRPLANE
WHITE RABBIT
*RCA*

▲ 8
🔟 2
—/500

Jefferson Airplane were one of the first album-oriented rock acts. They scored five consecutive Top 20 LPs in the late 1960s and had two Top 10 singles in the 'summer of love'. Their last major hit before evolving into Jefferson Starship (who later became Starship) was an *Alice In Wonderland* inspired tale that lead vocalist Grace Slick penned and originally recorded with the group Great Society. Perhaps surprisingly, this ground-breaking outfit had only a cult following in the UK during the decade.

# UNITED KINGDOM
# JULY 1967

## TURTLES
SHE'D RATHER BE
WITH ME
*London American*

▲ 4
🔟 1
415/500

See US entry (June).

## MONKEES
ALTERNATE TITLE
*RCA*

▲ 2
🔟 3
283/500

'Randy Scouse Git' was the original title of the extremely popular group's first self-written hit. The title was inspired by the UK TV series *Till Death*

*Do Us Part*, on which, incidentally, the later successful US series *All In The Family* was based.

## YOUNG RASCALS
GROOVIN'
*Atlantic*

▲ 8
🔟 1•
—/500

See US entry (May).

## VIKKI CARR
IT MUST BE HIM
*Liberty*

▲ 2
🔟 1•
266/500

See US entry (October).

## TOPOL
IF I WERE A RICH MAN
*CBS*

*Fiddler On The Roof* was one of the most successful musicals of the late 1960s. In the UK, the London cast album of the Sheldon Harnick and Jerry Bock-composed show reached the Top 5. This single taken from that recording gave the show's star, noted stage and film actor Topol, his only singles chart entry.

## BEATLES
ALL YOU NEED IS LOVE
*Parlophone*

Four hundred million people in over two dozen countries watched The Beatles' debut performance of this flower power anthem. It was the UK's contribution to the first worldwide live TV show, *Our World*. Joining in on the chorus were members of The Rolling Stones, The Who and The Hollies as well as Donovan, Marianne Faithfull and several other celebrities.

## PINK FLOYD
SEE EMILY PLAY
*Columbia*

In the 1960s, these pioneers of the psychedelic scene were a UK-only phenomenon. The act that helped rewrite the manual on live shows delivered four albums into the Top 10 before the decade ended. Their biggest single of the period was written by original front man Syd Barrett (who left them in 1968) and had initially been called 'Games For May'. The group, whose LP *Dark Side Of The Moon* holds the US chart longevity record, were still frequently topping the transatlantic charts 30 years later in the mid-1990s.

## ARETHA FRANKLIN
RESPECT
*Atlantic*

See US entry (May).

## SCOTT McKENZIE
SAN FRANCISCO (BE SURE TO WEAR FLOWERS IN YOUR HAIR)
*CBS*

See US entry (June).

## YOUNG IDEA
WITH A LITTLE HELP FROM MY FRIENDS
*Columbia*

With a little help from The Beatles, this UK vocal duo had a brief spell in the spotlight with their fourth release. Their timely cover of a popular track from the Liverpool quartet's record-breaking *Sgt Pepper* album opened the door to one-hit wonderland for Tony Cox and Douglas McCrae-Brown. In 1968 Joe Cocker's far more aggressive version topped the UK chart.

## JOHNNY MANN SINGERS
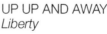
UP UP AND AWAY
*Liberty*

One of the US's busiest session groups of the decade had the UK hit version of the acclaimed Jim Webb composition that Fifth Dimension had registered with in the US. In his homeland, Mann's recording won a Grammy for Best Performance by a Chorus.

## DAVE DAVIES
DEATH OF A CLOWN
*Pye*

Astoundingly, the only member of The Kinks to have solo hits was not the group's celebrated lead singer Ray Davies but his guitar-playing younger brother Dave. In 1967, Dave had two major hits in the UK, the biggest being a song he penned with Ray.

# UNITED STATES
# AUGUST 1967

## BEATLES
ALL YOU NEED IS LOVE
*Capitol*

▲ 1
🔟 23
191/500

See UK entry (July).

## MONKEES
PLEASANT VALLEY
SUNDAY
*Colgems*

▲ 3
🔟 4
421/500

Carole King and Gerry Goffin composed the song that The Monkees promoted on their sell-out US tour. It came from the quartet's fourth successive No 1 album, *Pisces, Aquarius, Capricorn & Jones Ltd*.

## HOLLIES
CARRIE-ANNE
*Epic*

▲ 9
🔟 3
—/500

See UK entry (June).

## YOUNG RASCALS
A GIRL LIKE YOU
*Atlantic*

▲ 10
🔟 3
—/500

Group members Felix Cavaliere and Eddie Brigati (who had both been in hit maker Joey Dee's backing band The Starliters) penned the noted New York group's fifth single to reach the Top 20.

## ARETHA FRANKLIN
BABY I LOVE YOU
*Atlantic*

▲ 4
🔟 3
474/500

Ronnie Shannon, who composed Lady Soul's debut Top 10 hit, also wrote the Memphis-born performer's third million-selling single in four months.

## BOBBIE GENTRY
ODE TO BILLIE JOE
*Capitol*

▲ 1
🔟 1•
35/500

This Mississippi miss (born Roberta Streeter) originally recorded the intriguing self-penned ode as the B side to another southern saga, 'Mississippi Delta'. The song, which made Billie Joe McAllister and the Tallahatchee Bridge famous, put three Grammy Awards on the polished performer's shelf. Instrumental versions by The Kingpins (featuring King Curtis) and Ray Bryant also sold well that year. In 1976 (four years after the actual bridge had collapsed), Gentry re-recorded the track for the film of the same name and both of her versions reached the US chart.

## JAMES BROWN
COLD SWEAT (PT 1)
*King*

▲ 7
🔟 4
—/500

After a relatively quiet sales period, Brown returned with a single many consider to be the first real funk record. He penned this track with the new leader of his band, Alfred Ellis.

## DIANA ROSS &
## THE SUPREMES
REFLECTIONS
*Motown*

▲ 2
🔟 13
289/500

Their first single giving Diana Ross solo billing ended the golden group's run of four No 1 hits (interestingly its record number was Motown 1111). 'Reflections' was also the trio's first single without founder member Florence Ballard.

## TEMPTATIONS
YOU'RE MY EVERYTHING
*Gordy*

▲ 6
🔟 5
—/500

Norman Whitfield wrote and produced the single that gave this influential soul group their fourth Top 10 entry in a row.

# UNITED KINGDOM
# AUGUST 1967

### TOM JONES
I'LL NEVER FALL
IN LOVE AGAIN
*Decca*

An emotional ballad that had proved far from successful for composer Lonnie Donegan became the first of three UK No 2 hits in a row for the Welsh song wizard. Surprisingly, Jones' heartfelt rendition only reached the US Top 10 in 1969.

### STEVIE WONDER
I WAS MADE TO
LOVE HER
*Tamla Motown*

See US entry (July).

### ANITA HARRIS
JUST LOVING YOU
*CBS*

Six years after she made her solo recording bow, this one-time skating star and member of the Cliff Adams Singers scored the first of her three UK Top 40 singles. The Somerset-born singer and TV personality's highest-placed single was composed by Tom Springfield, who had previously written big hits for The Springfields and The Seekers.

### TREMELOES
EVEN THE BAD TIMES
ARE GOOD
*CBS*

The quartet from Essex had their third successive Top 5 single with a bouncy pop opus penned by top British tunesmiths Mitch Murray and Peter Callendar. In the US it was the last of the group's three Top 40 entries.

### ALAN PRICE SET
THE HOUSE THAT
JACK BUILT
*Decca*

Price's first self-composed single took the keyboard-playing vocalist from Durham into the Top 20 for the fourth time in succession. The founder member of The Animals added to his hit tally in the 1970s, when he also made a name for himself as a film score composer.

### MAMAS & THE PAPAS
CREEQUE ALLEY
*RCA*

See US entry (May).

# UNITED STATES
# SEPTEMBER 1967

## BOBBY VEE & THE STRANGERS
COME BACK WHEN YOU GROW UP
*Liberty*

▲ 3
🔟 6•
325/500

This one-time teen idol made his Top 10 comeback after almost five years away with a folk-flavoured song penned by Nashville composer Martha Sharp (who in 1966 had written two Top 20 entries for Sandy Posey). Incidentally, it had earlier been recorded but not released by Freddie & The Dreamers.

## BOX TOPS
THE LETTER
*Mala*

▲ 1
🔟 1
44/500

For four weeks this Memphis band's first chart entry topped the US list. Wayne Carson Thompson wrote the song, which debuted as his first big hit, 'Do It Again, A Little Bit Slower' by Jon & Robin, departed. The track was produced by Muscle Shoals mainstay Dan Penn. 'The Letter' also entered the US Top 20 in 1969 by The Arbors and in 1970 by Joe Cocker.

## JAY & THE TECHNIQUES
APPLES PEACHES PUMPKIN PIE
*Smash*

▲ 6
🔟 1•
—/500

In late 1967, this multi-racial septet from Pennsylvania put two consecutive singles into the US Top 20. The first and biggest seller was a bouncy pop/R&B tune composed by Maurice Irby Jr. Jerry Ross produced the track and veteran group vocalist Jay Proctor sang lead.

## ERIC BURDON & THE ANIMALS
SAN FRANCISCAN NIGHTS
*MGM*

▲ 9
🔟 3•
—/500

See UK entry (November).

## WILSON PICKETT
FUNKY BROADWAY
*Atlantic*

▲ 8
🔟 2•
—/500

Pickett was not only one of the most successful soul singers of the 1960s, he was also one of the genre's true greats. Among his eight transatlantic chart entries in the decade was a stand-out rendition of a funk track that composer Dyke (Arlester Christian) and his group The Blazers had taken into the R&B Top 20 some months before. In 1991, Pickett was elected into the Rock and Roll Hall of Fame.

## ASSOCIATION
NEVER MY LOVE
*Warner*

▲ 2
🔟 4
229/500

Singer/songwriters Don & Dick Addrisi composed the beautiful ballad that almost guided this California combo to the top for the third time in a year. The song also reached the US Top 20 by the Fifth Dimension (1971) and Blue Swede (1974), and has received over five million radio plays in the US.

## JACKIE WILSON
(YOUR LOVE KEEPS LIFTING ME) HIGHER AND HIGHER
*Brunswick*

▲ 6
⑩ 6•
—/500

The unmistakable vocalist's forty-fifth chart entry gave him his last major US hit, and amazingly reached the UK Top 40 in 1969, 1975 and 1987. The song also climbed into the US Top 10 in 1977 by Rita Coolidge. Wilson went into a coma in 1975 and died in 1984. Among his posthumous UK chart entries was the 1957 recording 'Reet Petite', which returned to top the singles list in 1986.

## PETER, PAUL & MARY
I DIG ROCK AND ROLL MUSIC
*Warner*

▲ 9
⑩ 5
—/500

The platinum-selling folk act reappeared in the Top 10 after a four-year hiatus with a song part-written by member Paul Stookey.

## VAN MORRISON
BROWN EYED GIRL
*Bang*

▲ 10
⑩ 1
—/500

Noted US R&B producer/songwriter Bert Berns was at the helm for Morrison's first solo hit. The Belfast-born artist penned the first of his five US Top 40 singles, as well as the vast majority of tracks on his numerous chart albums over the years. Few people were surprised when he was inducted into the Rock and Roll Hall of Fame in 1993, or when he received a BRITS award for Outstanding Contributions to UK Music in 1994.

---

# UNITED KINGDOM
# SEPTEMBER 1967

---

## ENGELBERT HUMPERDINCK
THE LAST WALTZ
*Decca*

▲ 1
⑩ 3
9/500

One of the most-performed British compositions of all time was written by Les Reed and Barry Mason and sold over a million in the UK alone by this internationally renowned entertainer. It was also the title track to the singer's second US Top 10 album.

## ROLLING STONES
WE LOVE YOU/ DANDELION
*Decca*

▲ 8
⑩ 11
—/500

Even though John Lennon and Paul McCartney joined in on the chorus, this 'All You Need Is Love'-influenced flower power opus was the Stones' least successful transatlantic hit since 1964.

## KEITH WEST
EXCERPT FROM A TEENAGE OPERA
*Parlophone*

▲ 2
⑩ 1•
234/500

'Tommy' was not the first rock opera hero. Over a year earlier, an excerpt from Keith West's planned teenage opera made 'Grocer Jack' famous, albeit briefly. However, when the second excerpt, 'Sam', stalled at the bottom of the Top 40, West (born Keith Hopkins) and co-writer/producer Mark Wirtz decided not to continue further with their operatic project.

## SMALL FACES
ITCHYCOO PARK
*Immediate*

It was eighth time lucky for one of the UK's most distinctive bands when this tongue-in-cheek psychedelic rock song shot them into the US Top 20 for the first (and only) time. In the UK the single, with its revolutionary phased drum sound, returned to the Top 10 again in 1975.

## FLOWERPOT MEN
LET'S GO TO
SAN FRANCISCO
*Deram*

With tongues firmly in their cheeks, top songwriters John Carter and Ken Lewis named this session group after a popular children's puppet TV show. The quartet, formed solely to front the flower-power cash-in song, included such note-worthies as Tony Burrows and Neil Landon. In the US, where the record sold poorly, they were renamed The Flowerpots.

## BEACH BOYS
HEROES AND VILLAINS
*Capitol*

Erratic musical genius Brian Wilson penned the universally popular band's latest transatlantic Top 20 entry with the critically acclaimed singer/songwriter Van Dyke Parks.

## DIANA ROSS &
## THE SUPREMES
REFLECTIONS
*Tamla Motown*

See US entry (August).

## MOVE
FLOWERS IN THE RAIN
*Regal Zonophone*

The first track to be played on the newly launched BBC Top 40 station, Radio One, gave the controversial performers their third Top 5 hit of the year. As the psychedelic-slanted single charted, the group toured the UK with Jimi Hendrix and Pink Floyd.

## TRAFFIC
HOLE IN MY SHOE
*Island*

Dave Mason wrote and sang this influential and acclaimed act's most successful single. In 1984, a tongue-in-cheek remake by neil (sic), actor Nigel Planer from TV's *The Young Ones* took the archetypal hippy song into the runner-up position for the second time.

## CLIFF RICHARD
THE DAY I MET MARIE
*Columbia*

Soon after he was again voted Top UK Male Singer, Cliff clicked with a song penned by Shadows stalwart Hank Marvin. The award-winning vocalist considers 'The Day I Met Marie' to be one of his favourite recordings.

# UNITED STATES
# OCTOBER 1967

## BILL COSBY
LITTLE OLE MAN
(UPTIGHT-EVERYTHING'S
ALRIGHT)
*Warner*

▲ 4
🔟 1•
—/500

His parody of Stevie Wonder's smash 'Uptight (Everything's Alright)' gave this multiple Grammy and Emmy award-winning entertainer his biggest hit single. The track came from the Philadelphia-born superstar's first vocal album, *Bill Cosby Sings/Silver Throat*. Incidentally, the multi-millionaire performer's previous five LPs had all turned gold.

## YOUNG RASCALS
HOW CAN I BE SURE
*Atlantic*

▲ 4
🔟 4
—/500

This memorable self-penned ballad was the third Top 10 single spawned from the regular US hit makers' *Groovin'* album. A revival by David Cassidy topped the UK chart in 1972.

## BRENTON WOOD
GIMME LITTLE SIGN
*Double Shot*

▲ 9
🔟 1•
—/500

Nine years after his first recording, Wood, who was born Alfred Smith in Louisiana, had three US Top 40 entries. The R&B performer's transatlantic Top 10 hit was a catchy pop-slanted ditty that he wrote with his producers Joe Hooven and Jerry Winn.

## LULU
TO SIR WITH LOVE
*Epic*

▲ 1
🔟 1•
20/500

In her homeland, Lulu's biggest US hit was hidden away on the B side of 'Let's Pretend'. 'To Sir With Love', which sold over two million copies in the US, was the title song from a British-based Sidney

Poitier movie in which she played a school girl. Surprisingly, in the UK, the consistently popular performer did not top the chart until 1993.

## SAM & DAVE
SOUL MAN
*Stax*

▲ 2
🔟 1
242/500

Sam (Moore) & Dave's (Prater) unique vocal interplay created the template for soul duos in the late 1960s. Their sixth R&B Top 10 entry launched them into the pop Top 10 for the first time and earned them a Grammy. Like the act's earlier hits, it was composed by another of the great R&B duos, producers/songwriters Isaac Hayes and David Porter. A retread by actors/singers the Blues Brothers reached the US Top 20 in 1978. In 1986, Sam re-recorded the track with rock star Lou Reed.

## SOUL SURVIVORS
EXPRESSWAY TO YOUR HEART
*Crimson*

▲ 4
🔟 1•
452/500

One of soul music's premier partnerships, producers/songwriters Kenny Gamble and Leon Huff, were behind this blue-eyed soul band's biggest hit. The track, which incorporated traffic noises, also drove the East Coast outfit into the R&B Top 5. In the 1970s, the act's recordings on Gamble & Huff's TSOP and Philly International labels made little headway.

## VIKKI CARR
IT MUST BE HIM
*Liberty*

▲ 3
🔟 1•
400/500

Not surprisingly, Texas-born Florencia Bisenta De Casillas Martinez Cardona used a stage name when she started recording. The emotive song stylist, who had released the original version of The Crystals' hit 'He's A Rebel', charted in both Australia and the UK before her homeland. Her only transatlantic success was a French ballad (originally titled 'Seul Sur Son Etoile') composed by Gilbert Becaud, with English lyrics by Mack David. A quarter of a century later, Carr is still a top-selling artist in the Latin market.

### MARVIN GAYE & TAMMI TERRELL
YOUR PRECIOUS LOVE
*Tamla*

The biggest-selling soul duo of the era clocked the first of four Top 10 singles with a song composed by another noted duo Valerie Simpson and Nick Ashford.

### ARETHA FRANKLIN
A NATURAL WOMAN (YOU MAKE ME FEEL LIKE)
*Atlantic*

Aretha's producer Jerry Wexler composed her fourth successive gold record with regular hit composers Carole King and Gerry Goffin. The track was later included on her No 2 album, *Aretha: Lady Soul*.

### STRAWBERRY ALARM CLOCK
INCENSE AND PEPPERMINTS
*UNI*

Frank Slay, who had earlier achieved many hits with partner Bob Crewe, produced this track as the B side of The Sixpences' 'The Birdman of Alkatrash' on the All-American label. The flower power opus, which started life as an instrumental entitled 'The Happy Whistler', was picked up by UNI and released under the group's more psychedelic new name. Oddly, the lead singer on the West Coast act's only smash single, 16-year-old Greg Munford, was not in the band. He was was just a friend who happened to be in the studio!

---

# UNITED KINGDOM
# OCTOBER 1967

---

### BEE GEES
MASSACHUSETTS
*Polydor*

One of the most popular recording acts of the rock era had their fourth US Top 20 entry with a self-penned single that had given them the first of five UK No 1 singles. The group co-produced the track in New York with manager Robert Stigwood. Interestingly, they had never been to Massachusetts when they wrote the song.

### BOX TOPS
THE LETTER
*Stateside*

See US entry (September).

### FRANKIE VAUGHAN
THERE MUST BE A WAY
*Columbia*

The very popular cabaret entertainer scored the last of his 16 Top 20 entries with an update of a 1945 composition that Joni James had taken into the US Top 40 in 1959. The singer, whose work for charity was legendary, had received an OBE from the Queen two years earlier.

### PROCOL HARUM
HOMBURG
*Regal Zonophone*

Classical rock pioneers Procol Harum followed worldwide hit 'A Whiter Shade Of Pale' with another grandiose Keith Reid and Gary Booker composed track. The album-oriented act, who evolved from UK R&B band The Paramounts, continued to add to their transatlantic chart tally for a further ten years, but never returned to the heights they achieved in 1967.

### HERD
FROM THE UNDERWORLD
*Fontana*

Successful producers/songwriters Ken Howard and Alan Blaikley turned this underground rock act into one of the UK's most popular teeny bop bands of the late 1960s. The group, voted Brightest Hope for 1968 in the *Disc* poll, first charted with a heavily orchestrated adaptation of Virgil's 'Orpheus In The Underworld'.

### FOUNDATIONS
BABY, NOW THAT I
FOUND YOU
*Pye*

This London-based multi-racial group topped the chart with their first release. The infectious pop/R&B song gave composers Tony MacAulay and John MacLeod the first of two consecutive UK No 1s. The MacAulay-produced track also cracked the US Top 20 and was a rare UK visitor to the US R&B chart. Lead singer Clem Curtis' 1987 re-recording (with a new line-up of Foundations) found few buyers.

### DAVE DEE, DOZY, BEAKY, MICK & TICH
ZABADAK!
*Fontana*

Dave Dee's oddly named outfit had their seventh UK Top 20 entry in 18 months with an innovative West Indian-influenced track which featured a hypnotic, if near-gibberish, chorus. It also whisked the Wiltshire quintet into the US Top 100 for the only time.

# UNITED STATES
# NOVEMBER 1967

### COWSILLS
THE RAIN, THE PARK
& OTHER THINGS

▲ 2
⑩ 1
228/500

*MGM*

During the late 1960s, America's 'First Family Of Music', as they were then tagged, were one of the most popular acts in the US. After a couple of less than successful singles, this clean-cut combo clicked with a song co-written by their producer Artie Kornfield. Only The Monkees' massive 'Daydream Believer' stood between the family septet's debut hit and the top spot.

### BOBBY VINTON
PLEASE LOVE ME
FOREVER

▲ 6
⑩ 7
—/500

*Epic*

A heartfelt ballad, that had charted for Tommy Edwards in 1958 and Cathy Jean & The Roommates in 1961, reinstalled Vinton in the Top 10 after a three-year absence.

## DIONNE WARWICK
I SAY A LITTLE PRAYER
*Scepter*

▲ 4
⑩ 4
470/500

One of Bacharach & David's most memorable compositions added to Warwick's praiseworthy portfolio of hits. A year later, a funkier version by Aretha Franklin reached the transatlantic Top 10, and in 1988 the song entered the UK Top 10 by Bomb The Bass.

## WHO
I CAN SEE FOR MILES
*Decca*

▲ 9
⑩ 1•
—/500

See UK entry.

## MONKEES
DAYDREAM BELIEVER
*Colgems*

▲ 1
⑩ 5
29/500

In 1967, The Monkees were the world's most successful act. They achieved a record-breaking four No 1 LPs in the period, and as the year ended they topped the singles chart with this captivating John Stewart composition. Anne Murray put the song back into the US Top 20 in 1980, and in 1986 The Monkees' original version reappeared in the US Top 100.

# UNITED KINGDOM
# NOVEMBER 1967

## KINKS
AUTUMN ALMANAC
*Pye*

▲ 3
⑩ 11
468/500

One of the decade's most popular and influential UK acts had their eighth consecutive Top 10 entry with another top-drawer Ray Davies composition. The group, whose fan base remained loyal long after most beat boom bands had faded into history, were rightfully inducted into the Rock and Roll Hall of Fame in 1990.

## TROGGS
LOVE IS ALL AROUND
*Page One*

▲ 5
⑩ 5•
—/500

As a contrast to their earlier semi-suggestive songs, The Troggs' last major transatlantic hit was a romantic ballad composed by charismatic front man Reg Presley. It was the seventh UK Top 20 entry in 18 months for the band who inspired and influenced many later groups. In 1994, Wet Wet Wet's revival headed the UK charts for an amazing 15 weeks!

## ERIC BURDON & THE ANIMALS
SAN FRANCISCAN NIGHTS
*MGM*

▲ 7
⑩ 8•
—/500

The unmistakable rough-hewn vocalist's second line-up of Animals was more favourably received in the US than in the UK. Their only transatlantic Top 10 entry came with a self-composed slice of psychedelia that cleverly captured the feel of the flower power era.

## DONOVAN
THERE IS A MOUNTAIN
*Pye*

▲ 8
⑩ 5
—/500

This influential Glasgow-born performer reached the transatlantic Top 20 for the third time with another of his well-crafted compositions. As the record hit, an album of his earlier folk favourites, *Universal Soldier*, went into the UK Top 5.

## LONG JOHN BALDRY
LET THE HEARTACHES
BEGIN
*Pye*

John MacLeod produced the emotional ballad that rocketed this respected UK R&B veteran to the top and gave him and his writing partner Tony MacAulay two successive No 1s. The powerful-voiced lanky Londoner, whose previous bands had included later superstars Rod Stewart and Elton John, also placed his biggest hit into the US Top 100.

## WHO
I CAN SEE FOR MILES
*Track*

Astoundingly, this classic Pete Townshend composition was the award-winning UK foursome's only US Top 10 singles hit. They did, however, manage a further seven Top 20 singles and nine Top 10 albums.

## DAVE CLARK FIVE
EVERYBODY KNOWS
*Columbia*

Two years after their single 'Everybody Knows' entered the US Top 20, the photogenic fivesome had a high-flying UK hit with a different song of the same title.

## VAL DOONICAN
IF THE WHOLE WORLD
STOPPED LOVING
*Pye*

As his album *Val Doonican Rocks But Gently* headed to the top spot, the Irish entertainer visited the Top 10 singles for the last time. Country tunesmith Ben Peters wrote this sing-along song with SSS International Records' head honcho Shelby Singleton. In total, the amiable singer had seven Top 20 singles and five Top 10 LPs in the 1960s.

---

# UNITED STATES
# DECEMBER 1967

---

## GLADYS KNIGHT & THE PIPS
I HEARD IT THROUGH
THE GRAPEVINE
*Soul*

Marvin Gaye, The Miracles and the Isley Brothers reportedly recorded this R&B classic before Knight, although her version was the first released. The outstanding Norman Whitfield and Barrett Strong soul song was the esteemed group's biggest hit of the 1960s. Later in the decade Gaye's interpretation fared even better and topped the transatlantic charts.

## VICTOR LUNDBERG
AN OPEN LETTER TO
MY TEENAGE SON
*Liberty*

Among the decade's most patriotic singles was this father's plea to his son not to burn his draft card but to go to Vietnam and fight. The narrator, Lundberg, was a World War II veteran who now worked as an advertising executive. The record encouraged many teenage boys to release answer versions eloquently explaining why they were not going. The most successful was 'A Letter To Dad' by Every Father's Teenage Son.

## SMOKEY ROBINSON & THE MIRACLES
I SECOND THAT EMOTION
*Tamla*

▲ 4
⑩ 4
390/500

The unmistakable group finally cracked the UK Top 40 with their self-penned twenty-sixth US chart entry. The record was also the vocal team's sixteenth US Top 10 R&B hit.

## BEATLES
HELLO GOODBYE
*Capitol*

▲ 1
⑩24
78/500

See UK entry.

## DIANA ROSS & THE SUPREMES
IN AND OUT OF LOVE
*Motown*

▲ 9
⑩14
—/500

The 1960's most successful female act notched up a record-breaking ninth Top 10 entry in a row. It was also the trio's last major hit penned by Holland, Dozier & Holland – who had written every one of their bestsellers to date.

## FANTASTIC JOHNNY C
BOOGALOO DOWN BROADWAY
*Phil LA Of Soul*

▲ 7
⑩ 1•
—/500

Johnny Corley may not have been fantastic, but he did manage to have one of the year's biggest dance hits with a song penned and produced by his manager, Jesse James. Among the South Carolina soul singer's later and less remembered releases was the similarly themed 'Cool Broadway'.

## CHER
YOU BETTER SIT DOWN KIDS
*Imperial*

▲ 9
⑩ 2
—/500

Cher's last major hit of the decade was a tale of a family break-up produced and penned by her husband Sonny Bono – this single came seven years before the couple divorced. Cher went on to become an Oscar-winning actress, a top TV personality and one of the most successful female singers of the rock era.

## UNION GAP FEATURING GARY PUCKETT
WOMAN, WOMAN
*Columbia*

▲ 4
⑩ 1
351/500

Jerry Fuller, best-known for his work in the early 1960s with Ricky Nelson, produced this San Diego-based band who reportedly sold more singles than The Beatles in the US in 1968. The group wore Civil War uniforms, named themselves after the site of a famous Civil War battle and were fronted by 'General' Gary Puckett from Minnesota. They first made their mark with a 'cheating song' that its composer, country singer Jimmy Payne, had originally recorded some months before.

## JOHN FRED & HIS PLAYBOY BAND
JUDY IN DISGUISE (WITH GLASSES)
*Paula*

▲ 1
⑩ 1•
106/500

Nine years after first charting, this blue-eyed soul singer (born John Fred Gourrier) from Louisiana had his second hit with his sixteenth single. The song, which he and band member Andrew Bernard originally called 'Beverly in Disguise', was inspired by 'Lucy In The Sky' by The Beatles (John originally misheard it as 'Lucy In Disguise'). The record dethroned The Beatles at the top of the US chart and reached the UK Top 3. Later releases, including a cover of The Beatles 'Back in the USSR', failed to reinstate them in the Top 40.

## ARETHA FRANKLIN
CHAIN OF FOOLS
*Atlantic*

▲ 2
⑩ 5
263/500

In just eight months this gospel-rooted R&B vocalist put five singles into the US Top 10. The latest link in her golden chain of major hits was composed by fellow soul star Don Covay.

## AMERICAN BREED
BEND ME, SHAPE ME
*Acta*

▲ 5
⑩ 1•
487/500

Gary Loizzo fronted this multi-racial Chicago rock quartet, who had previously recorded as Gary & The Nitelites. Their fourth release on Acta was the biggest of the act's three US Top 40 singles. The song that they are primarily remembered for was composed by singers/songwriters Scott English and Larry Weiss and had been released earlier by The Models. In the UK, a cover by Amen Corner grabbed the majority of sales. An offshoot of American Breed evolved into 1970s hit act Rufus.

commercial proposition, he also released several noteworthy novelties. The man they called 'The Rapper' returned to the Top 10 after three years of mid-table hits with a humorous self-penned song featuring studio-recorded 'live' audience reaction.

### JOE TEX
SKINNY LEGS AND ALL
*Dial*

▲ 10
⑩ 2
—/500

Joe Tex not only made soulful monologues a

# UNITED KINGDOM
# DECEMBER 1967

### GENE PITNEY
SOMETHING'S GOTTEN HOLD OF MY HEART
*Stateside*

▲ 5
⑩ 10
—/500

British tunesmiths Roger Cook and Roger Greenaway wrote the striking song that gave the transatlantic star his last UK Top 10 entry for 22 years. In 1989, together with Marc Almond, he hit the No 1 spot (for the first time!) with a million-selling update of this same number. Amazingly, neither recording graced the US Top 100.

### CLIFF RICHARD
ALL MY LOVE
*Columbia*

▲ 6
⑩ 35
—/500

Cliff's second Italian-composed Top 10 entry (the first was 'Constantly') became his most successful single of 1967. The song's English lyric was written by noted British composer Peter Callander.

### BEATLES
HELLO GOODBYE
*Parlophone*

▲ 1
⑩ 15
20/500

The Beatles said goodbye to 1967 and hello to 1968 in the top spot on both sides of the Atlantic. It was the group's first release after the death of their manager Brian Epstein and came soon after EMI announced that they had sold over 200 million records.

### DES O'CONNOR
CARELESS HANDS
*Columbia*

▲ 6
⑩ 1
—/500

One of the UK's most popular entertainers debuted on the charts ten years after he had released his first single. The song that elevated the London-born comedian and TV personality to hit star status was composed by Bob Hilliard and Carl Sigman and had given jazz vocalist Mel Torme a US No 1 in 1949.

### BEE GEES
WORLD
*Polydor*

When Polydor signed them they called this (then) quintet 'The most significant act since The Beatles'. The Australian-raised group's third UK Top 20 single of 1967 was penned by their mainstays, the Gibb brothers.

### TOM JONES
I'M COMIN' HOME
*Decca*

Only 'Hello Goodbye' from The Beatles stopped the celebrated Welsh all-round entertainer from taking this Les Reed and Barry Mason song to the top.

## TRAFFIC
HERE WE GO ROUND THE
MULBERRY BUSH
*Island*

The title song from a film starring Barry Evans and Judy Geeson became this critically acclaimed act's last hit single. However, it was by no means the end of the line for the multi-talented Traffic. Despite frequent personnel changes, the group clocked up six US and three UK Top 20 albums before disbanding in the mid-1970s. A US comeback tour in 1994 was a big financial success.

## SCAFFOLD
THANK U VERY MUCH
*Parlophone*

Paul McCartney's brother Mike was a member of this unique trio, whose stage act cleverly combined songs, comedy and poetry. The outfit's first hit came with their third release, a novelty penned by Mike (under his stage name McGear), which gave thanks for a wide variety of things including the late Brian Epstein ('The Aintree Iron') and even people who actually bought the record.

## BEATLES
MAGICAL MYSTERY TOUR
(DOUBLE EP)
*Parlophone*

In the US, the soundtrack from The Beatles' slated TV film *Magical Mystery Tour* was a No 1 album. In the UK, it was released on a double EP, which only the group's 'Hello Goodbye' stopped from topping the chart. Tracks on the EP included 'I Am A Walrus' and 'Fool On The Hill'.

## MONKEES
DAYDREAM BELIEVER
*RCA*

See US entry (November).

## FOUR TOPS
WALK AWAY RENEE
*Tamla Motown*

A song that Left Banke had taken into the US Top 10 in 1966 was this legendary foursome's biggest UK hit of the year. Due to its UK success, the single was released in their homeland, where it also reached the Top 20.

# UNITED STATES
# JANUARY 1968

## LEMON PIPERS
GREEN TAMBOURINE
*Buddah*

▲ 1
⑩ 1•
172/500

Buddah Records liked this Paul Leka and Shelley Pinz-penned bubblegum opus and told psychedelic pop group The Lemon Pipers that if they didn't record the song they would be dropped from the label. The Ohio outfit dutifully obliged. The single shot them into the Top 10 on both sides of the Atlantic. However, their flirtation with fame was to be brief, and the Ivan Brown-fronted quintet had disbanded before the end of the decade.

## MARVIN GAYE &
## TAMMI TERRELL
IF I COULD BUILD MY
WHOLE WORLD
AROUND YOU
*Tamla*

▲ 10
⑩6/2
—/500

Marvin's early mentor, Harvey Fuqua, penned his third Top 20 entry in succession with Philadelphia

born Terrell (born Tammy Montgomery), who had earlier recorded with James Brown.

## CLASSICS IV
SPOOKY
*Imperial*

▲ 3
⑩ 1
324/500

Before the Atlanta-based quintet started a string of US-only hits, they had released several small-selling singles and backed many acts on disc. Their breakthrough recording was a vocal version of a sax instrumental that its composer Mike Sharpe had taken halfway up the Top 100 the previous year.

# UNITED KINGDOM
# JANUARY 1968

## SIMON DUPREE &
## THE BIG SOUND
KITES
*Parlophone*

▲ 9
⑩ 1•
—/500

Scottish-born Derek Shulman fronted this R&B-based band, which included his brothers Ray &

Phil. Their fourth single was the act's only noticeable success. It was an ethereal flower power opus penned by earlier 1960s hit writer Lee Pockriss and originally recorded by the Rooftop Singers. Derek became a leading music business executive in the US in the 1990s.

## GEORGIE FAME
BALLAD OF BONNIE
AND CLYDE
*CBS*

Larry Parnes' one-time protégé had his only transatlantic Top 10 single with a song inspired by (but not heard in) the hit film *Bonnie And Clyde*. Mike Smith produced the Mitch Murray and Peter Callander composition, which gave the talented performer his third UK chart topper of the decade.

## LOVE AFFAIR
EVERLASTING LOVE
*CBS*

Controversy raged when this cherubic teenage quintet from London admitted that they did not play on their debut hit. Like the previous chart topper by Georgia Fame, it was produced by Mike Smith. A re-issue of the original version by Robert Knight finally made the UK Top 20 in 1974, as did updates by Worlds Apart in 1993 and Gloria Estefan in 1995. In the US, a version by Carl Carlton reached the Top 10 in 1974.

## ENGELBERT HUMPERDINCK
AM I THAT EASY
TO FORGET
*Decca*

Headliner Humperdinck added to his hits with a revival of a 1959 country bestseller by Carl Belew. Coincidentally, Esther Phillips, whose

arrangement of 'Release Me' helped inspire Englebert's version, had earlier revived this ballad.

## JOHN FRED & HIS PLAYBOY BAND
JUDY IN DISGUISE
(WITH GLASSES)
*Pye International*

See US entry (December 1967).

## SMALL FACES
TIN SOLDIER
*Immediate*

The group, now handled by the Stones' manager Andrew Loog Oldham, returned with another slice of commercial psychedelia penned by their vocalist Steve Marriott and bass player Ronnie 'Plonk' Lane.

## PLASTIC PENNY
EVERYTHING I AM
*Page One*

Their powerful interpretation of this melodic Dan Penn and Spooner Oldham ballad was the high spot of the quintet's career. Lead vocalist Brian Keith gave a stand-out performance of the song that had originally been recorded as the B side of 'Neon Rainbow' by the Box Tops. Incidentally, the group's drummer Nigel Olsson later found fame in Elton John's backing band.

# UNITED STATES
# FEBRUARY 1968

## PAUL MAURIAT
LOVE IS BLUE
*Philips*

*Blooming Hits* was an album of instrumental cover versions by French conductor, arranger,

songwriter and producer Mauriat. Among the tracks were entries from the recent Eurovision Song Contest: the UK winner 'Puppet On A String' and the fourth-placed entry from Luxembourg, 'L'Amour Est Bleu'. Amazingly, the latter track and the album itself topped the US charts – the only

French recordings ever to do so. The single also reached the UK Top 20, beating several other versions, including one by Jeff Beck.

## HUMAN BEINZ
NOBODY BUT ME
*Capitol*

This Cleveland rock quartet's commercial success centred around their interpretation of two R&B hits from 1962. The group's biggest seller was a song originally recorded by its composers the Isley Brothers on Wand. The follow-up, a rocking version of Bobby Bland's 'Turn on Your Love Light', was the psychedelic-dressed combo's only other Top 100 entry.

## LETTERMEN
GOIN' OUT OF MY HEAD/CAN'T TAKE MY EYES OFF YOU
*Capitol*

The popular album act reappeared in the singles Top 10 with a medley of hits. 'Goin' Out Of My Head' had been big for Little Anthony & The Imperials in 1964, and 'Can't Take My Eyes Off You' had taken Frankie Valli into the Top 3 just months earlier. Even though they sold millions of records in the US, the trio failed to dent the UK charts at all.

## TEMPTATIONS
I WISH IT WOULD RAIN
*Gordy*

The group's fifteenth Top 40 entry was the first of many written for them by their producer Norman Whitfield and Barrett Strong. A few months later Gladys Knight & The Pips returned it to the R&B Top 20.

## DIONNE WARWICK
(THEME FROM) VALLEY OF THE DOLLS
*Scepter*

The New Jersey-born vocalist had her biggest hit of the decade with the title song of an Oscar-winning movie. Top conductor Andre Previn composed it with his ex-wife Dory.

## OTIS REDDING
(SITTIN' ON) THE DOCK OF THE BAY
*Volt*

Astoundingly, this influential and innovative soul singer never had a Top 10 single in his lifetime. He recorded the wistful, haunting ballad just three days before his death in a plane crash. The Reddings (who included Otis' sons Dexter and Otis III) took the Grammy-winning song back into the US chart in 1982, and in 1988 Michael Bolton reinstated it in the Top 20. Redding, who replaced Elvis as the World's Top Male Singer in the 1967 *MM* poll, was inducted into the Rock and Roll Hall of Fame in 1989.

## TOMMY BOYCE & BOBBY HART
I WONDER WHAT SHE'S DOING TONIGHT
*A&M*

In the early 1960s both Boyce and Hart released solo singles on several labels without success. Before recording as a duo they had written Top 10 entries for such acts as The Monkees and Jay & The Americans. Not surprisingly, they also composed the biggest of their three US-only Top 40 entries. Boyce added to his hits in the 1970s as both a writer and producer, and together with Hart joined the reformed Monkees in 1975. Sadly, he committed suicide in 1994.

## 1910 FRUITGUM CO
SIMON SAYS
*Buddah*

Bubblegum music peaked in 1968, and its foremost exponents were this New Jersey quintet. The good-time group amassed five US Top 40 entries in eighteen months, all of which were produced by the masterminds behind the much-maligned musical genre, Jerry Kasenetz and Jeff Katz. In the UK, the novelty track, based on the famous children's game (aka O'Grady Says), reached the runner-up position and gave them their only UK hit.

## UNITED KINGDOM
# FEBRUARY 1968

**AMEN CORNER**
BEND ME SHAPE ME
*Deram*

Many of the late 1960s most popular teeny bop acts in the UK sold few records Stateside. Among this number were the Welsh septet fronted by the photogenic Andy Fairweather-Low. The group's second Top 20 entry came with their rendition of a song originally recorded by The Models, which had been taken into the US Top 10 by The American Breed.

**MANFRED MANN**
MIGHTY QUINN
*Fontana*

Manfred Mann's only big US hit featuring vocalist Mike D'Abo also gave them their third UK No 1 of the 1960s. Composer Bob Dylan had supposedly been inspired to write the song after seeing Anthony Quinn playing an Eskimo in the film *The Savage Innocents*.

**SOLOMON KING**
SHE WEARS MY RING
*Columbia*

This powerful-voiced MOR performer was the latest US artist to uproot and move to the UK in order to find fame. The singer, who had won a Sacred Special Merit Award in the US in 1965, was signed by manager Gordon Mills. Unlike his managerial stablemates, Tom Jones and Engelbert Humperdinck, King did not have a string of hits. His only major chart success was a revival of a Felice & Boudleaux Bryant song (based on the classical piece 'Golandrina'), which Jimmy Bell had recorded in 1960.

**TREMELOES**
SUDDENLY YOU LOVE ME
*CBS*

Peter Callander (who co-wrote their 'Even The Bad Times Are Good') penned the English lyrics to this happy Italian song, which started life as 'Uno Tranquillo'. It was the last Tremeloes single to crack the US Top 100.

**BRENTON WOOD**
GIMME LITTLE SIGN
*Liberty*

See US entry (October 1967).

**STATUS QUO**
PICTURES OF
MATCHSTICK MEN
*Pye*

Few people in 1968 could have foreseen that in time this South London band would amass more UK chart singles than any other group. The first of the quartet's 22 Top 10 entries came with their fifth release (the first as Status Quo), which was a slab of psychedelia composed by guitarist/vocalist Francis Rossi. Amazingly, it was the only single by the revered rockers to make its mark in the US.

**MOVE**
FIRE BRIGADE
*Regal Zonophone*

Despite their impressive run of top UK hits, this inventive and imaginative combo never graced the US Top 100 in the 1960s. The outstanding pop/rock track was composed by the group's eccentric co-leader Roy Wood.

## ESTHER & ABI OFARIM
CINDERELLA ROCKAFELLA
*Philips*

▲ 1
🔟 1•
90/500

One of the year's biggest UK novelty hits was recorded by an Israeli couple, who had come to the public's attention when they appeared on the TV shows of both Eamonn Andrews and Rolf Harris. This cute retro-sounding chart topper was composed and earlier recorded by Mason Williams (whose own single 'Classical Gas' was a transatlantic smash later in the year) and Nancy Ames. Abi (born Abraham Reichstadt) co-produced this and their Top 20 follow-up 'One More Dance'.

# UNITED STATES
# MARCH 1968

## FIRST EDITION
JUST DROPPED IN (TO SEE WHAT CONDITION MY CONDITION WAS IN)
*Reprise*

▲ 5
🔟 1
—/500

Ten years after he had started recording as a rock'n'roll vocalist, Kenny Rogers finally found himself on the chart. He was the leader of this folk/rock quartet which comprised ex-members of the New Christy Minstrels. Nashville songwriter Mickey Newbury composed the semi-psychedelic song (reportedly with Jerry Lee Lewis in mind) that kick started one of the most successful careers in the rock era.

## FIREBALLS
BOTTLE OF WINE
*Atco*

▲ 9
🔟 2•
—/500

In 1963, Jimmy Gilmer & The Fireballs topped the chart with 'Sugar Shack' and folk singer Tom Paxton penned 'Bottle Of Wine'. Five years later, Paxton's rousing folk opus transported the New Mexico combo into the Top 10 for the last time.

## ASSOCIATION
EVERYTHING THAT TOUCHES YOU
*Warner*

▲ 10
🔟 5•
—/500

These late 1960s US chart regulars had their last noticeable hit with a song composed by multi-talented lead singer Terry Kirkman. Despite a most impressive run of Top 10 singles and albums in the US, the group were relatively unknown across the Atlantic.

## DELFONICS
LA-LA MEANS I LOVE YOU
*Philly Groove*

▲ 4
🔟 1
441/500

One of the bestselling R&B groups of the late 1960s were this trio from Philadelphia. The smooth soul team scored 11 Top 20 R&B chart entries from 1968–1974. Their biggest hit came with a memorable ballad penned by member William Hart and producer Thom Bell. In the UK, the group's record finally cracked the Top 20 in 1971, and an updated treatment from Swing Out Sister was a Top 40 entry in 1994.

## MONKEES
VALLERI
*Colgems*

▲ 3
🔟 6•
423/500

Eighteen months after first crashing into the charts, the record-breaking quartet's sixth and last US Top 10 entry was a Tommy Boyce and Bobby Hart song which the band had considered to be substandard. Before the decade ended, the group with the Midas touch had disbanded. A comeback in the mid-1980s proved successful, albeit briefly, and seven of the act's previous albums charted concurrently.

## ARETHA FRANKLIN
(SWEET SWEET BABY)
SINCE YOU'VE
BEEN GONE
*Atlantic*

The song stylist who scooped the Grammy for Best R&B Vocal Performance every year from 1967–1974 had her highest-ranked single of 1968 with her first self-composed hit.

## SAM & DAVE
I THANK YOU
*Stax*

Before recording a string of gold albums as an artist, Isaac Hayes (together with Dave Porter) penned and produced numerous hits for Stax artists. Among these was their second successive million seller for the dynamic soul duo Sam & Dave. In 1980, a retread by ZZ Top also entered the US Top 40.

## GEORGIE FAME
THE BALLAD OF BONNIE
AND CLYDE
*Epic*

See UK entry (January).

## UNION GAP FEATURING
## GARY PUCKETT
YOUNG GIRL
*Columbia*

Not only did this dramatic ballad top the UK chart in 1968, it also reappeared in the UK Top 10 six years later. In the US, the song, which was written by their producer Jerry Fuller, lifted the quintet into the runner-up slot for three weeks.

## BEATLES
LADY MADONNA
*Capitol*

See UK entry.

---

# UNITED KINGDOM
# MARCH 1968

---

## DAVE DEE, DOZY,
## BEAKY, MICK & TICH
LEGEND OF XANADU
*Fontana*

The flamboyant band had their sole chart topper with another inventive and imaginative left-field song penned by talented managers Ken Howard and Alan Blaikley. The group, known for their intriguing use of sound effects, featured whip cracks on this Latin-laced mini-epic.

## BEE GEES
WORDS
*Polydor*

This instantly recognizable harmony group clocked up a fourth transatlantic Top 20 entry with a well-sculptured, self-composed ballad which they sang on their first Ed Sullivan TV show appearance.

## DON PARTRIDGE
ROSIE
*Columbia*

If any singer in the 1960s could be termed 'streetwise' it was this Bournemouth-born one-man band who, for a living, busked (sang and played) in the streets of London. The media loved the controversial and opinionated character, who boasted that his self-composed debut hit cost him only £5 ($12) to record.

### DONOVAN
JENNIFER JUNIPER
*Pye*

▲ 5
🔟 6
—/500

As his acclaimed album *A Gift From A Flower To A Garden* headed towards gold status, this regular transatlantic chart visitor added another self-penned single to his haul of hits.

### LEMON PiPERS
GREEN TAMBOURINE
*Pye International*

▲ 7
🔟 1•
—/500

See US entry (January).

### TOM JONES
DELILAH
*Decca*

▲ 2
🔟 7
218/500

One of the very influential performer's most requested songs was his third Top 3 hit composed by Les Reed. The dramatic 'Delilah' was also the title track to the Welsh superstar's first UK No 1 album. In 1975, an updated version by The Sensational Alex Harvey Band returned this karaoke classic to the Top 10.

### OTIS REDDING
(SITTIN' ON) THE DOCK
OF THE BAY
*Stax*

▲ 3
🔟 1•
383/500

See US entry (February).

### LULU
ME THE PEACEFUL HEART
*Columbia*

▲ 9
🔟 4
—/500

In the year that Lulu was voted Top UK Female Singer and hosted her own TV series, the Scottish lass (born Marie Lawrie) charted with this impressive Tony Hazzard composition.

### LOUIS ARMSTRONG
WHAT A WONDERFUL
WORLD
*HMV*

▲ 1
🔟 4•
28/500

Astoundingly, the UK's Top Single of 1968 was an uplifting though dated ballad sung by an entertainer who had made his first recording 45

years earlier. As amazing, is the fact that it finally reached the US Top 40 in 1988 – 17 years after the legendary performer's death.

### BEATLES
LADY MADONNA
*Parlophone*

▲ 1
🔟 17
175/500

While the other Beatles were meditating in India with Maharishi Mahesh Yogi, Paul McCartney recorded the self-composed song that gave them their fourteenth UK chart topper. 'Lady Madonna' was the act's first hit after the *Sgt Pepper* LP had netted them a staggering four Grammy awards.

### CLIFF RICHARD
CONGRATULATIONS
*Columbia*

▲ 1
🔟 36
140/500

Britain's best-known vocalist had his first chart topper for three years with a bubbly composition that grabbed the runner-up slot at the Eurovision Song Contest. The song was composed by Bill Martin and Phil Coulter, who had penned the previous year's winner, 'Puppet On A String'. It was Cliff's biggest-selling single to date and easily passed the million sales mark in Europe.

### FOUR TOPS
IF I WERE A CARPENTER
*Tamla Motown*

▲ 7
🔟 5
—/500

The quartet, whose personnel has remained unchanged for 40 years, had their sixth and last transatlantic Top 20 entry with an R&B treatment of Tim Hardin's noted folk composition. As the record charted, the group's *Greatest Hits* LP became the first album by an African-American act to head the UK Top 10. The Four Tops were inducted into the Rock and Roll Hall of Fame in 1990.

# UNITED STATES
# APRIL 1968

## BOX TOPS
CRY LIKE A BABY
*Mala*

Producer Dan Penn composed the critically lauded group's second and last transatlantic Top 20 entry with his long-time collaborator Lindon 'Spooner' Oldham. The record, which featured outstanding electric sitar work from Reggie Young, earned the combo their second gold disc. Since they disbanded in 1970, lead singer Alex Chiltern has become something of a cult hero to many rock fans.

## BOBBY GOLDSBORO
HONEY
*UA*

This top-notch tearjerker was the biggest record of Goldsboro's long career. 'Honey' was a country No 1 and the first of his two dozen hits on that chart. Unlike most of his singles, it was not self-penned; it was composed by Bobby Russell and had been released first by ex-Kingston Trio member Bob Shane. Margaret Lewis released an answer version entitled 'Honey (I Miss You Too)'. Amazingly, in the UK, this death disc reached the runner-up position in both 1968 and 1975.

## MANFRED MANN
MIGHTY QUINN
*Mercury*

See UK entry (February).

## SLY & THE FAMILY STONE
DANCE TO THE MUSIC
*Epic*

There is no doubt that this West Coast band, who introduced psychedelic-soul to the world, helped shape the sound and direction of 1970s soul music. The group's main focal point was Sylvester Stewart, who previously had Top 10 success as a producer (Beau Brummels and Bobby Freeman), although his own earlier records (released under a variety of guises) had hardly made a ripple. This innovative single was the act's only transatlantic Top 10 entry in the 1960s.

## JAMES BROWN
I GOT THE FEELIN'
*King*

The 'Godfather of Funk' added another US million seller to his enviable collection with this influential self-composed track. However, it sold few copies in the UK.

## ARCHIE BELL & THE DRELLS
TIGHTEN UP
*Atlantic*

Vietnam veteran Bell was still in the army when his re-recording of a track he originally cut in 1964 topped the US chart. This group-composed dance track, which was initially slated to be the B side of 'Dog Eat Dog', was the first of 20 R&B hits for the Texas quartet.

# UNITED KINGDOM
# APRIL 1968

## CILLA BLACK
STEP INSIDE LOVE
*Parlophone*

▲ 8
⑩ 8
—/500

The theme from the Liverpool vocalist's first TV series returned her to the Top 10 after an absence of almost two years. 'Step Inside Love', written by Lennon & McCartney, became one of her most popular songs.

## JOHN ROWLES
IF I ONLY HAD TIME
*MCA*

▲ 3
⑩ 1•
342/500

New Zealand's best-known solo singer of the 1960s had two UK-only Top 20 entries with MOR-slanted ballads. The highest placed was his rendition of the French song 'Je N'Aurai Pas Le Temps'. It was written and originally recorded by Michael Fugain, with English lyrics from chart regular Jack Fishman. In the US a cover by Nick DeCaro entered the Top 100. As the single climbed, Rowles toured the UK with Herman's Hermits and Amen Corner.

## 1910 FRUITGUM CO
SIMON SAYS
*Pye International*

▲ 2
⑩ 1•
228/500

See US entry (February).

## HOLLIES
JENNIFER ECCLES
*Parlophone*

▲ 7
⑩13
—/500

Group members Allan Clarke and Graham Nash concocted the title of this hit from their wife's names. Clarke's spouse was called Jennifer, Mrs Nash's maiden name being Eccles. The track was The Hollies' last Top 10 entry before Graham Nash left the act.

## ANDY WILLIAMS
CAN'T TAKE MY EYES
OFF YOU
*CBS*

▲ 5
⑩ 4
—/500

A year after Frankie Valli had scored with this memorable song in the US, top-selling MOR artist Williams clicked with it in the UK. In 1982, a Hi-NRG update of the Bob Gaudio and Bob Crewe composition by the Boystown Gang was a big hit, and in 1991 the Pet Shop Boys piloted it into the UK Top 5 for the third time.

## HONEYBUS
I CAN'T LET MAGGIE GO
*Deram*

▲ 8
⑩ 1•
—/500

Pete Dello (born Peter Blumsom) was the mastermind behind the quartet whose only claim to fame was this flyaway hit which he both penned and produced. It was the group's third release on Deram, and after one more single Dello said goodbye to the band. The song is perhaps best known to many as the theme music to the Nimble bread commercial.

## SMALL FACES
LAZY SUNDAY
*Immediate*

▲ 2
⑩ 7
304/500

A memorable Kinks-influenced cockney rock song gave these famous faces their biggest UK hit on Immediate. 'Lazy Sunday' was one of the tracks on the group's critically acclaimed UK chart-topping album *Ogdens' Nut Gone Flake* (which had a unique round sleeve). This summertime sing-along reappeared in the UK Top 40 In 1976. In 1969, Marriott formed Humble Pie and the remaining members evolved into the even more successful Faces.

# UNITED STATES
# MAY 1968

## INTRUDERS
COWBOYS TO GIRLS
*Gamble*

The Intruders joined fellow Philadelphia R&B groups The Delfonics and The Drells in the US Top 10. The vocal quartet, who started recording in 1961, had the first of a dozen R&B Top 20 entries in 1966, when Gamble and Huff took them under their wing. This million seller, and many of the act's other hits, was both written and produced by that prolific pair.

## HUGO MONTENEGRO & HIS ORCHESTRA
THE GOOD, THE BAD & THE UGLY
*RCA*

From 1955, this New York-born conductor/arranger/composer played a prominent role in MOR music – his orchestra backed many major RCA acts including Harry Belafonte. Montenegro's biggest sellers were the album *Music From A Fistful Of Dollars, For A Few Dollars More & The Good, The Bad & The Ugly*, and the title track from the latter Clint Eastwood spaghetti western. The first American instrumental to top the UK charts for six years featured an unforgettable ocarina introduction played by Arthur Smith, plus grunts from maestro Montenegro himself.

## RASCALS
A BEAUTIFUL MORNING
*Atlantic*

At the group's request, the word Young was finally dropped from their name, and the act's first release as The Rascals earned them a third gold record.

## IRISH ROVERS
THE UNICORN
*Decca*

An Irish-born, Canadian-based folk quintet, which featured brothers Will and George Millar, had their only taste of US Top 10 fame with a novelty number about the mythical one-horned animal. The song was composed by Shel Silverstein, who later penned hits for Johnny Cash and Dr Hook.

## SIMON & GARFUNKEL
MRS ROBINSON
*Columbia*

A song Paul Simon penned for the film *The Graduate* rushed the instantly recognizable duo back to the top in the US. In the UK, both the single and an EP of the same name also cracked the Top 10.

## TROGGS
LOVE IS ALL AROUND
*Fontana*

See UK entry (November 1967).

## DIONNE WARWICK
DO YOU KNOW THE WAY TO SAN JOSÉ
*Scepter*

Warwick picked up the Grammy for Best Female Vocal Performance for her eighth Top 20 single of the decade. The transatlantic smash was taken from her highest-charting album *Valley Of The Dolls*.

## MARVIN GAYE & TAMMI TERRELL
AIN'T NOTHING LIKE THE REAL THING
*Tamla*

The top US R&B idol first cracked the UK Top 40 with this soulful sing-along duet penned by Ashford & Simpson. The song returned to the US Top 40 in 1977 by Donny and Marie Osmond.

## STEVIE WONDER
SHOO-BE-DOO-BE-DOO-DA-DAY
*Tamla*

The highly touted multi-talented entertainer added to his impressive roster of chart hits with a hook-filled song he composed with Henry Cosby and Sylvia Moy.

---

# UNITED KINGDOM
# MAY 1968

---

## ENGELBERT HUMPERDINCK
A MAN WITHOUT LOVE
*Decca*

This easy-listening superstar's fifth consecutive UK Top 5 single was in fact the title track from his third transatlantic Top 20 album.

## HERD
I DON'T WANT OUR LOVING TO DIE
*Fontana*

Eighteen-year-old Peter Frampton fronted the popular act whose third UK Top 20 entry in a row came with a foot-tapping Ken Howard and Alan Blaikley composition. The group disbanded in 1969 after Frampton, voted 'The Face of 1968', had left to form Humble Pie.

## GARY PUCKETT & THE UNION GAP
YOUNG GIRL
*CBS*

See US entry (March).

## BOBBY GOLDSBORO
HONEY
*UA*

See US entry (April).

## JACKY
WHITE HORSES
*Philips*

Veteran British session singer Jackie Lee, who had been recording since the mid-1950s, had two Top 20 singles with themes from UK children's TV shows. The one-time member of The Squadronaires and The Raindrops had her first solo success with this Michael Carr composition. For the record books, the vocalist's 1971 hit 'Rupert' was released under her full name.

## LOVE AFFAIR
RAINBOW VALLEY
*CBS*

How did these UK teen idols follow their chart-topping cover version of Robert Knight's 'Everlasting Love'? Simple: with another cover of a Robert Knight record that also came from the prolific pens of Buzz Cason and Mac Gayden.

# UNITED STATES
# JUNE 1968

## OHIO EXPRESS
YUMMY YUMMY YUMMY
*Buddah*

▲ 4
🔟 1•
466/500

Lead singer Joey Levine co-wrote this pop pearl with noted songsmith Arthur Resnick. It was the second of the Ohio outfit's four Kasenetz and Katz-produced US Top 40 entries in the late 1960s. The instantly infectious track, which also cracked the UK Top 5, was the epitome of bubblegum music – an innocent childlike lyric with a good beat and a happy and irresistible hook.

## TOMMY JAMES & THE SHONDELLS
MONY MONY
*Roulette*

▲ 3
🔟 4
366/500

A foot-stomping song, whose title was inspired by the large neon sign on top of the Mutual of New York (MONY) Insurance company building, gave this group their only transatlantic Top 10 entry. Billy Idol's 1987 version also entered the Top 10 on both sides of the Atlantic.

## HERB ALPERT
THIS GUY'S IN LOVE WITH YOU
*A&M*

▲ 1
🔟 3
37/500

Before finding fame as an instrumentalist, this top trumpeter had released several overlooked vocal records under the name Dore Alpert. His first vocal hit was penned by Burt Bacharach and Hal David. It was the Top US Single of 1967 and also his biggest transatlantic success. A year later Dionne Warwick reinstated the romantic ballad in the Top 10.

## RICHARD HARRIS
MACARTHUR PARK
*Dunhill*

▲ 2
🔟 1•
321/500

See UK entry (July).

## ARETHA FRANKLIN
THINK
*Atlantic*

▲ 7
🔟 7
—/500

Soul music's all-time No 1 female singer co-wrote the song that took her to the top of the R&B chart for the sixth time in 15 months. The track appeared on Franklin's fourth US Top 5 album in just over a year (which was also her only UK Top 10 LP), *Aretha Now*.

## SERGIO MENDES & BRASIL '66
THE LOOK OF LOVE
*A&M*

▲ 4
🔟 1
475/500

Brazilian-born pianist Mendes and his easy-on-the-ear combo amassed five Top 40 albums in the US from 1966–69. The act's highest-placed single of the era was their interpretation of a beautiful Burt Bacharach and Hal David ballad from the James Bond movie *Casino Royale*. Intriguingly, it was even more successful than Dusty Springfield's original version had been a year earlier.

## MERRILEE RUSH
ANGEL OF THE MORNING
*Bell*

▲ 7
🔟 1•
—/500

With help from Paul Revere, this Seattle songstress and her band The Turnabouts were seen on *Happening '68* and signed by Bell. Rush's five minutes of fame came courtesy of her fourth release, a cover of a song Evie Sands had recorded for Cameo (it was one of the once-great label's last releases) in 1967. In the UK, a soulful cover by P.P. Arnold made the Top 40. Juice Newton's update of the celebrated Chip Taylor composition entered the US Top 5 in 1981.

## FRIEND AND LOVER
REACH OUT OF
THE DARKNESS
*Verve*

▲10
⑩1•
—/500

Joe South co-produced the track that gave this hippy married couple their sole trip into the Top 40, and fellow Atlanta resident Ray Stevens played piano. Texan Jim Post was inspired to write the song after attending a New York love-in with his Chicago-born wife Cathy (nee Conn). Later releases as both Friend And Lover and Jim & Cathy sold poorly.

## CLIFF NOBLES & CO
THE HORSE
*Phil LA Of Soul*

▲2
⑩1•
278/500

To cut costs, producer/songwriter Jesse James decided to use an instrumental version (featuring several noted Philly session musicians) of his danceable composition 'Love Is All Right' on the B side of vocalist Nobles' recording. Quite unexpectedly, this throwaway track, retitled 'The Horse', caught the public's imagination and raced up the chart. 'The Horse' was not the Alabama band's first release, but it was their only memorable hit. Similar follow-ups including 'Horse Fever', 'The Camel' and 'Pony The Horse' stalled at the starting post.

## SHORTY LONG
HERE COMES THE JUDGE
*Soul*

▲8
⑩1•
—/500

Amazingly, comedian Pigmeat Markham's catch phrase 'Here Comes The Judge' inspired four different chart entries of that title in the summer of '68. Markham's own song reached the Top 20, but was surpassed in sales by the one co-written and co-produced by Frederick 'Shorty' Long. The multi-instrumentalist and vocalist, who recorded the original version of 'The Devil With The Blues Dress On' (a hit for Mitch Ryder in 1966), never returned to the chart. He died in a boating accident in 1969.

# UNITED KINGDOM
# JUNE 1968

## SCOTT WALKER
JOANNA
*Philips*

▲7
⑩1•
—/500

The photogenic front man (born Noel Scott Engel) from the top-selling trio The Walker Brothers had his biggest solo hit with a Tony Hatch and Jackie Trent-penned ballad. This unmistakable baritone, who first recorded as a 13-year-old in 1957, was regarded as a cult hero by many later acts. The influential balladeer had four Top 10 solo albums in the late 1960s, and comeback albums in 1984 and 1995 also charted.

## DIONNE WARWICK
DO YOU KNOW THE WAY
TO SAN JOSÉ
*Pye International*

▲8
⑩2
—/500

See US entry (May).

## JULIE DRISCOLL, BRIAN AUGER & THE TRINITY
THIS WHEEL'S ON FIRE
*Marmalade*

▲5
⑩1•
—/500

Without doubt, Driscoll was one of the most photographed performers of the year. Therefore it was no surprise when she was chosen as both 'Face of 68' and Top Female Singer of the Year in the UK music press. The only shock was that her treatment of this underrated Bob Dylan composition was her only chart entry – especially as she was backed by Brian Auger's critically lauded jazz/rock combo.

## ROLLING STONES
JUMPING JACK FLASH
*Decca*

After a two-year absence, The Stones returned to the top with a Jagger and Richard composition that is rightfully regarded as one of the classic rock records of all time. Jimmy Miller produced the track, which was voted Top Single of 1968 in *MM*.

## DON PARTRIDGE
BLUE EYES
*Columbia*

For the second time in three months, this street busker reached the Top 5. His sophomore single was composed by Richard Kerr (who later wrote several hits for Barry Manilow). Partridge was never at home as a pop star, and before the end of the decade 'The King of the Street Singers' was back entertaining crowds outside theatres rather than inside.

## DONOVAN
HURDY GURDY MAN
*Pye*

Donovan, a recent convert to Eastern religion, was inspired to write his fifth successive UK Top 10 entry by a dream. Interestingly, Jeff Beck played guitar on the track, and the hurdy gurdy sound was made by Indian instrument, the tambura.

## EQUALS
BABY COME BACK
*President*

Jamaican-born twins Derv and Lincoln Gordon, together with Eddie (Eddy) Grant from Guyana, fronted this visually striking multi-racial pop/ska band. The first of their three Top 10 entries was a repetitive and hypnotic Grant-penned track that had been ignored when originally released in 1966. It was re-issued after it charted in Germany

and the Netherlands. A revival by Pato Banton in 1994 also reached No 1 in the UK.

## DES O'CONNOR
I PRETEND
*Columbia*

Les Reed, who had composed chart toppers for both Tom Jones and Engelbert Humperdinck, wrote this all-round entertainer's only No 1 with Barry Mason. The MOR ballad spent 36 weeks on the bestsellers list, and his album of the same name also climbed into the Top 10.

## O.C. SMITH
SON OF HICKORY
HOLLER'S TRAMP
*CBS*

Well-respected MOR jazz vocalist Smith had been recording for 12 years before making his chart debut with his interpretation of a controversial Dallas Frazier song. The country composition, which concerned a mother who turned to prostitution to support her son, was originally released by Johnny Darrell. Although only a minor Top 40 hit in the US, the one-time vocalist with the Count Basie Orchestra steered this single into the runner-up position in the UK.

## MARMALADE
LOVIN' THINGS
*CBS*

Seven years after the group debuted as Dean Ford & The Gaylords, and four years after they were first voted Scotland's No 1 band, this Glasgow quintet had the first of their eight UK Top 10 hits. The song that finally turned the unpretentious pop act into national stars was composed by Americans Jet Loring and Arthur Shroeck. 'Lovin' Things' reached the US Top 100 in 1969 by the Grass Roots.

# UNITED STATES
# JULY 1968

## ROLLING STONES
JUMPIN' JACK FLASH
*London*

▲ 3
⑩ 11
344/500

See UK entry (June).

## HUGH MASEKELA
GRAZING IN THE GRASS
*UNI*

▲ 1
⑩ 1•
151/500

South African trumpet virtuoso Masekela reached his commercial peak with a jazzy instrumental composed by Philemon Hou and produced by Stewart Levine. The band leader, who was helped on the road to success by both Johnny Dankworth and Harry Belafonte, also entered the US Top 20 with the album *The Promise Of A Future*, which contained this million-selling single. A vocal version by the Friends Of Distinction also made it to the Top 3 a year later.

## GARY PUCKETT & THE UNION GAP
LADY WILLPOWER
*Columbia*

▲ 2
⑩ 3
266/500

Their distinctive lead singer Gary Puckett was given front billing on the group's third million seller in succession. Like its predecessor, 'Young Girl', it peaked at No 2 in the US and reached the UK Top 5.

## 5TH DIMENSION
STONED SOUL PICNIC
*Soul City*

▲ 3
⑩ 2
346/500

This easy-listening R&B vocal group from Los Angeles had their fifth Top 40 entry with a song producer Bones Howe found on singer/songwriter Laura Nyro's album, *Eli And The Thirteenth Confession*.

## COWSILLS
INDIAN LAKE
*MGM*

▲ 10
⑩ 2
—/500

Rhode Island's best-known family returned to the Top 10 with a bouncy pop nugget composed by Tony Romeo – who later wrote hits for Cowsills-clones The Partridge Family. Freddy Weller took the song into the country Top 5 in 1971.

## DONOVAN
HURDY GURDY MAN
*Epic*

▲ 5
⑩ 3
—/500

See UK entry (June).

## MASON WILLIAMS
CLASSICAL GAS
*Warner*

▲ 2
⑩ 1•
300/500

Soon after his composition 'Cinderella Rockafella' topped the UK chart, this multi-talented singer/guitarist had a transatlantic Top 10 entry with a self-composed classics-meets-rock-meets-country instrumental. The Grammy-winning track and its Top 20 parent album, *The Mason Williams Phonograph Record*, were produced by Mike Post. Although Williams never became a chart regular, he was still much in demand in the 1990s as a songwriter, scriptwriter and musician.

## DOORS
HELLO, I LOVE YOU
*Elektra*

▲ 1
⑩ 2
121/500

The fifth of their eight US Top 40 entries lifted the legendary group into the top slot for the second time. Although this commercial self-composed cut (which conjured up images of The Kinks) missed the UK Top 10, it was the legendary quartet's biggest UK hit of the 1960s. The track was extracted from The Doors' only No 1 LP, *Waiting For The Sun*.

# UNITED KINGDOM
# JULY 1968

## CUPID'S INSPIRATION
YESTERDAY HAS GONE
*Nems*

Like The Beatles, this Lincolnshire quintet were signed to Nems and had played many times at Hamburg's famous Star Club. However, unlike the Liverpool lads, they were unable to score more than one major hit, despite lead singer Terry Rice-Milton being dubbed 'The Face of 1969' in the UK music media. The song that briefly lifted them into the winner's circle was written by 1950s headliner Teddy Randazzo and had earlier been recorded by Little Anthony & The Imperials.

## MANFRED MANN
MY NAME IS JACK
*Fontana*

One of the most consistently commercial groups of the 1960s hit the heights with a song about the fictitious Greta Garbo Children's Home, which its composer John Simon had originally recorded.

## OHIO EXPRESS
YUMMY YUMMY YUMMY
*Pye International*

See US entry (June).

## TOMMY JAMES & THE SHONDELLS
MONY MONY
*Major Minor*

See US entry (June).

## RICHARD HARRIS
MACARTHUR PARK
*RCA*

Soon after the soundtrack album from the film *Camelot* had taken this celebrated Irish actor into the US Top 20, he had his sole transatlantic hit single. It was a melodramatic seven-minute track penned and produced by Jim Webb. The track was recorded in LA with Harris' vocals added in London. The song, which Webb originally offered to The Association, was written about a LA park where he often met his girlfriend. A disco remake in 1981 by Donna Summer also parked itself in the transatlantic Top 5.

## CRAZY WORLD OF ARTHUR BROWN
FIRE
*Track*

One of the summer's hottest new acts owed something to Screaming Jay Hawkins, and opened the door for similar eccentric artists such as Alice Cooper. The underground group's second single topped the UK chart and almost emulated that feat in the US, while their eponymous LP was a transatlantic Top 10 entry. The outrageously outfitted singer (born Arthur Wilton in Yorkshire), who sported heavy face make-up and a burning head-dress, co-wrote the track with member Vincent Crane. However, interest in this crazy combo cooled surprisingly quickly.

## HERB ALPERT
THIS GUY'S IN LOVE WITH YOU
*A&M*

See US entry (June).

## SIMON & GARFUNKEL
MRS ROBINSON
*CBS*

See US entry (May).

# UNITED STATES
# AUGUST 1968

## VOGUES
TURN AROUND
LOOK AT ME
*Reprise*

After rejecting 'Happy Together' (No 1 for The Turtles) this pop/MOR quartet scored with their treatment of a song that had given Glen Campbell his first hit in 1961. The composer Jerry Capehart was best-known for his work with the late Eddie Cochran.

## CREAM
SUNSHINE OF YOUR LOVE
*Atco*

Cream were arguably the most lauded and influential new group of the late 1960s. The trio, which included ex-Yardbird Eric Clapton, quickly built up a large following on both sides of the Atlantic. Their fifth UK Top 40 single became the act's biggest US hit when re-issued six months after it first cracked the US Top 40. The track was extracted from Cream's first transatlantic Top 5 album, *Disraeli Gears*. While the record was riding high, the trio announced they were to disband.

## RASCALS
PEOPLE GOT TO BE FREE
*Atlantic*

In the late 1960s, few American groups outsold the quartet whose third chart topper was also their last major hit. Interestingly, Atlantic did not initially consider this thought-provoking song (inspired by the assassinations of Martin Luther King and Robert Kennedy) as a suitable single for them. In 1970, the Rascals signed a five-year million-dollar deal with Columbia, but disbanded two years later.

## STEPPENWOLF
BORN TO BE WILD
*Dunhill*

Group member Mars Bonfire (born Dennis Edmonton) composed the rebellious biker's anthem that is regarded as one of the all-time classic hard rock records. 'Born To Be Wild', which included the phrase 'Heavy metal thunder', was the Canadian group's second single as Steppenwolf after several releases as Sparrow. The track, which was subsequently used in the film *Easy Rider,* came from their eponymous Top 10 LP.

## JOSÉ FELICIANO
LIGHT MY FIRE
*RCA*

Since the mid 1960s this blind Puerto Rican singer/guitarist has been one of the biggest-selling recording artists in the Spanish-speaking world. He won the Grammy for Best New Artist of 1968 when his flamenco-flavoured renditions of previous pop hits briefly made him an international star. His distinctive treatment of the recent Doors smash shot the song into the transatlantic Top 10 (a feat The Doors had failed to pull off) and helped the album *Feliciano!* to achieve the same heights.

## ARCHIE BELL & THE DRELLS
I CAN'T STOP DANCING
*Atlantic*

Top Philadelphia producers Kenny Gamble and Leon Huff penned this funky dance track, which lead singer Bell recorded while on a 15-day pass from the army. It was the second US-only Top 10 entry in a row for the group named Best New Singles Act of 1968 by *Billboard*. Interestingly, the combo were far more successful in the UK pop charts in the 1970s.

## DELLS
STAY IN MY CORNER
*Cadet*

At a time when most people had written them off as has-beens, this Chicago vocal quintet returned with a string of top-selling singles. Their first pop Top 40 entry was a re-recording of an intense and dramatic soul ballad that they had first cut in 1965. The soul classic, 'Stay In My Corner', came from the pens of Barrett Strong, Wade Flemons (Earth, Wind & Fire's first lead vocalist) and producer Bobby Miller.

## VANILLA FUDGE
(YOU KEEP ME)
HANGIN' ON
*Atco*

This New York quartet, who specialized in slowing down and stretching-out well-known songs, described their music as 'psychedelic-symphonic rock'. The group's innovative style earned them four US Top 20 albums before they disbanded in 1970. Their only transatlantic Top 20 single was a reworking of an earlier Supremes chart topper that came from the prolific pens of Holland, Dozier & Holland.

## JEANNIE C. RILEY
HARPER VALLEY PTA
*Plantation*

Before finding fame as a country singer, Tom T. Hall composed this tale about a mini-skirted mother, which rocketed Texan Riley (born Jeannie C. Stephenson) to the top. The single sold over 1.5 million in the first ten days and made a record jump from 81 to 7 on the US chart. Riley, who thought this song was 'too pop', had her only other hits in the country field. The Grammy-winning ode, which was first recorded by Alice Joy, inspired a later movie and TV series.

## MARVIN GAYE & TAMMI TERRELL
YOU'RE ALL I NEED
TO GET BY
*Tamla*

The last of the dynamic duo's five consecutive Top 20 singles was the fourth composed by soulful singers/songwriters Nick Ashford and Valerie Simpson. The single gave Gaye his first UK Top 20 entry. Later versions by Aretha Franklin (1971) and Dawn (1975) also graced the US Top 40.

---

# UNITED KINGDOM
# AUGUST 1968

---

## DUSTY SPRINGFIELD
I CLOSE MY EYES AND
COUNT TO TEN

*Philips*

This infectious up-tempo number was the transatlantic hit maker's third UK Top 10 entry penned by Clive Westlake. The single was also her fifth UK Top 10 entry that failed to crack the US Top 100.

## DAVE DEE, DOZY, BEAKY, MICK & TICH
LAST NIGHT IN SOHO

*Fontana*

Even though they amassed 13 UK Top 40 entries in the late 1960s, this imaginative UK act failed to break into the US Top 40. As usual, Howard and Blaikley composed the well-crafted pop song which increased the group's run of Top 20 singles to nine. Before the decade ended, Dee went solo and the band continued as DBM & T, with neither extending their hit run into the 1970s.

## TOM JONES
HELP YOURSELF
*Decca*

▲ 3
⑩ 8
362/500

The darling of the international cabaret circuit registered his seventh successive Top 10 entry with a song that started life in Italy as 'Gli Occhi Miei'. 'Help Yourself' was also the title track to the superstar's first US Top 5 album.

## HERMAN'S HERMITS
SUNSHINE GIRL
*Columbia*

▲ 8
⑩ 7
—/500

Surprisingly, the record that ended the golden group's run of 19 consecutive US hits started a run of UK Top 10 successes for them. John Carter of the Ivy League composed this good-time song with Geoff Stevens.

## SLY & THE FAMILY STONE
DANCE TO THE MUSIC
*Direction*

▲ 7
⑩ 1•
—/500

See US entry (April).

## BEACH BOYS
DO IT AGAIN
*Capitol*

▲ 1
⑩ 8
164/500

A stand-out song that reminisced about their surfing days, took the US's foremost group to the top for the second time in a country where the combo's early surf singles had floundered.

## BEE GEES
I'VE GOTTA GET A
MESSAGE TO YOU
*Polydor*

▲ 1
⑩ 4
148/500

Brothers Barry, Maurice and Robin Gibb composed this captivating song about a man on death row. The record returned them to the top of the UK chart and gave them their first US Top 10 entry after five previous Top 20 singles.

## AMEN CORNER
HIGH IN THE SKY
*Deram*

▲ 6
⑩ 2
—/500

Amen Corner's last recording on Decca gave one of 1968's most successful new UK bands their fourth chart single in a year. Soon afterwards, these burgeoning teen idols joined Andrew Oldham's Immediate label.

## ARETHA FRANKLIN
I SAY A LITTLE PRAYER
*Atlantic*

▲ 4
⑩ 2
478/500

See US entry (October).

## UNITED STATES
# SEPTEMBER 1968

### ARETHA FRANKLIN
THE HOUSE THAT
JACK BUILT
*Atlantic*

For the only time in her long and supremely successful career, the soul singer with the Midas touch had a double-sided Top 10 hit. This side was her distinctive treatment of a song previously recorded by Thelma Jones.

### 1910 FRUITGUM CO
1, 2, 3, RED LIGHT
*Buddah*

Session singer Joey Levine handled the vocal chores for both 1910 Fruitgum Co and their equally successful label-mates Ohio Express. Like the act's debut hit, 'Simon Says', this was a danceable, easy-to-learn song with a pre-teen-targeted lyric.

### DEEP PURPLE
HUSH
*Tetragrammaton*

In the 1960s, this UK rock band's only success came across the Atlantic. The track that introduced them to the US public was a revival of a song previously recorded by its composer Joe South. Thanks in part to personnel changes, the group went from strength to strength in the 1970s and 1980s, and engraved their own chapter in the history of rock.

### BEATLES
HEY JUDE
*Apple*

At 7 minutes 10 seconds, this is the longest single to top the US chart. Its Top 100 entry at position 10 was a record at the time. Also see UK entry.

### SERGIO MENDES & BRASIL '66
THE FOOL ON THE HILL
*A&M*

A song taken from The Beatles album *Magical Mystery Tour* lifted this Latin MOR ensemble into the Top 10 for the second time in a row. It was the title track of their second successive Top 10 album – an LP that also headed the jazz charts. The 1970s were relatively bleak for Mendes (despite a name change to Brasil '77), but he reappeared in the Top 10 in the 1980s as a solo artist.

### BEE GEES
I'VE GOTTA GET A
MESSAGE TO YOU
*Atco*

See UK entry.

### CRAZY WORLD OF ARTHUR BROWN
FIRE
*Track*

See UK entry (July).

### O'KAYSIONS
GIRL WATCHER
*ABC*

Raspy-voiced Donny Weaver fronted the blue-eyed soul group from Carolina, who first released this single on the North State label before ABC turned it into a nationwide hit. It was the only occasion that they managed to reach the Top 40. Among the answer records it inspired was 'Boy Watcher' by Pat Parker. In 1985, a new line-up of O'Kaysions released 'Girl Watcher'/'Boy Watcher' on their own I-Katcher label.

## CLARENCE CARTER
SLIP AWAY
*Atlantic*

▲ 6
⑩ 1
—/500

From 1961–1966 this blind R&B vocalist recorded in a duo with Calvin Scott. As a soloist he had two successive million sellers in 1968, 'Slip Away' and his own composition 'Too Weak To Fight', both of which were produced in Muscle Shoals by Rick Hall. The Alabama-born performer had his only transatlantic hit in 1970 with 'Patches'. The one-time husband of singer Candi Staton received a Pioneer Award from the R&B Foundation in 1994.

# UNITED KINGDOM
# SEPTEMBER 1968

## JOHNNY NASH
HOLD ME TIGHT
*Regal Zonophone*

▲ 5
⑩ 1
—/500

See US entry (November).

## BEATLES
HEY JUDE
*Apple*

▲ 1
⑩ 18
100/500

The first release on their Apple label hogged the US No 1 spot for nine weeks. Depending on who is telling the tale, 'Jude' was reported to be either Julian Lennon, John Lennon or Paul McCartney! A soulful version by Wilson Pickett reached the UK Top 20 a year later.

## MARY HOPKIN
THOSE WERE THE DAYS
*Apple*

▲ 1
⑩ 1
17/500

Top model Twiggy tipped off Paul McCartney when she saw this Welsh vocalist singing 'Turn! Turn! Turn!' on TV's *Opportunity Knocks*. He produced her first Apple release, which replaced 'Hey Jude' at the top of the UK lists and reached the runner-up spot behind that Beatles single in the US. The track was based on a favourite Russian folksong 'Darogoi Dimmoyo' and had English lyrics by Gene Raskin, whose group The Limeliters had recorded it for their 1962 album *Folk Matinee*.

## CANNED HEAT
ON THE ROAD AGAIN
*Liberty*

▲ 8
⑩ 1
—/500

A blues-based rock quartet from LA who named themselves after a late 1920s blues song, had two consecutive transatlantic Top 20 entries with updates of old blues numbers. The first and biggest of these was their reworking of a hypnotic song that Floyd Jones recorded in the early 1950s as 'On The Road'. Canned Heat, who starred at both the Monterey Pop Festival in 1967 and Woodstock, cooled off in the early 1970s after lead singer Al Wilson died of a drug overdose.

## CASUALS
JESAMINE
*Decca*

▲ 2
⑩ 1•
221/500

This British pop quartet had been three times winners on TV's *Opportunity Knocks* and made a name for themsleves in Italy before taking their sole trip into the UK Top 20. The song, which was previously recorded by The Bystanders, was co-written by early rock star Marty Wilde. Coincidentally, the only act that halted the single's progress to the top was another winner from that same TV show, Mary Hopkin. The Casuals, who were voted Most Promising Group of 1968, were renamed the British Casuals in the US.

## GARY PUCKETT & THE UNION GAP
LADY WILLPOWER
*CBS*

▲ 5
⑩ 2
—/500

See US entry (July).

## LEAPY LEE
LITTLE ARROWS
*MCA*

▲ 2
⑩ 1•
226/500

Even though British record buyers voted this Albert Hammond-composed novelty the Most Disliked Record of 1968 in the *RM* poll, it was one of a decreasing number of UK singles to reach the Top 20 on both sides of the Atlantic. Not only that, but Hampshire-born actor/singer Lee (born Lee Graham) was only the second UK artist ever to crack the US country Top 20. 'Little Arrows' sold over three million worldwide, but none of his other releases hit the bull's-eye.

# UNITED STATES
# OCTOBER 1968

## O.C. SMITH
LITTLE GREEN APPLES
*Columbia*

▲ 2
⑩ 1•
239/500

Soon after Bobby Russell's No 1 song 'Honey' exited the charts, his captivating composition 'Little Green Apples' gave veteran vocalist Smith his biggest US hit. Only The Beatles prevented this classy Jerry Fuller production from reaching the summit. The song had been a mid-table pop chart entry earlier in the year by country superstar Roger Miller. Smith narrowly missed the Top 40 in 1969 with a rendition of 'Honey'.

## ARETHA FRANKLIN
I SAY A LITTLE PRAYER
*Atlantic*

▲ 10
⑩ 9
—/500

America's Top Singles Artist of 1968 chalked up her ninth successive US Top 10 entry with a memorable Bacharach & David ballad that Dionne Warwick had taken into the Top 5 a year earlier. During her long career, Aretha has had more than 40 Top 40 singles, amassed a staggering 14 gold singles and won numerous Grammy awards. She also received a Lifetime Achievement award from the R&B Foundation and was the first female inducted into the Rock and Roll Hall of Fame.

## GRASS ROOTS
MIDNIGHT CONFESSIONS
*Dunhill*

▲ 5
⑩ 2
—/500

Despite a long run of US chart entries, San Francisco's Grass Roots never cracked the UK lists. Even their outstanding treatment of this commercially compelling Lou Josie composition failed to ignite interest across the Atlantic. Group member Warren Ettner is now the manager of top-rated alternative rock band Faith No More.

## VOGUES
MY SPECIAL ANGEL
*Reprise*

▲ 7
⑩ 4•
—/500

This Pennsylvania quartet, who clocked up eight US Top 40 hits in the late 1960s, earned few fans outside the US with their old school vocal-style recordings. The group, who specialized in revivals, were last seen in th Top 10 with an update of a song Bobby Helms had flown high with in 1957.

## GARY PUCKETT & THE UNION GAP
OVER YOU
*Columbia*

Few American groups were as popular on both sides of the Atlantic in the late 1960s as this pop/rock quintet. They notched up their fourth US Top 10 entry in a row with a stand-out song penned by producer Jerry Fuller.

## JAMES BROWN
SAY IT LOUD–I'M BLACK AND I'M PROUD
*King*

The most influential African-American artist of all time scored his sixth R&B No 1 of the decade with a barrier-breaking black pride opus that helped set soul music's agenda for the 1970s. The performer, who inspired such stars as Prince, Michael Jackson and The Rolling Stones,

continued to add to his amazing collection of hits in the 1970s and 1980s. Brown, who greatly influenced both rap and hip hop, was one of the first acts inducted into the Rock and Roll Hall of Fame.

## MARY HOPKIN
THOSE WERE THE DAYS
*Apple*

See UK entry (September).

## TURTLES
ELENORE
*White Whale*

Howard Kaylan and Mark Volman, who were the nucleus of The Turtles, co-wrote the group's third transatlantic Top 20 entry in a row. Interestingly, in the 1970s the pair re-recorded the song as Flo & Eddie.

# UNITED KINGDOM
# OCTOBER 1968

## DAVE CLARK FIVE
RED BALLOON

*Columbia*

One of the biggest-selling UK bands of the 1960s had their last major hit of the decade with a cover version of a song written and first recorded by UK pop/country artist Raymond Froggatt.

## TREMELOES
MY LITTLE LADY
*CBS*

Group member Len 'Chip' Hawkes co-wrote the English lyrics to the Italian song originally known as 'Non Illuderti Mai'. It was composed by the same writers as their previous Top 10 hit, 'Suddenly You Love Me'.

## STATUS QUO
ICE IN THE SUN

*Pye*

Early 1960s British rock star Marty Wilde co-wrote the psychedelic pop opus that gave the quartet their last big seller of the decade. The group re-invented themselves in the early 1970s, and in 1973 they re-emerged as a 12-bar-boogie-band and started a staggering run of UK hit singles and albums.

## MASON WILLIAMS
CLASSICAL GAS
*Warner*

See US entry (July).

## ENGELBERT HUMPERDINCK
### LES BICYCLETTES DE BELSIZE
*Decca*

▲ 5
🔟 6
—/500

Despite its French title, the frequent chart visitor's latest international hit was a UK song written for him by Les Reed and Barry Mason – who had penned his earlier multi-million seller 'The Last Waltz'.

## LOVE AFFAIR
### A DAY WITHOUT LOVE
*CBS*

▲ 6
🔟 3
—/500

One of the UK's most popular groups in the late 1960s had their third Top 10 entry in a row with a song composed by Philip Goodhand-Tait from fellow British band the Stormsville Shakers.

## JOSE FELICIANO
### LIGHT MY FIRE
*RCA*

▲ 6
🔟 1•
—/500

See US entry (August).

## HUGO MONTENEGRO & HIS ORCHESTRA
### THE GOOD, THE BAD AND THE UGLY
*RCA*

▲ 1
🔟 1•
32/500

See US entry (May).

---

# UNITED STATES
# NOVEMBER 1968

---

## JOHNNY NASH
### HOLD ME TIGHT
*Jad*

▲ 5
🔟 1
—/500

Eleven years after he had made his US Top 100 debut, this multi-talented Texan singer/actor registered his first Top 10 entry. He not only composed the transatlantic pop reggae smash, but it was also released on Nash's own label, Jad. The single, which was produced in Jamaica by Byron Lee, was the first of three consecutive Top 10 entries in the UK for the distinctive vocalist.

## DIANA ROSS & THE SUPREMES
### LOVE CHILD
*Motown*

▲ 1
🔟 15
50/500

As the decade came to an end, the lyrics of many Motown releases were becoming more socially aware. One of the first hits from this new era,

'Love Child', sent The Supremes to the top for the eleventh time. It was written and produced by 'The Clan', which included Canadian-born white singer/songwriter R. Dean Taylor.

## CREAM
### WHITE ROOM
*Atco*

▲ 6
🔟 2•
—/500

A track taken from the blues rock superstars' chart-topping double album, *Wheels Of Fire*, returned them to the heights in the US as they performed their last dates. Twenty-five years later they briefly reunited to play when they were inducted into the Rock and Roll Hall of Fame.

## STEPPENWOLF
### MAGIC CARPET RIDE
*Dunhill*

▲ 3
🔟 2
348/500

Their German-born lead singer John Kay (real

name Joachim Krauledat) co-wrote the LA-based hard rock band's second successive million seller, which was extracted from the act's highest-placed album, *The Second*.

## JOHNNIE TAYLOR
WHO'S MAKING LOVE
*Stax*

▲ 5
⑩ 1
490/500

One of soul music's most recognizable performers had his highest-placed hit of the decade with a cheating song penned for him by one of Stax Records' in-house writing teams. It was the Arkansas soul man's third R&B Top 20 entry, and the first of his eight successive R&B Top 10 entries. 'Who's Making Love' was one of the biggest soul singles of the year and inspired several answers, recordings including 'I'm Making Love' by Little Frankie Lee.

## DION
ABRAHAM, MARTIN
AND JOHN
*Laurie*

▲ 4
⑩ 9•
399/500

After a five-year absence, the early 1960s superstar reappeared at the top end of the chart with a moving Dick Holler composition about great men who had died while serving their people. In the UK, Marvin Gaye had a hit with the song in 1970. Over the coming years Dion briefly reunited with The Belmonts, made spasmodic solo

comebacks and achieved a name for himself in the gospel field.

## GLEN CAMPBELL
WICHITA LINEMAN
*Capitol*

▲ 3
⑩ 1
286/500

Top songsmith Jim Webb composed the memorable ballad (originally for actor/singer Paul Petersen) that gave the singer and guitarist his seventh country Top 20 single and his first major pop hit. Before the public acquired a taste for the Arkansas-born entertainer, he had been a much-in-demand session musician and backing vocalist, as well as a member of the Beach Boys and The Crickets. Campbell's *Wichita Lineman* album was the first country LP to head the pop chart.

## STEVIE WONDER
FOR ONCE IN MY LIFE
*Tamla*

▲ 2
⑩ 7
222/500

A perennially popular tune, which celebrated balladeer Tony Bennett had taken into the Top 100 in 1967, 'For Once In My Life' narrowly missed the top spot by one of the decade's most successful artists.

# UNITED KINGDOM
# NOVEMBER 1968

## JOE COCKER
WITH A LITTLE HELP
FROM MY FRIENDS
*Regal Zonophone*

▲ 1
⑩ 1
189/500

Soul superstar Ray Charles greatly influenced this power-house vocalist from Yorkshire, who became one of rock's most revered performers. Cocker's

breakthough hit was a unique interpretation of a song from The Beatles' *Sgt Pepper* LP. Intriguingly, it was not the first Lennon & McCartney composition he had cut – his forgotten first release in 1965 had been 'I'll Cry Instead'. Among Cocker's friends on the timeless track were Jimmy Page and ex-Orlon Rosetta Hightower. Wet Wet Wet's 1988 rendition also topped the chart.

## MARBLES
ONLY ONE WOMAN
*Polydor*

Among the year's most interesting new artists was this blue-eyed soul duo which consisted of Graham Bonnet and Trevor Gordon. The Marbles' best-remembered track was written and produced by The Bee Gees, who were cousins of Bonnet. Coincidentally, in their early days The Bee Gees had backed Gordon on record. The duo, who were voted second Most Promising British Group of 1968, split in 1970. Bonnet later found gold as vocalist in Ritchie Blackmore's group Rainbow.

## BARRY RYAN
ELOISE
*MGM*

In the UK, one of the most popular new teen-appeal acts of the mid-1960s were Yorkshire born twins Paul and Barry Ryan (whose mother Marion Ryan had been a pop star in the 1950s). Barry (born Barry Sapherson) went solo in 1968 and had his biggest hit with a riveting pop/rock song penned by brother Paul, which sold over two million copies in Europe. A reworking in 1986 by The Damned gave the pioneer punk act their best-selling single.

## ISLEY BROTHERS
THIS OLD HEART OF MINE
*Tamla Motown*

Among the many Motown tracks that charted late in the UK was this hook-heavy Holland, Dozier & Holland composition, which had climbed into the US Top 20 in early 1966. It was the first notable UK hit for the exuberant R&B veterans, whose earlier recordings of 'Shout' and 'Twist & Shout' were legendary. In 1975, Rod Stewart reinstated the song in the UK Top 10, and in 1990 a revival teaming Stewart with Ronald Isley reached the US Top 10.

## JIMI HENDRIX EXPERIENCE
ALL ALONG THE WATCHTOWER
*Track*

Surprisingly, the legendary rock hero's unique interpretation of an impressive Bob Dylan composition was his only Top 20 single in his homeland. The track was taken from the double album *Electric Ladyland,* which topped the US chart. Hendrix, who clocked up four transatlantic Top 10 albums in the late 1960s, was still one of the world's most popular performers when he died from drug-related causes in 1970.

## BANDWAGON
BREAKIN' DOWN THE WALLS OF HEARTACHE
*Direction*

Despite achieving only minor success in their homeland, this American R&B outfit collected three UK Top 10 singles from 1968–70. The song that introduced them to the chart was a catchy up-tempo track written by noted composers Sandy Linzer and Denny Randell. On the group's other two major hits, lead singer Johnny Johnson was allocated front billing.

## TURTLES
ELENORE
*London American*

See US entry (October).

## NINA SIMONE
AIN'T GOT NO – I GOT LIFE/DO WHAT YOU GOTTA DO
*RCA*

One of the most recognizable song stylists of the rock era chalked up her biggest UK hit with a medley of two numbers from the musical *Hair*. It came nine years after the jazz/R&B singer/pianist from South Carolina (born Eunice Waymon) had enjoyed her only US Top 20 entry, 'I Love You, Porgy'. The equally popular Jim Webb-penned B side reappeared in the UK Top 20 the following year by the Four Tops.

## SCAFFOLD
LILY THE PINK
*Parlophone*

▲ 1
🔟 2
37/500

This tongue-in-cheek trio headed the chart with a self-composed novelty which they based on a traditional folk tune. The song, which extolled the virtues of Lily's magical medicinal compound, was the last of a record-breaking 27 No 1 singles for producer Norrie Paramor.

## LULU
I'M A TIGER
*Columbia*

▲ 9
🔟 5
—/500

Early UK rock star Marty Wilde composed the effervescent Scottish vocalist's seventh Top 20 entry. Incidentally, it was her last hit before marrying Bee Gee Maurice Gibb.

# UNITED STATES
# DECEMBER 1968

## MARVIN GAYE
I HEARD IT THROUGH
THE GRAPEVINE
*Tamla*

▲ 1
🔟 9
7/500

The soul superstar scored his only transatlantic No 1 with an unforgettable soul classic, co-written and produced by Norman Whitfield. The often-recorded song had reached the US Top 3 a year earlier by Gladys Knight & The Pips. The track gave Gaye his eighteenth solo Top 40 entry in the US and his first in the UK. In 1986, the perennially popular single returned to the UK Top 10 after being used in a TV commercial.

## CLASSICS IV
## FEATURING
## DENIS YOST
STORMY
*Imperial*

▲ 5
🔟 2
—/500

Buddy Buie, the group's producer and arranger, co-wrote this soft-rock song with lead guitarist James Cobb. For the first time, the Classics IV credited their Detroit-born lead singer Denis Yost on the label.

## BOBBY VINTON
I LOVE HOW YOU
LOVE ME
*Epic*

▲ 9
🔟 8
—/500

His update of a 1961 Top 10 hit by The Paris Sisters pushed Vinton's tally of Top 40 entries up to 24 for the decade. 'I Love How You Love Me' was also the title track of his seventh Top 40 album of the 1960s. Despite the fact that he was one of the era's top sellers in the US, Vinton had to wait until 1990 to finally crack the UK Top 10.

## JUDY COLLINS
BOTH SIDES NOW
*Elektra*

▲ 8
🔟 1•
—/500

When this clear-voiced soprano from Seattle turned her attention from traditional folk songs to material from her contemporaries, she moved from cult heroine to commercial hit maker. The single that opened the door for Collins on both sides of the Atlantic was her interpretation of fellow folk queen Joni Mitchell's outstanding composition 'Both Sides Now'. The album it was taken from, *Wildflowers*, was the first and biggest-selling of the vocalist's eight US Top 40 entries.

## DIANA ROSS, SUPREMES & TEMPTATIONS
I'M GONNA MAKE YOU LOVE ME
*Motown*

▲ 2
🔟 16/7
230/500

When the decade opened, these two groups worked together as The Primettes and The Primes. As the 1960s closed, they recorded several successful projects together. Soon after their remake of Dee Dee Warwick's 1966 single entered the Top 10, two joint albums were situated in the Top 3.

## TEMPTATIONS
CLOUD NINE
*Gordy*

▲ 6
🔟 8
—/500

Motown's first Grammy-winning record was also the track that introduced the award-winning group's new Sly Stone-influenced psychedelic soul sound. As the single slipped, an instrumental version by Mongo Santamaria climbed into the Top 40.

---

# UNITED KINGDOM
# DECEMBER 1968

---

## DES O'CONNOR
ONE TWO THREE O'LEARY
*Columbia*

▲ 4
🔟 3
480/500

Veteran songwriter Michael Carr teamed with chart regular Barry Mason to write this popular performer's third Top 10 entry in a year. In the US, where O'Connor's records fell on deaf ears, the song was covered by noted jazz vocalist Oscar Brown Jr. O'Connor, whose voice was, unfairly, the butt of many jokes, had two more Top 20 entries in the 1960s, but did not reappear in the Top 10 until 1986.

## MALCOLM ROBERTS
MAY I HAVE THE NEXT DREAM WITH YOU
*Major Minor*

▲ 8
🔟 1•
—/500

One of the last big-voiced MOR balladeers to crack the charts was a striking-looking UK cabaret entertainer whose earlier records for RCA had been ignored by buyers. The retro-sounding song that put Roberts among the winners was written by veteran US tunesmiths Charles, Harry and Henry Tobias. His follow-up, the Les Reed and

Barry Mason composition 'Love Is All', was the last UK hit for the performer, who soon after relocated successfully to Brazil.

## FOUNDATIONS
BUILD ME UP BUTTERCUP
*Pye*

▲ 2
🔟 2
245/500

Manfred Mann's lead singer Mike D'Abo co-wrote this outstanding Motown-influenced pop/R&B song with Tony MacAulay. The single, which also attained a Top 3 placing in the US, earned the multi-racial UK team their second gold record.

## BONZO DOG DOO-DAH BAND
I'M THE URBAN SPACEMAN
*Liberty*

▲ 5
🔟 1•
493/500

Their appearance in The Beatles' *Magical Mystery Tour* helped introduce this quirky and eccentric ensemble to the public. Although they were an extremely popular live act, the band's mix of musical and lyrical satire with New Vaudeville

Band-styled music worked less well on singles. The Bonzo's only chart entry came with a left-field opus produced by Apollo C. Vermouth (better known as Paul McCartney) and penned by front man Neil Innes, who in later life was a member of Beatles spoof-band, The Ruttles.

## LOVE SCULPTURE
SABRE DANCE
*Parlophone*

After a name change from the Human Beans, this Welsh rock trio released two small-selling singles before they achieved their only hit. It was a fast-moving instrumental adaptation of Arim Khachaturian's famous classical work (from the 'Gayaneh Ballet Suite') which briefly lifted them into the limelight. After they split in 1969, vocalist/guitarist Dave Edmunds had a string of successes as a solo artist and producer.

## GUN
RACE WITH THE DEVIL
*CBS*

Adrian and Paul Gurvitz and Louie Farrell comprised British hard rock trio Gun, whose opening salvo on the chart was also their last. The group's sole hit was written by Adrian, who with brother Paul formed the Baker-Gurvitz Army (with Cream's drummer Ginger Baker) when other Gun records failed to shoot chartwards.

## MARMALADE
OB-LA-DI OB-LA-DA
*CBS*

The first Scottish band to top the UK chart did so with their version of a sing-along song from The Beatles' (*White Album*) double album. This Mike Smith-produced track was the first of six successive Top 10 entries for the teen-appeal act.

# UNITED STATES
# JANUARY 1969

## YOUNG–HOLT UNLIMITED
SOULFUL STRUT
*Brunswick*

▲ 3
⑩ 1•
387/500

Before his group The Chi-lites started their run of pop hits, lead singer Eugene Record co-penned and produced this instrumental combo's biggest seller. The infectious 'Soulful Strut' was a showcase for bassist Eldee Young and drummer Isaac 'Red' Holt, who had both previously been in the successful Ramsey Lewis Trio. 'Am I The Same Girl', a vocal version of the song, scored in the States in 1969 by Barbara Acklin (using Young–Holt Unlimited's backing track), and in the UK by Dusty Springfield in 1969 and Swing Out Sister in 1992.

## B.J. THOMAS
HOOKED ON A FEELING
*Scepter*

▲ 5
⑩ 2
—/500

Thomas' fifth Top 40 entry was a hooky pop opus penned and first recorded by its composer Mark James. Twelve years later Thomas won a lengthy battle for back royalties earned by 'Hooked On A Feeling' and his other Scepter tracks. The song was taken to the top of the US chart in 1974 by Blue Swede, with a cover of Jonathan King's unique interpretation of it.

## TOMMY JAMES & THE SHONDELLS
CRIMSON & CLOVER
*Roulette*

▲ 1
⑩ 5
53/500

James returned to the top with a self-penned slice of psychedlia. Thirteen years later, Joan Jett & The Blackhearts brought this hypnotic song back into the Top 10.

## DOORS
TOUCH ME
*Elektra*

▲ 3
⑩ 3•
307/500

This revered rock band's last significant single of the decade was a noteworthy self-composed cut from the fourth of their six successive Top 10 albums, *Soft Parade*. Controversial and often confrontational leader Jim Morrison died in mysterious circumstances soon after leaving the group in 1970. The legendary quartet's records have remained popular on both sides of the Atlantic, and they were inducted into the Rock and Roll Hall of Fame in 1993.

## BROOKLYN BRIDGE
WORST THAT COULD HAPPEN
*Buddah*

▲ 3
⑩ 1•
369/500

Johnny Maestro (born John Maestrangelo), who had previously charted as leader of doo-wop group The Crests and as a soloist, fronted this 11-man New York-based ensemble. The act, which included members of the Del Satins (who had backed Dion on several solo hits), had the highest placed of their seven US charter songs with their second release. The track was produced by Wes Farrell and the song, which Jim Webb composed, had previously been recorded by The 5th Dimension on the group's second album *The Magic Carpet*.

## DUSTY SPRINGFIELD
SON-OF-A PREACHER MAN
*Atlantic*

▲ 10
⑩ 3
—/500

See UK entry.

## SLY & THE FAMILY STONE
EVERYDAY PEOPLE
*Epic*

▲ 1
🔟 2
30/500

One of the few acts who appealed to both R&B and pop record buyers registered the first of their three R&B and pop chart toppers with a mind-numbingly infectious Sly Stone composition. The song was also the basis of Arrested Development's 1992 transatlantic Top 10 entry 'People Everyday'.

## BEE GEES
I STARTED A JOKE
*Atco*

▲ 6
🔟 2
—/500

This US-only single (taken from the group's third transatlantic Top 20 album, *Idea*) gave the internationally renowned act their highest placed US hit of the decade.

# UNITED KINGDOM
# JANUARY 1969

## FLEETWOOD MAC
ALBATROSS
*Blue Horizon*

▲ 1
🔟 1
117/500

Before they became the darlings of the US AOR set, Fleetwood Mac were one of the best-respected blues bands in the UK. It might surprise the group's US fans to learn that their biggest UK hit was a moody guitar instrumental written by original front man Peter Green. This hypnotic track, which never graced the US Top 100, topped the UK chart in 1969 and very nearly repeated that feat in 1973 – three years after Green had left the band.

## DUSTY SPRINGFIELD
SON-OF-A
PREACHER MAN
*Philips*

▲ 9
🔟 10
—/500

The UK's most soulful female singer in the 1960s reached the transatlantic Top 10 with a track from her acclaimed *Dusty In Memphis* album. The LP was produced by Jerry Wexler, who was also responsible for many of Atlantic Records' top R&B sellers. It was Springfield's last major hit until the late 1980s, when the Pet Shop Boys helped bring her back into the limelight.

## HERMAN'S HERMITS
SOMETHING'S HAPPENING
*Columbia*

▲ 6
🔟 8
—/500

The group clocked up their fourteenth UK Top 20 hit with a bouncy Italian song (originally known as 'Luglio'), with English lyrics by top songsmith Jack Fishman.

## STEVIE WONDER
FOR ONCE IN MY LIFE
*Tamla Motown*

▲ 3
🔟 2
339/500

See US entry (November 1968).

## JUDY CLAY & WILLIAM BELL
PRIVATE NUMBER
*Stax*

▲ 8
🔟 1•
—/500

Even though only a minor pop hit in the US, this soulful duet gave these two respected R&B artists their sole UK Top 20 entry, and was one of Stax Records' biggest UK sellers. Memphis-born Bell (real name William Yarborough) co-wrote the number with noted keyboard player Booker T. Jones. Interestingly, New Yorker Clay (born Judy Guion) is a member of the same family as Dionne Warwick and Whitney Houston.

## MOVE
BLACKBERRY WAY
*Regal Zonophone*

This psychedelic sing-along song was the biggest of the creative combo's nine UK Top 20 entries. Jimmy Miller produced their fifth consecutive Top 5 entry, which was written by Roy Wood. The group disbanded in the early 1970s, and offshoots included frequent chart makers ELO and Wizzard.

## MANFRED MANN
FOX ON THE RUN
*Fontana*

Tony Hazzard, who had penned the top quintet's earlier hit 'Ha Ha Said The Clown', composed their third Top 10 single of the year. In 1976 Tom T. Hall steered the song into the country Top 10.

# UNITED STATES
# FEBRUARY 1969

## FOUNDATIONS
BUILD ME UP
BUTTERCUP
*UNI*

See UK entry (December 1968).

## BOOKER T. & THE MGs
HANG 'EM HIGH
*Stax*

After six years away, the innovative instrumental combo returned to the Top 10 with their unique treatment of the title song from a Clint Eastwood western.

## TYRONE DAVIS
CAN I CHANGE MY MIND
*Dakar*

Tyrone The Wonder Boy was the name this stylish Mississippi-born soul singer first recorded under in 1965. His impressive run of 21 Top 20 R&B hits started with a distinctive mid-tempo track composed by Carl Woolfolk and Barry Despenza. However, despite his quarter of a century as a US chart visitor, Davis has never graced the UK bestsellers.

## TURTLES
YOU SHOWED ME
*White Whale*

Jim McGuinn and Gene Clark wrote 'You Showed Me' for their group The Byrds. The Turtles' version took them into the US Top 40 for the ninth and last time. In 1989, the latter act sued rappers De La Soul for allegedly using samples from this single without permission.

## JAY & THE AMERICANS
THIS MAGIC MOMENT
*UA*

A Pomus and Shuman song that The Drifters had taken into the Top 20 in 1960 transported this talented vocal team into the Top 10 for the first time since 1965. In all, the group amassed 17 US chart entries during the decade, none of which, perhaps surprisingly, dented the UK list.

## CREEDENCE CLEARWATER REVIVAL
PROUD MARY
*Fantasy*

'Swamp Rock' was the term used to describe the sound of the most popular new US group of the late 1960s. The first of the Californian quartet's six transatlantic Top 20 entries was a tale about a Mississippi riverboat penned by leader John Fogerty who, at the time, had never even seen the famous river. The song also reached the US chart in the same year by R&B acts Solomon Burke and Checkmates Ltd, and in 1971 steamed back into the Top 5 courtesy of Ike & Tina Turner.

## DIANA ROSS & THE SUPREMES
I'M LIVIN' IN SHAME
*Motown*

▲ 10
🔟 17
—/500

Berry Gordy headed Motown's anonymous production and songwriting 'clan', who were behind this socially aware single which the all-time No 1 girl group launched on *The Ed Sullivan Show*.

# UNITED KINGDOM
# FEBRUARY 1969

## JOHNNY NASH
YOU GOT SOUL
*Major Minor*

▲ 6
🔟 2
—/500

In 1968, Bill Johnson's (from Sam & Bill) recording of this catchy Nash-penned pop/soul song on Johnny's label Jocida went nowhere. The label owner then cut the track himself, and his reggae-influenced rendition returned him to the top end of the UK charts.

## MARTHA & THE VANDELLAS
DANCING IN THE STREET
*Tamla Motown*

▲ 4
🔟 1•
—/500

See US entry (September 1964).

## NINA SIMONE
TO LOVE SOMEBODY
*RCA*

▲ 5
🔟 2
—/500

The song that returned the 'The High Priestess Of Soul' to the heights was written by Barry and Robin Gibb, and had been a US Top 20 hit for the Bee Gees in 1967. 'To Love Somebody', which was originally written for Otis Redding, revisited the UK Top 20 in 1990 by Jimmy Somerville and reached the transatlantic Top 20 once again in 1992 by Michael Bolton.

## DIANA ROSS & THE SUPREMES & THE TEMPTATIONS
I'M GONNA MAKE YOU LOVE ME
*Tamla Motown*

▲ 3
🔟 1
424/500

See US entry (December 1968).

## DONALD PEERS
PLEASE DON'T GO
*Columbia*

▲ 3
🔟 1•
367/500

One of the most popular singers in the UK in the 1940s and early 1950s reappeared in the chart after an extended 18-year absence. The song that briefly brought the MOR legend back into the spotlight was a retro-sounding ballad (adapted from the 'Barcarolle' from Offenbach's 'The Tales Of Hoffman'), penned by Les Reed and popular TV host Jackie Rae.

## SIMON & GARFUNKEL
MRS ROBINSON (EP)
*CBS*

▲ 9
🔟 3
—/500

Soon after putting three LPs in the US Top 5, Simon & Garfunkel charted in the UK with an EP of songs from *The Graduate*. The tracks were 'Mrs Robinson', 'Scarborough Fair-Canticle', 'Sounds Of Silence' and 'April She Will Come'.

## AMEN CORNER
(IF PARADISE IS)
HALF AS NICE
*Immediate*

Veteran Jack Fishman composed the English lyric to the Italian song 'Il Paradiso Belavista', which became the Welsh teen idols' only chart topper. In 1976, this praiseworthy pop record briefly reappeared in the UK Top 40.

## PETER SARSTEDT
WHERE DO YOU GO
TO MY LOVELY
*UA*

Six years after he started recording as Wes Sands, the brother of early-60s hit maker Eden Kane reached the top of the UK charts in his own right. Eden's one-time roadie became flavour-of-the-month thanks to a continental-sounding self-composed ballad about a poor little rich girl. It won the prestigious Ivor Novello Award for Song of the Year and was a minor success in the US (where Sarstedt later relocated).

## ENGELBERT HUMPERDINCK
THE WAY IT USED TO BE
*Decca*

Roger Greenaway and Roger Cook composed the English lyrics to the Italian song that gave the MOR hit machine his seventh UK Top 5 entry in a row.

---

# UNITED STATES
# MARCH 1969

---

## SMOKEY ROBINSON & THE MIRACLES
BABY, BABY DON'T
YOU CRY
*Tamla*

Robinson, who had penned bestsellers for label-mates such as The Temptations, Marvin Gaye and Mary Wells, co-wrote the stand-out quintet's last major hit of the decade. In the early 1970s Robinson successfully went solo, and also became vice-president of Motown Records.

## TOMMY ROE
DIZZY
*ABC*

One of the biggest-selling American male singers of the 1960s had his only transatlantic No 1 with a bubblegum song he wrote with Freddy Weller (of Paul Revere & The Raiders). Steve Barri (composer of 'Eve of Destruction') produced it, and early rocker Sid King played guitar on the track. Coincidentally, when pop fame faded for them, both Roe and Weller recorded for the country market.

## DIONNE WARWICK
THIS GIRL'S IN LOVE
WITH YOU
*Scepter*

Less than a year after Herb Alpert had taken Bacharach & David's enduring love ballad to the top, this distinctive song stylist reinstated it into the Top 10. Warwick continued to add to her hit tally during the 1970s and 1980s, and was still a major recording artist when her noteworthy niece, Whitney Houston, started her record-breaking career.

## 1910 FRUITGUM CO
INDIAN GIVER
*Buddah*

▲ 5
⑩ 3•
—/500

Bobby Bloom, Bo Gentry and Ritchie Cordell, who had composed numerous chart entries for Tommy James & The Shondells, penned the bubblegum gurus' third Top 5 entry in a year. It was, however, to be the group's last major hit, as their bubble burst soon afterwards.

## CLASSICS IV FEATURING DENIS YOST
TRACES
*Imperial*

▲ 2
⑩ 3•
337/500

For the third time in just over a year, this commercial quintet reached the Top 10 with a song whose title contained just one word. However, the group's run of Top 40 hits did not stretch into the 1970s, but in 1974 their producer Buddy Buie and a couple of group members formed the successful Atlanta Rhythm Section.

## ZOMBIES
TIME OF THE SEASON
*Date*

▲ 3
⑩ 3•
371/500

This musically adventurous track was recorded in 1967 as part of the quintet's experimental *Odessey And Oracle* (sic) album. The group then disbanded and the album died. However, in 1969 this Rod Argent-penned single came to life in the US, but despite some lucrative offers The Zombies refused to reform. Both lead singer Colin Blunstone and Argent had hits of their own in the 1970s, and in later years Argent became a successful producer.

## TEMPTATIONS
RUN AWAY CHILD, RUNNING WILD
*Gordy*

▲ 6
⑩ 9
—/500

Motown's boundary-stretching quintet added to their most impressive hit tally with a commercially appealing and socially conscious Norman Whitfield and Barrett Strong song. The track was extracted from the group's Top 5 album *Cloud Nine*.

## 5TH DIMENSION
AQUARIUS/LET THE SUNSHINE IN
*Soul City*

▲ 1
⑩ 3
8/500

Producer Bones Howe's idea of linking two show-stopping songs from the rock musical *Hair* was inspired. The single headed the US charts for six weeks and gave the polished vocal team their first and biggest UK hit.

## GLEN CAMPBELL
GALVESTON
*Capitol*

▲ 4
⑩ 2
444/500

Apparently, only The Beatles outsold this country-oriented performer in the US in 1969. The host of TV's *The Glen Campbell Goodtime Hour* collected up his third Country No 1 in a year with a melodic Jim Webb ballad that also returned him to the transatlantic pop Top 20. Its parent album *Galveston* reached runner-up position in the US. Campbell continued to add to his portfolio of hits in later decades.

## DAVID RUFFIN
MY WHOLE WORLD ENDED (THE MOMENT YOU LEFT ME)
*Motown*

▲ 9
⑩ 1
—/500

This may have been the Mississippi-born singer's first solo hit but his voice had already been heard on many bestsellers by The Temptations. Like his brother, Jimmy, he clocked up the first of two Top 10 entries in the soulful sixties. The archetypal Motown song that put him into the Top 10 was written by a quartet of Detroit's finest, including Johnny Bristol and Harvey Fuqua.

## JERRY BUTLER
ONLY THE STRONG SURVIVE
*Mercury*

▲ 4
⑩ 3•
454/500

The smooth R&B vocalist's thirteenth Top 40 entry was a soul song he penned with the record's producers Kenny Gamble and Leon Huff. Butler, one of the most successful R&B artists of the 1960s, received a Pioneer Award from the R&B Foundation in 1994.

# UNITED KINGDOM
# MARCH 1969

## GLEN CAMPBELL
WICHITA LINEMAN
*Ember*

▲ 7
⑩ 1
—/500

See US entry (November 1968).

## MARV JOHNSON
I'LL PICK A ROSE
FOR MY ROSE
*Tamla Motown*

▲ 10
⑩ 2•
—/500

Despite the fact that this catchy self-composed Motown cut had been totally ignored in the Detroit R&B singer's homeland, it returned him to the UK Top 10. Interestingly, Johnson's only hits of the 1960s came in the first and last years of the decade.

## CILLA BLACK
SURROUND YOURSELF
WITH SORROW
*Parlophone*

▲ 3
⑩ 9
407/500

Bill Martin and Phil Coulter, who had penned the UK's last two Eurovision Song Contest entries 'Puppet On A String' and 'Congratulations', composed the personable vocalist's biggest hit of the year.

## MARVIN GAYE
I HEARD IT THROUGH
THE GRAPEVINE
*Tamla Motown*

▲ 1
⑩ 1
70/500

See US entry (December 1968).

## SANDIE SHAW
MONSIEUR DUPONT
*Pye*

▲ 6
⑩ 8•
—/500

In the final year of the decade, Shaw scored the last of her 10 UK Top 20 singles with a German song that had English lyrics penned by Peter

Callander. In the 1980s, the singer, who barely put a foot wrong in the swinging sixties, made a chart comeback in the company of indie rock superstar Morrissey.

## DEAN MARTIN
GENTLE ON MY MIND
*Reprise*

▲ 2
⑩10•
217/500

Twenty years after his first Top 10 entry, one-time heartthrob Martin had the UK hit version of a ballad that Glen Campbell had taken up the US chart. It was the universally acclaimed entertainer's last top-selling single. Composed by folk performer John Hartford, this outstanding song has had more than five million plays on US radio.

## BEE GEES
FIRST OF MAY
*Polydor*

▲ 6
⑩ 5
—/500

Shortly before this top-selling act temporarily split up, they added to their impressive list of UK hits with another top-notch song composed by members Barry, Maurice and Robin Gibb.

## RIGHTEOUS BROTHERS
YOU'VE LOST THAT
LOVIN' FEELIN'
*London American*

▲ 10
⑩ 2
5/500

See US and UK entries (January 1965).

## HOLLIES
SORRY SUZANNE
*Parlophone*

▲ 3
⑩14
450/500

Leading UK tunesmiths Tony Macaulay and Geoff Stevens wrote the ever-successful act's penultimate Top 10 entry of the decade. 'Sorry Suzanne' was their first hit featuring new guitarist/singer Terry Sylvester, who joined from the Swinging Blue Jeans.

## JOE SOUTH
GAMES PEOPLE PLAY
*Capitol*

Eleven years after he first appeared on the US Top 100, this relatively youthful singer, songwriter, producer and top session guitarist (born Joe Souter) from Atlanta had his only transatlantic Top 20 entry as a performer. It was the third major US hit he had composed in the late 1960s, following 'Down In The Boondocks' and 'Hush'. Even though it failed to reach the US Top 10, the instantly infectious song earned the Grammy for Best Song of 1969.

## LULU
BOOM BANG-A-BANG
*Columbia*

This archetypal Eurovision Song Contest entry won the prestigious competition for the UK. 'Boom Bang-A-Bang' was Lulu's most successful UK single of the decade and her last major hit for five years. In the US, her version and a cover by previous chart topper Peggy March were chart casualties.

## TEMPTATIONS
GET READY
*Tamla Motown*

Surprisingly, America's leading male soul group only reached the UK Top 10 once in the decade, and that was with a three-year-old Smokey Robinson-produced and written track which had been one of their smaller US hits. In the US, this anthemic song finally cracked the Top 10 in 1970 by Motown's rock band Rare Earth.

# UNITED STATES
# APRIL 1969

## BLOOD SWEAT & TEARS
YOU'VE MADE ME SO VERY HAPPY

*Columbia*

The US's most successful new group of 1969 chalked up the first of three No 2 hits in a row with their unique interpretation of a Berry Gordy composition that co-writer Brenda Holloway had taken into the Top 40 in 1967. The track came from the pioneering jazz/rock fusion ensemble's chart-topping self-titled second album.

## ISLEY BROTHERS
IT'S YOUR THING
*T-Neck*

As the trio's old Motown recordings registered in the UK, they launched a new funkier image with the first release on their own T-Neck label. The innovative self-penned track won them a Grammy and became the act's biggest US hit to date. The exuberant group, who first found fame in the 1950s, were one of the 1970s top-selling album artists.

## COWSILLS
HAIR
*MGM*

A couple of months after rejecting roles in a TV series loosely based on their lives, this clean-cut family act recorded the title song from the revolutionary rock musical *Hair*. The resulting record gave Barbara Cowsill and her six children their last major hit. Intriguingly, The Cowsills' career faded as the stars of this TV series, The Partridge Family, become internationally successful. The Cowsills, who disbanded in 1972, re-formed in the early 1990s and were surprisingly voted Best Unsigned Band in LA in 1992.

### EDWIN STARR
TWENTY-FIVE MILES
*Gordy*

▲ 6
⑩ 1
—/500

Gutsy vocalist Starr, born Charles Hatcher in Nashville, had a couple of noteworthy R&B chart entries on Detroit's Ric Tic label before it was swallowed up in 1967 by Motown, its universally acclaimed hometown rival. His biggest hit of the decade came with a self-written Stax-styled stomper that the era's hottest R&B label originally rejected. He re-recorded 'Twenty-five Miles' in 1980 for 20th Century and ten years later for the UK label Motorcity, but neither version went the distance.

### STEPPENWOLF
ROCK ME
*Dunhill*

▲ 10
⑩ 3•
—/500

UK sales by Steppenwolf may have been negligible but in the US this track, composed by leader John

Kay, was their third Top 10 entry in a row. 'Rock Me', which was featured in the film *Candy*, came from the album *At Your Birthday Party*, which also completed a trio of Top 10 hits for the hard rockers.

### BOOKER T. & THE MGs
TIME IS TIGHT
*Stax*

▲ 6
⑩ 3•
—/500

The noted instrumental combo had their biggest transatlantic hit of the decade with the group-penned theme from the movie *Uptight*. In 1991 they were inducted into the Rock and Roll Hall of Fame, and four years later picked up a R&B Pioneer Award and a Grammy for Best Instrumental Performance of 1994.

### TOMMY JAMES & THE SHONDELLS
SWEET CHERRY WINE
*Roulette*

▲ 7
⑩ 6
—/500

This Pittsburgh quintet's eleventh Top 40 entry in three years was a psychedelic pop opus penned by their charismatic lead vocalist.

---

# UNITED KINGDOM
# APRIL 1969

---

### DESMOND DEKKER & THE ACES
ISRAELITES
*Pyramid*

▲ 1
⑩ 1
169/500

Before Bob Marley made his mark, his friend Dekker (born Desmond Dacris) was the world's No 1 reggae performer. The Jamaican-born singer/songwriter scored with a strongly patois-oriented opus which was partly unintelligible to most listeners. 'Israelites' was the first reggae record to top the UK chart and the first to break into the US Top 10. When the undeniably

infectious song was re-issued in 1975 it also reached the UK Top 10.

### FOUNDATIONS
IN THE BAD BAD OLD DAYS
*Pye*

▲ 8
⑩ 3•
—/500

The group's manager Tony MacAulay co-wrote the cosmopolitan combo's fourth Top 20 single in 18 months with talented veteran John MacLeod. It was the last noticeable hit for the group, who disbanded in 1970.

## MARY HOPKIN
GOODBYE
*Apple*

▲ 2
🔟 2
267/500

Paul McCartney penned and produced the second of the Welsh songstress' four successive UK Top 10 entries. Coincidentally, the only act that kept this single from the top spot was The Beatles. Ironically, the aptly named 'Goodbye' was the last major US hit for the performer who had been voted Best New Singer of 1968.

## WHO
PINBALL WIZARD
*Track*

▲ 4
🔟 9
481/500

One of the decade's most explosive acts ended the 1960s by successfully introducing rock opera on both sides of the Atlantic. 'Pinball Wizard', the biggest hit from the award-winning *Tommy*, also entered the UK Top 20 by the New Seekers in 1973 and Elton John in 1976. The Roger Daltrey-fronted quartet went on to sell many more millions of records before disbanding in 1982. They were inducted into the Rock and Roll Hall of Fame in 1989 and a US reunion tour later that year grossed a staggering $30 million.

## BEACH BOYS
I CAN HEAR MUSIC
*Capitol*

▲ 10
🔟 9
—/500

A catchy Phil Spector, Ellie Greenwich and Jeff Barry song, which had been a minor hit for The Ronettes in 1966, fared better in the UK for the California superstars than in their homeland. Incidentally, the writers also penned the Beach Boys' earlier UK smash 'Then He Kissed Me'.

## NOEL HARRISON
WINDMILLS OF
YOUR MIND
*Reprise*

▲ 8
🔟 1•
—/500

In his homeland, the son of celebrated British actor Rex Harrison had the hit of the Oscar-winning theme from the Steve McQueen and Faye Dunaway movie *The Thomas Crown Affair*. In the US, Harrison's soundtrack recording of this meritorious ballad was outpaced by compatriot Dusty Springfield's interpretation, which reached the Top 40.

## BEATLES WITH
## BILLY PRESTON
GET BACK
*Apple*

▲ 1
🔟 19
25/500

R&B singer/keyboard player Billy Preston was the only act to receive joint artist billing on a Beatles' hit. Amazingly, this retro-rock song was the only single by the group to enter the UK chart at No 1.

## CLODAGH RODGERS
COME BACK AND
SHAKE ME
*RCA*

▲ 3
🔟 1
408/500

This photogenic Irish vocalist, who had been recording with no noticeable success since 1962, finally clicked with her ninth single. The bouncy ditty was produced and penned for her by noted American Kenny Young. For the next two years Rodgers was the top-selling British female artist in the UK.

# UNITED STATES
# MAY 1969

## VENTURES
HAWAII FIVE-O
*Liberty*

▲ 4
⑩ 3•
—/500

The theme from the popular TV series whisked the Washington-based band into the Top 40 for the sixth and last time. 'Hawaii Five-O' was also the title track to their thirty-second US chart album – a tally that few acts can better.

## SIMON & GARFUNKEL
THE BOXER
*Columbia*

▲ 7
⑩ 5
—/500

Soon after Paul Simon and Art Garfunkel grabbed three Grammy Awards for their music from *The Graduate,* they returned to the Top 10 with another outstanding Simon composition. It was the first single from the act's award-winning transatlantic No 1 album, *Bridge Over Troubled Water.*

## DONOVAN
ATLANTIS
*Epic*

▲ 7
⑩ 4•
—/500

As this well-respected flower child had his only US Top 10 album with a collection of past hits, he journeyed into the US Top 10 with a self-composed tale about the lost land of Atlantis. Nevertheless, his days as a chart maker were numbered and he sold relatively few records after the 1960s.

## BEATLES WITH
## BILLY PRESTON
GET BACK
*Apple*

▲ 1
⑩27
23/500

The last of their 15 Top 5 hits in a row equalled the highest entry record when it debuted at No 10. Also see UK entry (April).

## MERCY
LOVE (CAN MAKE YOU HAPPY)
*Sundi*

▲ 2
⑩ 1•
272/500

Jack Sigler Jr fronted the soft rock group from Florida who guided his haunting composition into the runner-up spot behind 'Get Back' by The Beatles. 'Love (Can Make You Happy)' was one of the first successful singles produced by Steve Alaimo and Brad Shapiro, who in the 1970s produced a string of pop and R&B hits. Neither Mercy nor the Sundi label ever revisited the Top 40.

## RAY STEVENS
GITARZAN
*Monument*

▲ 8
⑩ 2
—/500

After a seven-year absence, the multi-talented entertainer reappeared in the Top 10 with a humorous ode that he had written with saxophonist Bill Justis of 'Raunchy' fame. Stevens, who is arguably the most successful novelty recording artist of the rock era, had two chart-topping singles in the 1970s, and frequently headed the music video bestsellers list in the 1990s.

## GUESS WHO
THESE EYES
*RCA*

▲ 6
⑩ 1
—/500

Canada's most successful rock group of the early 1970s started recording as Chad Allen & The Reflections at the dawn of the 1960s. They adopted the name Guess Who in the mid-1960s and earned a gold record with the third single from their album *Wheatfield Soul.* The top-notch composition, written by lead singer Burton Cummings and lead guitarist Randy Bachman, returned to the US Top 20 later in the year by Jr Walker & The All Stars.

## EDWIN HAWKINS SINGERS
OH HAPPY DAY
*Pavilion*

Gospel music's biggest hit of the 1960s was not intended for commercial release. This 40-plus ensemble, originally known as the Northern California State Youth Choir, recorded an album, *Let Us Go Into The House Of The Lord*, cheaply on a two-track machine in their church's basement. One of the 1,000 copies pressed reached a pop DJ and the rest is history. The uplifting opus, that briefly made his choir international stars, was penned by musical director Hawkins and the lead vocalist was Dorothy Combs Morrison.

## ELVIS PRESLEY
IN THE GHETTO
*RCA*

His first newly recorded transatlantic Top 5 entry for six years showed the pop world that the King was back with a vengeance. The Mac Davis-penned

social message song heralded the end of his film career and the start of a new run of hits for the most influential singer of the century.

## FRIENDS OF DISTINCTION
GRAZIN' IN THE GRASS
*RCA*

In less than a year this smooth and soulful MOR vocal quartet from LA put three singles into the Top 20. The biggest seller of these was a version of South African Hugh Masekela's 1968 instrumental No 1, with lyrics by member Harry Elston. Incidentally, the group were friends of The 5th Dimension, whose vocal style was reminiscent of their own.

# UNITED KINGDOM
# MAY 1969

## JOHNNY NASH
CUPID
*Major Minor*

A song that had taken composer Sam Cooke into the transatlantic Top 20 in 1961 gave the Cooke-influenced vocalist his third UK Top 10 entry in a row. This renowned pop/reggae performer continued his run of hits into the 1970s when, among the things, he introduced the songs of Bob Marley to the chart.

## BOB & EARL
HARLEM SHUFFLE
*Island*

A re-issue of an R&B stomper (arranged by newcomer Barry White) that narrowly missed the US Top 40 in 1963, rocketed the veteran LA duo up the UK charts. After its UK success, they re-recorded their composition on The Turtles' label White Whale – but it sank without trace. Incidentally, Earl (Earl Lee Nelson) had reached the US Top 10 in 1965 as Jackie Lee with 'The Duck'. A revival of 'Harlem Shuffle' by the Rolling Stones in 1985 entered the transatlantic Top 20.

## HERMAN'S HERMITS
MY SENTIMENTAL FRIEND
*Columbia*

▲ 2
⑩ 9
350/500

Ex-Ivy League vocalist John Carter, who co-wrote the first US Top 10 hit for Herman's Hermits ('Can't You Hear My Heartbeat'), also part-penned their last UK Top 10 entry of the decade. The universally acclaimed British act, who were even more popular in the US, sold over 40 million records in the 1960s.

## FLEETWOOD MAC
MAN OF THE WORLD
*Immediate*

▲ 2
⑩ 2
274/500

Only The Beatles prevented Fleetwood Mac from getting back to the top spot for the second time in four months. The mournful but compelling ballad was composed by the group's guitar wizard Peter Green. It was the quintet's only release on Immediate.

## ISLEY BROTHERS
BEHIND A PAINTED SMILE
*Tamla Motown*

▲ 5
⑩ 2
—/500

Even though this achetypal Motown track failed to ignite interest in the US when it was released in 1968, it returned the visually exciting trio to the top end of the UK lists.

## FRANK SINATRA
MY WAY
*Reprise*

▲ 5
⑩ 9
—/500

The multi-award-winning entertainer's 'national anthem' started life in France as 'Comme d'habitude'. Paul Anka penned the English lyric with Sinatra in mind, and the outstanding song soon became a must-record for literally thousands of acts. Ol' Blue Eyes' original version spent an unprecedented 124 weeks in the UK chart.

## SIMON & GARFUNKEL
THE BOXER
*CBS*

▲ 6
⑩ 4
—/500

See US entry.

## TOMMY ROE
DIZZY
*Stateside*

▲ 1
⑩ 4•
163/500

See US entry (March).

## MANFRED MANN
RAGAMUFFIN MAN
*Fontana*

▲ 8
⑩13
—/500

The one-time trend-setting R&B band's last release completed a run of four consecutive Top 10 entries. They disbanded shortly after releasing this bouncy Mitch Murray and Peter Callander composition, which the group personally disliked. In the 1970s, an offshoot, Manfred Mann's Earth Band, had several hits on both sides of the Atlantic.

## TOM JONES
LOVE ME TONIGHT
*Decca*

▲ 9
⑩ 9
—/500

Few solo artists in the 1960s could keep up with Jones when it came to hit making. He collected his sixth transatlantic Top 20 entry with a top-notch rendition of the Italian song, 'Alla Fine Della Strada', for which Barry Mason had provided English lyrics. This energetic showman has never been afraid of venturing down new musical paths, a fact that has helped him retain his position as one of the world's most respected entertainers.

# UNITED STATES
# JUNE 1969

## CREEDENCE CLEARWATER REVIVAL
BAD MOON RISING
*Fantasy*

One of the most popular live acts of the era clocked up the second of their five No 2 hits in the US with another contemporary rockabilly-based classic penned by leader John Fogerty. The record went one better on the other side of the Atlantic.

## HENRY MANCINI & HIS ORCHESTRA
LOVE THEME FROM ROMEO & JULIET
*RCA*

This multi-talented Cleveland-born composer, orchestra leader and pianist has won more Grammy and Oscar awards than any other pop performer. It is therefore surprising that the biggest single of his long and extremely successful career was not self-composed but written by Nino Rota. As amazing, was the fact that the theme to the award-winning film *Romeo And Juliet* was the first Mancini recording on which he had actually played piano.

## MARVIN GAYE
TOO BUSY THINKING ABOUT MY BABY
*Tamla*

According to *Cash Box* magazine, this hook-filled transatlantic Top 10 entry was the Top R&B single of the year in the US. In 1972, a pop version by Mardi Gras reached the UK Top 20.

## THREE DOG NIGHT
ONE
*Dunhill*

Danny Hutton, Cory Wells and Chuck Negron were three recording veterans who teamed up together

to produce one of the most successful American vocal groups of the rock era. The third single from their self-titled debut album was the first of 18 US Top 20 entries. 'One' also introduced composer Nilsson to the upper echelons of the chart.

## OLIVER
GOOD MORNING STARSHINE
*Jubilee*

Eddie Rambeau's recording of this popular song from the successful rock musical *Hair* failed to live up to expectations. It was then decided that Oliver (named after another hit musical) should add his vocal to Rambeau's backing track, and the result gave the pop singer from North Carolina a transatlantic Top 10 entry.

## BLOOD SWEAT & TEARS
SPINNING WHEEL
*Columbia*

British-born lead singer David Clayton Thomas (born David Thomsett) composed this innovative jazz/rock outfit's second Top 3 entry in three months. The trail-blazing act performed it to great effect at a handful of top-line festivals during the summer.

## DESMOND DEKKER & THE ACES
THE ISRAELITES
*UNI*

See UK entry (April).

# UNITED KINGDOM
# JUNE 1969

## BEATLES
BALLAD OF JOHN
AND YOKO
*Apple*

As the decade wound down, the 1960's most successful recording act logged their seventeenth and last UK No 1 with a true-life tale about John Lennon and his new wife. The track, which only featured John and Paul, was the group's smallest US hit – its progress being hampered when the so-called 'blasphemous lyrics' earned it many radio station bans.

## EDWIN HAWKINS SINGERS
OH HAPPY DAY
*Buddah*

See US entry (May).

## BOOKER T. & THE MGs
TIME IS TIGHT
*Stax*

See US entry (April).

## SMOKEY ROBINSON & THE MIRACLES
THE TRACKS OF
MY TEARS
*Tamla Motown*

By the time the instantly recognizable soul group debuted in the UK Top 20 they had 30 US hits under their belts. They finally broke through with a self-penned track which had been a US Top 20 entry four years earlier.

## JETHRO TULL
LIVING IN THE PAST
*Island*

Ian Anderson, a Fagin-like figure who played the flute while standing on one leg, fronted this progressive rock band who had few rivals when it came to selling albums in the first half of the 1970s. The unique group, whose visually striking live performances helped build up a vast following, had their biggest single hit with an Anderson original which finally cracked the US Top 20 more than three years later.

## CLIFF RICHARD
BIG SHIP
*Columbia*

After an unprecedented four successive Top 10 misses, Cliff reappeared with a song penned by country-oriented UK performer Raymond Froggatt, who had written the Dave Clark Five's last major hit, 'Red Balloon'.

## ELVIS PRESLEY
IN THE GHETTO
*RCA*

See US entry (May).

## THUNDERCLAP NEWMAN
SOMETHING IN THE AIR
*Track*

Pete Townshend (from The Who) not only helped assemble this band, he also produced and played bass on their chart-topping single. The captivating composition, that lyrically captured the feel of the time, was penned by the group's drummer John 'Speedy' Keen. 'Something In The Air', which was heard in Ringo Starr's film *The Magic Christian*, also cracked the US Top 40. When the distinctive-looking group's second single and debut album went nowhere, they disbanded.

## BEACH BOYS
BREAK AWAY
*Capitol*

One of the decade's most outstanding and successful acts chalked up their last major hit of the 1960s with another Brian Wilson-penned opus. As usual, it was a showcase for the 'Beach Boys sound' which they had made world-famous during the era. This veritable US institution continued to add to their chart tally in future years, and were rightfully inducted into the Rock and Roll Hall of Fame in 1988.

## CREEDENCE CLEARWATER REVIVAL
PROUD MARY
*Liberty*

See US entry.

---

# UNITED STATES
# JULY 1969

---

## TOMMY JAMES & THE SHONDELLS
CRYSTAL BLUE PERSUASION
*Roulette*

The regular chart entrants notched up their third Top 10 entry in a row with an easy-paced summer song composed by James and group members Mike Vale and Ed Gray. The track was included on the group's only Top 10 album, *Crimson And Clover*. Soon afterwards James embarked on a solo career, but found big hits harder to come by in the 1970s.

## ZAGER & EVANS
IN THE YEAR 2525 (EXORDIUM & TERMINUS)
*RCA*

Rick Evans penned this pessimistic peek into the future back in the year 1964, and the duo spent $500 producing it at ex-Cricket Tommy Allsup's studio in Texas. Initially, they pressed 1,000 copies on their own Truth label, and just weeks after RCA picked up the rights it was topping the charts on both sides of the Atlantic. Despite the fairytale start to their career, the future for these Nebraska natives was also bleak and they quickly returned to obscurity.

## WINSTONS
COLOUR HIM FATHER
*Metromedia*

Richard Spencer, the leader of this soft soul septet from Washington, penned their paean to the perfect pa. 'Colour Him Father' was the first single by the band, who had previously backed The Impressions on the road. To many people's surprise the sentimental pop-slanted opus won the Grammy for Best R&B Song of 1969. It was, however, to be a meteoric rise and fall for the group, whose future releases made little chart headway.

## BEATLES
BALLAD OF JOHN
AND YOKO
*Apple*

See UK entry (June).

## JR WALKER &
## THE ALL STARS
WHAT DOES IT TAKE TO
WIN YOUR LOVE
*Soul*

The US's Top Soul Single of 1969 gave the unique Indiana-based combo their ninth Top 10 R&B hit and ninth Top 40 pop entry of the decade. Although they never cracked the UK Top 10, this single was the second of the combo's four UK Top 20 singles. In 1995, the year Waller died, they were awarded a Pioneer Award from the R&B Foundation.

## STEVIE WONDER
MY CHERIE AMOUR
*Tamla*

After 'I Don't Know Why' dropped off the Top 40, its B side gave the talented performer one of his biggest transatlantic hits of the 1960s. To begin with, Wonder had titled the melodic song 'Oh My Marcia'.

## ANDY KIM
BABY I LOVE YOU
*Steed*

Composer Jeff Barry was a lucky omen for this Canadian singer/songwriter (born Andrew Joachim). Not only did they co-write one of the decade's biggest sellers, 'Sugar Sugar', but Barry also penned two of Kim's top hits and released them on his Steed label. The highest placed of the singer's four Top 40 singles in the 1960s was a Barry song that The Ronettes had scored with in 1964, and the first of his three Top 40 entries in 1970s was Barry's 'Be My Baby', another earlier Ronettes success.

# UNITED KINGDOM
# JULY 1969

## FAMILY DOGG
WAY OF LIFE
*Bell*

American producer Steve Rowland was the mastermind behind the mixed quartet, whose sole claim to fame was their recording of a noteworthy Roger Greenaway and Roger Cook composition. Rowland, who produced chart regulars Dave Dee, Dozy, Beaky, Mick & Tich and The Herd, was a member of the group, as was future hit writer Albert Hammond. Led Zeppelin's Jimmy Page reportedly played guitar on the track.

## PETER SARSTEDT
FROZEN ORANGE JUICE
*UA*

The hottest new UK singer/songwriter of 1969 followed his No 1 single with another self-composed track from his self-titled Top 10 album. Despite the promising start, Eden Kane's brother was unable to keep up the momentum, interest in him soon cooled and future releases proved far less fruitful.

## AMEN CORNER
HELLO SUSIE
*Immediate*

As this top-selling septet headed the star-studded Pop Prom at the Royal Festival Hall, they clocked up their fourth Top 10 entry in a row with a song composed by the Move's mastermind Roy Wood. A couple of months later the group split into two separate acts, neither of which could string together a similar run of hits.

## ROLLING STONES
HONKY TONK WOMEN
*Decca*

The Stones' last single of the 1960s was also the group's last UK chart topper. This rock masterpiece also earned the record-breaking band their fifth US No 1. Unlike arch rivals The Beatles, the Stones kept on rolling and are still regarded as the world's most successful live rock band.

## PLASTIC ONO BAND
GIVE PEACE A CHANCE
*Apple*

Only the Rolling Stones prevented John Lennon's first single outside of The Beatles from reaching the summit. The track was recorded live at a 'bed-in' at the Hotel Le Reine Elizabeth in Montreal, Canada. Reportedly among the members of the so-called Plastic Ono Band on the track were several celebrities including Petula Clark, Timothy Leary, Allen Ginsberg and Tommy Smothers. Soccer fans subsequently adapted the definitive pacifists' anthem, and for many years the chant of 'All we are saying is give us a goal' was heard at matches.

## DESMOND DEKKER & THE ACES
IT MEK
*Pyramid*

This reggae superstar followed his international smash 'Israelites' with another patois song composed with producer Leslie Kong. It was a re-recording of a track he had released with less success a year earlier, and a translation of the title would be 'That's Why It Happened'. The poll-winning Jamaican, who helped open many doors for reggae music, achieved several more UK Top 10 entries in the early 1970s.

## MARMALADE
BABY MAKE IT SOON
*CBS*

Leading UK songwriter Tony MacAulay wrote the last of this Glasgow quintet's hits on the CBS label. The clean-cut crew continued to add to their Top 10 tally in the 1970s despite several personnel changes and a career-threatening exposé about the act's off-stage activities in the tabloids.

## ROBIN GIBB
SAVED BY THE BELL
*Polydor*

His first single after temporarily leaving the Bee Gees only narrowly missed the top spot on the UK charts. The distinctive 19-year-old Manchester-born vocalist composed the emotional ballad that gave him his biggest hit away from his brothers.

## CLODAGH RODGERS
GOODNIGHT MIDNIGHT
*RCA*

For the second time in four months, this Northern Ireland songstress reached the Top 5 with a bouncy pop gem composed by her US producer Kenny Young. The singer, voted Best New Female Artist of 1969 in *NME*, said goodbye to the charts in 1971, the year she represented the UK in the Eurovision Song Contest.

# UNITED STATES
# AUGUST 1969

## KENNY ROGERS & THE FIRST EDITION
RUBY, DON'T TAKE YOUR LOVE TO TOWN
*Reprise*

The group's first transatlantic Top 10 entry held the runner-up position in the UK for six weeks. The song, which told the tale of a badly wounded Vietnam veteran, was composed by country star Mel Tillis and had been a Top 10 country hit in 1967 by Johnny Darrell. This single was the third of seven US Top 40 entries by the group. Rogers reappeared as a solo artist in 1977 and became one of the all-time top-selling acts.

## NEIL DIAMOND
SWEET CAROLINE
*UNI*

Diamond's move to UNI Records was not an instant success. However, after a few mid-table entries, this memorable composition brought the Brooklyn-born entertainer back into the Top 10. 'Sweet Caroline' also introduced him to the UK chart in 1971.

## ROLLING STONES
HONKY TONK WOMEN
*London*

See UK entry (July).

## JOHNNY CASH
A BOY NAMED SUE
*Columbia*

A track recorded live at San Quentin prison gave the legendary performer his only transatlantic Top 5 entry. It was the first time that he had sung this Shel Silverstein-composed novelty, which inspired several answer records including 'A Girl Named Sam', 'A Girl Named Johnny Cash' and even 'A Sioux Named Boy'. Its parent album *Johnny Cash At San Quentin* was the last country LP to head the pop chart for 22 years. Country Hall of Fame member Cash received a Lifetime Grammy in 1990.

## JACKIE DeSHANNON
PUT A LITTLE LOVE IN YOUR HEART
*Imperial*

This talented and prolific singer/songwriter (born Sharon Myers) from Kentucky had the biggest hit of her career with an impassioned plea for brotherhood, which she co-wrote with underrated R&B performer Jimmy Holiday and Randy Myers. The song reappeared in the US Top 10 in 1989 by Annie Lennox and Al Green.

## CREEDENCE CLEARWATER REVIVAL
GREEN RIVER
*Fantasy*

Amazingly, this John Fogerty composed retro-rocker returned the California quartet to the runner-up position for the third time in a row. However, nothing could stop their *Green River* album from reaching the top.

## TONY JOE WHITE
POLK SALAD ANNIE
*Monument*

Swamp rock pioneer White was one of the most innovative and interesting new artists of the late 1960s. The biggest hit of the Louisiana-born singer/songwriter's recording career was a self-composed bayou-beat gem, which Billy Swann helped produce. The song became one of the highlights of Elvis Presley's live show, and it was his version that cracked the UK Top 40 in 1973.

## YOUNGBLOODS
GET TOGETHER
*RCA*

▲ 5
⑩ 1•
—/500

Two years after it had been a minor hit, this 'peace and love' anthem earned the Californian folk-rock quartet their only gold single. Written by Dino Valenti, Youngbloods leader Jesse Colin Young (born Perry Miller) knew the song from Hamilton Camp's recording. Its use as background music to a nationwide promotion for Brotherhood Week gave the single a new lease of life. A rework of 'Get Together' took the Dave Clark Five into the UK Top 10 for the last time in 1970. In 1996 Big Mountain returned it to the US chart.

## GUESS WHO
LAUGHING
*RCA*

▲ 10
⑩ 2
—/500

Two months after the Canadian rock quartet's 'These Eyes' left the Top 10, the original B side 'Laughing' entered. Like the previous hit, it was composed by members Burton Cummings and Randy Bachman. The well-respected Winnipeg band amassed a half dozen more Top 20 entries before disbanding in 1975.

## ARCHIES
SUGAR SUGAR
*Calendar*

▲ 1
⑩ 1
13/500

Don Kirshner, who masterminded The Monkees, was behind the world's most successful single of 1969. Jeff Barry produced this catchy single and the song (a Monkees reject) was composed by Barry and Andy Kim. *The Archies* was a popular cartoon series. Singing on the fictional group's multi-million seller were Ron Dante and Toni Wine (composer of 'Groovy Kind Of Love'). Even though the TV series was not seen there, the record headed the UK charts for eight weeks. A disco update by Dante in 1975 went nowhere.

## BOB DYLAN
LAY LADY LAY
*Columbia*

▲ 7
⑩ 4•
—/500

Dylan, who wrote dozens of hits for other artists, penned 'Lay Lady Lay' with the Everly Brothers in mind. However, they rejected the semi-suggestive song that gave him his fourth and last transatlantic Top 10 entry as a singer. The globally popular performer, who also wrote several chapters in the history of music, was elected to the Rock and Roll Hall of Fame in 1988, and received a Lifetime Grammy award in 1991.

# UNITED KINGDOM
# AUGUST 1969

## JOE DOLAN
MAKE ME AN ISLAND
*Pye*

▲ 3
⑩ 1•
379/500

Ten years after he had launched the popular Drifters Showband in his native Ireland, pop/MOR vocalist Dolan amassed three UK Top 20 singles in a space of just nine months. The highest-ranking of these was his interpretation of a noteworthy Albert Hammond composition.

## STEVIE WONDER
MY CHERIE AMOUR
*Tamla Motown*

▲ 4
⑩ 3
449/500

See US entry (July).

## CILLA BLACK
CONVERSATIONS
*Parlophone*

▲ 7
⑩ 10
—/500

Few artists clocked up more big UK hits in the swinging sixties than the one-time cloakroom attendant at Liverpool's famous Cavern Club. Her tenth Top 10 entry in six years was composed by early 1960s chart regular Jerry Lordan and the hot writing team of Roger Greenaway and Roger Cook. When Black's pop star days ended, she went on to become one of the UK's most successful TV personalities.

## VANITY FARE
EARLY IN THE MORNING
*Page One*

One of the few British pop groups in the late 1960s who sold equally well across the Atlantic was this quartet from Kent fronted by Trevor Brice. The first of their two transatlantic Top 20 entries was an immediately infectious sing-along opus composed by Mike Leander and Eddie Seago.

## LOVE AFFAIR
BRINGING ON BACK THE
GOOD TIMES
*CBS*

Love Affair's fifth consecutive Top 20 entry was also their last chart single. Like the act's earlier hit 'A Day Without Love' it was composed by singer/songwriter Philip Goodhand-Tait. When popular lead singer Steve Ellis left the band soon afterwards, they changed their named to LA, hoping in vain to appeal to a hipper audience.

## MAX ROMEO
WET DREAM
*Unity*

Despite being banned by the BBC, this controversial British-recorded reggae song was the Jamaican performer's only UK pop hit. Romeo (born Max Smith) wrote the popular club track which opened the door for rude-reggae in the UK.

## ZAGER & EVANS
IN THE YEAR 2525
(EXORDIUM & TERMINUS)
*RCA*

See US entry (July).

## MARVIN GAYE
TOO BUSY THINKING
ABOUT MY BABY
*Tamla Motown*

See US entry (June).

## EQUALS
VIVA BOBBIE JOE
*President*

Colourful South London-based pop/ska band The Equals returned to the Top 10 with a catchy Eddy Grant composition, which was adopted by football fans as 'Viva Bobby Moore' (the captain of England's 1966 World Cup-winning side). Grant, who left the band in the early 1970s, later had a run of hits as a soloist.

## CREEDENCE CLEARWATER REVIVAL
BAD MOON RISING
*Liberty*

See US entry (June).

## BEE GEES
DON'T FORGET TO
REMEMBER
*Polydor*

One of the decade's best-selling bands narrowly missed the top with their last hit of the 1960s. When they trimmed down to a trio in the 1970s, the unmistakable British-born family group were even more successful. In the 1990s it was reported that the record-breaking multi-award-winning Gibb brothers had sold over 100 million records globally.

# UNITED STATES
# SEPTEMBER 1969

## THREE DOG NIGHT
EASY TO BE HARD
*Dunhill*

▲ 4
⑩ 2
405/500

The distinctive LA harmony trio had the hit version of one of the show-stopping songs from the lauded rock musical *Hair*. It was taken from the group's Top 20 album *Suitable For Framing*, which earned them their second of 12 successive gold albums.

## TOM JONES
I'LL NEVER FALL
IN LOVE AGAIN
*Parrot*

▲ 6
⑩ 3
—/500

See UK entry (August 1967).

## TEMPTATIONS
I CAN'T GET NEXT
TO YOU
*Gordy*

▲ 1
⑩10
61/500

Dennis Edwards sang lead on the group's ninth No 1 R&B hit of the decade. It also shipped the record-breaking quintet into the transatlantic Top 20 for the fourth time. In 1970, this Norman Whitfield and Barrett Strong song launched newcomer Al Green into the R&B Top 20.

## OLIVER
JEAN
*Crewe*

▲ 2
⑩ 2•
271/500

Composer/poet Rod McKuen wrote the song that lifted Oliver (born Williams Swafford) into the Top 10 for the second time in three months. The memorable ballad, penned for the Maggie Smith movie *The Prime Of Miss Jean Brodie*, was the vocalist's last notable hit.

## BOBBY SHERMAN
LITTLE WOMAN
*Metromedia*

▲ 3
⑩ 1
333/500

Before he started his impressive run of US-only hits, the last teen idol of the decade had recorded several forgettable flops for a handful of labels. The California-born star of TV's *Here Come The Brides* amassed three million-selling singles in six months. Both 'Little Woman' and the singer/actor/multi-instrumentalist's equally successful follow-up, 'La La La (If I Had You)' were written for him by Danny Janssen.

## SLY & THE
## FAMILY STONE
HOT FUN IN THE
SUMMERTIME
*Epic*

▲ 2
⑩ 3
291/500

Among the best-received performers at Woodstock was this much-imitated psychedelic soul combo from San Francisco. Coincidentally, the only act that stood between 'Hot Fun In The Summertime' and the top place were The Temptations, whose new sound owed much to the influential outfit. The group, who were even more successful in the 1970s, joined the Rock and Roll Hall of Fame in 1993.

## DELLS
OH WHAT A NITE
*Cadet*

▲ 10
⑩ 2•
—/500

A revival of a song that had given them their first hit in 1956 returned the soulful vocal group to the top of the R&B charts – a chart they scored on in four different decades. Among this underrated group's other outstanding singles were the similarly themed 'Oh What A Day' and 'Oh What A Good Nite'.

## UNITED KINGDOM
# SEPTEMBER 1969

### JANE BIRKIN & SERGE GAINSBOURG
JE T'AIME...MOI NON PLUS
*Fontana/Major Minor*

▲ 1
🔟 1•
121/500

The first foreign-language record to top the British chart was also the sexiest single of the swinging sixties. The two-million selling orgasmic ode was composed and performed by Frenchman Gainsbourg and Londoner Birkin. This influential sex-simulating single was banned by the BBC and dropped by Fontana when it reached No 2 – it was left to Major Minor to take it all the way. An instrumental version, 'Love At First Sight' by Sounds Nice, also entered the Top 20, and in 1975 Judge Dread reinstated it in the Top 10.

### HUMBLE PIE
NATURAL BORN BUGIE
*Immediate*

▲ 4
🔟 1•
—/500

Even though the main ingredients of Humble Pie were British-only hit makers Steve Marriott (from The Small Faces) and Peter Frampton (from The Herd), they sold more records in the US than the UK. The photogenic supergroup's Marriott-penned debut disc was their only UK chart single.

### OLIVER
GOOD MORNING STARSHINE
*CBS*

▲ 6
🔟 1•
—/500

See US entry (June).

### BOBBIE GENTRY
I'LL NEVER FALL IN LOVE AGAIN
*Capitol*

▲ 1
🔟 1
151/500

Despite the fact that this popular Las Vegas performer's version of the best-known song from Bacharach & David's musical *Promises, Promises* topped the UK chart, it lost out to Dionne Warwick's treatment in her homeland. In 1990 Deacon Blue brought the ballad back into the UK Top 3.

### JOHNNY CASH
A BOY NAMED SUE
*CBS*

▲ 4
🔟 1
470/500

See US entry (August).

# UNITED STATES
# OCTOBER 1969

## NILSSON
EVERYBODY'S TALKIN'
*RCA*

In the late 1960s, it seemed that everybody was talking about this New York-born performer (real name Harry Nelson III). It is therefore surprising that his biggest hit of the decade was the only non-original song on his album *Aerial Ballet*. The catchy 'Everybody's Talkin'' was composed and originally recorded by another singer/songwriter, Fred Neil. Nilsson's Grammy-winning version was first released in 1968, but was overlooked until it was heard in the box office smash *Midnight Cowboy*.

## GARY PUCKETT & THE UNION GAP
THIS GIRL IS A WOMAN NOW
*Columbia*

As the decade drew to a close, this unmistakable pop group notched up their sixth successive Top 20 entry. The act, whose first four hits all earned gold records, disbanded in 1971.

## ELVIS PRESLEY
SUSPICIOUS MINDS
*RCA*

Rock music's biggest-selling solo singer achieved his last US No 1 with a song written and originally recorded by Mark James. Interestingly, among the backing singers on Presley's first chart topper for seven years was later country superstar Ronnie Milsap.

## MARVIN GAYE
THAT'S THE WAY LOVE IS
*Tamla*

One of the best-known and biggest-selling R&B singers had his last hit of the soulful sixties with a stand-out Norman Whitfield and Barrett Strong song. During the following decade Gaye recorded some of the most outstanding and boundary-stretching tracks of the rock era. The singer, who was shot and killed by his father in 1984, left an indelible mark on the pop music scene.

## 5TH DIMENSION
WEDDING BELL BLUES
*Soul City*

Soon after group members Marilyn McCoo and Billy Davis married each other, Marilyn sang lead on the MOR vocal quintet's second chart topper, 'Wedding Bell Blues'. It was the third Laura Nyro composition that they had taken into the Top 20. The track came from their album *The Age Of Aquarius,* which reached the runner-up position. The distinctive group's run of single and album successes continued unto the mid-1970s, and then McCoo & Davis recorded as a duo.

## CUFF LINKS
TRACY
*Decca*

New Yorker Ron Dante (born Carmine Granito) was not only the lead vocalist of the chart-topping Archies but also the singer of this fictitious group's debut hit. In fact, all the many voices heard on the transatlantic Top 10 entry belong to Dante. The record was masterminded by one of the great pop teams of the decade, Lee Pockriss and Paul Vance. In retrospect, it seems hard to imagine that almost 20 labels rejected 'Tracy' before Decca snapped it up.

## SMITH
BABY IT'S YOU
*Dunhill*

Early 1960s chart regular Del Shannon arranged this Steve Barri produced remake of The Shirelles' 1962 Top 10 entry. The short-lived LA rock quintet's inventive interpretation of the memorable Bacharach & David ballad was their only Top 40 entry. When Smith split, St Louis-born singer Gayle McCormick had a couple of minor hits as a soloist.

## LOU CHRISTIE
I'M GONNA MAKE YOU MINE
*Buddah*

Only The Archies prevented Lou Christie's last major hit from topping the UK charts. Singing backing vocals on this Tony Romeo song were composer Ellie Greenwich and previous hit maker Linda Scott.

---

# UNITED KINGDOM
# OCTOBER 1969

---

## CLIFF & HANK
THROW DOWN A LINE
*Columbia*

The record-breaking singer, who had yet to crack the US Top 20, clocked up his thirty-third UK Top 10 entry of the decade. On the first of his many bestselling duets he was joined by the song's composer Hank Marvin. Cliff went on to notch up over 90 UK Top 20 hits, and was the first act to put 60 singles into the UK Top 10.

## MAMA CASS
IT'S GETTING BETTER
*Stateside*

This ex-Mamas and The Papas member (born Ellen Cohen) followed her successful revival of 'Dream A Little Dream Of Me' (which peaked at No 11 in both the US and the UK) with a Barry Mann and Cynthia Weil song that fared better in the UK than in her homeland. In 1974, the larger-than-life performer died of a heart attack at Harry Nilsson's London apartment (where Who drummer Keith Moon died in 1978).

## BOB DYLAN
LAY LADY LAY
*CBS*

See US entry (August).

## KAREN YOUNG
NOBODY'S CHILD
*Major Minor*

Her version of this tearjerking ode about an orphan transported the Sheffield-born MOR singer into the charts for the only time. 'Nobody's Child' was the sixth single by the cabaret entertainer who was discovered by The Bachelors in 1962. The oft-recorded folk/country favourite had been a mid-table country hit for Hank Williams Jr in 1967.

## LOU CHRISTIE
I'M GONNA MAKE YOU MINE
*Buddah*

See US entry.

## HOLLIES
HE AIN'T HEAVY,
HE'S MY BROTHER
*Parlophone*

A moving song penned by Bobby Scott and Bobby Russell (who died of cancer as the record hit) hurled The Hollies into the transatlantic Top 10 for the fourth and last time in the decade. The pianist on the track was the up-and-coming singer/songwriter Elton John. This heartfelt ballad had previously been recorded by both Kelly Gordon and Joe Cocker. Interestingly, The Hollies' single returned to top the UK chart in 1988 after being used in a TV advertisement for beer.

## DAVID BOWIE
SPACE ODDITY
*Philips*

One of the most innovative, influential and successful rock artists (born David Jones) first charted with a song about Major Tom, which he had written for a never seen TV film. 'Space Oddity' was produced by Gus Dudgeon and arranged by

Paul Buckmaster, who worked on many later Elton John hits. It finally docked in the US Top 20 in 1973, and rocketed to the top in the UK when re-issued in 1975. The trendsetting multi-million seller also piloted a sequel, 'Ashes To Ashes' to No 1 in the UK in 1980.

## FLEETWOOD MAC
OH WELL
*Reprise*

Five years before they exploded on to the US scene, the popular UK band had their first US Top 100 entry with an innovative and intriguing Peter Green-penned opus that helped them become the most successful chart act in the UK in 1969. It was the group's third UK Top 3 single in less than a year – each one being on a different label.

## ARCHIES
SUGAR SUGAR
*RCA*

See US entry (August).

---

## UNITED STATES
# NOVEMBER 1969

---

## BLOOD SWEAT & TEARS
AND WHEN I DIE
*Columbia*

Their interpretation of this noteworthy Laura Nyro composition was the last of a record-breaking three gold singles taken from the acclaimed group's triple platinum and triple Grammy-winning eponymous album. The ground-breaking band, who the *LA Times* felt 'May be the most important new pop group of the decade', retained their popularity in the early 1970s but never repeated the success of '69.

## FLYING MACHINE
SMILE A LITTLE SMILE
FOR ME
*Janus*

Top British songwriter/producers Tony MacAulay and Geoff Stevens used session singers to record this bouncy pop ditty, and the single flew up the US charts. When the US demanded a tour, the producers sent over the current line-up of Pinkerton's Assorted Colours, who had hit in the UK with 'Mirror Mirror' in 1966. The fictitious group then boarded a one-way flight to oblivion.

## R.B. GREAVES
TAKE A LETTER MARIA
*Atco*

Sam Cooke's Guyana-born nephew is one of a small number of artists raised on a US Indian reservation to have graced the charts. This California-based R&B performer almost joined the roll of No 1 hit makers with his self-penned cheating song, which was produced by veteran chart regular Ahmet Ertegun. In 1970, Anthony Armstrong Jones (named after Princess Margaret's then husband) delivered it into the country Top 10.

## STEAM
NA NA HEY HEY KISS
HIM GOODBYE
*Fontana*

When singer Garrett Scott (born Gary DeCarlo in Connecticut) needed a throwaway B side he quickly recorded a song he had written years earlier, and producer Paul Leka (who played with Scott in those early days) added the 'Na Na Hey Hey' chorus. When Fontana insisted it was an A side, Scott refused to let them release it under his name, and so Steam was born. The anthemic opus returned to the UK Top 10 in 1983 by Bananarama and to the US Top 20 in 1987 by acappella act The Nylons.

## STEVIE WONDER
YESTER-ME, YESTER-YOU,
YESTERDAY
*Tamla*

Ron Miller, who composed 'For Once In My Life' and 'A Place in The Sun' also penned Wonder's fourth transatlantic Top 10 entry of the decade. The artist's most successful UK single to date was produced by Johnny Bristol. In future years this innovative artist went on to collect numerous awards, play to packed stadiums around the globe and stockpile many more hit singles and albums.

## BEATLES
COME TOGETHER/
SOMETHING
*Apple*

Initally both sides entered the Top 5 separately, and the record then jumped to the top when the sales were combined. See also UK entry.

## PETER, PAUL & MARY
LEAVING ON A JET PLANE
*Warner*

The award-winning trio's biggest seller on either side of the Atlantic was the first hit penned by fellow folk performer John Denver. The song, which started life as 'Babe I Have To Go', was the last of 12 Top 40 entries by the 1960s superstar act that disbanded in 1971.

## CREEDENCE CLEARWATER REVIVAL
DOWN ON THE CORNER/
FORTUNATE SON
*Fantasy*

This universally acclaimed band ended the 1960s with a double-sided hit. Both of the outstanding songs came from the prolific pen of John Fogarty, whose departure from CCR in 1971 led to its demise soon afterwards. The swamp rock quartet, who were voted World's Top Group in UK polls in 1970, joined the elite in the Rock and Roll Hall of Fame in 1993.

## THREE DOG NIGHT
ELI'S COMING
*Dunhill*

Three Dog Night's third consecutive Top 10 entry meant that composer Laura Nyro had three songs simultaneously in the US Top 10! The unmistakable trio continued to chalk up top US hits in the early 1970s, although across the Atlantic they remained relatively unknown.

# UNITED KINGDOM
# NOVEMBER 1969

## UPSETTERS
THE RETURN OF
DJANGO/DOLLAR
IN THE TEETH
*Upsetter*

There was an upsurge of interest in reggae in the UK in late 1969. Three singles entered the Top 10, two of which featured The Upsetters. This top-ranking Jamaican session band, assembled by the multi-talented Lee Perry, not only had their own hit but also played on Harry J's 'Liquidator'. The group, whose personnel often changed, were among the busiest recording bands in the West Indies. The prolific Perry penned the influential 'The Return Of Django' which featured saxophonist player Val Bennett.

## FRANK SINATRA
LOVE'S BEEN GOOD
TO ME
*Reprise*

Sinatra was one of the surprise success stories of the late 1960s. The legendary performer, who had sung on the first US No 1 (Tommy Dorsey's 'I'll Never Smile Again' in 1940), ended the decade with a Top 10 ballad composed by Rod McKuen. The decade's top-selling male album artist was still adding to his collection of gold LPs in the 1990s.

## JOE COCKER
DELTA LADY
*Regal Zonophone*

A song that Leon Russell had written about singer Rita Coolidge returned this unmistakable vocalist to the heights in his homeland. Although it was only a minor hit single in the US, the track appeared on the Russell-produced *Joe Cocker!* album, which reached the Top 20. The surprise star of Woodstock continued to notch up transatlantic chart entries over the following decades.

## TREMELOES
(CALL ME) NUMBER ONE
*CBS*

Despite its title, the popular band only reached runner-up position with this potent pop opus composed by Alan Blaikley and the group's newly wed frontman 'Chip' Hawkes. Incidentally, 21 years later Chip's son Chesney topped the chart with another 'one' song, 'The One And Only'.

## BEATLES
SOMETHING/
COME TOGETHER
*Apple*

The Beatles' last hit of the decade was their sixty-first US chart entry in six years and the group's eighteenth No 1, breaking a record set by Elvis Presley. The oft-recorded George Harrison composition 'Something' was the act's first A side not written by Lennon & McCartney. Surprisingly, it was the group's lowest-ranking UK single since 'Love Me Do'. However, both songs reappeared in the UK Top 10: 'Something', which Joe Cocker had rejected earlier, charted for Shirley Bassey in 1970, and 'Come Together' clicked in 1992 courtesy of Michael Jackson.

## JIMMY CLIFF
WONDERFUL WORLD
BEAUTIFUL PEOPLE
*Trojan*

This Jamaican reggae performer (born James Chambers) followed in Desmond Dekker's footsteps, when his first release after leaving Island Records reached the Top 40 on both sides of the Atlantic. Grammy winner Cliff is probably the best-known living reggae performer. He has had hits of his own, written a handful of top sellers for other artists and appeared in several successful films.

## JETHRO TULL
SWEET DREAM
*Chrysalis*

Chrysalis Records' first major hit single came courtesy of a praiseworthy Ian Anderson composition. It gave his distinctive band the second of four UK Top 20 entries in succession. The record was released soon after the act, voted Best New Group of 1969 in the *NME* poll, had topped the UK LP chart with *Stand Up*. After this dream start they went from strength to strength, notching up a long string of transatlantic Top 20 albums in the 1970s.

## KENNY ROGERS &
## THE FIRST EDITION
RUBY, DON'T TAKE YOUR
LOVE TO TOWN
*Reprise*

See US entry (August).

## STEVIE WONDER
YESTER-ME, YESTER-YOU,
YESTERDAY
*Tamla Motown*

See US entry.

## HARRY J. &
## THE ALL STARS
LIQUIDATOR
*Trojan*

Successful Jamaican producer and keyboard player Harry Johnson teamed with his musical arranger Lee Perry's studio group The Upsetters to form this instrumental reggae quintet. 'Liquidator', which influenced The Staple Singers' 1972 US No 1 'I'll Take You There', also re-entered the UK chart in 1980. Harry J released a sequel, 'The Return Of The Liquidator', in 1992.

# UNITED STATES
# DECEMBER 1969

## DIANA ROSS &
## THE SUPREMES
SOMEDAY WE'LL
BE TOGETHER
*Motown*

Their final single with Diana Ross singing lead was the last of the record-breaking trio's dozen chart toppers. It was written and produced by Johnny Bristol, who had earlier released it as part of the duo Johnny & Jackey. Ross went on to become one of the world's top entertainers, and the Supremes clocked up a further three transatlantic Top 20 entries before disbanding in 1976. The group were inducted into the Rock and Roll Hall of Fame in 1988.

## B.J. THOMAS
RAINDROPS KEEP FALLIN'
ON MY HEAD
*Scepter*

A ballad that composers Bacharach & David initially wanted Ray Stevens to record gave this Texas-raised singer his biggest hit of the decade. The Academy Award-winning song came from the smash movie *Butch Cassidy & The Sundance Kid*. In the UK, Sacha Distell steered it into the Top 10. Thomas went on to have many more pop/country and gospel successes in future years.

## MEL & TIM
BACKFIELD IN MOTION
*Bamboo*

▲ 10
⑩ 1•
—/500

Many years before sisters Mel & Kim made a name for themselves with dance tracks, this similarly named family duo earned a gold disc with a self-composed booty-shaking floor-filler. The St Louis-based Mel Hardin and Tim McPherson's single was produced by R&B star Gene Chandler and was their second release on his Bamboo label. For the record books, the cousins' aptly named comeback hit 'Starting All Over Again' on Stax in 1972 was the act's last top seller.

## NEIL DIAMOND
HOLLY HOLY
*UNI*

▲ 6
⑩ 4
—/500

One of the rock era's biggest-selling superstars earned his second US gold disc in six months with another of his commercial compositions. Interestingly, although he had already scored several UK chart entries as a songwriter, Diamond had to wait until the 1970s before he had a UK hit of his own.

## JACKSON FIVE
I WANT YOU BACK
*Motown*

▲ 1
⑩ 1
120/500

In the last week of the decade, one of the most important acts of the rock era debuted in the Top 10. Gladys Knight initially alerted Berry Gordy to 11-year-old Michael Jackson and his four brothers from Indiana, and the label owner organized their momentous move from Steeltown Records to Motown. Gordy co-wrote and co-produced 'I Want You Back', which coincidentally was originally intended for Gladys Knight. It was the first of four consecutive US No 1s for the act who sold countless millions of records globally in the 1970s.

## LED ZEPPELIN
WHOLE LOTTA LOVE
*Atlantic*

▲ 4
⑩ 1•
409/500

Only The Beatles can claim more multi-platinum albums than these amazingly influential heavy rock pioneers. This group-composed rock anthem was extracted from the chart-topping *Led Zeppelin II* album – the first of the supergroup's eight consecutive transatlantic Top 3 albums. In the UK, where they refused to release singles, CCS had the hit. Intriguingly, Led Zeppelin were the first act to refuse to appear on *Top Of The Pops*; the successful British TV show which used 'Whole Lotta Love' as its theme tune.

# UNITED KINGDOM
# DECEMBER 1969

## ROLF HARRIS
TWO LITTLE BOYS
*Columbia*

▲ 1
⑩ 3
13/500

This turn-of-the-century music hall song was not only 1969's Top Single in the UK, but it made the multi-talented entertainer the first Australian solo artist to head the chart. The unique and innovative performer returned to the Top 10 in 1993 with a wobble board-driven version of Led Zeppelin's classic 'Stairway To Heaven'.

## BLUE MINK
MELTING POT
*Philips*

▲ 3
⑩ 1
314/500

Top songwriter Roger Cook hand picked the multi-racial band Blue Mink from the UK's top session musicians and vocalists. He and US R&B vocalist Madeline Bell fronted the group that amassed six UK-only Top 20 entries. This award-winning plea for universal brotherhood was composed by Cook and his long-term writing partner Roger Greenaway.

**ELVIS PRESLEY**
SUSPICIOUS MINDS
*RCA*

See US entry (October).

**ENGELBERT HUMPERDINCK**
WINTER WORLD OF LOVE
*Decca*

As the decade ended, one of the 1960's best-selling balladeers had his last transatlantic Top 20 entry with his third major hit composed by Les Reed and Barry Mason. The seasonal song was included on the cabaret king's first US Top 5 album, *Engelbert Humperdinck.*

**MARVIN GAYE & TAMMI TERRELL**
ONION SONG
*Tamla Motown*

One of the top-selling soul duo's least successful US singles gave them their biggest UK hit. Like the majority of Gaye and Terrell's duets, it was composed by Ashord and Simpson, who became a leading R&B vocal duo themselves in the 1980s.

**BOBBIE GENTRY & GLEN CAMPBELL**
ALL I HAVE TO DO IS DREAM
*Capitol*

The teaming of two of the late 1960s most acclaimed new easy-listening artists proved a wise commercial move. Their update of a beautiful Boudleaux Bryant rock ballad was especially successful in the UK. This often-recorded classic had previously reached the US Top 20 in 1963 by Richard Chamberlain, and in 1994 a duet by Phil Everly (whose version with brother Don had been a transatlantic topper in 1958) and Cliff Richard returned it to the UK Top 20.

**CUFF LINKS**
TRACY
*MCA*

See US entry (October).

# THE US
# TOP 100 ARTISTS
# IN 1960–69

1 BEATLES
2 SUPREMES
3 ELVIS PRESLEY
4 FOUR SEASONS
5 ROLLING STONES
6 BEACH BOYS
7 BRENDA LEE
8 HERMAN'S HERMITS
9 CONNIE FRANCIS
10 RAY CHARLES
11 TEMPTATIONS
12 BOBBY VINTON
13 MARVIN GAYE
14 CHUBBY CHECKER
15 ROY ORBISON
16 DION
17 STEVIE WONDER
18 ARETHA FRANKLIN
19 MONKEES
20 DAVE CLARK FIVE
21 TOMMY JAMES & THE SHONDELLS
22 YOUNG RASCALS
23 EVERLY BROTHERS
24 GARY LEWIS & THE PLAYBOYS
25 SHIRELLES
26 JOHNNY RIVERS
27 BOBBY VEE
28 PETULA CLARK
29 MAMAS & THE PAPAS
30 LOVIN' SPOONFUL
31 DIONNE WARWICK
32 FOUR TOPS
33 SIMON & GARFUNKEL
34 PETER, PAUL & MARY
35 RIGHTEOUS BROTHERS

36 TOMMY ROE
37 ASSOCIATION
38 RICKY NELSON
39 5TH DIMENSION
40 BOBBY DARIN
41 TURTLES
42 UNION GAP FEATURING GARY PUCKETT
43 NEIL SEDAKA
44 DINAH WASHINGTON & BROOK BENTON
45 MARTHA & THE VANDELLAS
46 JAMES BROWN
47 NANCY SINATRA
48 BOBBY RYDELL
49 CREEDENCE CLEARWATER REVIVAL
50 GARY U.S. BONDS
51 LESLEY GORE
52 MIRACLES
53 DONOVAN
54 DOORS
55 JACKIE WILSON
56 DRIFTERS
57 FRANK SINATRA
58 ROGER MILLER
59 JAN & DEAN
60 JAY & THE AMERICANS
61 JOHNNY TILLOTSON
62 BOB DYLAN
63 PAUL REVERE & THE RAIDERS
64 MARY WELLS
65 VOGUES
66 GENE PITNEY
67 SLY & THE FAMILY STONE
68 BLOOD SWEAT & TEARS

69 B.J. THOMAS
70 CRYSTALS
71 DEE DEE SHARP
72 HERB ALPERT
73 NEIL DIAMOND
74 DEL SHANNON
75 ORLONS
76 SAM COOKE
77 BUCKINGHAMS
78 CLASSICS IV
79 SHANGRI-LAS
80 CHIFFONS
81 ZOMBIES
82 SONNY & CHER
83 FLOYD CRAMER
84 COWSILLS
85 MARVIN GAYE & TAMMI TERRELL
86 MARVELETTES
87 BYRDS
88 STEVE LAWRENCE
89 VENTURES
90 1910 FRUITGUM CO
91 PETER & GORDON
92 DEAN MARTIN
93 STEPPENWOLF
94 LOU CHRISTIE
95 BOX TOPS
96 JERRY BUTLER
97 ANIMALS
98 THREE DOG NIGHT
99 FERRANTE & TEICHER
100 GENE MCDANIELS

# THE UK
# TOP 100 ARTISTS
# IN 1960–69

1 CLIFF RICHARD
2 BEATLES
3 ELVIS PRESLEY
4 ROLLING STONES
5 SHADOWS
6 HOLLIES
7 MANFRED MANN
8 ROY ORBISON
9 KINKS
10 ADAM FAITH
11 BEACH BOYS
12 BILLY FURY
13 TOM JONES
14 ENGELBERT HUMPERDINCK
15 CILLA BLACK
16 EVERLY BROTHERS
17 GENE PITNEY
18 SANDIE SHAW
19 DEL SHANNON
20 FRANK IFIELD
21 HERMAN'S HERMITS
22 DUSTY SPRINGFIELD
23 WHO
24 SUPREMES
25 BACHELORS
26 DAVE DEE, DOZY, BEAKY, MICK & TICH
27 PETULA CLARK
28 GERRY & THE PACEMAKERS
29 SEARCHERS
30 ANIMALS
31 SEEKERS
32 SMALL FACES
33 JIM REEVES
34 SHIRLEY BASSEY

35 BEE GEES
36 TREMELOES
37 HELEN SHAPIRO
38 DONOVAN
39 BOBBY VEE
40 BRENDA LEE
41 DAVE CLARK FIVE
42 ANTHONY NEWLEY
43 BOBBY DARIN
44 DUANE EDDY
45 BILLY J. KRAMER & THE DAKOTAS
46 MOVE
47 CONNIE FRANCIS
48 TROGGS
49 LONNIE DONEGAN
50 VAL DOONICAN
51 YARDBIRDS
52 BOB DYLAN
53 FOUR TOPS
54 MONKEES
55 FRANK SINATRA
56 EDEN KANE
57 LULU
58 KEN DODD
59 BRIAN POOLE & THE TREMELOES
60 SPENCER DAVIS GROUP
61 MATT MONRO
62 AMEN CORNER
63 STEVIE WONDER
64 CRAIG DOUGLAS
65 ACKER BILK
66 FREDDIE & THE DREAMERS
67 RAY CHARLES

68 TOMMY ROE
69 NEIL SEDAKA
70 GEORGIE FAME
71 WALKER BROTHERS
72 PETER & GORDON
73 LOVE AFFAIR
74 FLEETWOOD MAC
75 NANCY SINATRA
76 JET HARRIS & TONY MEEHAN
77 ROLF HARRIS
78 KENNY BALL
79 JIMI HENDRIX EXPERIENCE
80 DES O'CONNOR
81 FOUNDATIONS
82 P.J. PROBY
83 FRANKIE VAUGHAN
84 ANDY WILLIAMS
85 KARL DENVER
86 JOE BROWN & THE BRUVVERS
87 MARVIN GAYE
88 MARIANNE FAITHFULL
89 SIMON & GARFUNKEL
90 MARMALADE
91 FOUR SEASONS
92 MARY HOPKIN
93 MAMAS & THE PAPAS
94 CHRIS MONTEZ
95 BRIAN HYLAND
96 JIMMY JONES
97 TORNADOS
98 TRAFFIC
99 DAVE BERRY
100 JOHN LEYTON

# THE US
# TOP 500 SINGLES
# 1960–69

**1 THE TWIST**
CHUBBY CHECKER
*PARKWAY*

**2 HEY JUDE**
BEATLES
*APPLE*

**3 THEME FROM 'A SUMMER PLACE'**
PERCY FAITH
*COLUMBIA*

**4 TOSSIN' AND TURNIN'**
BOBBY LEWIS
*BELTONE*

**5 I WANT TO HOLD YOUR HAND**
BEATLES
*CAPITOL*

**6 I'M A BELIEVER**
MONKEES
*COLGEMS*

**7 I HEARD IT THROUGH THE GRAPEVINE**
MARVIN GAYE
*TAMLA*

**8 AQUARIUS/LET THE SUNSHINE IN**
FIFTH DIMENSION
*SOUL CITY*

**9 ARE YOU LONESOME TONIGHT?**
ELVIS PRESLEY
*RCA*

**10 IT'S NOW OR NEVER**
ELVIS PRESLEY
*RCA*

**11 RAINDROPS KEEP FALLIN' ON MY HEAD**
B.J. THOMAS
*SCEPTER*

**12 I CAN'T STOP LOVING YOU**
RAY CHARLES
*ABC PARAMOUNT*

**13 SUGAR SUGAR**
ARCHIES
*CALENDAR*

**14 LOVE IS BLUE**
PAUL MAURIAT
*PHILIPS*

**15 BIG GIRLS DON'T CRY**
FOUR SEASONS
*VEE JAY*

**16 IN THE YEAR 2525 (EXORDIUM & TERMINUS)**
ZAGER & EVANS
*RCA*

**17 SUGAR SHACK**
JIMMY GILMER & THE FIREBALLS
*DOT*

**18 CATHY'S CLOWN**
EVERLY BROTHERS
*WARNER*

**19 BIG BAD JOHN**
JIMMY DEAN
*COLUMBIA*

**20 TO SIR WITH LOVE**
LULU
*EPIC*

**21 HONEY**
BOBBY GOLDSBORO
*UA*

**22 PEOPLE GOT TO BE FREE**
RASCALS
*ATLANTIC*

**23 GET BACK**
BEATLES
*APPLE*

**24 HONKY TONK WOMEN**
ROLLING STONES
*LONDON*

**25 (SITTIN' ON) THE DOCK OF THE BAY**
OTIS REDDING
*VOLT*

**26 ROSES ARE RED (MY LOVE)**
BOBBY VINTON
*EPIC*

**27 SHERRY**
FOUR SEASONS
*VEE JAY*

**28 STUCK ON YOU**
ELVIS PRESLEY
*RCA*

**29 DAYDREAM BELIEVER**
MONKEES
*COLGEMS*

**30 EVERYDAY PEOPLE**
SLY & THE FAMILY STONE
*EPIC*

**31 I'M SORRY**
BRENDA LEE
*DECCA*

**32 WINDY**
ASSOCIATION
*WARNER*

**33 DOMINIQUE**
SINGING NUN (SOEUR SOURIRE)
*PHILIPS*

**34 (I CAN'T GET NO) SATISFACTION**
ROLLING STONES
*LONDON*

**35 ODE TO BILLIE JOE**
BOBBIE GENTRY
*CAPITOL*

**36 PEPPERMINT TWIST (PT 1)**
JOEY DEE & THE STARLITERS
*ROULETTE*

**37 THIS GUY'S IN LOVE WITH YOU**
HERB ALPERT
*A&M*

**38 GROOVIN'**
YOUNG RASCALS
*ATLANTIC*

**39 RUNAWAY**
DEL SHANNON
*BIG TOP*

**40 HE'S SO FINE**
CHIFFONS
*LAURIE*

**41 SOMETHIN' STUPID**
NANCY & FRANK SINATRA
*REPRISE*

**42 WONDERLAND BY NIGHT**
BERT KAEMPFERT
*DECCA*

**43 THERE I'VE SAID IT AGAIN**
BOBBY VINTON
*EPIC*

**44 THE LETTER**
BOX TOPS
*MALA*

**45 RUNNING BEAR**
JOHNNY PRESTON
*MERCURY*

**46 BABY LOVE**
SUPREMES
*MOTOWN*

**47 WINCHESTER CATHEDRAL**
NEW VAUDEVILLE BAND
*FONTANA*

**48 CAN'T BUY ME LOVE**
BEATLES
*CAPITOL*

**49 LIGHT MY FIRE**
DOORS
*ELEKTRA*

**50 LOVE CHILD**
DIANA ROSS & THE SUPREMES
*MOTOWN*

**51 HELLO, DOLLY!**
LOUIS ARMSTRONG
*KAPP*

**52 SAVE THE LAST DANCE FOR ME**
DRIFTERS
*ATLANTIC*

**53 CRIMSON & CLOVER**
TOMMY JAMES & THE SHONDELLS
*ROULETTE*

**54 HAPPY TOGETHER**
TURTLES
*WHITE WHALE*

**55 SHE LOVES YOU**
BEATLES
*SWAN*

**56 PONY TIME**
CHUBBY CHECKER
*PARKWAY*

**57 HEY PAULA**
PAUL & PAULA
*PHILIPS*

**58 DIZZY**
TOMMY ROE
*ABC*

**59 OH PRETTY WOMAN**
ROY ORBISON
*MONUMENT*

**60 BLUE VELVET**
BOBBY VINTON
*EPIC*

**61 I CAN'T GET NEXT TO YOU**
TEMPTATIONS
*GORDY*

**62 YESTERDAY**
BEATLES
*CAPITOL*

**63 SOLDIER BOY**
SHIRELLES
*SCEPTER*

**64 MY BOYFRIEND'S BACK**
ANGELS
*SMASH*

**65 TELSTAR**
TORNADOS
*LONDON*

**66 THE LION SLEEPS TONIGHT**
TOKENS
*RCA*

**67 (YOU'RE MY) SOUL AND INSPIRATION**
RIGHTEOUS BROTHERS
*VERVE*

**68 DUKE OF EARL**
GENE CHANDLER
*VEE JAY*

**69 LEAVING ON A JET PLANE**
PETER, PAUL & MARY
*WARNER*

**70 MY HEART HAS A MIND OF ITS OWN**
CONNIE FRANCIS
*MGM*

**71 TURN! TURN! TURN!**
BYRDS
*COLUMBIA*

**72 SUKIYAKI**
KYU SAKAMOTO
*CAPITOL*

**73 HEY! BABY**
BRUCE CHANNEL
*SMASH*

**74 MRS BROWN YOU'VE GOT A LOVELY DAUGHTER**
HERMAN'S HERMITS
*MGM*

**75 WEDDING BELL BLUES**
FIFTH DIMENSION
*SOUL CITY*

**76 YOU'VE LOST THAT LOVIN' FEELIN'**
RIGHTEOUS BROTHERS
*PHILLES*

**77 FINGERTIPS (PT 2)**
STEVIE WONDER
*TAMLA*

**78 HELLO GOODBYE**
BEATLES
*CAPITOL*

**79 MRS ROBINSON**
SIMON & GARFUNKEL
*COLUMBIA*

**80 BLUE MOON**
MARCELS
*COLPIX*

**81 I WILL FOLLOW HIM**
LITTLE PEGGY MARCH
*RCA*

**82 I CAN'T HELP MYSELF**
FOUR TOPS
*MOTOWN*

**83 TEEN ANGEL**
MARK DINNING
*MGM*

**84 RUNAROUND**
SUE DION
*LAURIE*

**85 WE CAN WORK IT OUT**
BEATLES
*CAPITOL*

**86 WIPE OUT**
SURFARIS
*DOT*

**87 GOOD VIBRATIONS**
BEACH BOYS
*CAPITOL*

**88 CALCUTTA**
LAWRENCE WELK
*DOT*

**89 HOUSE OF THE RISING SUN**
ANIMALS
*MGM*

**90 WALK LIKE A MAN**
FOUR SEASONS
*VEE JAY*

**91 COME SEE ABOUT ME**
SUPREMES
*MOTOWN*

**92 DOWNTOWN**
PETULA CLARK
*WARNER*

**93 CHAPEL OF LOVE**
DIXIE CUPS
*RED BIRD*

**94 I GET AROUND**
BEACH BOYS
*CAPITOL*

**95 WHERE DID OUR LOVE GO**
SUPREMES
*MOTOWN*

**96 I FEEL FINE**
BEATLES
*CAPITOL*

**97 MONDAY MONDAY**
MAMAS & THE PAPAS
*DUNHILL*

**98 EVERYBODY'S SOMEBODY'S FOOL**
CONNIE FRANCIS
*MGM*

**99 JOHNNY ANGEL**
SHELLEY FABARES
*COLPIX*

**100 GO AWAY LITTLE GIRL**
STEVE LAWRENCE
*COLUMBIA*

**101 HELP!**
BEATLES
*CAPITOL*

**102 MICHAEL**
HIGHWAYMEN
*UA*

**103 TAKE GOOD CARE OF MY BABY**
BOBBY VEE
*LIBERTY*

**104 STRANGER ON THE SHORE**
ACKER BILK
*ATCO*

**105 DO WAH DIDDY DIDDY**
MANFRED MANN
*ASCOT*

**106 JUDY IN DISGUISE (WITH GLASSES)**
JOHN FRED & HIS PLAYBOY BAND
*PAULA*

**107 SUMMER IN THE CITY**
LOVIN' SPOONFUL
*KAMA SUTRA*

**108 TRAVELIN' MAN**
RICKY NELSON
*IMPERIAL*

**109 MY GUY**
MARY WELLS
*MOTOWN*

**110 IF YOU WANNA BE HAPPY**
JIMMY SOUL
*SPQR*

**111 WILL YOU LOVE ME TOMORROW**
SHIRELLES
*SCEPTER*

**112 CHERISH**
ASSOCIATION
*VALIANT*

**113 I GOT YOU BABE**
SONNY & CHER
*ATCO*

**114 NA NA HEY HEY KISS HIM GOODBYE**
STEAM
*FONTANA*

**115 LOVE THEME FROM ROMEO & JULIET**
HENRY MANCINI & HIS ORCHESTRA
*RCA*

**116 QUARTER TO THREE**
GARY U.S. BONDS
*LEGRAND*

**117 TIGHTEN UP**
ARCHIE BELL & THE DRELLS
*ATLANTIC*

**118 A HARD DAY'S NIGHT**
BEATLES
*CAPITOL*

**119 THIS DIAMOND RING**
GARY LEWIS & THE PLAYBOYS
*LIBERTY*

**120 I WANT YOU BACK**
JACKSON FIVE
*MOTOWN*

**121 HELLO, I LOVE YOU**
DOORS
*ELEKTRA*

**122 STOP! IN THE NAME OF LOVE**
SUPREMES
*MOTOWN*

**123 SOMEDAY WE'LL BE TOGETHER**
DIANA ROSS & THE SUPREMES
*MOTOWN*

**124 HIT THE ROAD JACK**
RAY CHARLES
*ABC PARAMOUNT*

**125 BREAKING UP IS HARD TO DO**
NEIL SEDAKA
*RCA*

**126 COME TOGETHER/ SOMETHING**
BEATLES
*APPLE*

**127 GOOD LUCK CHARM**
ELVIS PRESLEY
*RCA*

**128 HE'S A REBEL**
CRYSTALS
*UA*

**129 SURRENDER**
ELVIS PRESLEY
*RCA*

**130 RAG DOLL**
FOUR SEASONS
*PHILIPS*

**131 I'M LEAVING IT UP TO YOU**
DALE & GRACE
*MONTEL*

**132 RESPECT**
ARETHA FRANKLIN
*ATLANTIC*

**133 WILD THING**
TROGGS
*FONTANA/ATCO*

**134 YOU CAN'T HURRY LOVE**
SUPREMES
*MOTOWN*

**135 HARPER VALLEY PTA**
JEANNIE C. RILEY
*PLANTATION*

**136 MONSTER MASH**
BOBBY 'BORIS' PICKETT & THE CRYPT KICKERS
*GARPAX*

**137 SURF CITY**
JAN & DEAN
*LIBERTY*

**138 MR LONELY**
BOBBY VINTON
*EPIC*

**139 IT'S MY PARTY**
LESLEY GORE
*MERCURY*

**140 REACH OUT I'LL BE THERE**
FOUR TOPS
*MOTOWN*

**141 96 TEARS**
? (QUESTION MARK) & THE MYSTERIANS
*CAMEO*

**142 INCENSE AND PEPPERMINTS**
STRAWBERY ALARM CLOCK
*UNI*

**143 KIND OF A DRAG**
BUCKINGHAMS
*USA*

**144 WALK RIGHT IN**
ROOFTOP SINGERS
*VANGUARD*

**145 THE BALLAD OF THE GREEN BERETS**
SSG. BARRY SADLER
*RCA*

**146 EASIER SAID THAN DONE**
ESSEX
*ROULETTE*

**147 EVERYBODY LOVES SOMEBODY**
DEAN MARTIN
*REPRISE*

**148 THE STRIPPER**
DAVID ROSE & HIS ORCHESTRA
*MGM*

**149 PAINT IT BLACK**
ROLLING STONES
*LONDON*

**150 SHEILA**
TOMMY ROE
*ABC PARAMOUNT*

**151 GRAZING IN THE GRASS**
HUGH MASEKELA
*UNI*

**152 GET OFF OF MY CLOUD**
ROLLING STONES
*LONDON*

**153 LAST TRAIN TO CLARKSVILLE**
MONKEES
*COLGEMS*

**154 ALLEY-OOP**
HOLLYWOOD ARGYLES
*LUTE*

**155 HELP ME, RHONDA**
BEACH BOYS
*CAPITOL*

**156 YOU KEEP ME HANGIN' ON**
SUPREMES
*MOTOWN*

**157 I HEAR A SYMPHONY**
SUPREMES
*MOTOWN*

**158 WHEN A MAN LOVES A WOMAN**
PERCY SLEDGE
*ATLANTIC*

**159 MY GIRL**
TEMPTATIONS
*GORDY*

**160 HANKY PANKY**
TOMMY JAMES & THE
  SHONDELLS
*ROULETTE*

**161 THE LOCOMOTION**
LITTLE EVA
*DIMENSION*

**162 ITSY BITSY TEENIE
  WEENIE YELLOW
  POLKA DOT BIKINI**
BRIAN HYLAND
*LEADER*

**163 MY LOVE**
PETULA CLARK
*WARNER*

**164 MOTHER-IN-LAW**
ERNIE K-DOE
*MINIT*

**165 PLEASE MR
  POSTMAN**
MARVELETTES
*TAMLA*

**166 THESE BOOTS ARE
  MADE FOR WALKIN'**
NANCY SINATRA
*REPRISE*

**167 THE SOUNDS OF
  SILENCE**
SIMON & GARFUNKEL
*COLUMBIA*

**168 PAPERBACK
  WRITER**
BEATLES
*CAPITOL*

**169 I'M TELLING YOU
  NOW**
FREDDIE & THE DREAMERS
*TOWER*

**170 EIGHT DAYS A
  WEEK**
BEATLES
*CAPITOL*

**171 POOR SIDE OF
  TOWN**
JOHNNY RIVERS
*IMPERIAL*

**172 GREEN
  TAMBOURINE**
LEMON PIPERS
*BUDDAH*

**173 DEEP PURPLE**
NINO TEMPO & APRIL
  STEVENS
*ATCO*

**174 SO MUCH IN LOVE**
TYMES
*PARKWAY*

**175 SUSPICIOUS MINDS**
ELVIS PRESLEY
*RCA*

**176 HANG ON SLOOPY**
McCOYS
*BANG*

**177 GOOD LOVIN'**
YOUNG RASCALS
*ATLANTIC*

**178 MR TAMBOURINE
  MAN**
BYRDS
*COLUMBIA*

**179 A WORLD WITHOUT
  LOVE**
PETER & GORDON
*CAPITOL*

**180 WOODEN HEART**
JOE DOWELL
*SMASH*

**181 SUNSHINE
  SUPERMAN**
DONOVAN
*EPIC*

**182 RUBY TUESDAY**
ROLLING STONES
*LONDON*

**183 LOVE ME DO**
BEATLES
*TOLLIE*

**184 RINGO**
LORNE GREENE
*RCA*

**185 I WANT TO BE
  WANTED**
BRENDA LEE
*DECCA*

**186 MR CUSTER**
LARRY VERNE
*ERA*

**187 STRANGERS IN THE
  NIGHT**
FRANK SINATRA
*REPRISE*

**188 EVE OF
  DESTRUCTION**
BARRY McGUIRE
*DUNHILL*

**189 MOODY RIVER**
PAT BOONE
*DOT*

**190 OUR DAY WILL
  COME**
RUBY & THE ROMANTICS
*KAPP*

**191 ALL YOU NEED IS
  LOVE**
BEATLES
*CAPITOL*

**192 DON'T BREAK THE
  HEART THAT LOVES
  YOU**
CONNIE FRANCIS
*MGM*

**193 TICKET TO RIDE**
BEATLES
*CAPITOL*

**194 LOVE IS HERE AND
  NOW YOU'RE GONE**
SUPREMES
*MOTOWN*

**195 LIGHTNIN' STRIKES**
LOU CHRISTIE
*MGM*

**196 I'M HENRY VIII I AM**
HERMAN'S HERMITS
*MGM*

**197 THE HAPPENING**
SUPREMES
*MOTOWN*

**198 LEADER OF THE
  PACK**
SHANGRI-LAS
*RED BIRD*

**199 OVER AND OVER**
DAVE CLARK FIVE
*EPIC*

**200 GAME OF LOVE**
WAYNE FONTANA & THE
  MINDBENDERS
*FONTANA*

**201 BACK IN MY ARMS
  AGAIN**
SUPREMES
*MOTOWN*

**202 STAY**
MAURICE WILLIAMS & THE
  ZODIACS
*HERALD*

**203 RUNNING SCARED**
ROY ORBISON
*MONUMENT*

**204 GEORGIA ON MY
  MIND**
RAY CHARLES
*ABC PARAMOUNT*

**205 HE'LL HAVE TO GO**
JIM REEVES
*RCA*

**206 PENNY LANE**
BEATLES
*CAPITOL*

**207 LIMBO ROCK**
CHUBBY CHECKER
*PARKWAY*

**208 EXODUS**
FERRANTE & TEICHER
*UA*

**209 LAST DATE**
FLOYD CRAMER
*RCA*

**210 RETURN TO
  SENDER**
ELVIS PRESLEY
*RCA*

**211 MASHED POTATO
  TIME**
DEE DEE SHARP
*CAMEO*

**212 WOOLLY BULLY**
SAM THE SHAM & THE
  PHARAOHS
*MGM*

**213 HANDY MAN**
JIMMY JONES
*CUB*

**214 GREENFIELDS**
BROTHERS FOUR
*COLUMBIA*

**215 WALK–DON'T RUN**
VENTURES
*DOLTON*

**216 LOUIE LOUIE**
KINGSMEN
*WAND*

**217 BRISTOL STOMP**
DOVELLS
*PARKWAY*

**218 CRYSTAL BLUE
  PERSUASION**
TOMMY JAMES & THE
  SHONDELLS
*ROULETTE*

**219 I HEARD IT
  THROUGH THE
  GRAPEVINE**
GLADYS KNIGHT & THE
  PIPS
*SOUL*

**220 YOUNG GIRL**
UNION GAP FEATURING
  GARY PUCKETT
*COLUMBIA*

**221 LITTLE BIT O' SOUL**
MUSIC EXPLOSION
*LAURIE*

**222 FOR ONCE IN MY
  LIFE**
STEVIE WONDER
*TAMLA*

**223 CAN'T TAKE MY
  EYES OFF YOU**
FRANKIE VALLI
*PHILIPS*

**224 RAMBLIN' ROSE**
NAT 'KING' COLE
*CAPITOL*

**225 ONLY THE LONELY**
ROY ORBISON
*MONUMENT*

**226 WILD ONE**
BOBBY RYDELL
*CAMEO*

**227 CHAIN GANG**
SAM COOKE
*RCA*

**228 THE RAIN, THE
  PARK & OTHER
  THINGS**
COWSILLS
*MGM*

**229 NEVER MY LOVE**
ASSOCIATION
*WARNER*

**230 I'M GONNA MAKE
  YOU LOVE ME**
DIANA ROSS & THE
  SUPREMES & THE
  TEMPTATIONS
*MOTOWN*

**231 HAIR**
COWSILLS
*MGM*

**232 RAINDROPS**
DEE CLARK
*VEE JAY*

**233 THOSE WERE THE
  DAYS**
MARY HOPKIN
*APPLE*

**234 LAST KISS**
J. FRANK WILSON & THE
  CAVALIERS
*JOSIE*

**235 THE BOLL WEEVIL
  SONG**
BROOK BENTON
*MERCURY*

**236 SNOOPY VS THE
  RED BARON**
ROYAL GUARDSMEN
*LAURIE*

**237 CAN'T HELP
  FALLING IN LOVE**
ELVIS PRESLEY
*RCA*

**238 SPINNING WHEEL**
BLOOD SWEAT & TEARS
*COLUMBIA*

**239 LITTLE GREEN
  APPLES**
O.C. SMITH
*COLUMBIA*

**240 TELL IT LIKE IT IS**
AARON NEVILLE
*PAR-LO*

**241 A BOY NAMED SUE**
JOHNNY CASH
*COLUMBIA*

**242 SOUL MAN**
SAM & DAVE
*STAX*

**243 GREEN RIVER**
CREEDENCE CLEARWATER
  REVIVAL
*FANTASY*

**244 GEORGY GIRL**
SEEKERS
*CAPITOL*

**245 FIRE**
CRAZY WORLD OF ARTHUR
  BROWN
*TRACK*

246 LIL' RED RIDING
  HOOD
SAM THE SHAM & THE
  PHARAOHS
*MGM*

247 IT'S YOUR THING
ISLEY BROTHERS
*T-NECK*

248 SHE'S NOT THERE
ZOMBIES
*PARROT*

249 THE WANDERER
DION
*LAURIE*

250 TWIST AND SHOUT
BEATLES
*TOLLIE*

251 RUN TO HIM
BOBBY VEE
*LIBERTY*

252 (THEME FROM)
  *VALLEY OF THE DOLLS*
DIONNE WARWICK
*SCEPTER*

253 THE GOOD, THE
  BAD & THE UGLY
HUGO MONTENEGRO & HIS
  ORCHESTRA
*RCA*

254 SWEET SOUL
  MUSIC
ARTHUR CONLEY
*ATCO*

255 POETRY IN MOTION
JOHNNY TILLOTSON
*CADENCE*

256 LET'S HANG ON!
FOUR SEASONS
*PHILIPS*

257 I WAS MADE TO
  LOVE HER
STEVIE WONDER
*TAMLA*

258 CAN'T GET USED
  TO LOSING YOU
ANDY WILLIAMS
*COLUMBIA*

259 BORN TO BE WILD
STEPPENWOLF
*DUNHILL*

260 PUFF THE MAGIC
  DRAGON
PETER, PAUL & MARY
*WARNER*

261 BAD MOON RISING
CREEDENCE CLEARWATER
  REVIVAL
*FANTASY*

262 CRY LIKE A BABY
BOX TOPS
*MALA*

263 CHAIN OF FOOLS
ARETHA FRANKLIN
*ATLANTIC*

264 THE END OF THE
  WORLD
SKEETER DAVIS
*RCA*

265 WASHINGTON
  SQUARE
VILLAGE STOMPERS
*EPIC*

266 LADY WILLPOWER
GARY PUCKETT & THE
  UNION GAP
*COLUMBIA*

267 PROUD MARY
CREEDENCE CLEARWATER
  REVIVAL
*FANTASY*

268 DEDICATED TO THE
  ONE I LOVE
SHIRELLES
*SCEPTER*

269 A THOUSAND
  STARS
KATHY YOUNG WITH THE
  INNOCENTS
*INDIGO*

270 THE WAH-WATUSI
ORLONS
*CAMEO*

271 JEAN
OLIVER
*CREWE*

272 LOVE (CAN MAKE
  YOU HAPPY)
MERCY
*SUNDI*

273 PUPPY LOVE
PAUL ANKA
*ABC PARAMOUNT*

274 BREAD AND
  BUTTER
NEWBEATS
*HICKORY*

275 AND WHEN I DIE
BLOOD SWEAT & TEARS
*COLUMBIA*

276 MIDNIGHT IN
  MOSCOW
KENNY BALL
*KAPP*

277 1-2-3
LEN BARRY
*DECCA*

278 THE HORSE
CLIFF NOBLES & CO
*PHIL LA OF SOUL*

279 I LIKE IT LIKE THAT
  (PT 1)
CHRIS KENNER
*INSTANT*

280 TAKE A LETTER
  MARIA
R.B. GREAVES
*ATCO*

281 DANCING IN THE
  STREET
MARTHA & THE
  VANDELLAS
*GORDY*

282 YOU'VE MADE ME
  SO VERY HAPPY
BLOOD SWEAT & TEARS
*COLUMBIA*

283 RHYTHM OF THE
  RAIN
CASCADES
*VALIANT*

284 CRYIN'
ROY ORBISON
*MONUMENT*

285 BOBBY'S GIRL
MARCIE BLANE
*SEVILLE*

286 WICHITA LINEMAN
GLEN CAMPBELL
*CAPITOL*

287 MELLOW YELLOW
DONOVAN
*EPIC*

288 APACHE
JORGEN INGMANN
*ATCO*

289 REFLECTIONS
DIANA ROSS & THE
  SUPREMES
*MOTOWN*

290 BE MY BABY
RONETTES
*PHILLES*

291 HOT FUN IN THE
  SUMMERTIME
SLY & THE FAMILY STONE
*EPIC*

292 RUBY BABY
DION
*COLUMBIA*

293 19TH NERVOUS
  BREAKDOWN
ROLLING STONES
*LONDON*

294 SHOP AROUND
MIRACLES
*TAMLA*

295 BLOWIN' IN THE
  WIND
PETER, PAUL & MARY
*WARNER*

296 A LOVER'S
  CONCERTO
TOYS
*DYNOVOICE*

297 BUILD ME UP
  BUTTERCUP
FOUNDATIONS
*UNI*

298 DAYDREAM
LOVIN' SPOONFUL
*KAMA SUTRA*

299 MEMPHIS
JOHNNY RIVERS
*IMPERIAL*

300 CLASSICAL GAS
MASON WILLIAMS
*WARNER*

301 SUNNY
BOBBY HEBB
*PHILIPS*

302 CAN'T YOU HEAR
  MY HEARTBEAT
HERMAN'S HERMITS
*MGM*

303 HELLO MUDDUH,
  HELLO FADDUH
ALLAN SHERMAN
*WARNER*

304 DEDICATED TO THE
  ONE I LOVE
MAMAS & THE PAPAS
*DUNHILL*

305 DOWN ON THE
  CORNER/FORTUNATE
  SON
CREEDENCE CLEARWATER
  REVIVAL
*FANTASY*

306 RED RUBBER BALL
CYRKLE
*COLUMBIA*

307 TOUCH ME
DOORS
*ELEKTRA*

308 SIXTEEN REASONS
CONNIE STEVENS
*WARNER*

309 YOU DON'T OWN
  ME
LESLEY GORE
*MERCURY*

310 GOODBYE CRUEL
  WORLD
JAMES DARREN
*COLPIX*

311 A LITTLE BIT ME, A
  LITTLE BIT YOU
MONKEES
*COLGEMS*

312 DO YOU WANT TO
  KNOW A SECRET
BEATLES
*VEE JAY*

313 BANG BANG (MY
  BABY SHOT ME
  DOWN)
CHER
*IMPERIAL*

314 DID YOU EVER
  HAVE TO MAKE UP
  YOUR MIND
LOVIN' SPOONFUL
*KAMA SUTRA*

315 SALLY, GO 'ROUND
  THE ROSES
JAYNETTS
*TUFF*

316 YELLOW
  SUBMARINE
BEATLES
*CAPITOL*

317 NORTH TO ALASKA
JOHNNY HORTON
*COLUMBIA*

318 A GROOVY KIND OF
  LOVE
MINDBENDERS
*FONTANA*

319 A HUNDRED
  POUNDS OF CLAY
GENE MCDANIELS
*LIBERTY*

320 DON'T WORRY
MARTY ROBBINS
*COLUMBIA*

321 MACARTHUR PARK
RICHARD HARRIS
*DUNHILL*

322 SLOW TWISTIN'
CHUBBY CHECKER
*PARKWAY*

323 SINK THE
  BISMARCK
JOHNNY HORTON
*COLUMBIA*

324 SPOOKY
CLASSICS IV
*IMPERIAL*

325 COME BACK WHEN
  YOU GROW UP
BOBBY VEE & THE
  STRANGERS
*LIBERTY*

326 GOOD TIMIN'
JIMMY JONES
*CUB*

327 YOU'RE THE
  REASON I'M LIVING
BOBBY DARIN
*CAPITOL*

328 TREAT HER RIGHT
ROY HEAD
*BACK BEAT*

329 COUNT ME IN
GARY LEWIS & THE
  PLAYBOYS
*LIBERTY*

330 ONLY LOVE CAN
  BREAK A HEART
GENE PITNEY
*MUSICOR*

**331 RAINY DAY WOMEN # 12 & 35**
BOB DYLAN
*COLUMBIA*

**332 LIKE A ROLLING STONE**
BOB DYLAN
*COLUMBIA*

**333 LITTLE WOMAN**
BOBBY SHERMAN
*METROMEDIA*

**334 DADDY'S HOME**
SHEP & THE LIMELITES
*HULL*

**335 BURNING BRIDGES**
JACK SCOTT
*TOP RANK*

**336 I GOT YOU (I FEEL GOOD)**
JAMES BROWN
*KING*

**337 TRACES**
CLASSICS IV
*IMPERIAL*

**338 ALL ALONE AM I**
BRENDA LEE
*DECCA*

**339 SAVE YOUR HEART FOR ME**
GARY LEWIS & THE PLAYBOYS
*LIBERTY*

**340 CRYING IN THE CHAPEL**
ELVIS PRESLEY
*RCA*

**341 MY BOY LOLLIPOP**
MILLIE SMALL
*SMASH*

**342 NORMAN**
SUE THOMPSON
*HICKORY*

**343 SURFIN' USA**
BEACH BOYS
*CAPITOL*

**344 JUMPIN' JACK FLASH**
ROLLING STONES
*LONDON*

**345 YOU DON'T KNOW ME**
RAY CHARLES
*ABC PARAMOUNT*

**346 STONED SOUL PICNIC**
FIFTH DIMENSION
*SOUL CITY*

**347 PALISADES PARK**
FREDDY CANNON
*SWAN*

**348 MAGIC CARPET RIDE**
STEPPENWOLF
*DUNHILL*

**349 DAWN (GO AWAY)**
FOUR SEASONS
*PHILIPS*

**350 PLEASE PLEASE ME**
BEATLES
*VEE JAY*

**351 WOMAN, WOMAN**
UNION GAP FEATURING GARY PUCKETT
*COLUMBIA*

**352 A BEAUTIFUL MORNING**
RASCALS
*ATLANTIC*

**353 IT KEEPS RIGHT ON A-HURTIN'**
JOHNNY TILLOTSON
*CADENCE*

**354 SUSPICION**
TERRY STAFFORD
*CRUSADER*

**355 LOVE POTION NUMBER NINE**
SEARCHERS
*KAPP*

**356 LOVE ME WITH ALL YOUR HEART**
RAY CHARLES SINGERS
*COMMAND*

**357 YOU WERE ON MY MIND**
WE FIVE
*A&M*

**358 GOOD MORNING STARSHINE**
OLIVER
*JUBILEE*

**359 LIGHT MY FIRE**
JOSÉ FELICIANO
*RCA*

**360 POPSICLES AND ICICLES**
MURMAIDS
*CHATTAHOOCHEE*

**361 THE BIRDS AND THE BEES**
JEWEL AKENS
*ERA*

**362 BARBARA ANN**
BEACH BOYS
*CAPITOL*

**363 THE NIGHT HAS A THOUSAND EYES**
BOBBY VEE
*LIBERTY*

**364 I KNOW (YOU DON'T LOVE ME NO MORE)**
BARBARA GEORGE
*AFO*

**365 SEALED WITH A KISS**
BRIAN HYLAND
*ABC PARAMOUNT*

**366 MONY MONY**
TOMMY JAMES & THE SHONDELLS
*ROULETTE*

**367 GREEN ONIONS**
BOOKER T. & THE MG's
*STAX*

**368 DEVIL WITH A BLUE DRESS ON & GOOD GOLLY MISS MOLLY**
MITCH RYDER & THE DETROIT WHEELS
*NEW VOICE*

**369 WORST THAT COULD HAPPEN**
BROOKLYN BRIDGE
*BUDDAH*

**370 I AM A ROCK**
SIMON & GARFUNKEL
*COLUMBIA*

**371 TIME OF THE SEASON**
ZOMBIES
*DATE*

**372 WHERE OR WHEN**
DION & THE BELMONTS
*LAURIE*

**373 (YOU'RE THE) DEVIL IN DISGUISE**
ELVIS PRESLEY
*RCA*

**374 SEE YOU IN SEPTEMBER**
HAPPENINGS
*B.T. PUPPY*

**375 WHEELS**
STRING-A-LONGS
*WARWICK*

**376 YOU CAN'T SIT DOWN**
DOVELLS
*PARKWAY*

**377 EVERYBODY**
TOMMY ROE
*ABC PARAMOUNT*

**378 CANDY GIRL**
FOUR SEASONS
*VEE JAY*

**379 NO MATTER WHAT SHAPE (YOUR STOMACH'S IN)**
T-BONES
*LIBERTY*

**380 IN THE GHETTO**
ELVIS PRESLEY
*RCA*

**381 SWEET NOTHIN'S**
BRENDA LEE
*DECCA*

**382 THE MOUNTAIN'S HIGH**
DICK & DEEDEE
*LIBERTY*

**383 I KNOW A PLACE**
PETULA CLARK
*WARNER*

**384 COME TOGETHER**
BEATLES
*APPLE*

**385 IF I HAD A HAMMER**
TRINI LOPEZ
*REPRISE*

**386 BLUE ON BLUE**
BOBBY VINTON
*EPIC*

**387 SOULFUL STRUT**
YOUNG-HOLT UNLIMITED
*BRUNSWICK*

**388 FOOL # 1**
BRENDA LEE
*DECCA*

**389 THE NAME GAME**
SHIRLEY ELLIS
*CONGRESS*

**390 I SECOND THAT EMOTION**
SMOKEY ROBINSON & THE MIRACLES
*TAMLA*

**391 I GOT RHYTHM**
HAPPENINGS
*B.T. PUPPY*

**392 LAST NIGHT**
MAR-KEYS
*SATELLITE*

**393 WHAT'S NEW PUSSYCAT?**
TOM JONES
*PARROT*

**394 DO YOU LOVE ME**
CONTOURS
*GORDY*

**395 BABY I NEED YOUR LOVIN'**
JOHNNY RIVERS
*IMPERIAL*

**396 I LOVE YOU BECAUSE**
AL MARTINO
*CAPITOL*

**397 NOWHERE MAN**
BEATLES
*CAPITOL*

**398 THE LITTLE OLD LADY (FROM PASADENA)**
JAN & DEAN
*LIBERTY*

**399 ABRAHAM, MARTIN AND JOHN**
DION
*LAURIE*

**400 IT MUST BE HIM**
VIKKI CARR
*LIBERTY*

**401 SOUTH STREET**
ORLONS
*CAMEO*

**402 DA DOO RON RON**
CRYSTALS
*PHILLES*

**403 SHE'S JUST MY STYLE**
GARY LEWIS & THE PLAYBOYS
*LIBERTY*

**404 SECRET AGENT MAN**
JOHNNY RIVERS
*IMPERIAL*

**405 EASY TO BE HARD**
THREE DOG NIGHT
*DUNHILL*

**406 HELLO STRANGER**
BARBARA LEWIS
*ATLANTIC*

**407 TIE ME KANGAROO DOWN, SPORT**
ROLF HARRIS
*EPIC*

**408 SLOOP JOHN B**
BEACH BOYS
*CAPITOL*

**409 WHOLE LOTTA LOVE**
LED ZEPPELIN
*ATLANTIC*

**410 CALIFORNIA GIRLS**
BEACH BOYS
*CAPITOL*

**411 THIS IS MY SONG**
PETULA CLARK
*WARNER*

**412 NIGHT**
JACKIE WILSON
*BRUNSWICK*

**413 KING OF THE ROAD**
ROGER MILLER
*SMASH*

**414 BECAUSE**
DAVE CLARK FIVE
*EPIC*

**415 COME A LITTLE BIT CLOSER**
JAY & THE AMERICANS
*UA*

**416 OUT OF LIMITS**
MARKETTS
*WARNER*

**417 CALIFORNIA DREAMIN'**
MAMAS & THE PAPAS
*DUNHILL*

**418 I WISH IT WOULD RAIN**
TEMPTATIONS
*GORDY*

**419 I'VE TOLD EVERY LITTLE STAR**
LINDA SCOTT
*CANADIAN AMERICAN*

**420 SIMON SAYS**
1910 FRUITGUM CO
*BUDDAH*

**421 PLEASANT VALLEY SUNDAY**
MONKEES
*COLGEMS*

**422 I THINK WE'RE ALONE NOW**
TOMMY JAMES & THE SHONDELLS
*ROULETTE*

**423 VALLERI**
MONKEES
*COLGEMS*

**424 I'LL NEVER FIND ANOTHER YOU**
SEEKERS
*CAPITOL*

**425 SWEET CAROLINE**
NEIL DIAMOND
*UNI*

**426 HOTEL HAPPINESS**
BROOK BENTON
*MERCURY*

**427 YOU DON'T HAVE TO BE A BABY TO CRY**
CARAVELLES
*SMASH*

**428 FIVE O'CLOCK WORLD**
VOGUES
*CO & CE*

**429 BREAK IT TO ME GENTLY**
BRENDA LEE
*DECCA*

**430 LADY MADONNA**
BEATLES
*CAPITOL*

**431 KICKS**
PAUL REVERE & THE RAIDERS
*COLUMBIA*

**432 LOVERS WHO WANDER**
DION
*LAURIE*

**433 SHE'D RATHER BE WITH ME**
TURTLES
*WHITE WHALE*

**434 THINGS**
BOBBY DARIN
*ATCO*

**435 JAVA**
AL HIRT
*RCA*

**436 WE'LL SING IN THE SUNSHINE**
GALE GARNETT
*RCA*

**437 ON THE REBOUND**
FLOYD CRAMER
*RCA*

**438 UPTIGHT (EVERYTHING'S ALRIGHT)**
STEVIE WONDER
*TAMLA*

**439 WHAT DOES IT TAKE TO WIN YOUR LOVE**
JR WALKER & THE ALL STARS
*SOUL*

**440 SINCE I FELL FOR YOU**
LENNY WELCH
*CADENCE*

**441 LA-LA MEANS I LOVE YOU**
DELFONICS
*PHILLY GROOVE*

**442 HEAT WAVE**
MARTHA & THE VANDELLAS
*GORDY*

**443 DUM DUM**
BRENDA LEE
*DECCA*

**444 GALVESTON**
GLEN CAMPBELL
*CAPITOL*

**445 THERE'S A MOON OUT TONIGHT**
CAPRIS
*OLD TOWN*

**446 BUSTED**
RAY CHARLES
*ABC PARAMOUNT*

**447 HEY LITTLE COBRA**
RIP CHORDS
*COLUMBIA*

**448 UNDER THE BOARDWALK**
DRIFTERS
*ATLANTIC*

**449 LISTEN PEOPLE**
HERMAN'S HERMITS
*MGM*

**450 TOO BUSY THINKING ABOUT MY BABY**
MARVIN GAYE
*TAMLA*

**451 YOU TALK TOO MUCH**
JOE JONES
*ROULETTE*

**452 EXPRESSWAY TO YOUR HEART**
SOUL SURVIVORS
*CRIMSON*

**453 MY TRUE STORY**
JIVE FIVE
*BELTONE*

**454 ONLY THE STRONG SURVIVE**
JERRY BUTLER
*MERCURY*

**455 SHOTGUN**
JR WALKER & THE ALL STARS
*SOUL*

**456 DON'T HANG UP**
ORLONS
*CAMEO*

**457 WALK ON BY**
LEROY VAN DYKE
*MERCURY*

**458 BEAUTY IS ONLY SKIN DEEP**
TEMPTATIONS
*GORDY*

**459 UNCHAINED MELODY**
RIGHTEOUS BROTHERS
*PHILLES*

**460 WHERE THE BOYS ARE**
CONNIE FRANCIS
*MGM*

**461 BECAUSE THEY'RE YOUNG**
DUANE EDDY
*JAMIE*

**462 RELEASE ME (AND LET ME LOVE AGAIN)**
ENGELBERT HUMPERDINCK
*PARROT*

**463 WHAT IN THE WORLD'S COME OVER YOU**
JACK SCOTT
*TOP RANK*

**464 THAT'S LIFE**
FRANK SINATRA
*REPRISE*

**465 CRY BABY**
GARNET MIMMS & THE ENCHANTERS
*UA*

**466 YUMMY YUMMY YUMMY**
OHIO EXPRESS
*BUDDAH*

**467 RESCUE ME**
FONTELLA BASS
*CHECKER*

**468 GTO**
RONNY & THE DAYTONAS
*MALA*

**469 SAN FRANCISCO (BE SURE TO WEAR FLOWERS IN YOUR HAIR)**
SCOTT MCKENZIE
*ODE*

**470 I SAY A LITTLE PRAYER**
DIONNE WARWICK
*SCEPTER*

**471 VOLARE**
BOBBY RYDELL
*CAMEO*

**472 YOU DON'T HAVE TO SAY YOU LOVE ME**
DUSTY SPRINGFIELD
*PHILIPS*

**473 FORGET HIM**
BOBBY RYDELL
*CAMEO*

**474 BABY I LOVE YOU**
ARETHA FRANKLIN
*ATLANTIC*

**475 THE LOOK OF LOVE**
SERGIO MENDES & BRASIL '66
*A&M*

**476 MY CHERIE AMOUR**
STEVIE WONDER
*TAMLA*

**477 BITS AND PIECES**
DAVE CLARK FIVE
*EPIC*

**478 CARA MIA**
JAY & THE AMERICANS
*UA*

**479 PIPELINE**
CHANTAYS
*DOT*

**480 IT'S ALL RIGHT**
IMPRESSIONS
*ABC PARAMOUNT*

**481 CALENDAR GIRL**
NEIL SEDAKA
*RCA*

**482 SURFIN' BIRD**
TRASHMEN
*GARRETT*

**483 PUT A LITTLE LOVE IN YOUR HEART**
JACKIE DESHANNON
*IMPERIAL*

**484 GOOD THING**
PAUL REVERE & THE RAIDERS
*COLUMBIA*

**485 HE'LL HAVE TO STAY**
JEANNE BLACK
*CAPITOL*

**486 ONE**
THREE DOG NIGHT
*DUNHILL*

**487 BEND ME, SHAPE ME**
AMERICAN BREED
*ACTA*

**488 LET ME IN**
SENSATIONS
*ARGO*

**489 LET'S DANCE**
CHRIS MONTEZ
*MONOGRAM*

**490 WHO'S MAKING LOVE**
JOHNNIE TAYLOR
*STAX*

**491 BUT I DO**
CLARENCE 'FROGMAN' HENRY
*ARGO*

**492 TELL HIM**
EXCITERS
*UA*

**493 THE JOLLY GREEN GIANT**
KINGSMEN
*WAND*

**494 YOU DON'T KNOW WHAT YOU GOT (UNTIL YOU LOSE IT)**
RAL DONNER
*GONE*

**495 THEY'RE COMING TO TAKE ME AWAY HA-HAAA!**
NAPOLEON XIV
*WARNER*

**496 THE PIED PIPER**
CRISPIAN ST PETERS
*JAMIE*

**497 YELLOW BIRD**
ARTHUR LYMAN
*HI FI*

**498 ANGEL BABY**
ROSIE & THE ORIGINALS
*HIGHLAND*

**499 WONDERFUL WORLD**
HERMAN'S HERMITS
*MGM*

**500 OH HAPPY DAY**
EDWIN HAWKINS SINGERS
*PAVILION*

# THE UK
# TOP 500 SINGLES
# 1960–69

**1 SHE LOVES YOU**
BEATLES
*PARLOPHONE*

**2 SUGAR SUGAR**
ARCHIES
*RCA*

**3 I REMEMBER YOU**
FRANK IFIELD
*COLUMBIA*

**4 WONDERFUL LAND**
SHADOWS
*COLUMBIA*

**5 YOU'VE LOST THAT LOVIN' FEELIN'**
RIGHTEOUS BROTHERS
*LONDON AMERICAN*

**6 IT'S NOW OR NEVER**
ELVIS PRESLEY
*RCA*

**7 TEARS**
KEN DODD
*COLUMBIA*

**8 GREEN GREEN GRASS OF HOME**
TOM JONES
*DECCA*

**9 THE LAST WALTZ**
ENGELBERT HUMPERDINCK
*DECCA*

**10 FROM ME TO YOU**
BEATLES
*PARLOPHONE*

**11 TELSTAR**
TORNADOS
*DECCA*

**12 CATHY'S CLOWN**
EVERLY BROTHERS
*WARNER*

**13 TWO LITTLE BOYS**
ROLF HARRIS
*COLUMBIA*

**14 RELEASE ME (AND LET ME LOVE AGAIN)**
ENGELBERT HUMPERDINCK
*DECCA*

**15 THE YOUNG ONES**
CLIFF RICHARD
*COLUMBIA*

**16 WOODEN HEART**
ELVIS PRESLEY
*RCA*

**17 THOSE WERE THE DAYS**
MARY HOPKIN
*APPLE*

**18 DISTANT DRUMS**
JIM REEVES
*RCA*

**19 LOVESICK BLUES**
FRANK IFIELD
*COLUMBIA*

**20 HELLO GOODBYE**
BEATLES
*PARLOPHONE*

**21 ROCK-A-HULA-BABY**
ELVIS PRESLEY
*RCA*

**22 APACHE**
SHADOWS
*COLUMBIA*

**23 A WHITER SHADE OF PALE**
PROCOL HARUM
*DERAM*

**24 GOOD LUCK CHARM**
ELVIS PRESLEY
*RCA*

**25 GET BACK**
BEATLES
*APPLE*

**26 I WANT TO HOLD YOUR HAND**
BEATLES
*PARLOPHONE*

**27 HONKY TONK WOMEN**
ROLLING STONES
*DECCA*

**28 WHAT A WONDERFUL WORLD**
LOUIS ARMSTRONG
*HMV*

**29 RUNAWAY**
DEL SHANNON
*LONDON AMERICAN*

**30 WHY**
ANTHONY NEWLEY
*DECCA*

**31 SAN FRANCISCO (BE SURE TO WEAR FLOWERS IN YOUR HAIR)**
SCOTT McKENZIE
*CBS*

**32 THE GOOD, THE BAD AND THE UGLY**
HUGO MONTENEGRO & HIS ORCHESTRA
*RCA*

**33 YOU DON'T KNOW**
HELEN SHAPIRO
*COLUMBIA*

**34 PLEASE DON'T TEASE**
CLIFF RICHARD
*COLUMBIA*

**35 DAY TRIPPER/WE CAN WORK IT OUT**
BEATLES
*PARLOPHONE*

**36 YOU'LL NEVER WALK ALONE**
GERRY & THE PACEMAKERS
*COLUMBIA*

**37 LILY THE PINK**
SCAFFOLD
*PARLOPHONE*

**38 STRANGER ON THE SHORE**
MR ACKER BILK
*COLUMBIA*

**39 I FEEL FINE**
BEATLES
*PARLOPHONE*

**40 WALKIN' BACK TO HAPPINESS**
HELEN SHAPIRO
*COLUMBIA*

**41 I LIKE IT**
GERRY & THE PACEMAKERS
*COLUMBIA*

**42 THE CARNIVAL IS OVER**
SEEKERS
*COLUMBIA*

**43 YOUNG GIRL**
GARY PUCKETT & THE UNION GAP
*CBS*

**44 THE NEXT TIME**
CLIFF RICHARD
*COLUMBIA*

**45 STRANGERS IN THE NIGHT**
FRANK SINATRA
*REPRISE*

**46 I'M A BELIEVER**
MONKEES
*RCA*

**47 WALK RIGHT BACK**
EVERLY BROTHERS
*WARNER*

**48 JOHNNY REMEMBER ME**
JOHN LEYTON
*TOP RANK*

**49 MASSACHUSETTS**
BEE GEES
*POLYDOR*

**50 PUPPET ON A STRING**
SANDIE SHAW
*PYE*

**51 ONLY THE LONELY**
ROY ORBISON
*LONDON AMERICAN*

**52 HIS LATEST FLAME**
ELVIS PRESLEY
*RCA*

**53 HOW DO YOU DO IT?**
GERRY & THE PACEMAKERS
*COLUMBIA*

**54 ARE YOU LONESOME TONIGHT ?**
ELVIS PRESLEY
*RCA*

**55 MY OLD MAN'S A DUSTMAN**
LONNIE DONEGAN
*PYE*

**56 WHERE DO YOU GO TO MY LOVELY**
PETER SARSTEDT
*UA*

**57 GLAD ALL OVER**
DAVE CLARK FIVE
*COLUMBIA*

**58 SURRENDER**
ELVIS PRESLEY
*RCA*

**59 YOU'RE MY WORLD**
CILLA BLACK
*PARLOPHONE*

**60 IT'S OVER**
ROY ORBISON
*LONDON AMERICAN*

**61 YELLOW SUBMARINE/ELEANOR RIGBY**
BEATLES
*PARLOPHONE*

**62 COME OUTSIDE**
MIKE SARNE AND WENDY RICHARD
*PARLOPHONE*

**63 A HARD DAY'S NIGHT**
BEATLES
*PARLOPHONE*

**64 GOOD TIMIN'**
JIMMY JONES
*MGM*

**65 RETURN TO SENDER**
ELVIS PRESLEY
*RCA*

**66 I CAN'T STOP LOVING YOU**
RAY CHARLES
*HMV*

**67 MONY MONY**
TOMMY JAMES & THE SHONDELLS
*MAJOR MINOR*

**68 DO YOU LOVE ME**
BRIAN POOLE & THE TREMELOES
*DECCA*

**69 WELL I ASK YOU**
EDEN KANE
*DECCA*

**70 I HEARD IT THROUGH THE GRAPEVINE**
MARVIN GAYE
*TAMLA MOTOWN*

**71 THE SUN AIN'T GONNA SHINE (ANYMORE)**
WALKER BROTHERS
*PHILIPS*

**72 ALL YOU NEED IS LOVE**
BEATLES
*PARLOPHONE*

**73 TELL LAURA I LOVE HER**
RICKY VALANCE
*COLUMBIA*

**74 ANYONE WHO HAD A HEART**
CILLA BLACK
*PARLOPHONE*

**75 I'M ALIVE**
HOLLIES
*PARLOPHONE*

**76 OH PRETTY WOMAN**
ROY ORBISON
*LONDON AMERICAN*

**77 SHE'S NOT YOU**
ELVIS PRESLEY
*RCA*

**78 BABY COME BACK**
EQUALS
*PRESIDENT*

**79 OB-LA-DI OB-LA-DA**
MARMALADE
*CBS*

**80 HELP!**
BEATLES
*PARLOPHONE*

**81 NEEDLES AND PINS**
SEARCHERS
*PYE*

**82 SILENCE IS GOLDEN**
TREMELOES
*CBS*

**83 BAD MOON RISING**
CREEDENCE CLEARWATER REVIVAL
*LIBERTY*

**84 CONFESSIN'**
FRANK IFIELD
*COLUMBIA*

**85 REACH OUT I'LL BE THERE**
FOUR TOPS
*TAMLA MOTOWN*

**86 POOR ME**
ADAM FAITH
*PARLOPHONE*

**87 DIAMONDS**
JET HARRIS & TONY MEEHAN
*DECCA*

**88 POETRY IN MOTION**
JOHNNY TILLOTSON
*LONDON AMERICAN*

**89 TOWER OF STRENGTH**
FRANKIE VAUGHAN
*PHILIPS*

**90 CINDERELLA ROCKAFELLA**
ESTHER & ABI OFARIM
*PHILIPS*

**91 TICKET TO RIDE**
BEATLES
*PARLOPHONE*

**92 I LOVE YOU**
CLIFF RICHARD
*COLUMBIA*

**93 THREE STEPS TO HEAVEN**
EDDIE COCHRAN
*LONDON AMERICAN*

**94 MOON RIVER**
DANNY WILLIAMS
*HMV*

**95 RUNNING BEAR**
JOHNNY PRESTON
*MERCURY*

**96 CAN'T BUY ME LOVE**
BEATLES
*PARLOPHONE*

**97 SOMETHIN' STUPID**
NANCY & FRANK SINATRA
*REPRISE*

**98 BAD TO ME**
BILLY J. KRAMER & THE DAKOTAS
*PARLOPHONE*

**99 IN THE YEAR 2525 (EXORDIUM & TERMINUS)**
ZAGER & EVANS
*RCA*

**100 HEY JUDE**
BEATLES
*APPLE*

**101 I PRETEND**
DES O'CONNOR
*COLUMBIA*

**102 LONG LIVE LOVE**
SANDIE SHAW
*PYE*

**103 DO YOU MIND**
ANTHONY NEWLEY
*DECCA*

**104 THESE BOOTS ARE MADE FOR WALKIN'**
NANCY SINATRA
*REPRISE*

**105 SHAKIN' ALL OVER**
JOHNNY KIDD & THE PIRATES
*HMV*

**106 SWEETS FOR MY SWEET**
SEARCHERS
*PYE*

**107 DO WAH DIDDY DIDDY**
MANFRED MANN
*HMV*

**108 SUMMER HOLIDAY**
CLIFF RICHARD
*COLUMBIA*

**109 BALLAD OF JOHN AND YOKO**
BEATLES
*APPLE*

**110 THE LAST TIME**
ROLLING STONES
*DECCA*

**111 THIS IS MY SONG**
PETULA CLARK
*PYE*

**112 I'LL NEVER FIND ANOTHER YOU**
SEEKERS
*COLUMBIA*

**113 GOOD VIBRATIONS**
BEACH BOYS
*CAPITOL*

**114 WAYWARD WIND**
FRANK IFIELD
*COLUMBIA*

**115 SOMETHING IN THE AIR**
THUNDERCLAP NEWMAN
*TRACK*

**116 HAVE I THE RIGHT?**
HONEYCOMBS
*PYE*

**117 ALBATROSS**
FLEETWOOD MAC
*BLUE HORIZON*

**118 I'M INTO SOMETHING GOOD**
HERMAN'S HERMITS
*COLUMBIA*

**119 GET OFF OF MY CLOUD**
ROLLING STONES
*DECCA*

**120 LITTLE CHILDREN**
BILLY J. KRAMER & THE DAKOTAS
*PARLOPHONE*

**121 JE T'AIME...MOI NON PLUS**
JANE BIRKIN & SERGE GAINSBOURG
*FONTANA/MAJOR MINOR*

**122 I GOT YOU BABE**
SONNY & CHER
*ATLANTIC*

**123 PRETTY FLAMINGO**
MANFRED MANN
*HMV*

**124 EVERLASTING LOVE**
LOVE AFFAIR
*CBS*

**125 (THERE'S) ALWAYS SOMETHING THERE TO REMIND ME**
SANDIE SHAW
*PYE*

**126 BABY, NOW THAT I FOUND YOU**
FOUNDATIONS
*PYE*

**127 (I CAN'T GET NO) SATISFACTION**
ROLLING STONES
*DECCA*

**128 SUNNY AFTERNOON**
KINKS
*PYE*

**129 TEMPTATION**
EVERLY BROTHERS
*WARNER*

**130 BLUE MOON**
MARCELS
*PYE INTERNATIONAL*

**131 BABY LOVE**
SUPREMES
*STATESIDE*

**132 WITH A GIRL LIKE YOU**
TROGGS
*FONTANA*

**133 NUT ROCKER**
B. BUMBLE & THE STINGERS
*TOP RANK*

**134 MR TAMBOURINE MAN**
BYRDS
*CBS*

**135 JUMPING JACK FLASH**
ROLLING STONES
*DECCA*

**136 LET THE HEARTACHES BEGIN**
LONG JOHN BALDRY
*PYE*

**137 A WORLD WITHOUT LOVE**
PETER & GORDON
*COLUMBIA*

**138 REACH FOR THE STARS/CLIMB EV'RY MOUNTAIN**
SHIRLEY BASSEY
*COLUMBIA*

**139 MIGHTY QUINN**
MANFRED MANN
*FONTANA*

**140 CONGRATULATIONS**
CLIFF RICHARD
*COLUMBIA*

**141 IT'S ALL OVER NOW**
ROLLING STONES
*DECCA*

**142 MICHELLE**
OVERLANDERS
*PYE*

**143 DIANE**
BACHELORS
*DECCA*

**144 CRYING IN THE CHAPEL**
ELVIS PRESLEY
*RCA*

**145 YOU REALLY GOT ME**
KINKS
*PYE*

**146 DON'T THROW YOUR LOVE AWAY**
SEARCHERS
*PYE*

**147 MAKE IT EASY ON YOURSELF**
WALKER BROTHERS
*PHILIPS*

**148 I'VE GOTTA GET A MESSAGE TO YOU**
BEE GEES
*POLYDOR*

**149 YEH YEH**
GEORGIE FAME
*COLUMBIA*

**150 SAILOR**
PETULA CLARK
*PYE*

**151 I'LL NEVER FALL IN LOVE AGAIN**
BOBBIE GENTRY
*CAPITOL*

**152 FIRE**
CRAZY WORLD OF ARTHUR BROWN
*TRACK*

**153 FOOT TAPPER**
SHADOWS
*COLUMBIA*

**154 YOU'RE DRIVING ME CRAZY**
TEMPERANCE SEVEN
*PARLOPHONE*

**155 STARRY EYED**
MICHAEL HOLLIDAY
*COLUMBIA*

**156 KEEP ON RUNNIN'**
SPENCER DAVIS GROUP
*FONTANA*

**157 AS LONG AS HE NEEDS ME**
SHIRLEY BASSEY
*COLUMBIA*

**158 DANCE ON**
SHADOWS
*COLUMBIA*

**159 THE MINUTE YOU'RE GONE**
CLIFF RICHARD
*COLUMBIA*

**160 JULIET**
FOUR PENNIES
*PHILIPS*

**161 SOMEBODY HELP ME**
SPENCER DAVIS GROUP
*FONTANA*

**162 PAPERBACK WRITER**
BEATLES
*PARLOPHONE*

**163 DIZZY**
TOMMY ROE
*STATESIDE*

**164 DO IT AGAIN**
BEACH BOYS
*CAPITOL*

**165 IT'S NOT UNUSUAL**
TOM JONES
*DECCA*

**166 (IF PARADISE IS) HALF AS NICE**
AMEN CORNER
*IMMEDIATE*

**167 KING OF THE ROAD**
ROGER MILLER
*PHILIPS*

**168 GO NOW!**
MOODY BLUES
*DECCA*

**169 ISRAELITES**
DESMOND DEKKER & THE ACES
*PYRAMID*

**170 DEVIL IN DISGUISE**
ELVIS PRESLEY
*RCA*

**171 YOU DON'T HAVE TO SAY YOU LOVE ME**
DUSTY SPRINGFIELD
*PHILIPS*

**172 KON-TIKI**
SHADOWS
*COLUMBIA*

**173 MICHAEL**
HIGHWAYMEN
*HMV*

**174 LEGEND OF XANADU**
DAVE DEE, DOZY, BEAKY, MICK & TICH
*FONTANA*

**175 LADY MADONNA**
BEATLES
*PARLOPHONE*

**176 BLACKBERRY WAY**
MOVE REGAL
*ZONOPHONE*

**177 ALL OR NOTHING**
SMALL FACES
*DECCA*

**178 BALLAD OF BONNIE & CLYDE**
GEORGIE FAME
*CBS*

**179 OUT OF TIME**
CHRIS FARLOWE
*IMMEDIATE*

**180 CONCRETE AND CLAY**
UNIT 4 PLUS 2
*DECCA*

**181 A MESS OF BLUES**
ELVIS PRESLEY
*RCA*

**182 I WON'T FORGET YOU**
JIM REEVES
*RCA*

**183 TIRED OF WAITING FOR YOU**
KINKS
*PYE*

**184 HOUSE OF THE RISING SUN**
ANIMALS
*COLUMBIA*

**185 ON THE REBOUND**
FLOYD CRAMER
*RCA*

**186 LITTLE RED ROOSTER**
ROLLING STONES
*DECCA*

**187 PAINT IT BLACK**
ROLLING STONES
*DECCA*

**188 GET AWAY**
GEORGIE FAME
*COLUMBIA*

**189 WITH A LITTLE HELP FROM MY FRIENDS**
JOE COCKER
*REGAL ZONOPHONE*

**190 RUBY, DON'T TAKE YOUR LOVE TO TOWN**
KENNY ROGERS & THE FIRST EDITION
*REPRISE*

**191 WHERE ARE YOU NOW (MY LOVE)**
JACKIE TRENT
*PYE*

**192 HANDY MAN**
JIMMY JONES
*MGM*

**193 HELLO MARY LOU/TRAVELLIN' MAN**
RICKY NELSON
*LONDON AMERICAN*

**194 A PICTURE OF YOU**
JOE BROWN & THE BRUVVERS
*PICCADILLY*

**195 BECAUSE THEY'RE YOUNG**
DUANE EDDY
*LONDON AMERICAN*

**196 LET'S TWIST AGAIN**
CHUBBY CHECKER
*COLUMBIA*

**197 SAVE THE LAST DANCE FOR ME**
DRIFTERS
*LONDON AMERICAN*

**198 LET'S DANCE**
CHRIS MONTEZ
*LONDON AMERICAN*

**199 HALFWAY TO PARADISE**
BILLY FURY
*DECCA*

**200 FALL IN LOVE WITH YOU**
CLIFF RICHARD
*COLUMBIA*

**201 ARE YOU SURE**
ALLISONS
*FONTANA*

**202 THERE GOES MY EVERYTHING**
ENGELBERT HUMPERDINCK
*DECCA*

**203 SWISS MAID**
DEL SHANNON
*LONDON AMERICAN*

**204 SPEEDY GONZALES**
PAT BOONE
*LONDON AMERICAN*

**205 I'M LOOKING OUT THE WINDOW**
CLIFF RICHARD
*COLUMBIA*

**206 FROM A JACK TO A KING**
NED MILLER
*LONDON AMERICAN*

**207 I BELIEVE**
BACHELORS
*DECCA*

**208 I LOVE YOU BECAUSE**
JIM REEVES
*RCA*

**209 WIND ME UP (LET ME GO)**
CLIFF RICHARD
*COLUMBIA*

**210 TELL ME WHAT HE SAID**
HELEN SHAPIRO
*COLUMBIA*

**211 ROCKING GOOSE**
JOHNNY & THE HURRICANES
*LONDON AMERICAN*

**212 THE LOCOMOTION**
LITTLE EVA
*LONDON AMERICAN*

**213 I'LL NEVER FALL IN LOVE AGAIN**
TOM JONES
*DECCA*

**214 THINGS**
BOBBY DARIN
*LONDON AMERICAN*

**215 DOWNTOWN**
PETULA CLARK
*PYE*

**216 PLEASE PLEASE ME**
BEATLES
*PARLOPHONE*

**217 GENTLE ON MY MIND**
DEAN MARTIN
*REPRISE*

**218 DELILAH**
TOM JONES
*DECCA*

**219 AIN'T GOT NO - I GOT LIFE/DO WHAT YOU GOTTA DO**
NINA SIMONE
*RCA*

**220 ATLANTIS**
SHADOWS
*COLUMBIA*

**221 JESAMINE**
CASUALS
*DECCA*

**222 MIDNIGHT IN MOSCOW**
KENNY BALL
*PYE JAZZ*

**223 SUSPICIOUS MINDS**
ELVIS PRESLEY
*RCA*

**224 MORNINGTOWN RIDE**
SEEKERS
*COLUMBIA*

**225 IN THE GHETTO**
ELVIS PRESLEY
*RCA*

**226 LITTLE ARROWS**
LEAPY LEE
*MCA*

**227 THIS GUY'S IN LOVE WITH YOU**
HERB ALPERT
*A&M*

**228 SIMON SAYS**
1910 FRUITGUM CO
*PYE INTERNATIONAL*

**229 THEME FROM *A SUMMER PLACE***
PERCY FAITH
*PHILIPS*

**230 DO YOU WANT TO KNOW A SECRET**
BILLY J. KRAMER & THE DAKOTAS
*PARLOPHONE*

**231 DREAM BABY**
ROY ORBISON
*LONDON AMERICAN*

**232 VOICE IN THE WILDERNESS**
CLIFF RICHARD
*COLUMBIA*

**233 CRADLE OF LOVE**
JOHNNY PRESTON
*MERCURY*

**234 EXCERPT FROM A TEENAGE OPERA**
KEITH WEST
*PARLOPHONE*

**235 SAVED BY THE BELL**
ROBIN GIBB
*POLYDOR*

**236 MY BOY LOLLIPOP**
MILLIE SMALL
*FONTANA*

**237 WHAT WOULD I BE**
VAL DOONICAN
*DECCA*

**238 OH WELL**
FLEETWOOD MAC
*REPRISE*

**239 HONEY**
BOBBY
*GOLDSBORO UA*

**240 HEY LITTLE GIRL**
DEL SHANNON
*LONDON AMERICAN*

**241 DEDICATED TO THE ONE I LOVE**
MAMAS & THE PAPAS
*RCA*

**242 HIPPY HIPPY SHAKE**
SWINGING BLUE JEANS
*HMV*

**243 A MAN WITHOUT LOVE**
ENGELBERT HUMPERDINCK
*DECCA*

**244 BIG BAD JOHN**
JIMMY DEAN
*PHILIPS*

**245 BUILD ME UP BUTTERCUP**
FOUNDATIONS
*PYE*

**246 I'M GONNA BE STRONG**
GENE PITNEY
*STATESIDE*

**247 THEN HE KISSED ME**
CRYSTALS
*LONDON AMERICAN*

**248 SOMEONE SOMEONE**
BRIAN POOLE & THE TREMELOES
*DECCA*

**249 (CALL ME) NUMBER ONE**
TREMELOES
*CBS*

**250 I'M COMIN' HOME**
TOM JONES
*DECCA*

**251 MY GENERATION**
WHO
*BRUNSWICK*

**252 SCARLETT O'HARA**
JET HARRIS & TONY MEEHAN
*DECCA*

**253 BOBBY'S GIRL**
SUSAN MAUGHAN
*PHILIPS*

**254 YESTER-ME, YESTER-YOU, YESTERDAY**
STEVIE WONDER
*TAMLA MOTOWN*

**255 DON'T FORGET TO REMEMBER**
BEE GEES
*POLYDOR*

**256 FRIGHTENED CITY**
SHADOWS
*COLUMBIA*

**257 A GROOVY KIND OF LOVE**
MINDBENDERS
*FONTANA*

**258 IF THE WHOLE WORLD STOPPED LOVING**
VAL DOONICAN
*PYE*

**259 EDELWEISS**
VINCE HILL
*COLUMBIA*

**260 HOLE IN MY SHOE**
TRAFFIC
*ISLAND*

**261 FLOWERS IN THE RAIN**
MOVE
*REGAL ZONOPHONE*

**262 CAN'T GET USED TO LOSING YOU**
ANDY WILLIAMS
*CBS*

**263 BLUE BAYOU**
ROY ORBISON
*LONDON AMERICAN*

**264 GOD ONLY KNOWS**
BEACH BOYS
*CAPITOL*

**265 DON'T TALK TO HIM**
CLIFF RICHARD
*COLUMBIA*

**266 IT MUST BE HIM**
VIKKI CARR
*LIBERTY*

**267 GOODBYE**
MARY HOPKIN
*APPLE*

**268 SOMEONE ELSE'S BABY**
ADAM FAITH
*PARLOPHONE*

**269 SLOOP JOHN B**
BEACH BOYS
*CAPITOL*

**270 BITS AND PIECES**
DAVE CLARK FIVE
*COLUMBIA*

**271 ALMOST THERE**
ANDY WILLIAMS
*CBS*

**272 I'M THE ONE**
GERRY & THE PACEMAKERS
*COLUMBIA*

**273 IT'S ALL IN THE GAME**
CLIFF RICHARD
*COLUMBIA*

**274 MAN OF THE WORLD**
FLEETWOOD MAC
*IMMEDIATE*

**275 HAPPY BIRTHDAY, SWEET SIXTEEN**
NEIL SEDAKA
*RCA*

**276 SPANISH FLEA**
HERB ALPERT
*PYE INTERNATIONAL*

**277 THE PRICE OF LOVE**
EVERLY BROTHERS
*WARNER*

**278 HEY! BABY**
BRUCE CHANNEL
*MERCURY*

**279 THE WEDDING**
JULIE ROGERS
*MERCURY*

**280 PENNY LANE/STRAWBERRY FIELDS FOREVER**
BEATLES
*PARLOPHONE*

**281 I'M A BOY**
WHO
*REACTION*

**282 MAGICAL MYSTERY TOUR (DOUBLE EP)**
BEATLES
*PARLOPHONE*

**283 ALTERNATE TITLE**
MONKEES
*RCA*

**284 JUST ONE LOOK**
HOLLIES
*PARLOPHONE*

**285 BLACK IS BLACK**
LOS BRAVOS
*DECCA*

**286 RAG DOLL**
FOUR SEASONS
*PHILIPS*

**287 WAY DOWN YONDER IN NEW ORLEANS**
FREDDY CANNON
*TOP RANK*

**288 IT'LL BE ME**
CLIFF RICHARD
*COLUMBIA*

**289 SUN ARISE**
ROLF HARRIS
*COLUMBIA*

**290 ELOISE**
BARRY RYAN
*MGM*

**291 TRUE LOVE WAYS**
PETER & GORDON
*COLUMBIA*

**292 BEND IT**
DAVE DEE, DOZY, BEAKY, MICK & TICH
*FONTANA*

**293 THE RIVER**
KEN DODD
*COLUMBIA*

**294 GIVE PEACE A CHANCE**
PLASTIC ONO BAND
*APPLE*

**295 SON OF HICKORY HOLLER'S TRAMP**
O.C. SMITH
*CBS*

**296 I CAN'T CONTROL MYSELF**
TROGGS
*PAGE ONE*

**297 A WALK IN THE BLACK FOREST**
HORST JANKOWSKI
*MERCURY*

**298 YOU'VE GOT YOUR TROUBLES**
FORTUNES
*DECCA*

**299 A WORLD OF OUR OWN**
SEEKERS
*COLUMBIA*

**300 HEART FULL OF SOUL**
YARDBIRDS
*COLUMBIA*

**301 HERE COMES THE NIGHT**
THEM
*DECCA*

**302 FORGET ME NOT**
EDEN KANE
*DECCA*

**303 YOU WERE MADE FOR ME**
FREDDIE & THE DREAMERS
*COLUMBIA*

**304 LAZY SUNDAY**
SMALL FACES
*IMMEDIATE*

**305 ROSES ARE RED**
RONNIE CARROLL
*PHILIPS*

**306 BUT I DO**
CLARENCE 'FROGMAN' HENRY
*PYE INTERNATIONAL*

**307 TAKE GOOD CARE OF MY BABY**
BOBBY VEE
*LONDON AMERICAN*

**308 I-2-3**
LEN BARRY
*BRUNSWICK*

**309 WHERE DID OUR LOVE GO**
SUPREMES
*STATESIDE*

**310 YOU WERE ON MY MIND**
CRISPIAN ST PETERS
*DECCA*

**311 STOP STOP STOP**
HOLLIES
*PARLOPHONE*

**312 IF YOU GOTTA GO, GO NOW**
MANFRED MANN
*HMV*

**313 PEPE**
DUANE EDDY
*LONDON AMERICAN*

**314 MELTING POT**
BLUE MINK
*PHILIPS*

**315 ROBOT MAN**
CONNIE FRANCIS
*MGM*

**316 SEMI-DETACHED SUBURBAN MR JAMES**
MANFRED MANN
*FONTANA*

**317 WATERLOO SUNSET**
KINKS
*PYE*

**318 SHEILA**
TOMMY ROE
*HMV*

**319 GIMME SOME LOVING**
SPENCER DAVIS GROUP
*FONTANA*

**320 THIS IS MY SONG**
HARRY SECOMBE
*PHILIPS*

**321 WILD WIND**
JOHN LEYTON
*TOP RANK*

**322 MY SHIP IS COMING IN**
WALKER BROTHERS
*PHILIPS*

**323 I'M GONNA MAKE YOU MINE**
LOU CHRISTIE
*BUDDAH*

**324 OH HAPPY DAY**
EDWIN HAWKINS SINGERS
*BUDDAH*

**325 WALK TALL**
VAL DOONICAN
*DECCA*

**326 WILD THING**
TROGGS
*FONTANA*

**327 WHEN WILL I BE LOVED**
EVERLY BROTHERS
*LONDON AMERICAN*

**328 JEALOUSY**
BILLY FURY
*DECCA*

**329 THIS OLD HEART OF MINE**
ISLEY BROTHERS
*TAMLA MOTOWN*

**330 NOBODY NEEDS YOUR LOVE**
GENE PITNEY
*STATESIDE*

**331 ALL I HAVE TO DO IS DREAM**
BOBBIE GENTRY & GLEN CAMPBELL
*CAPITOL*

**332 ALL DAY AND ALL OF THE NIGHT**
KINKS
*PYE*

**333 A GIRL LIKE YOU**
CLIFF RICHARD
*COLUMBIA*

**334 PASADENA**
TEMPERANCE SEVEN
*PARLOPHONE*

**335 WE GOTTA GET OUT OF THIS PLACE**
ANIMALS
*COLUMBIA*

**336 SUNSHINE SUPERMAN**
DONOVAN
*PYE*

**337 THEME FOR A DREAM**
CLIFF RICHARD
*COLUMBIA*

**338 I ONLY WANT TO BE WITH YOU**
DUSTY SPRINGFIELD
*PHILIPS*

**339 FOR ONCE IN MY LIFE**
STEVIE WONDER
*TAMLA MOTOWN*

**340 DANCE WITH THE GUITAR MAN**
DUANE EDDY
*RCA*

**341 MATTHEW AND SON**
CAT STEVENS
*DERAM*

**342 IF I ONLY HAD TIME**
JOHN ROWLES
*MCA*

**343 BOOM BANG-A-BANG**
LULU
*COLUMBIA*

**344 EVERYBODY KNOWS**
DAVE CLARK FIVE
COLUMBIA

**345 ROMEO**
PETULA CLARK
*PYE*

**346 EVE OF DESTRUCTION**
BARRY MCGUIRE
*RCA*

**347 SHE WEARS MY RING**
SOLOMON KING
*COLUMBIA*

**348 NOT FADE AWAY**
ROLLING STONES
*DECCA*

**349 SEALED WITH A KISS**
BRIAN HYLAND
*HMV*

**350 MY SENTIMENTAL FRIEND**
HERMAN'S HERMITS
*COLUMBIA*

**351 GAME OF LOVE**
WAYNE FONTANA & THE MINDBENDERS
*FONTANA*

**352 AIN'T MISBEHAVIN'**
TOMMY BRUCE & THE BRUISERS
*COLUMBIA*

**353 DAYDREAM**
LOVIN' SPOONFUL
*PYE INTERNATIONAL*

**354 NIGHT OF FEAR**
MOVE
*DERAM*

**355 STRAWBERRY FAIR**
ANTHONY NEWLEY
*DECCA*

**356 LIKE I'VE NEVER BEEN GONE**
BILLY FURY
*DECCA*

**357 I CAN'T LET GO**
HOLLIES
*PARLOPHONE*

**358 PORTRAIT OF MY LOVE**
MATT MONRO
*PARLOPHONE*

**359 ITCHYCOO PARK**
SMALL FACES
*IMMEDIATE*

**360 FOR YOUR LOVE**
YARDBIRDS
*COLUMBIA*

**361 19TH NERVOUS BREAKDOWN**
ROLLING STONES
*DECCA*

**362 HELP YOURSELF**
TOM JONES
*DECCA*

**363 SUGAR AND SPICE**
SEARCHERS
*PYE*

**364 MONDAY MONDAY**
MAMAS & THE PAPAS
*RCA*

**365 NINE TIMES OUT OF TEN**
CLIFF RICHARD
*COLUMBIA*

**366 DON'T TREAT ME LIKE A CHILD**
HELEN SHAPIRO
*COLUMBIA*

**367 PLEASE DON'T GO**
DONALD PEERS
*COLUMBIA*

**368 IT MIGHT AS WELL RAIN UNTIL SEPTEMBER**
CAROLE KING
*LONDON AMERICAN*

**369 LET THERE BE DRUMS**
SANDY NELSON
*LONDON AMERICAN*

**370 LAZY RIVER**
BOBBY DARIN
*LONDON AMERICAN*

**371 RIVER DEEP MOUNTAIN HIGH**
IKE & TINA TURNER
*LONDON AMERICAN*

**372 WIMOWEH**
KARL DENVER
*DECCA*

**373 TOO SOON TO KNOW**
ROY ORBISON
*LONDON AMERICAN*

**374 BEND ME SHAPE ME**
AMEN CORNER
*DERAM*

**375 YESTERDAY MAN**
CHRIS ANDREWS
*DECCA*

**376 WHEN THE GIRL IN YOUR ARMS IS THE GIRL IN YOUR HEART**
CLIFF RICHARD
*COLUMBIA*

**377 LIKE I DO**
MAUREEN EVANS
*ORIOLE*

**378 SECRET LOVE**
KATHY KIRBY
*DECCA*

**379 MAKE ME AN ISLAND**
JOE DOLAN
*PYE*

**380 CALL UP THE GROUPS**
BARRON KNIGHTS
*COLUMBIA*

**381 SILHOUETTES**
HERMAN'S HERMITS
*COLUMBIA*

**382 AM I THAT EASY TO FORGET**
ENGELBERT HUMPERDINCK
*DECCA*

**383 (SITTIN' ON) THE DOCK OF THE BAY**
OTIS REDDING
*STAX*

**384 DELAWARE**
PERRY COMO
*RCA*

**385 ON A SLOW BOAT TO CHINA**
EMILE FORD & THE CHECKMATES
*PYE*

**386 SWEET NOTHIN'S**
BRENDA LEE
*BRUNSWICK*

**387 I JUST DON'T KNOW WHAT TO DO WITH MYSELF**
DUSTY SPRINGFIELD
*PHILIPS*

**388 MY HEART HAS A MIND OF ITS OWN**
CONNIE FRANCIS
*MGM*

**389 THAT'S WHAT LOVE WILL DO**
JOE BROWN & THE BRUVVERS
*PICCADILLY*

**390 THE SOUND OF SILENCE**
BACHELORS
*DECCA*

**391 STUCK ON YOU**
ELVIS PRESLEY
*RCA*

**392 YOU'RE SIXTEEN**
JOHNNY BURNETTE
*LONDON AMERICAN*

**393 SHA LA LA LA LEE**
SMALL FACES
*DECCA*

**394 IF YOU GOTTA MAKE A FOOL OF SOMEBODY**
FREDDIE & THE DREAMERS
*COLUMBIA*

**395 BROWN EYED HANDSOME MAN**
BUDDY HOLLY
*CORAL*

**396 WILL YOU LOVE ME TOMORROW**
SHIRELLES
*TOP RANK*

**397 I WOULDN'T TRADE YOU FOR THE WORLD**
BACHELORS
*DECCA*

**398 FIRE BRIGADE**
MOVE
*REGAL ZONOPHONE*

**399 TOSSING AND TURNING**
IVY LEAGUE
*PICCADILLY*

**400 GOODNESS GRACIOUS ME**
PETER SELLERS & SOPHIA LOREN
*PARLOPHONE*

**401 BARBARA ANN**
BEACH BOYS
*CAPITOL*

**402 I'M TELLING YOU NOW**
FREDDIE & THE DREAMERS
*COLUMBIA*

**403 ZABADAK!**
DAVE DEE, DOZY, BEAKY, MICK & TICH
*FONTANA*

**404 WHEN WILL YOU SAY I LOVE YOU**
BILLY FURY
*DECCA*

**405 THE MORE I SEE YOU**
CHRIS MONTEZ
*PYE INTERNATIONAL*

**406 LITTLE DONKEY**
NINA & FREDERICK
*COLUMBIA*

**407 SURROUND YOURSELF WITH SORROW**
CILLA BLACK
*PARLOPHONE*

**408 COME BACK AND SHAKE ME**
CLODAGH RODGERS
*RCA*

**409 HE AIN'T HEAVY, HE'S MY BROTHER**
HOLLIES
*PARLOPHONE*

**410 GIRL DON'T COME**
SANDIE SHAW
*PYE*

**411 IF I HAD A HAMMER**
TRINI LOPEZ
*REPRISE*

**412 A LITTLE BIT ME, A LITTLE BIT YOU**
MONKEES
*RCA*

**413 THE NIGHT HAS A THOUSAND EYES**
BOBBY VEE
*LIBERTY*

**414 WHEN YOU WALK IN THE ROOM**
SEARCHERS
*PYE*

**415 SHE'D RATHER BE WITH ME**
TURTLES
*LONDON AMERICAN*

**416 THE WAY IT USED TO BE**
ENGELBERT HUMPERDINCK
*DECCA*

**417 DEATH OF A CLOWN**
DAVE DAVIES
*PYE*

**418 MORE THAN I CAN SAY**
BOBBY VEE
*LONDON AMERICAN*

**419 HOLD ME**
P.J. PROBY
*DECCA*

**420 I WANT TO STAY HERE**
STEVE LAWRENCE & EYDIE GORME
*CBS*

**421 YOU CAN'T HURRY LOVE**
SUPREMES
*TAMLA MOTOWN*

**422 CARRIE-ANNE**
HOLLIES
*PARLOPHONE*

**423 LOOKING THROUGH THE EYES OF LOVE**
GENE PITNEY
*STATESIDE*

**424 I'M GONNA MAKE YOU LOVE ME**
DIANA ROSS & THE SUPREMES & THE TEMPTATIONS
*TAMLA MOTOWN*

**425 SPEAK TO ME PRETTY**
BRENDA LEE
*BRUNSWICK*

**426 BLUE EYES**
DON PARTRIDGE
*COLUMBIA*

**427 LET'S HANG ON!**
FOUR SEASONS
*PHILIPS*

**428 PURPLE HAZE**
JIMI HENDRIX EXPERIENCE
*TRACK*

**429 WALK AWAY RENEE**
FOUR TOPS
*TAMLA MOTOWN*

**430 YOU'VE LOST THAT LOVIN' FEELIN'**
CILLA BLACK
*PARLOPHONE*

**431 LET'S SPEND THE NIGHT TOGETHER/RUBY TUESDAY**
ROLLING STONES
*DECCA*

**432 BANG BANG (MY BABY SHOT ME DOWN)**
CHER
*LIBERTY*

**433 I'LL NEVER GET OVER YOU**
JOHNNY KIDD & THE PIRATES
*HMV*

**434 JUDY IN DISGUISE (WITH GLASSES)**
JOHN FRED & HIS PLAYBOY BAND
*PYE INTERNATIONAL*

**435 HOLD TIGHT**
DAVE DEE, DOZY, BEAKY, MICK & TICH
*FONTANA*

**436 TAKE THESE CHAINS FROM MY HEART**
RAY CHARLES
*HMV*

**437 SHAZAM**
DUANE EDDY
*LONDON AMERICAN*

**438 GUITAR TANGO**
SHADOWS
*COLUMBIA*

**439 HAPPY JACK**
WHO
*REACTION*

**440 SAVE ME**
DAVE DEE, DOZY, BEAKY, MICK & TICH
*FONTANA*

**441 LAST NIGHT WAS MADE FOR LOVE**
BILLY FURY
*DECCA*

**442 ISLAND OF DREAMS**
SPRINGFIELDS
*PHILIPS*

**443 GINNY COME LATELY**
BRIAN HYLAND
*HMV*

**444 WINCHESTER CATHEDRAL**
NEW VAUDEVILLE BAND
*FONTANA*

**445 FOOTSTEPS**
STEVE LAWRENCE
*HMV*

**446 KEEP SEARCHIN' (WE'LL FOLLOW THE SUN)**
DEL SHANNON
*STATESIDE*

**447 HOW ABOUT THAT**
ADAM FAITH
*PARLOPHONE*

**448 VENUS IN BLUE JEANS**
MARK WYNTER
*PYE*

**449 MY CHERIE AMOUR**
STEVIE WONDER
*TAMLA MOTOWN*

**450 SORRY**
SUZANNE HOLLIES
*PARLOPHONE*

**451 EVIL HEARTED YOU/STILL I'M SAD**
YARDBIRDS
*COLUMBIA*

**452 DON'T LET ME BE MISUNDERSTOOD**
ANIMALS
*COLUMBIA*

**453 TWIST AND SHOUT**
BRIAN POOLE & THE TREMELOES
*DECCA*

**454 YOU'RE NO GOOD**
SWINGING BLUE JEANS
*HMV*

**455 DECK OF CARDS**
WINK MARTINDALE
*LONDON AMERICAN*

**456 HE'S IN TOWN**
ROCKIN' BERRIES
*PICCADILLY*

**457 WALK AWAY**
MATT MONRO
*PARLOPHONE*

**458 TWENTY FOUR HOURS FROM TULSA**
GENE PITNEY
*UA*

**459 LIVING IN THE PAST**
JETHRO TULL
*ISLAND*

**460 GEORGY GIRL**
SEEKERS
*COLUMBIA*

**461 SHAPES OF THINGS**
YARDBIRDS
*COLUMBIA*

**462 PRETTY BLUE EYES**
CRAIG DOUGLAS
*TOP RANK*

**463 BREAKIN' DOWN THE WALLS OF HEARTACHE**
JOHNNY JOHNSON & THE BANDWAGON
*DIRECTION*

**464 TERRY**
TWINKLE
*DECCA*

**465 TRACY**
CUFF LINKS
*MCA*

**466 SHA LA LA**
MANFRED MANN
*HMV*

**467 SO SAD (TO WATCH GOOD LOVE GO BAD)**
EVERLY BROTHERS
*WARNER*

**468 AUTUMN ALMANAC**
KINKS
*PYE*

**469 MAN OF MYSTERY**
SHADOWS
*COLUMBIA*

**470 A BOY NAMED SUE**
JOHNNY CASH
*CBS*

**471 JOHNNY WILL**
PAT BOONE
*LONDON AMERICAN*

**472 NO PARTICULAR PLACE TO GO**
CHUCK BERRY
*PYE INTERNATIONAL*

**473 SORROW**
MERSEYS
*FONTANA*

**474 WHEN A MAN LOVES A WOMAN**
PERCY SLEDGE
*ATLANTIC*

**475 NOBODY'S DARLIN' BUT MINE**
FRANK IFIELD
*COLUMBIA*

**476 IN DREAMS**
ROY ORBISON
*LONDON AMERICAN*

**477 EVEN THE BAD TIMES ARE GOOD**
TREMELOES
*CBS*

**478 I SAY A LITTLE PRAYER**
ARETHA FRANKLIN
*ATLANTIC*

**479 THE TIME HAS COME**
ADAM FAITH
*PARLOPHONE*

**480 ONE TWO THREE O'LEARY**
DES O'CONNOR
*COLUMBIA*

**481 PINBALL WIZARD**
WHO
*TRACK*

**482 WALK ON BY**
LEROY VAN DYKE
*MERCURY*

**483 TIME IS TIGHT**
BOOKER T. & THE MG's
*STAX*

**484 WILD IN THE COUNTRY**
ELVIS PRESLEY
*RCA*

**485 CATCH THE WIND**
DONOVAN
*PYE*

**486 CONSTANTLY**
CLIFF RICHARD
*COLUMBIA*

**487 LUCKY LIPS**
CLIFF RICHARD
*COLUMBIA*

**488 DAYDREAM BELIEVER**
MONKEES
*RCA*

**489 ROSIE**
DON PARTRIDGE
*COLUMBIA*

**490 LOOK THROUGH ANY WINDOW**
HOLLIES
*PARLOPHONE*

**491 DA DOO RON RON**
CRYSTALS
*LONDON AMERICAN*

**492 LIKE A ROLLING STONE**
BOB DYLAN
*CBS*

**493 I'M THE URBAN SPACEMAN**
BONZO DOG DOO-DAH BAND
*LIBERTY*

**494 COUNTING TEARDROPS**
EMILE FORD & THE CHECKMATES
*PYE*

**495 I'D NEVER FIND ANOTHER YOU**
BILLY FURY
*DECCA*

**496 THANK U VERY MUCH**
SCAFFOLD
*PARLOPHONE*

**497 THEME FROM 'THE LEGION'S LAST PATROL'**
KEN THORNE & HIS ORCHESTRA
*HMV*

**498 LITTLE TOWN FLIRT**
DEL SHANNON
*LONDON AMERICAN*

**499 FBI**
SHADOWS
*COLUMBIA*

**500 COME AND STAY WITH ME**
MARIANNE FAITHFULL
*DECCA*